Psychoanalysis of Behavior

Volume One

Psychoanalysis of Behavior

COLLECTED PAPERS

Volume One: 1922-1956

by

SANDOR RADO, M.D., D.P. Sc.

Former Clinical Professor of Psychiatry and Director of the Psychoanalytic Clinic for Training and Research, Columbia University

GRUNE & STRATTON

New York • London • 1956

Library of Congress Catalog Card No. 56–7550

Printed and bound in U. S. A.

CONTENTS

Preface

The papers collected in this volume were first published in German, English, and American scientific periodicals and books from 1922 to 1956. They are arranged in chronological order and divided into three periods. The first consists of contributions to classical psychodynamics; the second, of articles marked by the quest for a basic conceptual scheme; the third, of papers aimed at the development of an adaptational psychodynamics. Four papers of the third period have been revised in order to make a few additions and to remove some initial uncertainties of a slowly developing terminology. Save for the correction of errors and a more uniform arrangement of the references, the rest of the material is reprinted here unchanged.

For the permission to reprint these papers, I should like to express my sincere thanks to the following publications and publishers:

VIENNA
Internationale Zeitschrift fuer Psychoanalyse
Imago Zeitschrift fuer Anwendung der Psychoanalyse auf die Geisteswissenschaften
Internationaler Psychoanalytischer Verlag
LONDON
The International Journal of Psycho-Analysis
NEW YORK
The Psychoanalytic Quarterly
The New York Psychoanalytic Institute
The American Journal of Orthopsychiatry
Psychosomatic Medicine
The Journal of Nervous and Mental Disease
Research Publication of the Association for Research in Nervous and Mental Disease
International Universities Press, Inc.
Transactions of the New York Academy of Sciences
Grune & Stratton, Inc.
BALTIMORE, MARYLAND
American Journal of Psychiatry
CHICAGO, ILLINOIS
A.M.A. Archives of Dermatology and Syphilology

February, 1956   SANDOR RADO

Contributions to
Classical
Psychodynamics

The Paths of Natural Science in the Light of Psychoanalysis*

We have recently learned from our foremost investigators that a change of decisive significance is taking place in their conception of the ground-work of the mathematical sciences.[2, 15, 16, 17, 19, 20, 21, 23] The new position takes as its point of departure the province of physics, the findings of which have shaken the belief in the validity of the causality principle (better known to you as scientific determinism) and have inaugurated scientific methods that transcend the limitations of this basic law. I rather suppose that a turn of events of this kind surprises all of us—perhaps even imbues us, who are such strangers in the realm of physical research, with a decided uneasiness. Hitherto we understood the principle of determinism to be one of the pillars upon which the entire body of natural science was erected. The undreamed of results that consistent adherence to this principle afforded Freud's psychology need not be discussed before this audience. Indeed, all our scientific reasoning has become so intimately intertwined with the idea of determinism that a science lacking this concept is altogether unthinkable. Yet there exists a large number of facts which prove with indubitable certainty that this conviction is unfounded and that scientific research can tranquilly proceed, albeit the bed-rock of causality has been forsaken.

I intend to illustrate this circumstance most succinctly with an example borrowed from a paper by the well-known mathematician v. Mises. To this end, we must venture into the realm of mechanics which, on account of its strictly causal structure, serves as a model for all the physical sciences. Indeed, the so-called "mechanical view" of nature demands that science comprehend the entire physical world to be a mechanical phenomenon. Now we wish to see whether mechanics, which inspires us with such high hopes and which makes such great pretensions, can completely master at least its own domain—the phenomena of motion—with its causal methods.

You are acquainted with the Galton frame through its use in the form

* Authorized translation by Monroe A. Meyer. Read before the Seventh International Congress of Psychoanalysis, Berlin, September 25, 1922. First published in German in *Imago Zeitschrift fuer Anwendung der Psychoanalyse auf die Geisteswissenschaften*, 8: 401–417, 1922; in English, *The Psychoanalytic Quarterly*, 1: 683–700, 1932.

of the tivoli table. The entire surface of this frame is provided with equidistant rows of nails through which small circular discs can tumble down. The size of these discs corresponds exactly to the interval between the nails. Let us drop a fairly large number of these discs through one compartment in the top row and ask our expert to tell us in what distribution they will reach the bottom row, according to the principles of classical mechanics. Well, he is unable to answer our question, although it concerns a commonplace phenomenon—the motions of tangible masses. "The results of this proceeding," v. Mises assures us, "may in no wise be deduced from the propositions of classical mechanics; indeed, we have not the faintest notion how such a mathematical derivation might appear." The mechanist can idealize the problem by assuming that the frame and the discs have been constructed with absolute precision (the frame perfectly smooth, the nails and their intervals perfectly uniform, the discs perfectly circular), that no defects supervene, etc. In that case, however, his computations must come to naught, for, as a matter of fact, the result depends upon just those innumerable small factors that he has eliminated by his assumption. A mathematical manipulation of the problem in strict conformity with the facts is inconceivable. How should the necessary mass of data merely be collected, much less the endless calculations performed? What is the use of wanting to preserve determinism "in principle" by telling ourselves that the paths of the discs could be unequivocally determined if we knew the precise initial conditions of the experiment and all the adventitious factors? For we must immediately add that there is no prospect of ever obtaining this information. We would have had recourse to an assertion, the truth of which could never be put to the test, and would have in that way given a scientific principle the status of a dogma. It is much more straightforward and correct to pronounce the lot of the discs a matter of chance. Then the new task of studying the characteristics of fortuitous events arises.

Scientific research has done this. It developed the statistical method with the calculus of probabilities and, on the basis of certain premises, could wrest conformity to law from the chaos of chance. In our example, provided the number of discs and of rows of nails be sufficiently large, a distribution is observed that agrees well with the formula given by Gauss.

We must understand that it is by no means solely in the case of games of chance that deterministic mechanics breaks down. There is a host of problems—I mention only random motion in liquids and gases—which admit of entirely analogous points of view. A new mechanics, which v. Mises contrasts with the fixed, classical mechanics as "mechanical statistics" or "free mechanics," has sprung from work with these phenomena.

I should not care to tarry too long in the field of physics, a domain equally remote to you and to me; but I fear lest my meagre account lead you into a very natural misapprehension. Perhaps you are charging me with undue haste in the formation of my opinion of determinism. If the new procedure, too, permits us to confirm the fact that natural phenomena conform to laws, then it is precisely the old methods and not the principle of causality that has failed. This objection, however, misses the mark, for the fact that certain phenomena are expressible in laws is not identical with determinism, as, for example, Helmholtz believed, and as is frequently asserted to this very day.* We have only to realize the profound difference between conformity to law from the causal and from the statistical standpoints in order to clear up this question.

The deterministic view contemplates the individual event and the deterministic law definitely fixes the entire time-space course of a phenomenon. For example, if we have found that in the case of gravitation phenomena, Newton's law is valid within a certain limit of accuracy, the events investigated seem determined thereby in every respect, and we should expect a similar effect in every subsequent instance in which ponderable masses act upon one another.

The state of affairs is quite different in the case of statistical laws. From the standpoint of statistics, whether applied to atoms and molecules, to grossly perceptible masses or to living organisms, the individual factor sinks into insignificance. The statistical view always envisages aggregates of phenomena which it groups together under the empirical viewpoint of similarity. Hence, we can learn nothing about single occurrences from a statistical correlation. As for phenomena taken collectively, it tells us only the relative frequency of the possible issues. You will not be enlightened then in respect to individual happenings on the Galton frame by the frequency distribution function of Gauss. Each disc describes a course that is spatially and temporally independent of those of the other discs. We do not know what path a given disc will take. The formula embraces the total phenomenon and clarifies it in one respect by indicating the end result. It does so, however, only when certain restrictive conditions are satisfied. But the way in which such a result comes to pass remains unknown. The computation of probabilities achieves its results from so-called initial probabilities, hence from certain abstract auxiliary assumptions which one should indeed not understand as the "causes" or "conditions" of the process in question in the deterministic sense. The "conditions," in the deterministic

---

* Helmholtz—1881—(according to Exner, l. c.): "I realized only later that the principle of causality really was nothing more than the hypothesis that all natural phenomena happen according to law."

M. Schlick—1920—(l. c.): "The assertion that events are universally determinate in nature, predicated by the causality principle, is accordingly identical with the universal existence of natural laws."

sense of the term, resident in the fine structural inaccuracies of the apparatus are not touched at all by the probabilistic point of view and remain as before, unknown to us. The computation of probabilities is a neat construction which—expressed in deterministic language—spans a sea of unknown conditions and furnishes results which tally sufficiently with experience without disclosing to us either for what reasons or in what way the calculated results come about. I believe that now we see clearly that with the statistical method the deterministic manner of thinking ceases completely and that natural science has really trod a new path.

As a result of their general insight into this situation, investigators of today—more strictly speaking, some investigators—have been obliged to modify their evaluation of the causality principle from the standpoint of the theory of knowledge. They no longer deem it a fundamental law established for all time. Like many an apodeictical scientific tenet, the causality principle, too, has been allotted the more modest rôle of an hypothesis that is judged, maintained or abandoned solely on the basis of its serviceableness. Hitherto, the deterministic postulate was of surpassing importance to research. Now, however, it has reached the limit of its usefulness and it can be replaced by new scientific postulates. Freud once styled determinism a preconceived idea.[12] We are beginning to discern how profoundly significant this assertion is. Besides, the effects of the new conception are still more far-reaching. It is becoming more and more evident that causal laws themselves do not possess the exactness that fanatics ascribed to them. Stimulated especially by the investigations of Ernst Mach, science is proceeding to a "transvaluation" of deterministic principles. It is not our intention to pursue these lines of thought.

You are perhaps already impatient to learn of what direct interest our representations can be to the psychoanalyst. It is a well-known technical difficulty of applied psychoanalysis that all the unfamiliar material must be communicated before the psychoanalytic investigation itself can be instituted. The significance of the problem of determinism for psychoanalysis is surely one not to be underestimated. Yet we do not wish to take this consideration as our point of departure. First of all, our attention must be claimed by that psychological reaction which precipitated among scientists the change in principles alluded to—a change that is still in full swing today.

We may characterize this reaction as a perplexing one. After Maxwell (1859, in the kinetic theory of gases) and later, Boltzmann (1895, in the case of the second law of thermodynamics) had successfully introduced the probabilistic approach into physics and a physics based on statistics gradually began to develop, it was soon noticed that the statistical conception of phenomena clashed so to speak with deterministic physics. This

entailed a distressing discrepancy that scientists wanted to get rid of somehow. Worse than this discordance were certain purely emotional factors
that asserted themselves. Genuine confidence in scientific assertions that
were predicated "merely" on a statistical basis and that claimed only a
given degree of probability instead of deterministic certainty failed to arise.
Scientists felt their craving for knowledge, their "natural need of causality"
unsatisfied. They did not know where to accommodate the new points of
view in their reasoning. Social statistics always had to contend with similar
difficulties, and in this way, efforts emanating from both quarters were
instituted to reduce statistical formulations to a causal basis.[22] Every endeavor in that direction remained nevertheless unsuccessful and, since
physicists did not wish to give up the concept of causality, they heedlessly
ignored the very promising methods of statistics for decades. You can
readily judge what a checking of progress was produced at this juncture by
the deterministic point of view, otherwise so profitable. Although the very
beginnings of mechanical statistics date back more than sixty years, this
science must still struggle for recognition today, as the cited contribution
of v. Mises indicates. I can assure you that rational factors, perhaps a less
practical utilizability of statistical results, do not participate in this resistance to a degree worth mentioning. Physics presents a host of problems
that are inaccessible to deterministic treatment, in which the individual
events recede completely behind the phenomenon as a whole from the
standpoint of both our theoretical and practical interest.

In the history of science, the spectacle of men opposing a scientific innovation with the most intense resistances and of arresting the further
development of scientific inquiry for a long time, has repeated itself on
innumerable occasions. Freud's investigations have demonstrated that it
is always a matter of affective motives disguising themselves as an intellectual opposition. He was able to show us in the case of several excellent
examples what sensibilities were thus offended and how this provoked mankind's perverse behavior.[19] We have now received the impression that in
our mental life the principle of causality acquires an emotional coloring
that seems to us incongruous in the face of such an essentially prosaic
scientific abstraction. We already suspect that unconscious impulses are
at play here and we set ourselves the task of tracing the psychical origin of
the causality credo. In so doing, we must succeed in demonstrating the
hidden instinctual forces from which this mental construction receives its
affective cathexis.

Let us first cast a cursory glance upon the history of the notion of causality.[1] Its very beginnings may be traced as far back as ancient Greece.
However, it became the universal basis of natural philosophy only after
the theological era of the Middle Ages as a result of the labors of Bacon,

Galileo, Newton and the philosopher, Descartes. We can perhaps sum up its content as first formulated as follows: every effect arises from a cause; like causes produce like results. Then, in the course of time, it met with the most varied constructions and formulations. Its anthropomorphism, the obvious analogy of the idea of cause with man's will, repeatedly engaged the attention of thinkers. But they were less concerned with the psychologic origin of the notion than with its logical justification and the demonstration of its validity. I make mention of the fact that Hume, who explains the matter rather on a psychological basis, attributes the belief in causality to association, expectation and habit and hence disputes its capability of being verified and its strict validity. On the other hand, Kant conceives of it as an a priori category of thought, while Mill, Spencer and others derive it from experience and induction. These efforts concern us but little, as do similarly the later transformations that the causality principle underwent. Since the idea of cause contained in the original causality tenet is disposed of in the "conditionalism" of Verworn by the means of "conditions" (originated by Goethe) and since Ernst Mach replaces the whole formula with the mathematical-functional connection of sensational elements, the aim of this transformation becomes clear. It wishes to eliminate the objectionable anthropomorphic quality of the causality principle and lets it assume increasingly abstract forms, while the underlying idea remains unchanged.

If we subject the doctrine of an absolute causality in nature—the strict determinateness of all happenings—to a psychological examination, the parallel with the dogma of religious determinism forces itself upon us quite automatically. This spontaneous association has undoubtedly already made many individuals suspicious. We, however, ought not to be deterred from taking the idea seriously. We want to follow up its implications, with our psychoanalytic armamentarium. In the first place, the parallel shows that the idea of an unequivocal causal determining of cosmic processes is common to both formulations, the religious as well as the scientific. Then we find other points in respect of which they behave like opposites. Religion attributes all the processes of the universe to a single cause known to the faithful as the will of God. Science presumes the existence of different causes behind each variety of processes, which are not given it a priori, but which it must rather seek in each instance. Religion then does not stimulate research at all. It finds its complement in a "psychological technique" [11] that aims at obtaining God's grace. Man need not concern himself in what way the will of God then brings about what was requested of Him. Scientific determinism on the contrary actually invites research. It goes hand in hand with a materialistic technique that effects the desired changes by means of an actual intervention among natural processes. Besides, it no longer suffices to discover an answer to the question why an event happens; an interest is felt in learning how processes go on, what regulative principles govern them. With the awakening of this interest mankind took a step to which we rightly concede a decisive significance in the evolution of science.

It is not difficult to pass on from the comparative description of both systems of thought to a psychoanalytical understanding of them. We know that historically the one succeeded the other, and we need only introduce at this point the natural supposition that scientific determinism sprang from religious determinism thanks to a wave of repression. The process that produced this result could be more accurately called a mental revolt, for it embraces the entire gamut of psychical defense procedures: conscious opposition, condemnation, suppression and repression. However, repression is undoubtedly the most significant participant therein.

The mental revolt is aimed, as is clear, at the authority of God. The idea that He rules the world with His will is now negated and repressed. But it lives on basically unaltered. For mankind has scarcely freed itself from the thought of a single determinative Will, when it hastens to introduce a multiplicity of wills as a substitute into the cosmology that it had to create anew. It gives them, to be sure, the impersonal name of "natural forces." The substitute formation is not even an unique one. We have no difficulty in recognizing the new guise of the spirits and deities that the animistic age placed behind natural processes. In modern science, as we know, the most important question concerning forces appears displaced upon the work done by them, which we term energy. The case is altered thereby only to the extent that we can now designate the attitude of physics toward the universe a polyenergistic one. However, scientific inquiry does not rest satisfied with this situation. It is pervaded with an impulsion toward increasing unification and has set up an ideal worthy of pursuit in cosmological monism. This tendency received a brilliant and undoubtedly apposite rationalization through the "economic principle" of thought suggested by Ernst Mach. We, however, should recognize the return in scientific form of the recently repressed monotheistic conception under the guise of the desired monism. As is well known, the glowing scientific phantasy of the great astronomer, Laplace, anticipated the realization of the monistic scientific ideal. The intelligence, invented by him, that holds all natural laws condensed into a single mathematical-analytical formula and that derives past and future from any given situation flawlessly, conjures up in us with "uncanny" certitude the image of an omniscient and omnipotent God. Here, too, the repeated admonition of Freud should be quoted, not to expect science to replace the catechism. It is precisely in respect of certain monistic tendencies that we can confirm how justified this warning is.

Let us follow up the further explanations to which our assumption leads.

Religion, as we have learned from Freud, affords the true believer a gratification-situation.[6, 11] His intellect and his emotions are bound up with the person of his God, unto whom he has committed himself; in the presence of such a tie no genuine curiosity can arise. Whatever appears in the way of an impulse to investigate takes—since access to the physical world is blocked by divine authority—the person of God as its object and tries to fathom His mysterious nature. This mental activity engenders a "science" that is entirely removed from reality and that neither knows nor admits of an empirical check. The psychical revolt changes this picture. Divine authority is abolished and the defiant rebel is thrown upon his own resources. But now he is also free of the paralyzing influence that hitherto trammeled his thoughts and his feelings. Now he can attack the physical world with the full force of his pent-up thirst for knowledge and of his hankering. The phenomenal world (to be sure only an extension of the idea of earth) is thought of as his mother in his unconscious. The changed behavior can be understood in the light of the new psychical situation without difficulty.

If you are willing to take into account the fact that we investigate such complicated phenomena as the religious and scientific conceptions of the universe under the limitation imposed by our aim and that we also reduce them so to speak to an imaginary schema, then our description finds an excellent confirmation in the historical facts.

We have postulated a psychical revolt and should demonstrate the considerations that caused it. I wish to stress but two among the great array of these—the two that seem to be the most important. The one, an internal motive, is the hostility of old, inherent in the father complex. The other, externally operative, is the struggle for life. Indeed, it was only owing to the many inconsistencies in the religious view of the world that it contrived any adaptation to reality at all. This, however, fell increasingly short of social needs. After the psychical revolt came a hitherto undreamed of control over the struggle for existence. This is the basis of its very great significance in the development of civilization.

Having succeeded in tracing the origin of scientific determinism to its religious precursor, let us pursue its noble genealogy further. We know that monotheistic religion appropriated determinism from the animistic-mythological system of thought that preceded the former historically. We have already encountered polytheistic determinism in its modern guise in the form of "polyenergetics." We cannot take any special interest therein since the question of the genesis of religious determinism is most intimately linked with the general evolution of religion, and therefore eludes isolated treatment.

Let us then take the final step that leads back to the earliest stage of human development. Since Freud's investigations have rendered the principal part of pre-history psychologically understandable,[7, 11] we can enter this obscure field with a feeling of fortified assurance. Freud's reconstruction gives us to understand that the primal human community was arbitrarily ruled by an exceedingly powerful chief. We know, too, what kind of organization characterized this "primal horde" from the standpoint of group psychology. All the sons were fettered to the tyranny of the hostile and feared primal father by libidinal ties. The latter commanded their persons and fates with a plenitude of power never duplicated. His will governed their world, ordained their lives and their deaths. This furnished the situation in which mankind acquired the idea of determinism. It really required but a very small step for the primitive mentation of the sons to extend the inexorable omnipotence of the father of the horde to the rest of the universe. Compare with this the position that the person of the king receives even today in the thoughts of primitive peoples. Freud, referring to Fraser, states[11]: "Strictly speaking, he is a person who regulates the course of the world; his people have to thank him not only for rain and sunshine which allow the fruits of the earth to grow, but also for the wind which brings the ships to their shores and for the solid ground on which they set their feet." How faithfully the ontogenetic development of people repeats this situation is demonstrated by Ferenczi in his study of the infantile roots of hypnosis and of the stages in the development of the sense of reality.[3, 4]

If the overpowering will of the primal father is reflected in this manner in mankind's belief in causality, it is because his command was the first law—the prototype of all subsequent establishing of laws, including scientific ones. The ambivalent attitude of the sons toward the dictates of the primal father proved withal ineradicable, and having found expression in the sphere of religion, it constituted the basis of scientific scepticism.

It is as little possible for us to trace here the evolution that transformed primal determinism into the pluralistic system of the mythological level, as the advance from the animistic to the monotheistic formulation, which also eluded our discussion. Instead we can now supplement our conception of the origin of scientific determinism, which is our chief concern, in one respect. You will recall the description that Freud, assisted by Rank, gave us of the advance of the individual from group to individual psychology in the mental development of man.[7] After the murder of the primal father, during the period without master, "some individual, in the exigency of his longing, may have been moved to free himself from the group and take over the father's part. He who did this was the first epic poet; and the advance was achieved in his imagination. This poet disguised the truth with lies in accordance with his longing. He invented the heroic myth. . . .

The myth, then, is the step by which the individual emerges from group psychology." But the poet can find the way back to the group "for he goes and relates to the group his hero's deeds which he has invented."

I believe that the birth of science from the spirit of religion must have taken place in a similar manner at another stage in human development. The first scientists—history has recorded their names—follow in the wake of their predecessors, the poets, by freeing themselves from the communion of believers, by repeating the crime in phantasy and by supplanting the Father God. Whilst formerly it was His Divine Wisdom that gave the world laws, now this rôle is assumed by their human intelligence. They create the ideal of self-sufficient naturalists. In so doing, they have to destroy the "lying fancy" of their predecessors, the poets. Now, their own individuality, undisguised, takes the place of the fabled Hero God, while they replace the explanatory nature myth with a new invention, which will be much more in keeping with reality, and which on that account affords the mind very much less satisfaction. But the masses do not wish to be dragged down to reality from the heights of illusion. Since it is at first impossible for them to identify themselves with the person of the investigator, they stone him as soon as he dares to follow the example of his forefathers, the poets, and to venture into their midst. Respect for science and for the scientist appeared later, after the latter had succeeded in attracting the masses with the recompense of the usefulness of his lore.

Only now, I believe, can we appreciate in every particular the psychological significance of the deterministic fiction for science. It makes an identification with the psychically imperishable figure of the primal father easily possible for the investigator and all who are guided by him. It permits them to enjoy the reflected splendor of his omnipotence in an intellectual grasp of the world. To be sure, the more modest statistical approach leads also to an intellectual mastery of nature. However, by foregoing of necessity the fabrication of causal connections, it made the identification in question more difficult for the investigator, and in this way, it deprived him of a good part of his mental gratification.

Compared with this "thought-omnipotence" [11] afforded by science, the material power that the practical application of the latter offers man seems insignificant. We have recognized external necessity as a potent instigator of investigation. Now we see, however, that its mainspring is an internal pressure, from which it is intended to liberate mankind. Thus science fundamentally serves the same rôle in our mental life as does poetry, of which it is the ontogenetic offshoot and which it will perhaps one day wholly replace. [18] In the fictional world of art man remains on the archaic level of the pleasure principle, as Freud showed us [5]; whereas the world of science betokens to him the supreme triumph of the reality principle. To be sure, these are great extremes, and in art and science we are accustomed to perceive diametrical opposites. Here we found occasion to emphasize what is common to the psychical origin of both. Let us not forget that the reality principle, too, ultimately aims at pleasure. We are indebted to research for the pleasure in knowing, which—certainly much more difficult to attain—is closely related to the poetic delights of art. The former also proves to be to a high degree independent of satisfaction in the utility of knowledge, with which it is generally associated. The pleasure in knowing can easily change regressively into a purely artistic delight. This is the case when the investigator—often entirely unwittingly—passes over from a heuristic working hypothesis into an hedonistic speculation, which only illudes him with pseudo-knowledge. Freud called such speculations "scientific myths." They constitute that bit of fiction which in science supplements the truth. Let us confess that science would perforce become sadly impoverished, should it deny itself this liberty. Moreover, a later age often transforms the wishful dreams of research into knowledge to which no exception can be taken—ancient atomism and modern atomic physics provide an excellent example of this—and therein even the most sober critic of science may find solace.

Further insight, that may merit attention, is linked with our conclusions. We have learned that the idea of causality came into existence through primitive man's projection outward of an internal perception, that emanated from his reactions both as an individual and as a member of a group. We know that determinism has retained this "animistic" impress, even as a scientific principle. Upon occasion, I chanced the experiment of reducing highly evolved, abstract scientific conceptual constructions to their psychical substrates. In so doing I always arrived at the same result. The formation of concepts and theories in science quite regularly begins with self-perceptions, of a nature pertaining to both individual and group psychology, that are animistically shifted to the external world.* The choice of the psychical material that finds such utilization, as well as the way in which problems are put in science, appears to conform to the demands of the sexual instinct and of its attendant pleasure principle. Although Freud prepared us for the realization[11] that much contained in humanity's animistic conception of the world can still be demonstrated today "as the foundation of our language, our beliefs and our philosophy," this assertion may at first sound surprising

---

* Cf., the following passage from Freud's *Instincts and Their Vicissitudes*.[8] "The true beginning of scientific activity consists rather in describing phenomena and then in proceeding to group, classify and correlate them. Even at the stage of description it is not possible to avoid applying *certain abstract ideas to the material in hand, ideas derived from various sources and certainly not the fruit of the new experience only.*" (Italicized by myself.)

in the face of our materialistic predilection. Yet we soon perceive that it cannot indeed be otherwise and we take the liberty of appending to Freud's account the statement that our whole scientific conception of the universe, based as it is on research, is a legitimate derivative of the animistic system of thought. Moreover, we should be ever mindful of the fact that the materialistic sovereignty of natural science obtains only for our consciousness; in the unconscious animistic thinking indeed holds unlimited sway.

On the other hand, we do not wish, of course, to lose sight of the great dissimilarities that separate the animistic and the scientific systems of thought so pronouncedly when we evaluate them. We look to the analytic viewpoint to enlighten us as to the psychological basis of these differences.

I intend to touch upon this question, which constitutes a fundamental problem of the psychology of research, only cursorily. While animism projects the unalloyed products of internal perception, subject at most to the censorship of conscience, into the external world in the form of an explanation of nature, in the case of scientific thinking self-perceptions must pass through a complicated mental process. This process might be termed the "knowledge-work," since the study of it finds such an excellent model in the case of the well-known dream-work. A consideration of the data of sense-perception and of memory and, also, secondary elaboration are conspicuous for their significance in this connection. This assertion is, of course, identical with the predicating of a general reality-testing function, as well as of an "economic tendency" subordinated to the former. They distinguish scientific reasoning from all other forms of thinking.[5, 9, 13, 14]

Finally, I should not like to leave our theme before discussing briefly a question, that has presumably been stirring in your minds for some time. We have investigated the origin and significance of determinism, as well as the substitution of the statistical principle for it in natural science. In so doing we had confined ourselves to the physical disciplines. Now we can ask: what then may the situation be as regards determinism, in the case of psychoanalysis? I trust that a reliable and explicit answer can be given. Psychoanalysis has but recently begun to exploit the immeasurable advantages that the deterministic viewpoint affords it and it will have to work hard to exhaust the possibilities of that principle. In matters of science we should certainly not venture to make prophecies. We cannot foresee when and at what point in our work the statistical view, or one as yet unknown, will oust determinism from the domain of psychoanalysis. But I should not be surprised were psychoanalysis to succeed in attaining a complete understanding of our mental life with its deterministic manner of viewing things. Determinism has, to be sure, proved to be a truly anthropomorphic postulate. However, our mental life is an exquisitely anthropomorphic object of research; it is ἄνθρωπος himself. In the pre-psychoanalytical era we met with enough deterring examples of psychologies that approached the study of man's mental life with premises far removed from humanity.

REFERENCES

[1] EISLER, R.: *Handwörterbuch der Philosophie.* 1913.

[2] EXNER, F.: *Vorlesungen über die physikalischen Grundlagen der Naturwissenschaften.* 1919.

[3] FERENCZI, S.: Introjection and Transference. *Contributions to Psychoanalysis.* 1916.

[4] ——: Stages in the Development of the Sense of Reality. *Contributions to Psychoanalysis.* 1916.

[5] FREUD, S.: Formulations Regarding the Two Principles in Mental Functioning (1911). *Collected Papers, 4.*

[6] ——: From the History of an Infantile Neurosis (1918). *Collected Papers, 3.*

[7] ——: *Group Psychology and the Analysis of the Ego.* London, Hogarth, 1922.

[8] ——: Instincts and Their Vicissitudes (1915). *Collected Papers, 4.*

[9] ——: *The Interpretation of Dreams.*

[10] ——: One of the Difficulties of Psychoanalysis (1917). *Collected Papers, 4.*

[11] ——: *Totem and Taboo.* 1913.

[12] ——: *Über Psychoanalyse. Fünf Vorlesungen.* 2 Aufl. 1912. (Translated in *Am. J. Psychol.*, 1910.)

[13] MACH, ERNST: *Die Analyse der Empfindungen.* 1911.

[14] ——: *Erkenntnis und Irrtum.* 1906.

[15] MISES, R. v.: Über die gegenwärtige Krise in der Mechanik. *Die Naturwissenschaften,* 1922.

[16] NERNST, W.: Zum Gültigkeitsbereich der Naturgesetze. *Die Naturwissenschaften,* 1922.

[17] POINCARÉ, H.: *Wissenschaft und Hypothese.* 1904.

[18] RANK, O.: *Das Inzest-Motiv in Dichtung und Sage.* 1912.

[19] REICHENBACH, HANS: *Relitivitätstheorie und Erkenntnis a priori.* 1921.

[20] SCHOTTKY, W.: Das Kausalproblem der Quantentheorie als eine Grundfrage der modernen Naturforschung überhaupt. *Die Naturwissenschaften,* 1921.

[21] SCHLICK, MORITZ: Naturphilosophische Betrachtungen über das Kausalprinzip. *Die Naturwissenschaften,* 1920.

[22] TIMMERDING: *Die Analyse des Zufalls.* 1915.

[23] WEYL, H.: *Allgemeine Relativitätstheorie.* 1921.

The Economic Principle in Psycho-analytic Technique*

1. HYPNOSIS AND CATHARSIS†

Our interest in a systematic extension of analytic technique involves close investigation and theoretical appreciation of the phenomena occurring in the course of treatment. We must understand fully the relation between the methods employed and the results observed, which factors bring about the desired effect and through which channels they gradually become operative.

One has hardly settled down to these problems before it becomes apparent that the methods of treatment as carried out at the present time do not provide a suitable starting-point for the investigation. The technique of psycho-analysis, advancing tentatively along the lines of empirical observation, has already reached a stage where the analyst can achieve striking therapeutic (and pedagogic) results, but where the therapeutic conditions have become so complicated that it is by no means easy to dissect them or to present them in proper perspective. Following a hint given by Freud,[7] we shall exploit the advantages to be gained by a consideration of earlier procedures in psycho-therapeutics. Although the demands made on them were more modest and their possibilities more limited, these methods proved of good service and provided a satisfactory basis from which further advances were possible. I refer of course to those historic phases of development in technique, the use of ordinary hypnosis, the application of Breuer's cathartic hypnosis, of Freud's catharsis in a waking condition and 'analysis of symptoms' which laid the foundations of pure psycho-analysis. In so far as one views these fore-stages or forerunners of psycho-analysis as separate methods of treatment and practises them as such, consideration of them in the light of our present theoretical understanding becomes a plain necessity of immediate practical value.

* Contribution to the Symposium held at the Eighth International Psycho-Analytical Congress, Salzburg, April 21, 1924. First published in English translation in *The International Journal of Psycho-Analysis, 6:* 35–44, 1925; in German, *Internationale Zeitschrift fuer Psychoanalyse, 12:* 15–24, 1926.

† The contemplated Part 2 of this paper was never published. The entire problem of treatment technique is re-examined in *Recent Advances in Psychoanalytic Therapy* (1953) and *Adaptational Development of Psychoanalytic Therapy* (1955), both in this volume.

Coming first of all to the *clinical sequence of events* during treatment, we can begin by considering the fundamental principle established by Freud, viz. that the (classical) analytic technique is dominated by the manifestations of the artificial neurosis arising during treatment. Our treatment first transforms the patient's ordinary neurosis into a fresh 'transference neurosis' and we are thereupon faced with the task of reducing this fresh formation. The analyst did not deliberately set out to effect this new artificial formation; he merely observed that such a process took place and forthwith made use of it for his own purposes. This being so, the question naturally arises: Are we here dealing with a specific product of the classical technique or does something similar come about in the case of the earlier methods of treatment, all of which are related to the phenomenon of transference? If, moreover, this should prove to be the case, the further question arises: Since this therapeutic neurosis is not recognized and not consciously taken into consideration during treatment, what ultimately becomes of it?

Let us consider first of all the ordinary hypnotic therapy, on the psychological mechanisms of which light has already been thrown by psychoanalytic research. As is well known, the hypnotist activates in the patient the latter's infantile erotic relationships to the parents and once more accomplishes the educative effect which on an earlier occasion forced the child to control its instincts by the way of repression. At that time education opposed the child's tendency to direct gratification through action; now the hypnotist deals with the later distorted derivations of such actions, i.e. with the neurotic symptoms, which are for the patient a substitute for fulfillment of instinctual demands not capable of becoming conscious. At that time the child found compensation in parental love; now the patient consoles himself with the gratification implicit in love of the hypnotist, in hypnotic fascination. The symptoms which he must abandon are related to archaic phantasies of gratification, but the hypnotic situation actually brings about realization of the greatest of them on a living object as distinguished from an imagined object. We may assume that before the patient can repress his symptoms successfully he permits them to become *depleted* in favor of this potential gratification in actual (re-)experience. It is not quite clear how this withdrawn quantum of excitation is dealt with in the hypnotic experience, but according to the subjective sensations of the patient it is certain that it does become discharged, in all probability through the silent affective and somatic processes in hypnosis.

It would not constitute, one imagines, a departure from customary analytical modes of expression to suggest that this transference of libido from the symptoms to the hypnotic experience represents the formation of a hypnotic transference-neurosis: the new symptom-formation, fascination, exhibits quite definitely the characteristic of a compromise, in spite of the fact that this fascination provides the neurotic instinctual demands of the patient with a gratification that is, to be sure, inhibited in its aim but is none the less real and actual, and that, regarded as a social process, is lacking in certain of the characteristics of a symptom. It might be interpreted as a boundary-manifestation between the phenomena that we have to deal with, and could also be quite truly described as a kind of sublimation. The intensity of the affective discharge may be less than is usually obtained through the ordinary symptom, but this difference seems to be balanced by the actuality of the object.

One gathers from observation of patients who have previously been treated by hypnosis that after recovery they repeat over and over again this experience of fascination by elaboration in phantasy (and dreams), provided the fixation on the hypnotist and recovery from symptoms persist. Apart from the manifest adoration which such persons lavish on their saviour, these phantasies constitute the invisible symptom-formations arising from the experience of hypnotic cure.

Hence we may regard a hypnotic cure as a transformation of the ordinary neurosis into an artificial, hypnotic neurosis and can therefore endorse the hypnotist's logical endeavour to perpetuate this permanent symptom of recovery although it is in no way recognized in the technique. The advantage gained by the patient from this formation is illuminating: he has exchanged his original symptoms for symptoms which are more in keeping with the demands of his ego and is freed from the direct injury associated with his malady. Apart from this there has been no alteration in his disadvantageous libido-economy.

In the case of cathartic hypnosis the formation and ultimate issue of the neurosis occurring during treatment is much more apparent to us. Its development from the reactivated nucleus of the Oedipus complex is to begin with very similar to that occurring in ordinary hypnosis, but a fresh factor is introduced owing to an alteration in the attitude of the hypnotist. Here the latter exerts all his influence to release from the pressure of repression those instinctual demands which are represented in the neurotic symptoms. This displacement of energy must give rise to the disintegration of the symptoms concerned; it puts an end to the final process of symptom-formation and uncovers the raw material from which symptoms are constructed. The (partial) demolition of the symptoms sets free large charges of excitation which were previously 'bound'; these overflow into the motor system and by reason of their eruptive discharge give rise to dramatic scenes of 'abreaction' in the presence of the physician.

This 'abreaction', that is to say, catharsis, corresponds in every respect to an acute neurotic symptom. It presents in a marked degree the character of suffering, at the same time ensuring gratification of an intense kind which, although inhibited in its aim, is none the less real. The structure of the cathartic symptom is apparent, being constituted from two archaic situations of gratification (that of hypnosis and the situation contained in the disintegrated symptom) which are condensed through their common content (the Oedipus complex) and give rise to a unified process of discharge.

We see in abreaction the artificial counterpart of a hysterical fit and note that cure of a neurosis by catharsis comes about by its conversion into hysteria. This accords well with the fact that the cathartic method was built up from experience of hysterical cases and developed most rapidly with this neurosis.

Cathartic abreaction therefore changes the permanent symptoms of hysteria into hysterical seizures, and it goes without saying that the ordinary seizures of hysteria are converted into seizures of a different structure. Here a theoretically important question arises as to the economic difference between these two varieties of symptom, a question, however, which cannot be discussed at this juncture.

To judge from the many analogous circumstances it is probable that the enduring symptom-formations of cathartic treatment are formed in the same way as with hypnosis: it is a matter concerning which I have no personal experience.

Compared with simple hypnosis, cathartic hypnosis owes its greater practical results to the immeasurably greater intensity of substitutive satisfaction made possible through the disintegration of the symptoms. For the rest, cathartic hypnosis in the long run simply produces the situation of ordinary hypnosis: the release from repression is merely transitory and the discharge which results in the breakdown of symptoms is said to disappear from consciousness.

There is no notable difference between the special neurosis produced during treatment by catharsis in the waking state and that produced in ordinary hypnosis. The retention of ordinary consciousness during the cathartic procedure could not in itself lead to any special advantages: its historical importance depends on the fact that its possibilities were developed by the genius of Freud in a truly marvellous way.

To sum up the foregoing considerations, we may say that the therapeutic achievement of the earlier technical methods consisted in an unintended and unrecognized production and preservation of an advantageous neurosis during treatment.

Having so far oriented ourselves on the clinical characteristics of the hypnotic and cathartic therapy, we may turn our attention to the *metapsychological* understanding of the *therapeutic situation* involved in these methods.

Our insight into the topographical dynamics of the hypnotic situation depends on the principle, enunciated by Freud, that the hypnotist takes the place of the patient's ego-ideal, usurping the functions of the super-ego. As we know, in the case of ordinary hypnosis he exercises his authority in conformity with the tendencies of the old ideal: he assists the patient's ego to carry the existing repression a stage further on to the symptoms. From the point of view of the patient we might say that the latter borrows from the hypnotist the forces necessary for repression, thus regressing, as far as aims and means of instinctual mastery are concerned, to the stage of childhood at which the father's omnipotence is supreme. It seems remarkable in this connection that the hypnotist himself takes part in this regression, in that he gives a faithful rendering of the rôle attributed to him by the unconscious of the patient. Hypnosis with all its 'uncanny' procedure is without doubt a therapy based on the archaic stage of magic, one which offers substantial gratification of the patient's longing for omnipotence, to say nothing of a similar longing on the part of the physician. This narcissistic pleasure constitutes one of the factors which ensure the therapeutic results of hypnosis. I have singled out this factor because it throws some light on an aspect of hypnotic therapy to which sufficient attention has not been paid.* Hypnosis dazzles the patient's eyes with a vision of reality pleasing to his infantile attitude to life, which in other respects is quite useless, being entirely governed by the pleasure-principle; in so far as it counters his neurotic manifestations it does so by reinforcing their neurotic basis with all the impressiveness of actual experience. This contradiction which is implicit in hypnosis constitutes one of the most fundamental characteristics differentiating it from analysis.

In cathartic hypnosis the hypnotist plays a part which is completely opposed to the tendencies of the old ideal. He behaves like the leader of a successful revolutionary movement who overthrows the old constitution and repeals all the old legislative prohibitions. The cathartic excess which thereby comes about represents a triumph, as Freud has characterized it psychologically, a triumph which is celebrated by a 'crowd of two'. [8]

Returning to our fundamental proposition that the hypnotist plays the part of the super-ego, we have now to consider the method by which this is effected, to wit, the process of introjection. We shall study this process in its separate phases and differentiate its manifestations from the other transference-phenomena which characterize the hypnotic relationship.

Proceeding with our description, we may say that there is set up in the

---

* I might mention, however, a paper by Jones[11] which has come to my attention since writing: hypnotic therapy is there regarded from points of view similar to those given above and it is gratifying to me to find that many of his conclusions confirm my own.

ego of the hypnotized person an *ideational presentation* of the hypnotist who is first regarded as an outer object, i.e. a sort of result of actual sensory perception and of the instinctual forces in the mind aroused by excitation. This ideational presentation continues incessantly to receive fresh impressions from without and to be subjected to alterations in cathexis from within; through it mental processes can be influenced to a varying extent in the way of organization, direction and development, that is to say, it can continue the process of ego-alteration which we call identification. Should it now succeed in attracting to itself the natural cathexis of the topographically differentiated super-ego, its sphere of influence is thereby subjected to a new authority and the hypnotist is promoted from being an object of the ego to the position of a *parasitic super-ego*.

Incontrovertible clinical experience of hypnosis, e.g. awakening in response to suggestions of a criminal nature, show us that this withdrawal of cathexis cannot be complete. The super-ego, an organization genetically firmly established, seems to be equipped with a certain resistance against loss of power, nevertheless the residue of power it preserves is crippled through repression by its self-controlling 'double'.* The (relative) strength of cathexis of the introjected super-ego must vary; it provides a quantitative measure of the depth of hypnosis.

Belonging as it does to the ego-structure, the hypnotic super-ego seemingly usurps to itself the function of consciousness: at any rate its experiences are subjected, after the awakening of the ego, to counter-repression.

Let us now consider what ultimately happens in hypnosis to the object-cathexes directed by the ego on the hypnotist. This is closely associated with the origin and development of these strivings towards the object and the matter can only be settled by discussion of a somewhat wider scope.

We may recall here Freud's description of the means by which the infantile ego overcomes the Oedipus complex.[4, 9] 'The object-cathexes are abandoned and replaced by identification. Paternal or parental authority, introjected into the ego, forms there the core of the super-ego which, taking over its severity from the father, perpetuates the incest-prohibition and so guards the ego against the return of libidinal object-cathexes. The libidinal trends pertaining to the Oedipus complex are in part desexualized and sublimated, . . . partly inhibited as to aim and changed into feelings of tenderness.' 'The process in question represents something more than repression; under ideal conditions it is equivalent to a destruction and abro-

---

* This conception of the newly-formed super-ego in hypnosis as a 'parasitic double' was formed in my mind from the study of some of Freud's speculations which have hitherto been neglected.[10]

gation of the Oedipus complex. . . . If the ego has really not achieved much more than a repression of the complex, this latter persists unconsciously in the *id*, giving rise later to pathogenic manifestations.'

The neurotic, whose restoration to health is the concern of our therapy, illustrates this latter contingency: he has come to grief during childhood over the mastering of his Oedipus complex, has repressed the sexual trends pertaining to it and afterwards has had to put up with their reappearance in the form of symptoms. He finds himself in a situation of frustration, exhibits an intense craving for an object, the instinctual force of which is derived from the *id*, and which is due to the unconscious dominance of the Oedipus complex.

Hence it is the Oedipus libido of the *id* which at the commencement of hypnosis invests the person of the hypnotist and which, at the signal he gives, activates the 'feminine masochistic' attitude[6] present in the ego.* It is easy to conjecture the subsequent course of events. The ego takes alarm at the sudden intensity of the masochistic trend, even if it should at first give rein to this striving; stimulated by the active liberation of anxiety which follows, it takes flight, thus stultifying the endeavours of the hypnotist.

It must depend on certain characteristics of the masochistic trends, in all probability on their intensity and the durability of their manifest component, whether this eventuality is avoided and the road to hypnosis is finally traversed. If the ego is barred from both extremes (hasty repression or direct realization) it must of necessity strive to overcome the new (masochistic) demands of Oedipus libido on an infantile pattern by replacing the object through identification, desexualizing object-cathexes and binding this acute ego-alteration. This cannot be entirely successful: object-cathexis is in part retained but is transformed into an aim-inhibited feeling. Once accepted by the ego, this must endanger the unity of the ego, since its masochistic character is incompatible with the ego-alteration (identification) which takes place at the same time. This identification, the kernel of which arises from the ideational presentation of the hypnotist, separates itself eventually from the remaining masochistic content of the ego and retreats in the direction of the super-ego. Only after these preliminary steps have been taken is the identification in a position to deal with the super-ego in the manner already described, to establish itself by an extensive withdrawal of energy as a usurper of the super-ego's power.

Thus masochism ultimately gains a free hand in the ego and unites with the sadism of the introjected, parasitic super-ego to bring about the results

---

* The so-called 'mother-hypnosis' is best explained as a clever device which conceals the hypnotist's ultimate aims under a hypocritical mask which is psychologically well conceived.

The Psychic Effects of Intoxicants: An Attempt to Evolve a Psycho- analytical Theory of Morbid Cravings*

Intoxicants are substances varying very greatly in origin and chemical peculiarities (alkaloids, substances of the alcohol-group, etc.), which, when resorted to either occasionally or habitually, have stupefying, stimulating or exhilarating effects on the mental life. Pharmacology has conducted more or less exhaustive researches in connection with the influence of these substances upon the organic functions of body and mind and gives us some information with regard to the specific effects produced by intoxicants according to the manner and the quantity in which they are employed. Nevertheless, these investigations have only a rough (statistical) validity; we are quite unable to predict with any certainty how a given individual will react to an intoxicant. Pharmacology gives this fact due consideration by postulating a "constitutional factor." According to Lewin[8] every individual has his own peculiar "toxic equation"; this, however, is composed of elements of which we know nothing and which elude the investigations of the pharmacologist.

Everyday experience shows us how great this uncertainty is, particularly in regard to the specific effects of intoxicants. A very little alcohol suffices to intoxicate some people, whereas others can drink a large quantity and yet remain sober, though experiencing the physical effects of intoxication. Indeed, the behaviour of one and the same person in this respect may completely change as time goes on, without anyone being able to say why. Similar phenomena are observed when morphia and other narcotics are administered. Accordingly, the theory of the psychiatrists is that this unknown quantity—the individual's disposition or tendency to intoxication— plays a decisive part in the etiology of morbid cravings and allied states.

Let us try to penetrate this obscure region from the psychoanalytical point of view. Pharmacology classifies the manifold effects of intoxicants according to its own standpoints. We aim at a psychological (or, more

* First published in *Festschrift* for Sigmund Freud on the occasion of his seventieth birthday, of the *Internationale Zeitschrift fuer Psychoanalyse, 12:* 540–556, 1926; in English, *The International Journal of Psycho-Analysis, 7:* 396–413, 1926.

exactly, a metapsychological) orientation and ask ourselves: What are the peculiar properties of these substances, in virtue of which they are employed by the medical profession and in ordinary life? The answer is simple: they offer human beings in their need two things—help and gratification. This "help" may take one of two forms: the drugs have (a) an analgesic (sedative, hypnotic), and (b) a stimulating effect.

Hitherto these two modes of operation have not been investigated analytically. Let us put down the first things which strike us as characteristic of them.

(a) In order to discuss the pain-killing effect of the so-called "analgesics" we have to enter upon the problem of pain in general. Freud's view has provided a firm basis for a psychological conception of this difficult subject.[2] His theory is as follows: The specific mental distress of bodily pain arises when some influence breaks down the peripheral shield against stimuli, thus allowing a flow of continuous excitations from the affected area to the central mental apparatus. When the shield is broken through, pain, even when its onslaught is from without, assumes the characteristics of continuous inner stimuli (i.e. of the instincts), against which the measures designed to withstand stimuli are from the outset futile. Within the mental apparatus the pleasure-pain principle by which it is governed, by setting up anticathexes, binds the advancing volume of excitation and discharges it in motor activities. It is the quantitative factor which determines the measure of success attained by these defensive processes in the mastering of pain. Experience teaches us that when the painful excitation passes beyond a certain intensity the mental life succumbs to it helplessly. Moreover, the biological tendency of pain, which is to give warning of a danger threatening, is then altogether defeated.

We can now easily realize that, by diminishing or removing the sensation of pain, drugs supply exactly that which the mental organization lacks— namely, a shield against stimulation from within. This artificial shield functions *centrally*, at the sensory approaches to the mental apparatus, and acts, as we may say, as a second line of defence. The somatic process by which it is conditioned is invariably a diminution in function through paralysis of the excitable nerve-substance—a method which is sometimes also employed by the natural peripheral shield against stimuli.*

All medical practitioners seem to agree that morphia is still our most valuable analgesic, though chemists are working hard to produce new and specifically differentiated combinations. Recently, L. Lévy[7] published one of the few psychoanalytical contributions to this subject. He tells us that,

---

* What occurs in local anaesthesia is that the peripheral shield is so enormously strengthened that the sensory end-apparatus is benumbed and the function of receiving stimuli is wholly abrogated.

in a number of grave organic cases in which morphia had been administered with successful results, he observed a remarkable phenomenon: the patients in their phantasies *projected* their serious state of health on to persons in their environment. This discovery of Lévy's must be regarded as of great importance in the present connection. As we know, Freud has traced the origin of projection to the impulse to treat inner excitations "as if they were acting not from within but from without, so as to be able to employ against them the defensive measures of the shield against stimuli." [2] Now if, as I think, the analgesia produced by morphia is an artificial inner defence against stimuli, then Lévy's observation is actually an experimental proof of the close connection between the warding-off of stimuli and the process of projection.

The overcoming of sleeplessness by hypnotics or the inducing of sleep by means of toxins (narcosis) cannot for the present be described more exactly in analytical terms, because we know almost nothing about the specific characteristics of these states. When we consider that sleeplessness is due to the obduracy of inner excitations, which will not yield to the desire for sleep and cooperate in the general withdrawal of cathexis, we must suppose that the establishing of a shield against stimuli from within again plays a part in the hypnotic and sedative effect of the drugs. But in narcosis there must certainly be something more than that, psychologically.

(b) The specific effect of "stimulants" is the one most familiar to us and of the most general importance, because these substances, in the form of coffee, tea, etc., are part of our daily food. Nevertheless, an attempt to define the processes of stimulation psychologically meets with great difficulties. The usual explanation that stimulants have a quickening effect upon our intellectual functions obviously takes us little further. Pharmacology teaches us that, strictly speaking, there are no drugs which are pure stimulants, for all such substances work electively upon the different nervous centres, stimulating some and paralysing others. Perhaps the single exception is caffeine, which has an almost exclusively stimulating effect and is not succeeded by a phase of dullness. We must assume that the influence of these substances on the separate centers and functions of the brain is much more far-reaching and more finely graded electively than pharmacology can at present demonstrate. For psychological observation shows us that what constitutes the psychic effect of these substances is the alternation of stimulating and paralysing influences. We can see that the drugs produce feelings of tension and at the same time relieve already existing tensions—the final result being the conversion of painful into pleasurable tensions. Unfortunately, this simple explanation is even less valuable than it might be, because we know so little of these two kinds of sensations of tension.

On the other hand, we must not underrate the importance of the discovery that the promotion of our ego-functions by means of toxins is bound up with a reversal in the feeling-tone of our inner tensions. Behind this lie hidden the economic conditions of our ego-functions in general, into which we may possibly penetrate from this angle. Let us consider the situation in which the ego has recourse to toxins in order to function more freely. We have already said that it needs this help in the distress consequent upon the hard struggle to maintain itself. Freud has given us an impressive account of the "allegiances" which the ego owes.[3] The ego must always be alert to adapt itself satisfactorily to the demands of reality and at the same time to be true to its two inner masters: the libido of the id and the demands of conscience. Now self-observation shows us that both the libidinal instinctual tensions and also the tensions proceeding from conscience—the so-called sense of guilt—invariably announce themselves to consciousness (though it may be only as a nameless discomfort) when the ego has succeeded in warding off by repression the ideational contents of these affects or when these contents are from the outset incapable of becoming conscious. In the same way we see that the ucs phantasies by which the impulses of the object-libido are gratified and also those phantasies from which the self-complacent ideal (the super-ego) derives satisfaction make themselves felt in consciousness in the form of an inarticulate feeling of pleasure (a mood).* Sometimes we succeed in catching hold of such ucs products in analysis, and then we can also see how it is that stimulants bring about a reversal in the mind. They clear the way for hampered intentions, for they appease the hampering (inhibiting) influences—which are mainly the tensions produced by conscience—by giving them ucs gratification and thus get rid of them. Apparently this has the direct effect of reinforcing the function intended; at the same time the subject is enabled to draw upon instinctual sources, otherwise sealed to him, through an extensive fusion of the contents of the ego with the symbol-cathexes of the id. Or possibly, this fusion gives rise to a partial transition from the "bound" discharge of the secondary process to that of the primary process. This effect is principally brought about in the pcs; the rigid attachments of this system are loosened and its conductivity is increased. We note that what happens in stimulation is really a successful eroticizing of the ego-functions.

The second effect of intoxicants is the production of states of well-being (euphoria, stupefaction, and exhilaration), which vary greatly in intensity and quality. The variety of phenomena observed is enormously increased by the specific characteristics and secondary effects of the different in-

* These facts must also play an important part in the effect of music on our minds.

toxicants, by the manner in which they are employed and by all kinds of disturbances in the capacity of individuals to react to them. From amongst these many possibilities let us select the type of the *optimal* effect, as we see it in complete euphoria induced by morphia or in the untroubled ecstasy resulting from opium. The erotic nature of these states (to which Abraham drew attention long ago) is immediately obvious. But in following up this impression we may go much further and are bound to conclude that there is an essential agreement between the ideal, toxic inebriation and the end-pleasure obtained in natural sexual activities, i.e., orgasm. The distinctive characteristic of genital orgasm, which makes it rank high as a gratification *sui generis*, must be held to lie simply in the fact that the feeling of well-being succeeding on orgasm quickly loses its originally local character and, in a manner which we cannot apprehend more exactly, becomes diffused through the entire organism with the utmost intensity.* In the gratification of erotic component instincts and in the ordinary pleasure-sensations located in the erotogenic zones this is never the case; their local colour is retained throughout the discharge of excitation, and this discharge, so far as we know at present, is not capable of general diffusion. But precisely this feature of diffusion recurs in a marked form in the picture of intoxication. In our view this justifies us in calling the production of this feeling of well-being the *orgastic* effect of intoxicants. In comparison with the abrupt curve of genital orgasm, the course followed by pharmacotoxic or pharmacogenic orgasm is generally a long drawn-out one. We shall return later to this striking difference between the two phenomena.

The question arises whether this conception of the orgastic effect of intoxicants may be extended from the "optimal" to all other cases? The capacity of different drugs and of different individuals to achieve this effect certainly varies very greatly, but observation puts it almost beyond doubt that in every instance the process tends to the same final result. In practice, of course, we have to take into account all the varying degrees of intensity and further we must not be misled by those cases in which the orgastic effect is qualitatively impaired or wholly absent. After all, genital orgasm also is frequently enough subject to similar disturbances. Even "stimulation," which on theoretical grounds we differentiate so sharply from the pure pleasure-states, proves in the light of this knowledge to be an admirably graduated "minimal effect" of an orgastic process.

In pharmacogenic orgasm the subject becomes acquainted with a new kind of erotic gratification, which enters into rivalry with the natural modes of sexual gratification. It has certain characteristics which give it remarkable advantages and must appear the more attractive in proportion as the

---

* The extension of orgastic excitation to the whole vegetative nervous system has already been demonstrated from the physiological point of view.[9]

normal possibilities of gratification are prejudiced by neurosis or by un-favourable circumstances. The crisis occurs when the ego is enlisted on the side of the desire for intoxication, and thus brings to the experience of pharmacotoxic orgasm all the libido at its disposal. When once intoxication has become a sexual aim, the subject has fallen a victim to the craving; it is but seldom that anyone succeeds in arresting the further course of events. It makes very little difference whether the temptation is succumbed to of deliberate intention or whether the first unforgettable experience of the pleasure of intoxication is a secondary result of the medical administration of a drug. Only too often we observe an instructive initial stage, in which the drug addict denies to himself his desire for intoxication; he still uses the drug as a "medicine" to overcome suffering, to increase his efficiency or to heighten his potency, but in reality he has long ago succumbed to its orgastic influence and, departing from the reality-principle, is approaching dangerously near to blind obedience to instinct.

On the other hand we now comprehend how it comes about that im-bibing intoxicants does not always lead to intoxication or to any orgastic discharge. In the first place, because the longing, the desire for intoxication, is lacking. And secondly, because that desire may be replaced by a strong inhibition (in the form of a reaction of conscience, usually unconscious), which checks the instinctual transmutations and prevents intoxication, even though the dose be considerably increased.

When a person adopts the practice of pharmacotoxic gratification, mo-mentous consequences ensue to his whole psychic and somatic condition. The phenomena presented to the clinical observer in cases of morbid craving are so multifarious that in this brief survey we must confine our-selves to stressing certain fundamental characteristics. The changes are enacted principally, of course, in the abode of the libido, for erotic gratifi-cation by means of drugs is a violent attack on our biological sexual or-ganization, a bold forward movement of our "alloplastic" civilization. Let us confine ourselves to morphinism and to the most "fashionable" method of administering the poison by means of the Pravaz syringe. To put the matter in a nutshell, the whole peripheral sexual apparatus is left on one side as in a "short circuit" and the exciting stimuli are enabled to operate directly on the central organ. I propose to term this phenomenon, which deserves to be distinguished by a special name, "metaerotism."* With the advance of organic chemistry the manufacture of the most refined sub-stances for producing sexual gratification is assuredly only a matter of

---

* I prefer to use this term rather than the obvious "paraerotism," which I think should be reserved for the less questionable scientific designation of the perversions. My justification for proposing so many new terms in this paper must be that I am trying to treat of a wide range of facts which have not hitherto been dealt with in detail by psychoanalysis.

time, and it is easy to prophesy that in the future of our race this mode of gratification will play a part as yet incalculable.

Elimination of the genital and of the other erotogenic zones, with their complicated interplay and their cumbrous methods for discharging excitation, first and foremost undermines genital potency and then leads rapidly to a turning away from real love-objects, which are no longer of any interest. Like most intoxicants, morphia is a poison dangerous to potency and as a source of pleasure soon makes itself an absolute monarch. With the abandonment of sexual love a loosening of the relations to reality begins—of course, with the exception of the drug itself—and the whole psychic interest of the morphomaniac becomes gradually concentrated upon procuring the latter.

Metaerotism, however, not only destroys genital potency; it also robs of their value all other natural ways of attaining pleasure, substituting for them pharmacotoxic orgasm as a means of gratification. We must regard pharmacogenic orgasm as an executive process by which the discharge of the entire psychosexual excitation is accomplished, like the function of onanism in children.

Now what is the state in which the libido finds itself psychically after real love-objects and genital activity have been given up? As always happens when the genital primacy is demolished, the pregenital organizations come to their own. The erotic tendencies of the past are activated by a comprehensive regression, the Oedipus complex flares up and it depends in the first instance on the vicissitudes of infancy and the fixation-points of the libido what manner of impulses and desires make their appearance. Day-dreams and phantasies occur, quite comparable to masturbation-phantasies, the excitation of which is discharged in pharmacotoxic orgasm. In the blissful phantasy-images of opium-intoxication as described by certain writers, it is evident that the subject actually produces wish-fulfilling hallucinations. Thus every hidden source of pleasure which can conduce towards intensification of the ecstasy may contribute to the gratification. Even the genital libido, after being withdrawn from reality, may still be retained for a time in phantasy as an impulse belonging to the Oedipus complex. This is apparent in the symbolic value attached to the syringe, etc.

In many cases the significance of particular erotogenic zones is so marked that they take shelter, like refugees, under the metaerotic régime; they may then be retained as areas for and modes of application of the drug and take their place in the metaerotic organization, together with the excitation of which they are capable or with the symbolic cathexis attaching to them, as a kind of mechanism for preliminary pleasure. Incomparably the most important in this respect is the oral zone, the close connections of which with intoxicants are already known. Undoubtedly drinking was the earliest method by which intoxicants were imbibed and it is probably still the most widespread. We may say in general that there is scarcely any accessible region of the body which has not been used for the introduction of drugs, and the variety in the ways of their application is amazingly great.

If we have the courage to compare artificial metaerotism with the natural libidinal organizations we shall find certain further points which assist orientation in the bewildering abundance of phenomena. We then see clearly that pharmacogenic orgasm may be subject to disturbances and produce pathological reactions (as it were of a second order), just like any normal life process. First and foremost, owing to its great practical significance for the curability of the patient, is pharmacotoxic impotence—the failure to achieve pharmacotoxic orgasm though the intention to obtain gratification is present. It seems premature today to give a picture of the *psychic* forces and processes which may produce this state, sometimes even in the initial stages of the craving. In any case the fact should be specially stressed that with most drugs this failure inevitably occurs sooner or later from physiological reasons ("habituation") and cannot be overcome, however desperate the efforts of the patient. Another group of phenomena displays those products of unsuccessful attempts at defence or powerful reaction of conscience familiar to us from the theory of the neuroses. This defence impairs or wholly nullifies the pharmacogenic orgasm aimed at, but defensive process is directed against its psychic superstructure, the forbidden tendencies of the Oedipus complex activated by metaerotism. Thus the "neurotic" reverse side of blissful intoxication is manifested in the most terrible anxiety-states, torturing excitement, frightful visions, etc. The behaviour of different drugs varies greatly in this respect. With many of them (for instance, with cocaine) the specific effect is complicated by these phenomena. All these relations can only be cleared up by full and complete analyses, and the same is true of the vast field of allied phenomena accompanying abstention from the drug, with which we cannot deal here.

Several authors have already remarked on the emergence of the primitive libidinal organizations in the clinical picture of morbid cravings. Schilder[10] recently laid special emphasis on this point. To this we must add that the destruction of genital primacy may so strengthen certain pregenital erotisms that the result is sometimes (especially in periods of abstention from the drug) a manifest perversion. In particular, an important part is played here by homosexuality, the relations of which to alcoholism were described by Abraham long ago, and to the cocaine-habit recently by Hartmann.[6]

In grave cases of drug-mania the disruptive effect of metaerotism on the mental life goes much further still. We get the impression that, through the neglect of their somatic sources, the specific mental impulses of the component instincts gradually become exhausted also, and even that all the differentiated mental modes of erotic manifestation, with their richly diversified contents, progressively perish. A relentless process of mental devastation overtakes and destroys everything that has been created through psychogenesis in the individual—a mental state comparable only to certain features in the final stages of schizophrenia. We shall be entirely in accordance with facts if we construct theoretically a final phase in which the libido has lost all its genetically differentiated characteristics and forms of organization, and survives in mental life only as an *amorphous* erotic tension. The patient's mental life is then represented by a very simple formula: *desire for intoxication, intoxication, after-effects,* and so forth. This hypothesis seems to me to throw a searching light on certain grave forms of morbid craving, for it is indisputable that, unless failure through "habituation" previously takes place, this is the direction in which they tend. The whole mental personality, together with the drug, then represents an autoerotic pleasure-apparatus. The ego is completely subjugated and devastated by the libido of the id—one might almost say that it is converted back into the id; the outside world is ignored and the conscience disintegrated. We get a glimpse of the enormous importance the drug assumes as the sole piece of reality in which the subject has any interest, and we can realize how it is that from the very beginning of his illness the drug-addict throws overboard every legal and moral consideration in his attempts to procure it.

The picture I have outlined must now be supplemented by certain features which relate to one factor that I have so far left on one side. The continuous process of regression and deterioration which overtakes the libido in metaerotism must, according to Freud's conception, which is confirmed by all the experience acquired in studying the psychoneuroses, be accompanied by a far-reaching defusion of the instincts and liberation of the destructive component. It is easy to see that the facts fully bear out this theoretical expectation. The overthrow which I have described of the higher mental organizations and differentiations can only be the work of destructive forces liberated by defusion, and we still do not know what part this psychic factor plays in the somatic deterioration of the drug-victim, which runs parallel with his mental ruin. The destructive force, once let loose, finds a second stronghold within the super-ego in the faculty of conscience whose aggressive tendencies (according to Freud's view) are directed upon the ego in the form of a "conscience-instinct."* In the case

---

* It seems advisable to designate as the "conscience-instinct" the dynamic expression of the institution of conscience. According to Freud's discovery this instinct represents the phylogenetically most recent differentiation in human instinctual life and is mainly determined by its topographical strategical position. The phrase enables us to utilize in the psychology of the ego terminology already familiar from the theory of instinct, and as regards its content it is perfectly accurate and is also helpful.

of many drug-addicts (we do not as yet know of which type) we are forced to assume that the unconscious tension of conscience is actually intensified rapidly, and that this involves, amongst other things, a strong need for punishment. The result is a vicious circle, the patient being plunged deeper and deeper into his craving, and a *psychological* basis being supplied for the inevitable increase of the dose.

Although often, especially in the case of certain drugs, the aggressive tendency may also be directed outwards, undoubtedly it is far more significant when it is "turned round" upon the subject's own person. Here is a remarkable analogy: the drug-addict perishes as a result of the psychic disintegration due to his metaerotism, just as some lower animals perish as a result of their natural sexual activity.

Let us now turn to what is perhaps the most important question arising out of our discussion. After the drug has been first taken purely for medical purposes, what is it in a man's mind which oversteps the boundary between "help" and "pleasure," or what is it which first of all leads him to resort to drugs with the intention of procuring gratification?* In other words, what kind of person conceives the desire for intoxication and follows it along the path which leads to drug-mania?

The commonest factor in the etiology of morbid cravings is, of course, actual frustration of gratification with all its manifold accompanying phenomena, familiar to us from the etiology of the neurosis. We find nothing which might not occur as an "actual conflict" in the neuroses too, with at most this additional fact that any of the neuroses may also enter into the causation of morbid cravings. It often happens that frustration is followed first of all by a neurosis, and only later by such a craving, but this compli-

---

* The following table may make it easier to grasp the relations which I have been describing:

THE PSYCHIC EFFECTS OF INTOXICANTS

A. *Help rendered*
  (a) Protective shield against stimulus from within. (Analgetic, sedative, hypnotic and narcotic effects)
  (b) Promotion of ego-functions. (Stimulating effects)
	Internal relief for the ego in the service of reality

B. *Pleasure derived* Pharmacotoxic orgasm. (Intoxicating effects)	Subjugation of the ego by the id. Destruction of the relations of the ego to reality

cates matters only by one degree. The disposing factors which decide the choice of "flight into morbid craving" must therefore lie further back, and all our endeavours to bring this field of phenomena under the terms of Freud's theory of the libido lead us to the conclusion that these factors are to be sought in the libidinal development of the person concerned. Thus our attention was directed to oral erotism, whose etiological importance in dipsomania (already cited by Freud in his *Drei Abhandlungen zur Sexualtheorie*[4]) has been confirmed by all subsequent analytical experience. The surprising discovery was made that the psychic manifestations of oral erotism are always present in a marked form even in those cases of drug-mania in which the drug is not taken by mouth at all. One received the impression that some mysterious bonds exist between the oral zone and intoxication, and that the significance of these bonds is retained even when other erotogenic zones have replaced the oral in administering the drug, or when it is wholly independent of erotogenic zones. This fact is perhaps most clearly seen in cases of the latter type, where the Pravaz syringe is employed. It is as though intoxication remained an oral phenomenon, although precisely the most highly finished technique for producing it has emancipated itself from the oral zone. This conclusion is certainly not very satisfying, and the more so when we reflect how little it advances our knowledge. Abraham's classic researches have shown us how manifold are the operations and manifestations of oral erotism in our mental life, and we simply do not understand what there can be which disposes the subject to the production of states of intoxication, from which the mouth as an erotogenic zone is eliminated.

I admit that for many years this problem baffled me, until certain chance observations supplied me with the solution. Curiously enough, these were not in the first instance made in relation to drug-addicts at all. One day it struck me that the exciting process in oral erotism could not be restricted to the region of the mouth as the somatic source. When pleasant-tasting food has been eaten in abundance and with enjoyment, there follows a phase to which, physiologically, nothing but the beginning of digestion and absorption can correspond. In this phase the mental picture is dominated by the agreeable feeling of a full stomach (repletion) and by a general diffused feeling of well-being which extends far beyond that of repletion, the whole organism here taking its share.* Some people possess the capacity for experiencing this phenomenon intensely; in others the faculty has been more or less lost. There is no doubt that, in adults, this process is the sur-

---

* The phase of digestion announces itself, as we know, by a series of physiological indications in the *whole* organism (raising of the temperature, change in the composition of the blood, etc.).

vival of a psycho-physiological primary function which can only be termed an *alimentary orgasm*. I will show elsewhere by means of clinical material how great may be the significance of this orgastic mode of gratification in normal persons, and in certain of the neuroses. Such observations are easily made, when once attention has been drawn to the phenomenon. Let us pass on to consider the theoretical importance of this discovery.

It is only too plain that the oral organization of the sucking infant culminates in alimentary orgasm. Since the somatic processes on which this orgastic pleasure is based take place within the body, and are thus unperceived by the infant, his interest must be displaced on to the tangible oral zone, the excitation of which, as a fore-pleasure mechanism, sets in motion the process of gratification. We may assume that what the sucking infant really aims at is the repetition of orgastic gratification, and that he contents himself with such enjoyment as is restricted to the oral zone only as a surrogate satisfaction. Owing to the dependence of alimentary orgasm on the function of nutrition it is possible to repeat it at all only within the limits permitted by the physical condition of the digestive tract at the moment. Thus the enhanced erotic value of the oral zone would have to be traced to alimentary orgasm. In any case, however, there is deeply imprinted in the ucs the expectant surmise that stimulation of the oral zone may reproduce that hidden and mysterious pleasure. This may even have led some ancestor of ours with unusual oral endowment to the first discovery of a plant yielding an intoxicating substance.

Alimentary orgasm makes its appearance in mental life as a finished psycho-physiological mechanism, and in its further developments exercises a far-reaching influence on psycho-sexual evolution. With the cathexes which it contributes it enters into a whole series of infantile ideas and wish-images familiar to us. Thus, to mention only the most essential, it proves to be what really underlies the familiar sequence: *oral impregnation–abdominal pregnancy–anal birth*. These connections may be proved with certainty in analysis, and must be reckoned amongst the most important factual bases of our theory. It is only when we argue back to the sucking infant that we enter the realm of speculation, cogent though our argument seems to be. But why alimentary orgasm is the nucleus round which are grouped the "genital" ideas which enter into these infantile sexual theories so important in the symptomatology of the neuroses—this is a question which must be answered later. Here I would simply add the remark that the sexual excitation of such wish-phantasies (which belong to the Oedipus complex), given a certain disposition in the subject, is discharged *not* by means of onanism but through alimentary orgasm. Subsequently, when a defence is set up against the, now forbidden, incestuous tendencies, the repressive process extends to the executive function of alimentary orgasm and in *this* way brings about the familiar psychic disturbances of the function of nutrition (distaste for food, gastric and intestinal neuroses, etc.).

It is in alimentary orgasm with its psychic superstructure as outlined here that we shall find the specific fixation-point disposing the subject to morbid craving. Pharmacotoxic orgasm is seen to be a new edition of alimentary orgasm, in common with which it shares its diffused and retarded course and much besides, but which otherwise it far surpasses in pleasurable characteristics.* Here we have at one blow the solution of a number of problems which present themselves in our study of morbid cravings. The pregenital erotisms, so prominent in the clinical pictures, are the psychic garb of the alimentary orgasm of the infantile period. This gives us an intelligible psychological motivation for the prevalence of homosexuality, without being obliged to assume with Schilder[10] a mutual affinity between particular drugs and particular erotisms. We understand first of all from the psychological side why most morbid cravings are accompanied by great emaciation and by the neglect of the function of nutrition, and why, according to Lewin,[8] in the coca-chewer, for instance, 'for long periods of time, the under-nourished body feels no sensations of hunger.' The pharmacotoxic orgasm in its magnitude has swallowed up the rudiments of the alimentary orgasm which acts as a pleasure-premium and ensures nutrition and digestion.

To the unconscious 'tension of conscience' (sense of guilt), on the other hand, no specific rôle in the etiology of morbid cravings can be ascribed. Its importance in grave cases is similar to that which we must assign to it in grave cases of neuroses. Merely proving that it is present (important as this may be practically) makes us none the wiser as to why a given individual should have either succumbed to a neurosis, or fallen a victim to drug-mania, or become a criminal or a socially energetic philanthropist.

Before we leave this subject let us draw a brief comparison between the different modes of orgastic gratification which we have discovered. Here it is tempting to mention the phylogenetic standpoint. It seems hardly credible that the orgastic mode of gratification was first introduced as a novelty when the higher forms of animal life emerged and the organs of copulation were formed. If, then we discard this hypothesis, purely evolutionary reasons force us to adopt the view that alimentary orgasm represents the original form of orgastic gratification, and that, accordingly, the highest pleasure-function of primitive living beings is bound up with their

---

* A long series of foods and delicacies can be worked out, forming a regular gradation from ordinary foods up to pure intoxicants, so that we have also to take into consideration cases in which the two orgastic functions are blended.

most important self-preservative function.* Thus in the period when he is
an infant at the breast the individual recapitulates a version of that phase
of development, which then (and this is certainly only a repetition of a
phase in the evolution of the race—cf. beasts of prey) persists for a time in
formidable rivalry with the gradually maturing genitality.†

This would explain also the fact that in ontogenesis the complex of
'genital' phantasies (and often also the discharge of the accompanying sexual
excitation) is at the outset connected with alimentary orgasm. This latter
must obviously be based on the physiological-chemical processes of digestion and absorption. Following the theory suggested by Freud in relation to a sexual chemistry,[4] we assume that in these processes some
change (and perhaps also the production) of sexual substances takes place.
This would imply that alimentary orgasm is an (endo)-toxic phenomenon,
closely bound up with the nutritive process. According to Ferenczi's view,[1]
the development of 'genitality' in the phylogenetic process of progressive
differentiation is to be conceived of as the setting up and discriminating of
an erotic centre, whose function it is to relieve the processes of self-preservation from their secondary, erotic service. If we accept this view, we may
add to our argument that the genital has obviously wrested its orgastic
operation from the process of nutrition. In spite of its subservience to the
function of reproduction, genitality has without doubt a greater mobility
in the management of sexual substances than was the case in the act of
nutrition. For the present we do not understand how the toxic sexual substances have been so dealt with by genital erotism as to undergo *explosive*
transformation in the new, *genital* orgasm. But when man discovered
pharmacotoxic orgasm he played a trick on biology. He too has copied the
function of nutrition, has detached its accompanying sexual-toxic phenomena from their cumbrous alimentary prerequisites and raised them to
the status of an independent mode of orgastic gratification. Possibly we
shall at some future time succeed in imitating a genital orgasm by pharmacogenic means.

One factor common to all three forms of orgasm is that they induce sleep

---

* Biological considerations compel us to ascribe alimentary orgasm even to the
lowest protozoa, which take in nourishment with their whole, undifferentiated, uni-
cellular body. The conception of orgasm as an 'erotic primary function' and of the
cell as an 'orgastic unity' opens up an interesting biological perspective and should
throw light from a new angle upon the processes of cell-division and copulation, and
make them more accessible to experimental research.

† The transition from alimentary orgasm to genital erotism appears to be made
by way of the oral zone. For the relations existing between oral and genital erotism,
cf. the following writings: *Psychoanalyse der weiblichen Sexualfunctionen*, by Helene
Deutsch; *Psychologie des Säuglings*, by Bernfeld; 'Zur Genese der Genitalität,' by
Rank.

by equalizing the erotic tensions. In alimentary orgasm the destructive tendency, when liberated (mainly in the form of *chemical* aggression), is directed against the food which the subject has taken; in genital and pharmacogenic orgasm the destructive force attacks the subject's own bodily existence, though far less noticeably in the first than in the second.

In conclusion, I would say a few words on the subject of melancholia. Knowing, as we do, the significance of the function of oral incorporation in this disease, we should expect that the idea of alimentary orgasm would throw fresh light also on its pathology. We will confine ourselves here to a few brief suggestions. The similarity of mania and melancholia to intoxication and its depressing after-effects respectively is well known. I think that we can now show the biological prototypes of both pairs of phenomena; they are (a) alimentary orgasm and (b) long-continued hunger which has already produced a paralysing effect. When a starving man, in order to meet his need for fresh energy, destroys his own body, his aggression is ultimately directed against objects formerly belonging to the outside world, which have been incorporated by him and built into his frame. Though we are far from overestimating the importance of analogies of this sort, yet we cannot but be surprised to see how faithfully these processes are reproduced on purely psychological ground in melancholia. And further, we must not forget that rapid emaciation is one of the most striking clinical accompaniments of melancholia. Moreover, the constant lament of the melancholic patient that his body is decomposing and that his stomach or intestines have perished and so forth, betrays its deep biological meaning—a grave impairment of the orgastic alimentary function. Finally, it must be admitted in this connection that both with our ancestors in the brute creation, and to a great extent with infants at the present time, alimentary orgasm was and is preceded by a tormenting state of hunger, just as mania is preceded by melancholia.

References

[1] FERENCZI, S.: *Versuch einer Genitaltheorie.* 1924.
[2] FREUD, S.: *Beyond the Pleasure Principle.*
[3] ——: *Das Ich und das Es.*
[4] ——: *Drei Abhandlungen zur Sexualtheorie.*
[5] GOLDSCHEIDER: *Das Schmerzproblem.* Berlin, 1920.
[6] HARTMANN: Kokainismus und Homosexualitat. *Ztschr. f. die gesammte Psychiatrie und Neurologie,* 1925.
[7] LÉVY, L.: Zur Psychologie der Morphiumvirkung. *Int. Ztschr. f. Psychoanal.,* 10, 1924.
[8] LEWIN, L.: *Phantastica, Die betaübenden und erregenden Genussmittel.* Berlin, 1924.
[9] MÜLLER, L. R.: *Das Vegetative Nervensystem.* Berlin, 1920.
[10] SCHILDER: *Entwurf zu einer Psychiatrie auf psycho-analytischer Grundlage.* 1925.

An Anxious Mother: A Contribution to the Analysis of the Ego[*]

The scene was the beach of a small and quiet seaside resort. One day there appeared close to where I was lying a young woman with a little boy of perhaps five years old. They were strangers, and I never came to know them personally, but for several weeks I was an involuntary eye-witness and auditor of their behaviour. The little boy behaved just like the other children who thronged the beach. He played in the sand, ran about, fetched water in little buckets from the sea to his sand-castles, and so forth. The mother lay in a deck-chair; now and then she read a book or a newspaper and, for the rest, she passed the time with needlework. She was generally sunk in her phantasies, and only occasionally chatted a little with the other women. But, whatever she was doing, she glanced up anxiously every few minutes, sought her boy with a look of concern, and if she could not immediately detect his whereabouts, began to call in a despairing manner, 'Ma-a-a-ssimo, Ma-a-a-ssimo.' If the child had strayed just a few paces away from her, or if he was anywhere near the water's edge (he never went further, for he was plainly timid about the sea), she flew after him, seized his arm and dragged him back again to her. If he quarrelled with the other boys, or tried to resist his mother, she generally scolded him and gave him a sound slap, only to overwhelm him with violent hugs and kisses if he began to cry. So it went on, all day long: with the punctuality of clockwork the perpetual cry of 'Ma-a-ssimo, Ma-a-ssimo' made itself heard.

In such a situation a psychoanalyst really cannot prevent himself from thinking a little about such a mother. One seemed to read her dissatisfaction in her face; her emotional interests were obviously concentrated on her boy. There could be no doubt about the meaning of her exaggerated tenderness. She loved and hated the child at one and the same time, but she had repressed her hate out of her consciousness by an extreme over-accentuation of her devoted tenderness, and so put an end to the inner discord. Here we have a simple instance of the mechanism of 'repression by means of reaction-formation.' Again, the extension of this process (so familiar to the analyst), the 'return of the repressed,' was perfectly plain

* First published in German in *Internationale Zeitschrift fuer Psychoanalyse, 13:* 283–289, 1927; in English, *The International Journal of Psycho-Analysis, 9:* 219 ff., 1928.

in this woman. She tormented the child in spite of, or rather precisely with, her infatuated love. The more devoted she was in watching over and disciplining him, the more fully—but also the less noticeably—could she gratify thereby her secret pleasure in aggression.

Thus far the psychological situation is clear, but one's interest in the little episode is not exhausted by this much insight into it, and one is inclined to pursue the subject further. It occurs to us at once to consider it in the light of Freud's recent detailed discussion of the question of 'danger.' For it is obvious that the mother behaved as if her boy, when playing on the beach, were threatened with some unknown dangers, and must be shielded with the utmost caution from some harm. Her whole attitude to the child showed how deeply she must have been impressed with this conviction. The objective observer then judges the mother's apprehension to be 'exaggerated beyond all measure,' for in reality there could be no question of such dangers as she feared. The analyst need not impugn this statement, but he can correct it in an important respect. If the mother's fears had no foundation in reality, it means that they had another, purely psychic, origin. Thus understood, her fears were justified. The child was actually in peril, only the dangers threatening it lay not, as the mother thought, in the outside world, but in the depths of her own mind. Her anxiety was a reaction to her own unconscious hostility to her child. Really she was compelled to protect him from herself, to direct her precautions against her own person. But she knew nothing of this hostility; her ego had warded off the aggressive impulses by means of repression, and thus hampered in the struggle against the overwhelming force of the instinctual impulse, it employed other means. She displaced the evil spirits, which she detected, from within herself to the outside world, scenting dangers and menaces everywhere and combating them with tactics whose aggressive fury was directed outwards, above all against the very child whom she sought to protect.

The view set forth by Freud on 'danger' thus proves to yield useful results, for it reveals in the mother's mental life an act of projection, thus furnishing an incentive to and matter for further reflection. Projection plays a part in 'the return of the repressed'; thus it serves the purpose of 'substitute-formation.' We should like to know what are the other factors in this complicated process. It would be easy to tell if we were dealing with a person under analytic treatment who would give an account of herself to the analyst and supply him with exhaustive information about her mental life. But in the case in question we have only the meagre material which could be gleaned by one observing from a distance, without the knowledge and cooperation of the person under observation. Nevertheless, we need not be daunted in our attempt to reconstruct the process. Let us take as a starting-point one impression derived from my observation. The woman's whole behaviour betrayed marked ambition as a mother. The command that she should do her duty as a mother seemed actually to dominate her ego and swallow up every other interest. Her conscience clamoured in the most importunate fashion: 'You must be a faithful and devoted mother to your child.' Leaving out of account the deeper, genetic conditioning factors in the formation of conscience, this demand can be brought into conjunction with the mother's aggressive instinctual impulses.

We may assume that in this case the defensive measures of the ego have only to a partial extent had the result of repressing her pleasure in aggression. What has happened to another part of the aggressive instinct-components in that they have been 'directed against the self.' The aggressive tendency, thus turned inward, increases the severity of the woman's conscience towards her own ego and supports the moral demand, the protective (altruistic) intention of which has reference to the very object (the child) which was the object of the original aggression. This being the way in which the woman's maternal 'virtue' has originated, we can understand how it is that the aggressive tendency, unaltered by repression, so readily links up with its derivative, the demand of conscience, and thus reinforced, accomplishes its own purpose.

Thus it really is possible by means of Freud's theory to penetrate quite a considerable way into the mental mechanisms of a subject whom we have studied only, as it were, from outside. But now we are confronted with a fresh problem. We have seen that projection supplies a rationalistic motivation for the breaking-through of repressed hostility. By projection a perception of the repressed impulse within the ego is converted from an internal to an external perception: that is, it is a kind of erroneous perception and the secondary elaboration of it. Now, how is it that the ego does not correct the result of this pathological thought-process, seeing that the conclusion drawn is contrary to reality? Why did the mother not perceive that hundreds of children were playing peacefully on the beach and that the other mothers showed not a sign of concern, and she herself was the only one who had no peace of mind? Indeed, if anyone had tried to explain this simple fact to her, he would probably have found that it was impossible to make her realize it. She would prefer to believe that amongst several hundred careless mothers she was the only really conscientious one on the whole beach.

Obviously here some damage has been sustained by certain important functions of the ego—the reality-test and the function of critical judgement. But there is nothing in what has so far been arrived at about the different ways in which the instincts are transformed which throws any real light on the origin of this disturbance. We certainly cannot regard it as a necessary accompaniment of the process of projection. A tendency to projection occurs at times in normal mental life, but the critical function of the ego remains completely intact and soon sees to it that an erroneous conclusion is rejected. We must, then, look for some special cause of the disturbance, and it will not be difficult to find it. If every fulfilment of an ideal results in an enhancement of the self-regarding sentiment, the fulfilling of an obsessively accentuated demand of conscience (ambition in the role of mother) must afford the ego especially keen narcissistic enjoyment. For the pleasurable value of the fulfilment of ideals is based on a restoration of the infantile self-feeling and is clearly experienced by the ego in direct proportion to the amount of pain caused by the reduction of the original supposed grandeur of the ego during the formation and development of the super-ego. Anyone who observed the self-satisfied expression with which this woman resumed her seat every time she had enforced her disciplinary measures would have needed no further proofs of the correctness of this theoretical conclusion. And we shall have no hesitation in believing that an ego which stays on the level of narcissistic gratification will allow its critical reality-function to be paralysed. The ego behaves exactly as if it were deriving such gratification from assurances of love, from praise, flattery, and so on, coming from without.

Hence, it is the narcissistic satisfaction derived from the fulfilling of an ideal which benumbs the critical judgment of the ego, and secures gratification of the forbidden aggressive tendencies. This economic mechanism may be described as a kind of *narcissistic insurance*. By means of ideal-formation, according to Freud, the 'basest' is raised to the 'highest'; the satisfaction derived from the fulfilling of an ideal, acting as a narcissistic insurance, allows the ill-restrained 'base' element to accomplish its purpose once more in the midst of the 'highest.'

It is easy to see that the factor of 'narcissistic insurance' plays an important part in the mental economy in all other analogous cases in which a repressed instinctual impulse achieves gratification with the cooperation of the super-ego. Especially in the late symptoms of the obsessional neurosis, which have been so fully discussed by Freud, does this mechanism frequently manifest itself in a highly significant manner: the ego wallows in its hyper-morality and under cover of this gratifies the most despicable tendencies. This, however, is not the place in which to trace out this mechanism in the various fields of mental life. From the wealth of material which at once presents itself, let us take only that example in the history of civilization—the Crusaders. These heroes of an ideal were certainly prevented by an excessive self-feeling from realizing the true nature of the deeds which they perpetrated in the name of the religion of love.*

* One young woman whom I analysed had volunteered as a nurse during the war and by her goodness and loving devotion had won the name of 'a true Madonna.' Her analysis showed that in fulfilling this patriotic duty she had quite unsuspectingly gratified her aggressive desires on hundreds of wounded men in the course of her

I would point out that one advantage of this theory is that by it a certain substitute-formation achieved with the assistance of the super-ego is explained simply by the interaction of processes either within or having relation to the ego. Following Freud's conception in *The Ego and the Id*, it sets the ego in the very centre of the metapsychological picture, for it takes into consideration the instinctual forces which operate upon the ego from the id and the super-ego, together with the effect which they have upon it. It may be worth while to sum up our argument again from this point of view.

The ego comprehends the severity of the demands made by conscience, feels a constraint, and conceives a longing to raise its self-feeling to the happy heights where it dwelt in childhood. On the other hand, it keeps up a heavy expenditure of repression on the forbidden aggressive tendencies. This is the initial situation; it is here that the process of substitute-formation begins. The ego enhances its self-regarding feeling by continual fulfilling of its ideals. From the point of view of the ego's situation (narcissistic craving, great tension of conscience) this satisfaction has a rare value; the ego clings to it convulsively, and by this effort is diverted from its other aims—the service of reality. Since the repressed aggressive tendency retains its activity, a slackening of the ego's control of its instincts must cause this impulse to break through. This too takes place with the active cooperation of the ego. Lying wholly under the ban of its conscience (i.e. of its narcissistic craving), the ego employs two weapons to defend itself from the threatened perception of the aggressive impulse. Its more moderate trend (hostility) is seen as it were in the disguise of the promptings of conscience, is construed as a means for the fulfilment of an ideal, and thus its character is radically misunderstood. The most repugnant part of the impulse (the death-wish) is 'recognized' by the ego—always under the oppression of conscience—as located in the outside world (projection). From this counterfeit presentment of reality a rationalistic motivation is then deduced, which makes the work of 'disciplinary' aggression the easier. All this comes about because the ego, hard pressed on both sides and seduced by the pleasure of gratifying its impulses, performs incorrectly those of its functions which relate to reality (censorship, testing the reality of phenom-

---

'self-sacrificing' work. When her own brother (against whom she had had the very strongest castration-wishes in her childhood) received a serious head-wound, she exalted him as a hero, and, in her martial enthusiasm, received the news of the danger his life was in without a sign of distress. But she herself nearly caused her 'tenderly loved' father to lose his life. In her fanatic zeal she insisted that the old man, who was entrusted with a duty in a very exposed position, should remain at his post from 'a sense of duty' in a perfectly insane manner, even when the enemy broke through. He actually escaped certain death only at the very last moment.

ena, critical judgement). The result is a compromise, in which (entirely at the expense of its insight into reality) it frees itself from the tension of conscience and the urge of its aggressive impulse, and thereby experiences gratification. One single process is not involved in this construction, but it is one which does not belong to the substitute-formation, but to more remote genetic conditions. I mean the turning-in upon the ego of the aggression which is held back from reality and its inclusion in the drive of conscience. The analysis of the ego should be able to shew that the incentive for even this transformation of instinct in the depths of the mental apparatus proceeds from the ego.

In one direction this way of looking at the matter already leads us to a clear conclusion. We realize how energetically the self-regarding feelings enforce their claims in the decisions which the ego has to make in its business of mastering the instincts, and how extensively they obtrude themselves into the different activities of the ego. But what exactly are the self-regarding feelings? On the one hand they are the expression of the level of narcissistic gratification, i.e. *an economic index*; on the other hand they are the sum of the dynamic results produced within the ego by the narcissistic instinctual forces, that is, *a signal of a craving*. These properties account for their enormous importance in the behaviour of the ego. If, in addition, we assume in accordance with the psychoanalytical view, that the whole structure of the ego is cemented by narcissistic libido, then we cannot reject the assumption that the 'synthetic function' in the ego depends specifically upon the self-regarding feelings and performs its task (the establishing of a coherent ego) at the dictates of those feelings. It is true that the act of thinking in terms of reality and the function of critical judgement do play a considerable part in the synthesis of the ego; but the intellectual functions mature at a later phase of ego-development and throughout life they depend upon self-feeling, and are ready, in the event of conflict, to bow to its supremacy. On this premise rest, in particular, the syntheses of the neurotic ego during the process of symptom-formation. Perhaps we shall find that the idiosyncrasies in the (as yet unexplored) mode of operation of the 'synthetic function' form the nucleus of what may be described psychoanalytically as the 'character' of the ego.

It is quite in agreement with this view that we find that, where self-regarding feeling is carried to an extreme degree, the 'synthetic function' concocts an ego which can no longer do justice to all its three 'subordinate relationships' and—as Freud has shewn—recants from one or other of them. Once on the heights of an over-exalted self-feeling, the ego either gives up reality (in psychosis) or blends with the super-ego (in mania). The case is different when the self-regarding feelings are hurtled to the depths—as in the clinical picture of melancholia. In this disease (which we can describe only as a great despairing cry for love) the craving for self-feeling itself becomes over-mastering. The ego is prepared to relinquish its care for its own vegetal functions (to abandon itself) and submits to the cruellest torments, to the very point of self-destruction, in order thus to regain the blissful situation of being loved and, therewith, the measure of self-love which is normally necessary to a human being. But the process has little that is mysterious about it. Once the ego in an analogous situation—being abandoned by the mother and exhausted with impotent rage—was subjected to the *tortures of hunger*. But there followed with never-failing certainty the reappearance of the mother and the oral-narcissistic bliss experienced in drinking at her breast. It is in this primal series of experiences, which are later ranged into the pregnant context of *guilt–expiation–forgiveness*, that we discover the roots of the imaginary craving of the melancholic, and with it, the mechanism of his illness.*

---

* Cf. the remarks on melancholia in my paper: 'The Psychic Effects of Intoxicants.' [In this volume.]

The Problem of Melancholia[*]

The insight which psycho-analysis has gained into the clinical picture of melancholia is the result of the investigations of Freud and Abraham. Abraham was the first to turn his attention to this subject. As early as 1911 he asserted[1] that melancholia represents a reaction (comparable to that of grief) to the loss of love (the object). Some years later Freud, having in the interval begun his researches into the nature of narcissism, took the decisive step which led to the analytical elucidation of the subject of melancholia.[3] He recognized that in melancholia the object which has been renounced is set up again within the ego and that thus in his self-reproaches the patient is continuing his aggressive tendencies against that object. The first conditioning factor in this process he showed to be the regression from an object-relation to a narcissistic substitute for it and, next, the predominance of ambivalence, which replaces love by hate and oral incorporation. In a later work Freud[4] supplemented this hypothesis by the observation that the cruelty of the super-ego in melancholia results from the defusion of instincts which accompanies the act of identification. In 1923 Abraham[2] published a second and comprehensive work on melancholia. By a number of excellent individual observations he was able to confirm Freud's conclusions in all points and he added several important clinical discoveries. He emphasized the melancholiac's incapacity for love—an incapacity springing from his ambivalence—indicated the large part played in the mental productions of such patients by cannibalistic and oral instinctual impulses and revealed in the history of their childhood a 'primal depression' from which they had suffered at the height of their Oedipus development as a reaction to the double disappointment of their love for mother and father.

We now understand the mechanism of melancholia in so far as Freud has dissected it into its separate parts and Abraham has traced the forces at work in it to elementary impulses of the component instincts. But the plan according to which these separate mental acts are combined to form the whole structure of melancholia, its origin and its specific meaning are still wholly obscure.

I shall endeavour to indicate to you today how far the analysis of the

---

* Read before the Tenth International Psycho-Analytical Congress, Innsbruck, September 1, 1927. First published in *Internationale Zeitschrift fuer Psychoanalyse*, *13:* 439–455, 1927; in English, *The International Journal of Psycho-Analysis, 9:* 420–438, 1928.

ego and its narcissism enable us to penetrate deeper into the nature of melancholia.

The most striking feature in the picture displayed by the symptoms of depressive conditions is the fall in self-esteem and self-satisfaction.[†] The depressive neurotic for the most part attempts to conceal this disturbance; in melancholia it finds clamorous expression in the patients' delusional self-accusations and self-aspersions, which we call 'the delusion of moral inferiority'. On the other hand, there are in the behaviour of melancholiacs many phenomena which are in complete contradiction to the patient's general self-abasement. Freud[3] gives the following description of this re-markable inconsistency in such patients: 'they are far from evincing to-wards those around them the attitude of humility and submission that alone would befit such worthless persons; on the contrary, they give a great deal of trouble, perpetually taking offence and behaving as if they had been treated with great injustice.'

He adds the explanation that these latter reactions are still being roused by the mental attitude of rebellion, which has only later been converted into the contrition of the melancholiac. As observation shews, the acute phase of melancholia (or depressive conditions) is regularly preceded by such a period of arrogant and embittered rebellion. But this phase generally passes quickly and its symptoms are then merged into the subsequent melancholic phase. In the transitory symptoms which occur during analytic treatment we have an impressive picture of this process. Let us now endeavour to throw some light on this rebellious phase from the patient's previous history and a consideration of the type of persons who are subject to it.

We will begin by describing the characteristics which may be recognized in the ego of persons predisposed to depressive states. We find in them, above all, an intensely strong craving for narcissistic gratification and a very considerable narcissistic intolerance. We observe that even to trivial offences and disappointments they immediately react with a fall in their self-esteem. Their ego then experiences an urgent craving to relieve in some way or other the resulting narcissistic tension. Their ego may be completely absorbed by this and be paralysed for all further activities. A stronger individual, on the other hand, will scarcely react at all to such frustrations, will endure without harm trivial variations in the degree of his self-esteem and will accommodate himself to the inevitable delay in its restoration. Those predisposed to depression are, moreover, wholly reliant and depend-ent on other people for maintaining their self-esteem; they have not at-tained to the level of independence where self-esteem has its foundation in

---

[†] *Selbstgefühl*, usually translated by the neutral word 'self-regard', is used by this author in a more positive sense and is variously translated here, by 'self-respect, self-esteem and self-satisfaction,' as well as by 'self-regard' (ed.).

the subject's own achievements and critical judgement. They have a sense of security and comfort only when they feel themselves loved, esteemed, supported and encouraged. Even when they display an approximately normal activity in the gratification of their instincts and succeed in realizing their aims and ideals, their self-esteem largely depends on whether they do or do not meet with approbation and recognition. They are like those children who, when their early narcissism is shattered, recover their self-respect only in complete dependence on their love-objects.

Thus the favourite method employed by persons of this type for increasing their self-respect is that of attracting to themselves narcissistic gratification from *without*. Their libidinal disposition is easy to comprehend; the instinctual energies which they direct towards objects retain strong narcissistic elements, and therefore passive narcissistic aims prevail in their object-relations. Freud[8] postulated that the melancholiac's 'object-choice conforms to the narcissistic type'; this characteristic may be regarded as a special instance of my general statement.

Besides dependence on the love-object we find in persons prone to depressive states a number of secondary characteristics which must be present in order to make up this typical disposition. Such persons are never weary of courting the favour of the objects of their libido and seeking for evidences of love from them; they sometimes expend an astonishing skill and subtlety in this pursuit. This applies not only to the objects of their purely sexual feelings: they behave in exactly the same way in relations in which their sexual instinct is inhibited in its aim and sublimated. They are wont to have a considerable number of such relations, for they are most happy when living in an atmosphere permeated with libido. But as soon as they are sure of the affection or devotion of another person and have entered into a fairly secure relation with him or her their behaviour undergoes a complete change. They accept the devoted love of the beloved person with a sublime nonchalance, as a matter of course, and become more and more domineering and autocratic, displaying an increasingly unbridled egoism, until their attitude becomes one of full-blown tyranny. They cling to their objects like leeches (to use a phrase of Abraham's) and feed upon them, as though it were their intention to devour them altogether. But all this takes place without their self-critical faculty being aware of it; as a rule they are just as unaware of the wooing character of their attitude as of its subsequent reversal or of the tenacity with which their sadism fastens on their love-objects. Taking this attitude into consideration we can hardly wonder that they react with embittered vehemence to aggression on the part of others or to the threat of withdrawal of love and that they feel the final loss of the object of their tormenting love to be the greatest injustice in the world.

Such, approximately, is the process leading to the indignant rebellion which precedes the turning of the subject's aggressive tendencies against himself in melancholia. Let us for the moment leave out of consideration the introjection of the object, to which process Freud has traced the reversal of mood in this disease, and let us try to see how melancholia can be accounted for on the same psychological premises as have explained the patient's passing into the phase of rebellion. It will then be obvious that his contrition can only be a reaction to the failure of his rebellion—a fresh weapon (the last one) to which his ego has recourse in order to carry out its purpose. That which it could not accomplish by rebellion it now tries to achieve by remorseful self-punishment and expiation. The ego does penance, begs for forgiveness and endeavours in this way to win back the lost object. I once[9] described melancholia as a great despairing cry for love, and I believe that our present context justifies us in so conceiving of it.

But, you will object, this cannot be so, for the melancholiac has surely withdrawn his interest from the object; it exists for him no longer. How can he be striving to be reconciled to this object and to recapture its affection? You are right; but the melancholiac has transferred the scene of his struggle for the love of his object to a different stage. He has withdrawn in narcissistic fashion to the inner world of his own mind and now, instead of procuring the pardon and love of his object, he tries to secure those of his super-ego. We know that his relation to the object was marked by the predominance of the narcissistic desire to be loved, and it is quite easy for this aspiration to be carried over to his relation with his own super-ego. It is as if the ego of the melancholiac were to say to his super-ego: 'I will take all the guilt upon myself and submit myself to any punishment; I will even, by ceasing to care for my bodily welfare, offer myself as an expiatory sacrifice, if you will only interest yourself in me and be kind to me.' Thus it seems that in melancholia there is an attempt to decide the conflict with the object on a field other than the real one: there is a narcissistic flight from the object-relation to that with the super-ego and, by this regressive step, the ego is removed from reality.

From this behaviour of the melancholiac we may venture to divine the processes which once took place within him at the time when the formation of his super-ego was in progress. He was a child of a narcissistic disposition, whose self-esteem depended entirely on his parents' love. What an improvement in his mental situation when he began actively to reproduce their requirements in his own mind! He was then able to say to them: 'There is no need for you to correct me any more, for I tell myself what you expect of me and, what is more, I will do it.' But there were also times when he was naughty and his parents were very angry. Then he understood that he had only to pay the penalty and to ask for forgiveness, in order to be reconciled to them. The next time he offended, it occurred to him that he might do penance of his own accord and punish himself, in order quickly to win his parents' forgiveness. Incidents of this sort are related to us in our patients' analyses and children are known actually to carry out this idea. We can easily imagine that, later, this process takes place in the child without his knowing it. He begins *unconsciously* to reproduce within his mind the punishments anticipated from his parents and, in doing so, he unconsciously *hopes to win love*. Some unmerited narcissistic injury, e.g. an estrangement from his parents through no fault of his own, is probably the original motive for such an unconscious attempt at reparation. In some such way we may reconstruct the process by which the person who subsequently succumbs to melancholia (and certainly he is not alone in this respect) produces the mechanism of self-punishment.

But, as soon as the active reproduction of parental punishment ceases to have reference in the conscious mind to the parents themselves and is carried out unconsciously, the intention is no longer that the subject should be reconciled to them but to the super-ego, which is their internal mental representative. Instead of the early process of putting matters right in actual fact with the parents, we have the purely psychical process by which he puts them right with his super-ego, as happens later in melancholia. But in relation to external reality this inner process remains entirely ineffective. With the unconscious reproduction of parental punishments the oral-narcissistic process of introjection (the formation of the super-ego) has overstepped the limits of its social usefulness: self-punishment is a part of the infantile relation to the object, a survival which controverts reality and takes an inward direction. In its dread of losing love the infantile ego has clearly gone too far; its narcissistic craving remains unsatisfied, even when it submits itself to the destructive effects of self-punishment. In so far, then, as the ego in melancholia gives itself up to this mechanism, it has broken off its relations with reality and jeopardized its existence in vain.

We have seen how self-punishment takes place in the hope of absolution and has its origin in the longing for love. Now I am sure you will share my critical suspicion that the close connection between *guilt, atonement* and *forgiveness*, so deeply rooted in our mental life, cannot possibly owe its enormous importance simply to the experiences of the growing child in the course of his training. It is certainly a momentous step when the child begins to grasp the idea of guilt and to experience the peculiar quality of the sense of guilt. But it seems as though he were already prepared for this experience, so as to understand straight away the next conception: that of punishment and expiation and, above all, that of final forgiveness. Our study of melancholia enables us actually to see into the history of this mental structure—a history reaching back to the primal dawn of the mind—and to lay bare the ultimate foundations of experience upon which it is built. Here I may refer to a conclusion which I have already suggested elsewhere.[9] Briefly it is this: that, when the child passes from the period of suckling, he carries with him, indelibly stamped on his mind, a sequence of experiences which *later* he works over so as to form the connection: guilt–atonement–forgiveness. You can observe in the nursery how the infant, if its craving for nourishment awakens in the absence of the mother, flies into an impotent rage, kicks and screams, and then, exhausted by this reaction to its helplessness, falls wholly a prey to the torments of hunger. But you know also that this cruel experience is finally followed with *unfailing certainty* by the reappearance of the mother and that in drinking at her breast the child experiences that oral-narcissistic bliss which Freud is certainly right in describing as the prototype, never again attained to, of all subsequent gratification. The whole process constitutes a *single* sequence of experiences, countless times repeated, of whose responsibility in determining future development we surely need no further proofs. From the paroxysm of rage in the hungry infant proceed all the later forms of *aggressive reaction* to frustration (e.g. devouring, biting, striking, destroying, etc.) and it is on these that the ego, in the period of latency, concentrates its whole sense of guilt. The hyper-cathexis of the impulses of aggression with manifest feelings of guilt is the consequence of a normal advance in development, which the material produced in our analyses enables us to follow without effort, while the knowledge arrived at by Freud makes it easily intelligible. At the height of the phallic phase the infantile ego (intimidated by the dread of castration—loss of love) has to renounce its dangerous Oedipus wishes and to secure itself against their recurrence. To do this it forms out of the primary function of self-observation a powerful institution (the super-ego) and develops the capacity for becoming aware of the criticisms of this institution in the form of a dread of conscience (the sense of guilt). The newly-acquired reaction of conscience deals a death-blow to the Oedipus complex, but the impulses embodied in that complex undergo different fates. The genital impulse succumbs to repression; its motor elements are inhibited and the group of ideas (incest-phantasies, onanism) which were cathected by it vanish from consciousness and leave no trace behind them. The aggressive impulse, on the other hand, cannot be warded off in so effectual a manner. Its driving force is, it is true, paralysed by the setting up of a powerful anti-cathexis, but the ideas cathected by it are retained in consciousness. Evidently the ego is incapable of erecting a barrier against the manifestations of aggression as it does against those of gross sensuality. The former are constantly presented to it by the unavoidable impressions of daily life and not least by the aggressive measures adopted by those who train the child. Education must therefore content itself with *condemning* his acts of aggression in the most severe terms and causing him to attach to them the ideas of guilt and sin. The close relation between genitality and repression on the one hand and aggression and defence through reaction on the other—a relation to which Freud has recently drawn attention[6] —thus has its roots in the child's practical situation. Subsequently, the repressed guilt connected with genitality (i.e. the guilt which is incapable of entering consciousness) hides itself behind the guilt of aggression, which persists undisguised in the conscious mind; and thus the sadistic impulse (which, genetically, goes back to the infant's outbreak of rage) also becomes the manifest carrier of the whole feeling of incest-guilt, this being displaced from its genital source. The torments of hunger are the mental precursors of later 'punishments' and, by way of the discipline of punishment, they come to be the primal mechanism of self-punishment, which in melancholia assumes such a fatal significance. At the bottom of the melancholiac's profound dread of impoverishment there is really simply the dread of starvation (that is, of impoverishment in physical possessions), with which the vitality of such part of his ego as remains normal reacts to the expiatory acts which threaten the life of the patient in this disease. But drinking at the mother's breast remains the radiant image of unremitting, forgiving love. It is certainly no mere chance that the Madonna nursing the Child has become the emblem of a mighty religion and thereby the emblem of a whole epoch of our Western civilization. I think that if we trace the chain of ideas, *guilt–atonement–forgiveness*, back to the sequence of experiences of early infancy: *rage, hunger, drinking at the mother's breast*, we have the explanation of the problem why the hope of absolution and love is perhaps the most powerful conception which we meet with in the higher strata of the mental life of mankind.

According to this argument, the deepest fixation-point in the melancholic (depressive) disposition is to be found in the 'situation of threatened loss of love' [Freud,[6]] more precisely, in the hunger-situation of the infant. We shall learn more about it if we examine more closely that experience of 'oral-narcissistic bliss' which is vouchsafed to him in his extremity. I have elsewhere[10] tried to demonstrate that pleasurable stimulation of the mouth-zone does not constitute the whole of the oral-libidinal gratification but should rather be regarded as its more conspicuous antecedent. I thought there was reason to refer the climax of this enjoyment to the subsequent, invisible part of the process, which I termed 'the alimentary orgasm' and which I have assumed to be the precursor, along the road of evolution, of the later genital orgasm. We now see that the alimentary orgasm of the infant at the mother's breast is a phenomenon with important consequences, whose influence radiates out into the whole of his later life. It satisfies the egoistic cravings of the little human being for nourishment, security and warmth, fulfils the longings of his budding object-instincts and, by the blending of all these factors it induces in him a kind of narcissistic transport which is inseparably connected with them. It is perhaps more correct to say that this tremendous experience of gratification contains, as yet inextricably combined, all the components which subsequent development will differentiate and carry forward to different fates. But it comes to the same thing: we cannot fail to recognize that the infant's dawning ego acquires in this narcissistic gratification that mental quality which it will later experience as 'self-satisfaction'. This feeling is, in its origin, the reaction of the dawning ego to the experience which is biologically the most important to it, namely, that of alimentary orgasm. Later on the principal incentives for stimulating self-esteem will be the ego's developments in the direction of power and all the forms of activity by which it obtains gratification— we can actually distinguish within self-esteem a progress from the oral to a sadistic-anal and thence to a genital level (corresponding to the varying technique of acquisition)—but the peculiar quality of the experience persists as a specifically differentiated memory-symbol of that early ego-reaction which was conditioned by the alimentary orgasm.

If we take into consideration the fact that the quality of feeling which is experienced as self-esteem—as has already been described by Bernfeld[3] —can, by the addition of fresh factors, advance in successive stages to the pitch of exaltation, triumph, ecstasy and intoxication, we may feel that the chain of connected ideas is brought to a satisfactory end. I discovered already some time ago through another channel that states of intoxication in adults are derived from the experience of blissful repletion in the process of nutrition. Now it is precisely for melancholia that the genetic sequence here worked out: *alimentary orgasm—self-satisfaction—intoxication*—is of importance. As we have heard, the melancholiac tries to restore his seriously diminished self-esteem by means of love. His behaviour strikes us as morbid, because it is related not to the object but to his own super-ego. But it leads to a result which is entirely logical though none the less pathological. I refer to mania, in which disease, as Freud has recognized,[5] the ego is once more merged with the super-ego in unity. We may add that this process is the faithful, intra-psychic repetition of the experience of that fusing with the mother that takes place during drinking at her breast. The earliest (oral) technique for the renewal of self-satisfaction is revived on the psychic plane and results—as is psychologically perfectly correct—in the transports* of mania. The manic condition succeeds the phase of self-punishment with the same regularity with which formerly, in the biological process, the bliss* of satiety succeeded to hunger. We know, further, that the ego has

---

* *Rausch:* This word is the same as that used by the author for the effect of drugs, then and here too also translated by 'intoxication' (ed.).

yet another pathological method to which it can resort in order to bolster up its tottering self-esteem. This method also takes the alimentary orgasm as its prototype: it consists of a flight into the pharmacotoxic states to which the victims of drug-addiction have recourse.

Let us go back to our earlier statement that the ego, finding that its rebellion against the loss of its object is futile, changes its psychological technique, confesses that it is guilty and passes into a state of remorseful contrition. Here the question arises exactly why and of what does the ego feel itself guilty? In depressive neurotics we need to get through a great deal of work in order to answer this question with any certainty. With the melancholiac, however, who in this respect is so frank with us, we have only to listen attentively and then we easily arrive at the inner meaning of his self-reproaches. He feels guilty because by his aggressive attitude he has himself to blame for the loss of the object, and in this we certainly cannot contradict him. We observe, too, that this confession of guilt by the ego is modelled on infantile prototypes and its expression is strongly reinforced from infantile sources. Nevertheless, precisely the most striking characteristics of the melancholiac's atonement will still be incomprehensible were it not that we know that this behaviour is contributed to very largely from another quarter.

There is indeed another psychic process at work, parallel with the melancholic atonement. It has its origin in the sadistic trend of hostility to the object, which has already shown its force in the ambivalent character of the love-relation, which later supplied the fuel for rebellious reactions, and which brought the ego over to the other view, namely, that the object alone was to blame for the quarrel, having provoked the rigour of the ego by its caprice, unreliability and spite. Freud's discovery, which I mentioned at the beginning of this paper, revealed to us the surprising fact that in melancholia this overmastering aggressive tendency of the id proves stronger than the ego. When the latter has failed ignominiously to carry through the claims of its hostile impulses toward the object (i.e. when the phase of rebellion collapses) and thereupon adopts an attitude of masochistic remorse towards the super-ego, the aggressive tendency of the id goes over to the side of the super-ego and forces the ego itself, weakened by its expiatory attitude, into the position of the object. Thereafter the super-ego visits upon the ego all the fury which the ego would otherwise have been capable of visiting upon the object. In the past the ego sallied forth into the world in order to find gratification for its narcissistic craving for love, but the demands of its sadism brought it to grief; now, turning away from reality, it seeks for narcissistic gratification within the mind itself, but, here again, it cannot escape the overpowering force of the aggressive instinct. The self-punishments assume forms very different from that of the expiation which may have hovered before the imagination of the ego, and are carried to a degree far in excess of it. In its remorse the ego turned, full of confidence, to a benevolent being, whose punishments would be but light; now it has to bear the consequences of its infantile trustfulness and weakness. Since, in its perplexity, it cannot rid itself of the hope of the forgiveness which shall save it, it submits to the role of object, takes upon itself the whole guilt of the object and suffers without resistance the cruelties of the super-ego. Its own self is now almost annihilated—only its various dreads (expressed in distorted forms) betray that the core of the ego still exists. Such total capitulation on the part of the ego to the sadism of the id would be incomprehensible, if it were not that we realize that it falls a victim to the indestructible infantile illusion that only by yielding and making atonement can it be delivered from its *narcissistic* distress.

This, then, is the change of grouping which the 'synthetic function' brings about in the ego of the melancholiac. From instinctual processes whose origin and trend are diametrically opposed it succeeds in organizing the mental activities into one great and unified whole, these heterogeneous elements appearing as operative factors which are mutually dependent and complementary. The repentant ego desires to win the forgiveness of the offended object and, as an atonement, submits to being punished by the super-ego instead of by the object. In the undreamed-of harshness of the super-ego the old tendency of hostility to the object is expending its fury on the ego, which is thrust into the place of the hated object. Thus, the result of this synthetic process is a very extensive loss of the relation to reality and complete subjection of the ego to the unrestrained tyranny of the sadistic super-ego, which, as Freud remarks, has arrogated to itself the consciousness (and, we may now add, also the 'synthetic function') of the melancholic personality.

Here we must pause, for we cannot suppress our astonishment at this conclusion. This, so to speak, symmetrical solution which we have discovered for the conflicts of the ambivalent instinctual impulses is certainly tempting in form, and in content it is based in all its elements on assured data acquired by observation, but it appears to contain a hopeless contradiction. According to our construction the object would have to undergo two different processes of incorporation, being absorbed not only by the super-ego but by the ego—an idea which at first sight we cannot grasp and which we mistrust. Either our explanation is erroneous or we still lack insight into certain fundamental relations. I hope to be able to shew that the latter is true and that the difficulty can be solved. But, in order to do this, we must go back a little further.

Freud has assumed, for good reasons, that sensory perception is at the outset entirely controlled by the pleasure-principle. Only what is pleasurable is perceived; that which is painful is, as far as possible, ignored. It is a long time before this latter also gains psychic representation in the child. When it does so, the period begins in which the world clearly consists, in the child's view, of two kinds of ideas: those of things which are pleasurable and those of things which are painful. But there are certain tricky things which are sometimes a source of pleasure and sometimes of pain: the mother, for instance, according to whether she caresses her child with a happy smile or is angry and disregards or even hurts it. It is easy for us to say that it is one and the same mother in two different moods. It signifies an enormous advance when the child reaches the point of being able to make this synthesis; at first he is incapable of such an achievement of thought. He is still wholly dominated by the pleasure-principle, and he distinguishes between these two impressions as objects which are 'good' or 'bad', or, as we may say, as his 'good mother' or his 'bad mother'. The experiences and recollections connected with the mother do not form in the child's mind *one* continuous series, as we should expect in the case of adults. His perceptions and memory-images of the *one* real object produce *two* series, sharply differentiated according to their hedonic value.

This primitive mode of functioning of the dawning intellectual activity acquires a lasting importance in our mental life from the fact that it is connected with the ambivalence of instinctual life. The 'good' (pleasure-conferring) and the 'bad' (frustration-inflicting) mothers become for the child *isolated objects* (instinct-representations) of his love and his hate. This duality of the objects persists in such thinking as is instinctually controlled, even when the child from the purely intellectual standpoint grasps the complete idea of 'mother' (including both her 'good' and her 'bad' moods). As soon as he comes under the influence of a strong love-impulse his whole real knowledge about the bad side of his mother is simply blotted out; and, conversely, when his hate-impulses break through, there is nothing in the mother who is now 'bad' to remind him that this mother is also wont to be good. It is easy to understand this behaviour: it means that the still weak ego is avoiding the conflict of ambivalence by turning with its love to a mother who is *only* loveable and with its hate to another mother who deserves *only* hate. While in this condition the child, from his subjective standpoint, cannot yet be described as 'ambivalent' at all; ambivalence is established only when education succeeds in causing him to relate the two contrary discharges of instinct to the one real mother-object, that is, when he has 'learnt to know' what he is doing. By this means education compels him to repress at any rate the worst part of his aggressive tendencies. His aggression, warded off by the ego, then remains in the unconscious fastened upon the isolated representation 'bad mother', a fact which ensures the continuance of this partial idea. When the child has recognized the sad truth that his mother is sometimes 'good' and sometimes 'bad', there arises in him in his craving for love the constantly increasing longing for a mother who is 'always only good'. The isolated image of the 'good' mother now persists in his mind as a strongly-cathected *wish-idea.*

I would note here that persons who have the care of little children reveal in their behaviour an instinctive knowledge of the duality of the child's conception. When a nurse, after scolding her little charge, desires to soothe him, she makes use of a certain comforting expedient. 'The naughty boy has gone away,' she says, 'there is only our good boy here now.' Or if, perhaps, she perceives that she has been unjust to the little boy, she will give herself one or two slaps in front of him and then say of herself: 'Naughty Marie has gone away: there is only good Marie here now.' You observe how this innocent game confirms the child's instinctive view that bad people are there to be slain, for to be 'away' means to be dead. We may say, further, that in this double idea we have the origin of the good and evil spirits which primitive man conceives of as 'possessing' people or things, and also of the idea of a 'double' which in dreams, myths and other creation of the unconscious is so often met with as an expression of ambivalence.

The child's longing for a father and a mother who shall be always 'only good' is constantly being reinforced by the threats with which he is menaced (castration) and by painful punishments, and it finally provides the motive force for the formation of the super-ego. In saying this we are only expressing in a somewhat modified form a discovery of Freud's which has become familiar to us. Our formulation of it is designed to bring into prominence the part played in psychology by these pairs of ideas. We gain a clear picture of the situation in the phase in which the super-ego is being formed, if we attribute to the infantile ego the following train of thought:

'My parents must never punish me any more, they must *only* love me. Their image within my mind—my super-ego—will now see to it that they need never again be angry with me. Of course my super-ego also must love me. But if the function of my super-ego is to secure for me my parents' love, then it must be able to compel me to desist from certain actions. If necessary, it must be very severe with me and, nevertheless, I shall love it.'

According to this description the formation of the super-ego is an attempt of the ego to realize its desire to transform the alternately 'good' and 'bad' parents into parents who are 'only good'. In pursuit of this intention the ego must above all renounce its genital and sadistic impulses, in so far as they are directed against the parents (Oedipus libido of the id). Moreover, it must make up its mind to accord to the internalized parents (the super-ego) the right to be angry and severe on occasion; nevertheless, the ego will not cease to love them and to desire their love. In taking this decision the ego makes over to the super-ego the control of those instinctual energies of the id whose activity it has itself renounced.

Thus the parental institution set up within the mind (introjected) is in all points a creation of the ego. The ego in the first instance constructs this institution from its 'good parents' and also from the behaviour of the 'bad parents'. That is to say, the ego *loves* the internalized parents just as it loves its 'good parents' in reality, but it must not allow itself to *hate* them like its 'bad parents', even if they behave like 'bad parents'. We see then that the super-ego when it comes into being takes over from the ego the group of ideas relating to 'good parents' together with the cathexis pertaining to it, whilst it borrows from the group of ideas relating to the 'bad parents' only its *content*. The erotic and aggressive forces with which the super-ego has to work are placed at its disposal by the ego when the latter abandons its own right to employ them; they are drawn from the instinct-reservoir of the id. The sadistic tendency (of hostility to the parents), so far as it resists this fate, is banished by the ego unaltered into the realm of the repressed, where it already finds a representation in the isolated partial idea of the 'bad parents'. A similar fate overtakes that remainder of the crudely sensual sexual trend which refuses to be turned inwards (in the form of desexualization and surrender to the super-ego). Thus the ego strives earnestly to give to its old dream of parents who are 'only good' living realization in the real parents.

At this point I must again emphasize the one-sided orientation and the schematic character of the account which I have just given. My purpose was simply to define the type of individuals, feminine in their narcissism, to which persons of depressive disposition conform. With this type the mere 'danger of loss of love' is sufficient to compel formation of the super-ego. The purely masculine type, whose narcissism is of a different character and which surrenders only to the pressure of threatened castration, does not concern us here.

We can now return from this excursion back to the question of melancholic introjection. The individual who is later to succumb to melancholia retains all his life, in consequence of the exaggerated ambivalence of his instinctual disposition, very considerable residues of his infantile, duplicating mode of thinking. When he gives play alternately to his ambivalent impulses and thus succeeds in completely withdrawing his consciousness from the light or dark side of the object, as the occasion requires, he is behaving in a manner hardly different from that of the child. It is only clinical observation of this phenomenon, so entirely characteristic of neurotic ambivalence, which enables us by reasoning *a posteriori* to throw light upon the corresponding process in the development of the child. When, with the outbreak of melancholia, the strong current of regressive processes begins to flow, the subject's idea of his latest love-object, which has hitherto corresponded to reality, must also give way in the end to the archaic demands made on the function of thought by his ambivalence, which has now broken free of all restraint. The 'good object', whose love the ego desires, is introjected and incorporated in the super-ego. There, in accordance with the principle which, as we have just remarked, governs the formation of this institution, it is endowed with the prescriptive right (formerly so vehemently disputed in relation to the real object), to be angry with the ego—indeed, very angry. The 'bad object' has been split off from the object as a whole, to act, as it were, as 'whipping boy'. It is incorporated in the ego and becomes the victim of the sadistic tendency now emanating from the super-ego. As you see, the logical inconsistency is really entirely cleared up.

This conclusion now enables us to discover in its fullest implications the hidden meaning of the mechanism of melancholia. For consider: the worst fault by which the 'bad object' has incurred guilt, according to the reproach of the ego, is its ambivalence, by which it has 'provoked' the ego's hostility. Now if the 'bad object' which resides within the ego is chastised and finally destroyed, all that remains is the object purged of its 'bad' element, i.e. the 'good object'; moreover, the hostility of the ego (of the id) is satisfied and has spent itself. Nothing now stands in the way of the purified ego's uniting itself with the object, which is also purged of offence, in reciprocal love! When the subject swings over to mania this, the goal of the melancholic process (in the region of the pathological), is fully attained. The 'bad object'—as Abraham[2] recognized—is expelled from the ego by an anal act and this is synonymous with its being killed. The ego, freed of its own aggressive tendencies and its hated enemy, heaves a sigh of relief and with every sign of blissful transport unites itself with the 'good object', which has been raised to the position of the super-ego.

Thus we come to realize that the process of melancholia represents an attempt at reparation (cure) on a grand scale, carried out with an iron psychological consistency. It is designed to revive the ego's self-regard, which has been annihilated by the loss of love, to restore the interrupted love-relation, to be as it were a prophylactic measure against the ego's ever suffering such severe injury again and, with this end in view, to do away with the causes of mischief, namely, the ambivalence of the ego and that of the object. As to attaining any *real* effect by this line of action, the crucial point is that it does not take place on the right plane, in relation to the object-world, but is carried out, subject to a narcissistic regression, entirely between the separate institutions in the patient's mind. It cannot restore to the ego the lost object; the final reconciliation with the object (after this has been replaced by the super-ego) is accomplished not as a real process in the outside world but as a change of the situation (cathexis) in the psychic organization. From this purely psychic act, however, there ensues an important *real* result: the restoration of the subject's self-esteem —indeed, its leap into the exaltation of mania. The difference is clear to us: the melancholic process, set going by a grievous shattering of the subject's narcissism, can by means of a purely psychic shifting of cathexis attain to its *narcissistic* goal (the restoration of self-esteem), even though reality be thereby ignored. Once passed into the state of mania, the ego immediately finds its way back into the object-world. With all its energy released by the sudden change in cathexis it rushes upon reality and there expends its violence. What determines the behaviour of the manic patient is the oral derivation of the psychogenic transport; it is a striking fact that in mania the adult with his manifold potentialities of action and reaction reproduces the uninhibited instinctual manifestations which we observe in the euphoria of the satiated suckling. That the quality of the reactions of a period of life in which the super-ego did not as yet exist should be the pattern upon which is modelled the manic state (the basis of which is a temporary withdrawal of the super-ego) is exactly what we should expect.

The productive energy of the melancholic process is not exhausted when the manic phase has been brought about. When the last echoes of that phase have died away—or sometimes immediately on its passing—this energy finds outlet in the obsessive tinge which it imparts to the subject's character in the 'interval of remission'. One of Abraham's most memorable contributions to our knowledge is his discovery and description of this peculiarity of character.[2] This issue is due to the preponderance of sadistic-anal instinctual energies and is based on a renunciation of the oral restoration of self-esteem in mania. The ego has grown stronger and endeavours to avert in the sphere of reality the dangers with which it is threatened by its ambivalence. Thanks to the subject's full recognition of reality, this endeavour is crowned with considerable success in the direction of cure. The ego, its wits sharpened by its painful experiences, erects widely-flung psychic bulwarks to restrain its ambivalence; through this excess of reaction-formations its character now becomes like that of the obsessional neurotic. But this change in character does more than merely guard the ego against the perils of its ambivalence. By means of the extensive ideal-

formation the dangerous aggressive impulses are directed into social channels and thus, by way of fulfillment of the ideal, they minister to narcissistic gratification in accordance with reality. As we know, the power of
this mental structure to resist fresh strains varies extraordinarily with different individuals. But it would be premature to try to make any more
exact pronouncement at the present time either on this point or on the
other economic problems of the manifold courses taken by melancholia.

In conclusion I should like to devote a few remarks to the problem of
neurotic depression. Observation shows that the depressive process, in so
far as it has caught in its grip the ego of the person suffering from a transference-neurosis, is carried out in exact accordance with the mechanism of
true melancholia. That is to say that neurotic depression also has as its
basis a narcissistic turning-away from reality, the external object being
replaced by psychic institutions and an endeavour being made to solve
the conflicts on the intrapsychic plane instead of in the outside world, and
by means of a regressively activated oral technique. But there is this difference: these processes almost wholly consume the ego of the melancholic
and destroy those functions in him which relate to reality, while in a transference-neurosis they are as it were merely superimposed upon an ego which
is, indeed, neurotic but is more or less intact. In the depressive neurotic
the object and, with it, the relation to reality, are preserved: it is only that
the patient's hold on them is loosened and the weakly ego has begun to
give up the struggle with the world—a struggle which it feels to be unbearable—to turn inwards in a narcissistic fashion and to take refuge in the
oral-narcissistic reparation-mechanism. Thus, neurotic depression is a kind
of partial melancholia of the (neurotic) ego; the further the depressive
process extends within that ego at the cost of its relations to the object
and to reality, the more does the condition of narcissistic neurosis approximate to melancholia. Accordingly, in an acute access of depression we should
expect the issue to turn upon whether in the narcissistic machinery of the
ego the oral mechanisms gain the upper hand or whether the sadistic-anal
(and genital) mechanisms, whose hold upon the object-world is firmer, are
strong enough to safeguard the ego from the plunge into melancholia.

REFERENCES

[1] ABRAHAM, K.: Notes on the Psycho-Analytical Investigation and Treatment of
Manic-Depressive Insanity and Allied Conditions (1911). *Selected Papers on
Psychoanalysis.* London, Hogarth.

[2] ——: A Short Study of the Development of the Libido, Viewed in the Light of
Mental Disorders (1924). *Selected Papers on Psychoanalysis.* London, Hogarth.

[3] BERNFELD: *Psychologie des Säuglings.* Wien, 1925.

[4] FREUD, S.: *The Ego and the Id.* London, Hogarth, 1923.

[5] ——: *Group Psychology and the Analysis of the Ego.* London, Hogarth, 1921.

[6] ———: *Hemmung, Symptom und Angst.* 1926.

[7] ———: *Introductory Lectures on Psycho-Analysis* (1916–17). Allen and Unwin, 1922.

[8] ———: Mourning and Melancholia (1916). *Collected Papers, 4.*

[9] RADO, S.: An Anxious Mother. *Internat. J. Psycho-Analysis, 9,* 1928.

[10] ———: The Psychic Effects of Intoxicants (1926). *Internat. J. Psycho-Analysis, 9,* 1928.

The Psychoanalysis of Pharmacothymia (Drug Addiction)*

Clinical psychiatry regards the disorders known as alcoholism, morphinism, cocainism, etc.—for which, as an inclusive designation, we may provisionally use the term "drug addiction"—as *somatic intoxications*, and places them in the classificatory group "mental disorders of exogenous origin". From this point of view, the process of mental dilapidation presented in the clinical picture of the addiction would appear to be the mental manifestation of the injury to the brain produced by the poisons. The investigation of the addictions has imposed upon it by this theory, as its first task, the determination in detail of the cerebral effect of the noxious substance. Ultimately, its goal would be the exact correlation of the course of the mental disorder with the toxic processes in the brain. But this investigation, especially in its experimental aspects, is disturbingly complicated by the fact that the poisons in question attack not only the brain but the rest of the organism as well; therefore, injurious effects may be exerted upon the brain by changes in other organs through an impairment of the general metabolism. The problem thus includes not only the direct influence of the poison on the brain, but also its indirect influence. It is, consequently, not remarkable that the notion that the problem of addiction is a problem of somatic intoxication has borne so little fruit.

How did it happen, then, that psychiatry became so wedded to this idea? The obvious answer is that the idea was developed because infectious diseases were used as paradigms. To be sure, one could not ignore the fact that alcohol, for example, does not "cause" alcoholism in the same sense as the spirochaete causes luetic infection. The pathogenic microörganisms attack a person quite regardless of what his wishes or purposes in the matter may be. But the drugs in question attack him only if he purposely introduces them into his body. This distinction, however, has not sufficiently affected psychiatric thinking. In psychiatry, the idea was promulgated that a certain type of "uninhibited", "weak-willed" or "psychopathic" individual happens to develop a passion for using these drugs—which

* Authorized translation from the German manuscript by Bertram D. Lewin. Enlarged version of an address delivered before the Neurologic-Psychiatric Section of the New York Academy of Medicine, December 13, 1932. First published in English translation in *The Psychoanalytic Quarterly*, *2:* 1–23, 1933; in German, in *Internationale Zeitschrift fuer Psychoanalyse*, *20:* 16–32, 1934.

means, to read between the lines, that how these substances get into the body is of no importance: the problem is scientific and worth touching only after they are inside. It must be admitted that after the drugs have made their entry, there is, unquestionably, a certain similarity to the infections. But in so far as psychological questions, such as the susceptibility of an individual to develop a craving for drugs, were broached at all, one was groping in the dark. The intoxication theory furnished no point of departure for any solution of this type of problem. Indeed, even if all the problems relating to somatic intoxication were solved, there would still be no answer to this type of question.

The psychoanalytic study of the problem of addiction begins at this point. It begins with the recognition of the fact that not the toxic agent, but the impulse to use it, makes an addict of a given individual. We see that this unprejudiced description focuses our attention on the very feature, which, under the influence of premature analogical reasoning, was permitted to fall by the wayside. The problem then presents a different appearance. The drug addictions are seen to be psychically determined, artificially induced illnesses; they can exist because drugs exist; and they are brought into being for psychic reasons.

With the adoption of the psychogenetic standpoint, the emphasis shifts from the manifoldness of the drugs used to the singleness of the impulse which unleashes the craving. The ease with which an addict exchanges one drug for another immediately comes to mind; so that we feel impelled to regard all types of drug cravings as varieties of *one single* disease. To crystallize this theory, let me introduce the term "pharmacothymia" to designate the illness characterized by the craving for drugs. We shall have occasion later to explain our selection of this term.

The older psychoanalytic literature contains many valuable contributions and references, particularly on alcoholism and morphinism, which attempt essentially to explain the relationship of these states to disturbances in the development of the libido function. Reports of this type we owe to Freud, Abraham, Tausk, Schilder, Hartmann and others in Europe; and in this country, Brill, Jelliffe, Oberndorf and others. Two definite conclusions could be drawn from these studies, namely, the etiological importance of the erotogenic oral zone and close relationship to homosexuality. Several years ago, I outlined the beginnings of a psychoanalytic theory which aimed to include the whole scope of the problem of drug addiction.[*, 7]

---

* Since this, I have reported the progress of my views in a number of addresses: "Drug Addiction" at the First Congress for Mental Hygiene, at Washington, D. C., May 1930; "Intoxication and 'The Morning After' " at a meeting of the German Psychoanalytic Society in Berlin, November 1930; "Depressive and Elated States in Neuroses and in Drug Addiction", a lecture course at the Berlin Psychoanalytic Institute, Spring 1931.

Further, as yet unpublished, studies have led me to introduce the conception of pharmacothymia, to the preliminary description of which the present paper is devoted.

Since, for our purposes, suggestions derived from the theory of somatic intoxication are of no avail, we ourselves must select a suitable point of departure, taking our bearings from psychoanalysis. Our notion that despite the many drugs there is only one disease, suggests where we may begin. We must separate out of the abundant clinical findings those elements which are *constant* and determine their interrelationships empirically, and then from this material, formulate the general psychopathology, that is to say, the *schematic structure* of pharmacothymia. Generalizations which we can make in this way concerning the nature of the illness will discover for us the viewpoints and conceptions needed for the study of individual phenomena. If our outline is well founded, the more new details are added, the more will it reproduce living reality.

Pharmacothymia can occur because there are certain drugs, the "elatants", to give them an inclusive designation, which a human being in psychic distress can utilize to influence his emotional life. I have given a description of this influence in a previous communication (*loc. cit.*). Here I need only say that there are two types of effects. First, the analgesic, sedative, hypnotic and narcotic effects—their function is easily characterized: they allay and *prevent "pain"*. Secondly, the stimulant and euphoria-producing effects—these promote or *generate pleasure*. Both types of effect, the pain-removing and the pleasure-giving, serve the pleasure principle; together they both constitute what may be called "the pharmacogenic pleasure-effect". The capriciousness of the pharmacogenic pleasure-effect is well known; it vitiates the best part of the experimental work of the pharmacologists. I have found that in addition to the pharmacological factors (nature, dose and mode of administration of the substance), the pleasure-effect depends essentially on a psychological factor—a certain active preparedness with which the individual approaches the pleasure-effect.

The thing which the pharmacothymic patient wishes the toxic agent to give him is the pleasure-effect. But this is not to be obtained without cost. The patient must pay for his enjoyment with severe suffering and self-injury—often, indeed, with self-destruction. These are assuredly not the effects desired. If, notwithstanding this fact, he clings to the use of drugs, it must be either because the pleasure gained is worth the sacrifice of suffering, or he is in a trap and is forced to act as he does.

Then we must ask: What is the nature of the psychic situation which makes acute the demand for elatants? What is the effect of this indulgence upon the mental life? What is there in it that makes the patient suffer? And why, in spite of the suffering, can he not cease from doing as he does?

The previous history of those individuals who take to the use of elatants, in a general way reveals the following. There is a group of human beings who respond to frustrations in life with a special type of emotional alteration, which might be designated "tense depression". It sometimes happens, too, that the first reaction to the frustration takes the form of other types of neurotic symptoms, and that the "tense depression" appears only later. The intense, persistent suffering due to a severe physical illness may also lead to the same emotional state. The tense depression may change into other forms of depression; since pharmacothymia originates from the tense depression, let us designate it the "initial depression". It is marked by great "painful" tension and at the same time, by a high degree of intolerance to pain. In this state of mind, psychic interest is concentrated upon the need for relief. If the patient finds relief in a drug, in this state he is properly prepared to be susceptible to its effects. The rôle of the initial depression, then, is to *sensitize* the patient for the pharmacogenic pleasure-effect. It is immaterial whether the drug comes into his hands by accident or whether it is prescribed by his physician for therapeutic purposes, whether he was induced to use it or made the experiment on his own responsibility: he experiences a pharmacogenic pleasure-effect, which is in proportion to his longing for relief, and this event frequently, therefore, determines his future fate. If the substance and the dose were well chosen, the first pharmacogenic pleasure-effect remains as a rule the most impressive event of its kind in the whole course of the illness.

We must consider the pharmacogenic pleasure-effect, particularly this maiden one, more intensively. That which makes it so outstanding, when viewed from without, is the sharp rise in self-regard and the elevation of the mood—that is to say, elation.* It is useful to distinguish conceptually between the pharmacogenic elation and the pharmacogenic pleasure-effect, although they merge in the course of the emotional process. The elation would then represent the reaction of the ego to the pleasure-effect. After therapeutic medication, we observe countless instances of the pharmacogenic pleasure-effect which do *not* set up an elation in the patient. It is evident that in the evolution of a pharmacothymia, it is essential that an elation should be developed. In our outline, we must confine ourselves to a description of the outspoken forms, yet we should like to emphasize that the pharmacogenic elation is a protean phenomenon. It may remain so inconspicuous, externally viewed, that a casual observer could overlook it, and nevertheless be an experience which is psychologically an elation.

---

* "Elation" = *Rausch.* "Elatant" = *Rauschgift.* TR.

The elation also need not appear immediately after the first contact with the poison. The important thing is not, when it is experienced, but whether it is experienced.

What happens in a pharmacogenic elation can be understood only on the basis of further circumstantial discussion.

This individual's ego was not always so miserable a creature as we judge it to be when we encounter it in its "tense depression". Once it was a baby, radiant with self-esteem, full of belief in the omnipotence of its wishes, of its thoughts, gestures and words.[1] But the child's megalomania melted away under the inexorable pressure of experience. Its sense of its own sovereignty had to make room for a more modest self-evaluation. This process, first described by Freud,[4] may be designated the reduction in size of the original ego; it is a painful procedure and one that is possibly never completely carried out. Now, to be sure, the path to achievement opens for the growing child: he can work and base his self-regard on his own achievements. Two things become evident. In the first place, self-regard is the expression of self-love—that is to say, of narcissistic gratification.[5] Secondly, narcissism, which at the start was gratified "at command" with no labor (thanks to the care of the infant by the adults), is later compelled to cope more and more laboriously with the environment. Or we might put it, the ego must make over its psychology from that of a supercilious parasite into that of a well adjusted self-sustaining creature. Therefore, a complete recognition of the necessity to fend for itself becomes the guiding principle of the mature ego in satisfying its narcissistic needs, that is to say, in maintaining its self-regard. This developmental stage of the "narcissistic system" we may call the "realistic regime of the ego".*

There is no complete certainty that one can attain one's objectives in life by means of this realistic regime; there is always such a thing as bad luck or adversity. It is even worse, certainly, if the functional capacity of the ego is reduced through disturbances in the development of the libido function, which never fail to impair the realistic regime of the ego. The maladapted libido can wrest a substitute satisfaction from the ego in the shape of a neurosis, but then the self-regard usually suffers. An ego whose narcissism insists on the best value in its satisfactions, is not to be deceived in regard to the painfulness of real frustration. When it perceives the frustration, it reacts with the change in feeling we have described as "tense depression". Of interest to us in the deep psychology of this condition is the fact that the ego secretly compares its current helplessness with its original narcissistic stature,† which persists as an ideal for the ego, torments

* "Regime of the ego" = *Steuerung des Ichs*. TR.
† "Original narcissistic stature" = *narzisstische Urgestalt*. TR.

itself with self-reproaches and aspires to leave its tribulations and regain its old magnitude.

At this pass, as if from heaven, comes the miracle of the pharmacogenic pleasure-effect. Or rather, the important thing is that it does not come from heaven at all, but is *brought about by the ego itself*. A magical movement of the hand introduces a magical substance, and behold, pain and suffering are exorcized, the sense of misery disappears and the body is suffused by waves of pleasure. It is as though the distress and pettiness of the ego had been only a nightmare; for it now seems that the ego is, after all, the omnipotent giant it had always fundamentally thought it was.

In the pharmacogenic elation the ego regains its original narcissistic stature. Did not the ego obtain a tremendous *real* satisfaction by mere wishing, i.e., without effort, as only that narcissistic image can?

Furthermore, it is not only an infantile wish but an ancient dream of mankind which finds fulfilment in the state of elation. It is generally known that the ancient Greeks used the word "φάρμακον" to mean "drug" and "magical substance". This double meaning legitimates our designation; for the term "pharmacothymia", combining the significations of "craving for drugs" and "craving for magic", expresses aptly the nature of this illness.

At the height of the elation, interest in reality disappears, and with it any respect for reality. All the ego's devices which work in the service of reality—the ascertainment of the environment, mental elaboration of its data, instinctual inhibitions imposed by reality—are neglected; and there erupts the striving to bring to the surface and satisfy—either by fantasies or by floundering activity—all the unsatisfied instincts which are lurking in the background. Who could doubt that an experience of this sort leaves the deepest impression on the mental life?

It is generally said that a miracle never lasts longer than three days. The miracle of the elation lasts only a few hours. Then, in accordance with the laws of nature, comes sleep, and a gray and sober awakening, "the morning after". We are not so much referring to the possible discomfort due to symptoms from individual organs as to the *inevitable alteration of mood*. The emotional situation which obtained in the initial depression has again returned, but exacerbated, evidently by new factors. The elation had augmented the ego to gigantic dimensions and had almost eliminated reality; now just the reverse state appears, sharpened by the contrast. The ego is shrunken, and reality appears exaggerated in its dimensions. To turn again to real tasks would be the next step, but meanwhile this has become all the more difficult. In the previous depression there may have been remorse for having disregarded one's activities, but now there is in addition a sense of guilt for having been completely disdainful of real requirements, and an increased fear of reality. There is a storm of reproaches from all sides for the dereliction of duty toward family and work. But from yesterday comes the enticing memory of the elation. All in all, because of additional increments in "pain" the ego has become more irritable and, because of the increased anxiety and bad conscience, weaker; at the final accounting, there is an even greater deficit. What can be done, then? The ego grieves for its lost bliss and longs for its reappearance. This longing is destined to be victorious, for every argument is in its favor. What the pains of the pharmacogenic depression give birth to is, with the most rigorous psychological consistency, the craving for elation.

We obtain, thus, a certain insight into fundamental relationships. The transitoriness of the elation determines the return of the depression; the latter, the renewed craving for elation, and so on. We discover that there is a cyclic course, and its regularity demonstrates that the ego is now maintaining its self-regard by means of an artificial technique. This step involves an alteration in the individual's entire mode of life; it means a change from the "realistic regime" to a *"pharmacothymic regime"* of the ego. A pharmacothymic, therefore, may be defined as an individual who has betaken himself to this type of regime; the ensuing consequences make up the scope of the manifestations of pharmacothymia. In other words, this illness is a narcissistic disorder, a destruction through artificial means of the natural ego organization.[6] Later we shall learn in what way the erotic pleasure function is involved in this process, and how the appreciation of its rôle changes the appearance of the pathological picture.

Comparing life under the pharmacothymic regime with life oriented towards reality, the impoverishment becomes evident. The pharmacothymic regime has a definite course and increasingly restricts the ego's freedom of action. This regime is interested in only one problem: depression, and in only one method of attacking it, the administration of the drug.

The insufficiency of this method, which the ego at first believes infallible, is soon demonstrated by sad experience. It is not at all the case that elation and depression always recur with unfailing regularity in a cyclic course. The part that puts in its appearance punctually is the depression; the elation becomes increasingly more undependable and in the end threatens complete non-appearance. It is a fact of great importance that the pharmacogenic pleasure-effect, and particularly the elation induced by repeated medication, rapidly wanes. Thus, we encounter here the phenomenon of "diminishing return" in terms of elation. I cannot promise to explain the dynamics of this fall. It is doubtless ultimately dependent on organic processes, which are referred to as the "development of a tolerance" but which cannot as yet be given an accurate physiological interpretation.

During the past years an extensive study of this problem was initiated in this country. A comprehensive report of the results arrived at so far, has been published recently by the pharmacologists A. L. Fatum and M. H. Seevers in *Physiological Reviews* (Vol. XI, no. 2. 1931). A reading of this report shows that such an explanation has not yet been found. I should like to contribute a point in relation to this problem from the psychological side; namely, the assurance that in the phenomenon of "diminishing return" in elation a *psychological* factor is involved: the patient's fear that the drug will be inefficacious. This fear is analogous to the fear of impotent persons, and, similarly, reduces the chances of success even more. We shall learn, below, which deeper sources give sustenance to this fear.

The phenomenon of "diminishing return" intensifies the phase of depression, inasmuch as it adds to the tension the pain of disappointment and a new fear. The attempt to compensate the reduction of the effect by increasing the dosage proves to be worth while in the case of many drugs; a good example of this is morphine-pharmacothymia. With this develops the mad pursuit of the patients after the constantly increasing doses which become necessary. Moral obligations, life interests of other kinds are thrown to the winds, when it is a question of pursuing the satisfaction of this need, —a process of moral disintegration second to none.

Meanwhile, crucial alterations occur in the sexual life of the patient. In order to remain within the limits of this presentation, I must restrict my remarks to the most fundamental ones. All elatants poison sexual potency. After a transient augmentation of genital libido, the patient soon turns away from sexual activity and disregards more and more even his affectionate relationships. In lieu of genital pleasure appears the pharmacogenic pleasure-effect, which gradually comes to be the dominant sexual aim. From the ease with which this remarkable substitution is effected, we must conclude that pharmacogenic pleasure depends upon genetically preformed, elementary paths, and that old sensory material is utilized to create a new combination. This, however, is a problem which can be postponed. What is immediately evident is the fact that the pharmacogenic attainment of pleasure initiates an artificial sexual organization which is autoerotic and modeled on infantile masturbation. Objects of love are no longer needed but are retained for a time in fantasy. Later the activity of fantasy returns, regressively, to the emotional attachments of childhood, that is to say, to the oedipus complex. The pharmacogenic pleasure instigates a rich fantasy life; this feature seems especially characteristic of opium-pharmacothymia. Indeed, struck by this fact, the pharmacologist Lewin suggested that the "elatants" should be named "phantastica". The crux of the matter is, that it is the pharmacogenic pleasure-effect which discharges the libidinal tension associated with these fantasies. The phar-

macogenic pleasure process thus comes to replace the natural sexual executive. The genital apparatus with its extensive auxiliary ramifications in
the erotogenic zones falls into desuetude and is overtaken by a sort of
mental atrophy of disuse. The fire of life is gradually extinguished at that
point where it should glow most intensely according to nature and is
kindled at a site contrary to nature. Pharmacothymia destroys the psychic
structure of the individual long before it inflicts any damage on the physical
substrate.

The ego responds to this devaluation of the natural sexual organization
with a fear of castration only too justifiable in this instance. This warning
signal is due to the narcissistic investment of the genital; anxiety about
the genital should then compel abstention from the dangerous practice,
just as, at one time, it compelled abstention from masturbation. But the
ego has sold itself to the elatant drugs and cannot heed this warning. The
ego, to be sure, is not able to suppress the fear itself, but it perceives the
fear consciously as a dread of pharmacogenic failure. This switching of the
anxiety is, psychologically, entirely correct. Whoever secretly desires to
fail because he is afraid of succeeding, is quite right in being in dread of
failure. The effect of the fear is naturally in accordance with its original
intent; as we have learned, it reduces the pleasure-effect and the intensity
of the elation.

By frivolously cutting itself off from its social and sexual activities the
ego conjures up an instinctual danger, the extent of which it does not suspect. It delivers itself over to that antagonistic instinctual power within,
which we call masochism, and following Freud, interpret as a death instinct.
The ego had an opportunity to feel the dark power of this instinct in the
initial depression; partly for fear of it then, the ego took flight into the
pharmacothymic regime. The ego can defend itself successfully against the
dangers of masochistic self-injury only by vigorously developing its vitality
and thus entrenching its narcissism. What the pharmacothymic regime
bestowed upon the ego, was, however, a valueless inflation of narcissism.
The ego lives, then, in a period of pseudo-prosperity, and is not aware that
it has played into the hands of its self-destruction. The ego, in every neurosis, is driven into harmful complications by masochism; but of all methods
of combating masochism, the pharmacothymic regime is assuredly the
most hopeless.

It is impossible for the patient not to perceive what is happening. His
friends and relatives deluge him with warnings to "pull himself together"
if he does not wish to ruin himself and his family. And at the same time,
the elation diminishes in intensity continuously and the depression becomes
more severe. Physical illnesses, unmistakably due to the use of the poison,
afflict him with pains. Since the first temptation the picture has completely

changed. Then, everything was in favor of the elation, whereas now the hopes set upon it have been revealed as deluding. It might be supposed that the patient would reflect on this and give up the drug—but, no; he continues on his way. I must admit that for many years I could not grasp the economics of this state of mind until a patient himself gave me the explanation. He said: "I know all the things that people say when they upbraid me. But, mark my words, doctor, *nothing* can happen to *me*." This, then, is the patient's position. The elation has reactivated his narcissistic belief in his *invulnerability*, and all of his better insight and all of his sense of guilt are shattered on this bulwark.

Benumbed by this illusion, the ego's adherence to the pharmacothymic regime is strengthened all the more. The pharmacothymic regime still seems to be *the* way out of all difficulties. One day, things have progressed so far that an elation can no longer be provided to combat the misery of the depression. The regime has collapsed, and we are confronted by the phenomenon of the *pharmacothymic crisis*.

There are three ways out of this crisis: flight into a free interval, suicide and psychosis.

By voluntarily submitting to withdrawal therapy, the patient undertakes a flight into a free interval. It is out of the question that he is actuated by any real desire to recover his health. In those rare instances in which the patient really wishes to be delivered from his pharmacothymia, as I have occasionally been able to observe in my analytic practice, he sets great store upon executing his resolve by himself, and it does not occur to him to seek aid from others. But, if he submits to a withdrawal cure, as a rule, he wishes only to rehabilitate the depreciated value of the poison. It may be that he can no longer afford the money for the enormous quantity of the drug that he needs; after the withdrawal treatment he can begin anew with much less expense.

Since the withdrawal of the drug divests the ego of its elation—its protection against masochism—the latter can now invade the ego. There it seizes upon the physical symptoms due to abstinence and exploits them, frequently to the point of a true masochistic orgy; naturally with the opposition of the ego, which is not grateful for this type of pleasure. As a result, we have the familiar scenes which patients produce during the withdrawal period.

Suicide is the work of self-destructive masochism. But to say that the patient kills himself because of a masochistic need for punishment would be too one-sided a statement. The analysis of the suicidal fantasies and attempts of which our patients tell us, reveals the narcissistic aspect of the experience. The patient takes the lethal dose because he wishes to dispel the depression for good by an elation which will last *forever*. He does not kill himself; he believes in his *immortality*. Once the demon of infantile narcissism is unchained, he can send the ego to its death.

Furthermore, in suicide through drugs, masochism is victorious under the banner of a "feminine" instinctual demand. Remarkably enough, it is the deeply rooted high estimation which the male has for his sexual organ, his genital narcissism, which brings about this transformation and transmutes masochism into a feminine phenomenon. This sounds paradoxical but can readily be understood as a compromise. The ingestion of drugs, it is well known, in infantile archaic thinking represents an oral insemination; planning to die from poisoning is a cover for the wish to become pregnant in this fashion. We see, therefore, that after the pharmacothymia has paralyzed the ego's virility, the hurt pride in genitality, forced into passivity because of masochism, desires as a substitute the satisfaction of child bearing. Freud recognized the replacement of the wish to possess a penis by the wish to have a child as a turning point in the normal sexual development of women. In the case we are discussing, the male takes this female path in order to illude himself concerning his masochistic self-destruction by appealing to his genital narcissism. It is as though the ego, worried about the male genital, told itself: "Be comforted. You are getting a new genital." To this idea, inferred from empirical findings, we may add that impregnation biologically initiates a new life cycle: the wish to be pregnant is a mute appeal to the function of reproduction, to "divine Eros", to testify to the immortality of the ego.

The *psychotic episode* as an outcome of the crisis is known to us chiefly—though by no means exclusively—in alcohol-pharmacothymia. This is a large chapter. I can only indicate the framework around which its contents may be arranged.

The failure of the pharmacothymic regime has robbed the ego of its protective elation. Masochism then crowds into the foreground. The terrible hallucinations and deliria, in which the patient believes that he is being persecuted, or threatened—particularly by the danger of castration or a sexual attack—and the like are fantasies that gratify masochistic wishes. The masochism desires to place the ego in a situation where it will suffer, in order to obtain pleasure from the painful stimulation. The narcissistic ego offers opposition to this "pain-pleasure"; it desires the pleasure *without* pain. The wishes of its masochism inspire the ego with fear and horror. It can, to be sure, no longer prevent the eruption of the masochistic fantasies, yet it looks upon them through its own eyes. Thus, the latent *wish* fantasies of masochism are transformed into the manifest *terror*-fantasies of the ego. Now it is as though the danger proceeded from without; there, at least, it can be combated, and the terrified patient attempts to do this in the imaginations of his psychosis.

It is even worse if the anxiety which protects the ego from masochism breaks down. Then, the ego must accede to masochism. If the patient has arrived at this point, he suddenly announces his intention of destroying his genital organ or—substitutively—inflicting some other injury upon himself. He actually takes measures towards the blind execution of the biddings of his masochism; the patient's narcissism, defeated, can only insure that he will literally act blindly. It dims his gaze by means of delusion: the patient is not aware of the true nature of his masochism and refuses to recognize it. Instead, he asserts that he must rid himself of his organ because this organ is a nuisance to him, or has been a source of harm, or the like. If we read, for this statement, "because this organ has sinned against him", a path opens for the clarification of the latent meaning of this delusion. We may now compare it with another type of delusion of self-injury, in which the patient is well aware that he is engaged in harming himself yet persists in his designs nonetheless. This variant of the delusion usually appears in the guise of the moral idea of sin; the ego believes that it must inflict a merited punishment upon itself, in order to purify its conscience. The central feature in this "moralizing" type of delusional state is self-reproach. It may be assumed that in the "unconcerned" type of delusional state, previously described, the ego institutes a displacement of the guilt and directs its reproaches, not against itself, but against its genital organ. Primitive thought finds displacements of this sort very easy. We often hear small children say : "I didn't do it. My hand did it." The life of primitive peoples is replete with instances of this sort. The patient, then, is incensed with his genital organ, dispossesses it of the esteem previously lavished upon it (its narcissistic investment), and wishes to part with it. It is as though the ego said to the genital organ; "You are to blame for it all. First you tempted me to sin." (Bad conscience for infantile masturbation.) "Then your inefficiency brought me disappointment." (Lowering of self-esteem through later disturbances of potency.) "And therefore you drove me into my ill-omened drug addiction. I do not love you any more; away with you!" The ego does not castrate itself; it wrecks vengeance on its genital.*

---

* In Ferenczi's ingenious theory of genitality[2] the author calls attention to the fact that the relationship of the ego and the genital, in spite of all interests held in common, reflects profound biological antagonisms. The ego is, after all, the representative of the interests of the "soma"; and the genital, the representative of those of the "germ plasm". In so far as the ego feels itself at one with its genital libido, its genital organ impresses it as its most prolific source of pleasure; but for an ego that wishes peace, the genital becomes merely the bearer of oppressive tensions, which the ego wishes to shake off. From these and like premises, Ferenczi infers that—in the male—the act of procreation includes among its psychic qualities a "tendency towards autotomy of the genital".

In the "unconcerned" form of delusion of self-injury, the ego obviously is still experiencing an after-effect of the continuous elation; it is still "beclouded by original narcissism". To masochism—that is, to knowledge that it wishes to injure itself and that this is its sole objective—the ego is blind and deaf. It is as though, in the ego's state of grandeur, whether or not it has a genital is of no moment. The genital offended the ego—away with it!

The unconcerned type of delusion of self-injury occurs more frequently in schizophrenia than in pharmacothymia. In schizophrenia, the megalomania is responsible for the fact that the ego, under pressure of masochism, undertakes so easily to inflict the most horrible mutilations upon itself, such as amputations, enucleation of the eyeball, etc. The megalomania of schizophrenia and the megalomania of pharmacothymic elation are related manifestations of narcissistic regression. The former pursues a chronic course, the latter an acute, and they differ in regard to intellectual content and emotional tone; nevertheless, they both are based upon a regression to the "original narcissistic stature" of the ego.

Masochism in pharmacothymia may be attenuated into the passivity of a homosexual attitude. This fact gives us deep insight into the dynamics of homosexuality. The pharmacothymic regime has driven eroticism from its active positions and thereby, as a reaction, encouraged masochism. The genital eroticism which is on the retreat can then with the masochism enter into a compromise which will combine the genital aim of painless pleasure with the passive behavior of masochism, and the result of this combination, in men, is a homosexual choice of object.* The danger proceeding from the masochistic wish to be castrated, naturally remains extant. If it is of sufficient magnitude, the ego reacts to it with a fear of castration and represses the homosexual impulse, which afterwards in the psychosis may become manifest as a delusion of jealousy, or in the feminine erotic quality of the delusions of persecution.

The advantage of homosexuality as compared to masochism is its more ready acceptability to the ego. In overt homosexuality, the ego combats the masochistic danger of castration by denying the existence, in general, of any such thing as a danger of castration. Its position is: there is no such thing as castration, for there are no castrated persons; even the sexual partner possesses a penis. If the ego in pharmacothymia or after the withdrawal of the drug accepts homosexuality, this turn must be regarded as an attempt at autotherapy. The recrudescence of the genital function with a new aim, more readily attainable, psychologically speaking, permits the ego to return to, or fortify, the "realistic regime". After being reconciled to its homosexuality, the ego can subsequently take a new reparative step toward masculinity by progressing from a passive homosexual to an active

---

* I shall discuss the conditions in women in another article.

homosexual attitude. Thus, male heterosexual normality is changed into active homosexuality by a three-stage process: (1) weakening of genital masculinity (because of intimidation due to threats of castration, diversion of the libido into the pharmacothymia, etc.) and a corresponding reactive increase in the antagonistic masochism; (2) the confluence of genital pleasure and masochism in the compromise, passive homosexuality; and (3) the development of homosexuality from the passive to the active form as the result of a vigorous reparative action on the part of the ego. In corroboration of this idea is the finding, hitherto neglected, that the homosexuality which the ego rejects and combats by the formation of delusions (symptoms) is always passive homosexuality. These facts help to clarify clinical manifestations that appeared obscure and complex. Obviously, the ego may have become homosexual, because of analogous circumstances, even before the pharmacothymia began.

These views, as I have presented them here, seem to me to throw new light upon the problem of the relationship between homosexuality and pharmacothymia. The homosexual background became evident to psychoanalysis, first in alcoholism, later in cocainism, and finally in morphinism. Since I attribute homosexuality to the influence of masochism, and since, furthermore, every type of pharmacothymia attacks genitality and by reaction strengthens masochism, the opportunity to effect this compromise must naturally be present in every case of pharmacothymia.

The love life of pharmacothymics may present pathological features other than homosexuality. These all derive from the basic situation described above, in my outline of the development of homosexuality, as "stage (1)". The pharmacothymic whose potency is debilitated by masochism may find ways of preserving his heterosexuality. In the first place, he may choose another compromise solution and become oriented passively towards *women*. This erotic position is quite unstable; but it can be reënforced, by an infusion of fetishism, to withstand the onslaught of castration anxiety. With the aid of the fetishistic mechanism, the beloved woman is in imagination transmuted into the possessor of a penis and elevated to take the place of the "phallic mother".[3] With this alignment of the instincts, the persons chosen as objects are, by preference, women who have a prominent nose, large breasts, an imposing figure, or, too, a good deal of money, and the like. Correlated with this, the emotional tone in regard to the genital region of women is disturbed by a sort of discomfort, and the patient assiduously avoids looking at it or touching it. In mild cases of pharmacothymia, this passive orientation towards women with its fetishistic ingredient often plays a major rôle, but its distribution is by no means restricted to pharmacothymia. A further intensification of the masochistic wish to be castrated, or better, of the fear of castration aroused by this

wish, then forces the patient either to be abstinent or to follow the homosexual course and exchange the partner without a penis for one who possesses
a penis. (See "stage (2)" described above.) In the second place, the ego
may refuse to adopt as a solution the compromise of any passive orientation; it may respond to the danger proceeding from the masochistic instinct
by a reaction formation. It is no easy task to divine what special conditions
enable the ego to react in this way. But at any rate, the means used by the
ego are the strained exertion of its pleasure in aggression. Sadism is rushed
to the rescue of imperiled masculinity, to shout down, by its vehemence,
fear of castration and masochistic temptation. In this case, too, heterosexuality is preserved, but the ego must pay for this by entering the path
of sadistic perversion. In the dynamics of the perversion of sadism, the *vis
a tergo* of masochism is the crucial factor; in its construction, infantile and
recent experiences are jointly effective, in the usual familiar manner. The
appearance of this variant, that is, the production of a true sadistic perversion is not, to be sure, promoted by the pharmacothymia. I recognized this
mechanism in non-pharmacothymic cases, and I have mentioned it here
only because it may furnish us with the explanation of a conspicuous deformation of the character, which may be considered a counterpart of the
perversion of sadism, and which often may be found in pharmacothymia.
Particularly in drunkards, we are familiar with aggressive irritability, with
unprovoked outbursts of hate or rage against women, and the like, which
in apparently unpredictable fashion, alternate with states of touching
mollification. We can now understand that the accesses of brutality are the
substitutes for potency of the pharmacothymic who is fighting for his
masculinity, and that his sentimental seizures are eruptions of the masochism which his pharmacothymia has reactively intensified.

Pharmacothymia is not ineluctably bound to this basic course with its
terminal crisis. Many drugs, especially alcohol, admit of combating the
recurrent depression by overlapping dosage. The patient takes a fresh dose
before the effect of the previous one has ceased. If he does so, he renounces
"elation" in the narrower sense of this word; for elation is a phenomenon
dependent on contrast. Instead, he lives in a sort of "subdued continuous
elation" which differs from simple stupefaction probably only because of
its narcissistically pleasurable quality. This modified course leads through
a progressive reduction of the ego to the terminal state of pharmacogenic
stupor. A flaring up of the desire for a real elation or other reasons may
at any time bring the patient back to the basic course with its critical
complications.

This sketch of the theoretical picture of pharmacothymia roughly outlines the broad field of its symptomatology. One thing remains to be added.
In more severe, advanced cases, symptoms appear which are the result of

cerebral damage, and which are consequently to be interpreted with due consideration of the point of view of brain pathology. In this, we may expediently make use of the psycho-physiological point of view introduced into psychopathology by Schilder with the concept of "inroad of the somatic" ("*somatischer Einbruch*").* If the poisons consumed have damaged the brain substance, and permanently impaired cerebral activity, this is perceived in the mental sphere as a disturbance of the elementary psychological functions. The psychic organization reacts with an effort to adapt to this fact and correct the result. It is well to differentiate the

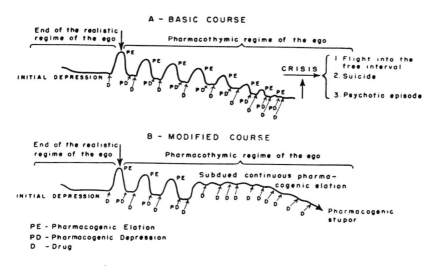

SCHEMATIZED COURSE OF PHARMACOTHYMIA.

phenomena which originate in this way, as the "secondary symptoms" of pharmacothymia, from those "primary" ones which we have been considering. The secondary symptoms are more characteristic of the brain lesions which determine them than of the illness in which they appear. This can be seen in the example of the Korsakoff syndrome, which occurs in other conditions as well as in pharmacothymia.

Finally, it might be pointed out that in addition to full-blown pharmacothymia there are obviously abortive forms of this illness. The patient may, generally speaking, retain the realistic regime, and use his pharmacothymic regime only as an auxiliary and corrective. He desires in this

---

* Schilder, Paul: *Über die kausale Bedeutung des durch Psychoanalyse gewonnenen Materials*. Wiener klin. Wchschr. 1921.—The theory of general paralysis formulated by Hollós and Ferenczi is based on a similar idea.

way to make up for the uncertainty in his realistic attitude and cover a deficit by means of counterfeit. By easy transitions we arrive at the normal persons who makes daily use of stimulants in the form of coffee, tea, tobacco, and the like.

REFERENCES

1 FERENCZI, S.: Stages in the Development of the Sense of Reality. *Contributions to Psychoanalysis*. (Translated by Jones). 1916.
2 ——: *Versuch einer Genitaltheorie*. 1924.
3 FREUD, S.: Fetishism, *Internat. J. Psycho-Analysis, 9*, 161, 1928.
4 ——: On Narcissism, an Introduction. *Collected Papers, 4*.
5 RADO, S.: An Anxious Mother. *Internat. J. Psycho-Analysis, 9*, 1928.
6 ——: The Problem of Melancholia. *Internat. J. Psycho-Analysis, 9*, 1928.
7 ——: The Psychic Effects of Intoxicants: An Attempt to Evolve a Psycho-analytical Theory of Morbid Cravings. *Internat. J. Psycho-Analysis, 7*, 1926.

Quest for a
Basic
Conceptual
Scheme

Fear of Castration in Women*

INTRODUCTION

The expression, "castration complex", which has achieved a certain amount of popularity, was coined by psychoanalysis. At first its application was limited to the male sex, and it was used as the generic designation of an important group of manifestations, which psychoanalysis had discovered in the psychic life of men. The insight obtained from the study of men sensitized the analyst in his observation of women, and it was soon evident that the new term could be applied profitably in female psychology as well. Abundant material justifying the expansion of the term was ably presented and summarized in 1921 by Abraham†,[1] in a classic study of the castration complex of women, and requires no repetition here. The manifestations in question were ideas and fantasies, attended by strong emotions, dealing with the possession or lack of a penis, the injury involved in being a woman, the desire to be a man, active and passive mutilative experiences, etc. The agreement of such ideas and certain ideas pertaining to the castration complex of men is unmistakable.

We get into difficulty when we are no longer satisfied merely to give descriptions of the empirical findings but attempt, in the spirit of our science, to proceed to an understanding of them.

In the case of the man, this task was easy. The man's genitality is characterized by two features: great narcissistic estimation of his own genital organ, and the fear, awakened by early experiences, that this valuable part may come to harm. All manifestations of the male castration complex

---

* Authorized translation from the German manuscript by Bertram D. Lewin. First published in English translation in *The Psychoanalytic Quarterly*, *2:* 425–475, 1933; in German, under the title of *Die Kastrationsangst des Weibes*, Internationaler Psychoanalytischer Verlag, Vienna, 1934.

The principal ideas contained in the present essay were first presented at a meeting of the American Psychoanalytic Association in New York City, on the 29th of December, 1931. Following this (January to March, 1933), the same topic was dealt with more extensively in a course of eight lectures held at the New York Psychoanalytic Institute. It would be a hopeless task to illustrate the widely distributed matter by means of clinical histories. The clinical material, moreover, is available to all practicing analysts. I can offer the assurance that every assertion contained in the following pages originates from the continuous and searching observations of patients. s. r.

† Of the earlier literature, see especially Van Ophuijsen, J. H. W.[19]

can be derived from these two fundamental facts. But in the woman these two elements are not present. Since women have no penis, they cannot experience a danger of castration, from which their castration complex might arise. We have, therefore, an obvious logical incompatibility. And it is this incompatibility that accounts ultimately for the obscurities to be found in the (otherwise valuable and competent) analytic literature on this topic.

Indeed, it was only in 1925 that Freud, in his paper, *Some Psychological Consequences of the Anatomical Differences between the Sexes*,[11] showed us a way out of this dilemma. Freud takes as his starting point the impression made on a child by the discovery of the genitalia of the opposite sex and compares the behavior in the two sexes. The boy sees in the "de-masculinized" female body a proof that the threat of castration is to be taken seriously. He develops a fear of castration, and later will be much put to it to emancipate his masculinity from its inhibiting effect. The little girl sees in the penis a great possession in which the boy surpasses her. Compared to the boy, she feels that she has come short—that she is as if castrated. She envies him his penis, and becomes possessed by the hope that she somehow is or will become like him. Much of her destiny as a woman will depend on the way in which she masters these importunate ideas.

Hence, according to Freud, the specific reaction to the anatomic experience discloses the difference in the castration complex of the two sexes: in men, the leading impulse in the complex is a *fear of castration*, whereas in women, this position is occupied by *penis envy*. Fear of castration is a warning, of which the effect is to safeguard threatened masculinity. Penis envy represents an attempt on the little girl's part to rebel against her anatomically attested "castration", and to persevere in her imagined masculinity. If she adapts herself to the anatomical facts opportunely, the antagonistic instinctual energy residing in penis envy is deflected into a biologically indicated wish for a child, and thus assists the girl to develop into a woman.

Freud, as it appears, gives the conception of the "female castration complex" a precise theoretical framework; and his theory enabled us properly to arrange in a cohesive system the observed data which at first seemed hopelessly disconnected. The logical incompatibility would also have been eliminated if it had been possible to conclude from Freud's theory that in women there is no fear of castration, but only penis envy. Unfortunately, it is impossible to make this deduction, for empirical analytic experience is sharply contradictory. The neuroses of women, with astonishing frequency, show characteristic anxiety symptoms and inhibitions; to give only the simplest examples, fear of dental or medical procedures, fear of having a haircut or a manicure, excessive sensitivity of certain body areas or organs, etc., which we interpret, when we find them in men, as displaced fears of castration. We have been accustomed to apply the same interpretation in the case of women, and the clinical facts have justified us. From the illustrations given, it must not be thought that we are expanding upon a trivial subject. The anxiety in question may attain almost unbearable degrees of intensity, produce grotesque and tormenting defensive symptoms, and only too frequently create a stubborn resistance to therapeutic efforts. So, practical and theoretical interests alike both compel us to face the riddle of castration fear in women.

We must ask how it happens that offshoots of a fear of castration do appear in women, even though this fear in its original form can never have existed. Here we meet the same logical difficulty which we thought we had settled. We saw that the nucleus of the castration complex in women is penis envy, but this information throws no light upon the fear. One could, of course, conclude that the two findings are mutually exclusive; for an envy of the penis depends on a castration performed and acknowledged, while a fear of castration depends on one merely imminent and expected. But it would be erroneous indeed to rely solely on this inference and conclude that Freud's construction is at fault. His theory groups facts that are clinical certainties; one group of facts simply confronts the other. It must be possible, therefore, to expand Freud's scheme of the castration complex, to make a place for and give an explanation of castration fear in women.

Since the publication of Freud's 1925 essay, I have paid consistent attention to this problem, and in addition to cases analyzed or supervised by myself, I have utilized for study the abundant case material presented in my Technical Seminars at the Berlin and New York Psychoanalytic Institutes. I am now reporting my conclusions.

I

THE ILLUSORY PENIS

The analysis of castration fear in women takes us back to the period of infancy when the penis is observed and its possession is envied. Our first clue comes from those cases in which a vigorous "masculinity complex" develops on the basis of this penis envy. The little girl, in this instance, becomes fixed in her belief that she is a boy; she ignores the evidence of her senses, and imagines that she has a penis. We must inquire further into this illusion. Let us call the organ which the girl gives herself in fantasy, the *"illusory penis"*,* her emotional gratification depends on this fantasy.

---

* Illusory penis = *Wunschpenis*. TR.

Unfortunately, I have not directly observed this process in children, but because of certain features of the "repetitive dreams" during analysis, I should like to draw the retrospective conclusion that the form in which the illusory penis first appears is that of a hallucinatory reproduction, at the proper place on the girl's own body, of the male organ that was seen. At any rate, the early form of illusory penis is short-lived. It must be abandoned, for it cannot be maintained against the refutation of the facts. For this reason, in one group of cases, the girl gradually dispenses entirely with her illusory penis, or tries some other way of renewing her illusion. But the cases that we have in mind take a different course. The illusory penis here is obviously too valuable for the girl to give up. She ceases to hallucinate and retires with her illusory penis into the realm of unconscious fantasies, where the test of reality can no longer so easily imperil her possession of it. The illusory penis is then withdrawn from the sphere of perception, but it has nevertheless unmistakably left its representative at some position or other on the surface of the body that recommends itself for this post (the nose, the eye or elsewhere) because of constitutional fitness or individual experience. The organ thus selected, though previously without sexual significance, is now entrusted by the unconscious with an accessory and essentially inappropriate function, and owing to this excessive unconscious investment behaves as the symbolic substitute for the illusory penis that was excluded from the possibility of conscious perception. We may assert then that the bodily region in question has been neurotically affected and has become the site of a conversion-hysteric symptom.

The mastery of penis envy is thus clearly divisible into two stages: an earlier stage of overt hallucinatory wish fulfilment and a second stage—brought about by the pressure of factual reality—in which the gratification is under cover, and results from the formation of a conversion symptom. It is not difficult to recognize a neurotically affected area of this description. It betrays itself by its oversensitiveness and the propensity to anxiety, which will develop for its protection. We then note that the connection between the unconscious illusory penis and its superficial substitute is not a rigid one. Along the surface, the unconscious investment is readily displaceable; new substitutes are formed, which either replace the other ones, or more frequently, persist alongside them. Indeed, the entire surface of the body may become a narcissistic substitute for a penis, as Hárnik[*, 13] has shown. Or, proceeding, the intellect may be utilized as a penis surrogate—a real or imaginary masculinization of the mental functions, which then may either persist as a symptom or become a sublimation. We infer these processes from the dreams of patients, which reveal the meaning of their flaring, wandering, local oversensitiveness and propensity to anxiety.

---

* For additional and confirmatory material see, Lewin, Bertram D.[15]

The anxiety which arises is marked by the typical features of "displaced" fear of castration. If we seek its origin, we find that the precipitating experiences are such commonplace things as wounds or injuries; and furthermore (not infrequently), that the little girl was present when a little boy was threatened with castration, or else heard of the threat. In view of such observations, one is tempted to formulate the girl's fear of castration as being borrowed from the boy; she has seen his penis, copied it, and consistently takes over the appropriate fear.

Examining the meager results of our considerations, we find that they are far from fulfilling our theoretical expectations. For our conclusion seems to be that it makes no difference whether one really has an organ or merely imagines that one has. This can hardly be true. The penis is an exceedingly pleasure-giving organ, and is, besides, the instrument by means of which a number of component impulses are gratified, as Horney,[14] in an early article, has ably demonstrated. The little girl can obtain no pleasure at all from an illusory penis, whereas with the organ she really has she can enjoy many satisfactions. The idea naturally arises that this illusory penis should be connected with pleasurable experiences in the clitoris, and that it somehow serves to maintain and assure this source of pleasure. But this suggestion cannot be supported. For in point of fact, it so happens that after the little girl has focussed her interest on her illusory penis, she abruptly loses all interest in her real genital and in masturbation. She is obviously forced to sacrifice her masturbation for the sake of her illusory penis. This process is readily intelligible: the ego has in fantasy corrected an unattractive bit of reality and consequently avoids coming into contact with it. Accordingly, the sole remaining impulse that might account for the illusory penis—that is to say, the one which has created it and finds satisfaction in it—is simply envy, or more accurately, injured self-love manifested as envy. Therefore, our suspicion is justified that so trivial a gratification cannot give the illusory penis the emotional value of the real organ. It must also not be forgotten that the boy's narcissistic pride in the penis has biology on its side, while the girl's narcissistic illusion of having a penis has biology against it.

This lengthy account enables us to deal more briefly with the problem of fear. If the only motive for the interest in the illusory penis is a narcissistic desire to quell envious feelings, then the terrific intensity of the fear of castration, which arises when the woman's illusory penis is threatened, is unintelligible—it remains a psychological riddle. The theory of the illusory penis is an incontestably true formulation of the observed clinical data, but the economic problem in women's castration fear is not solved by it.

II

THE MASOCHISTIC DEFORMATION OF THE GENITAL IMPULSE

The answer we need must obviously be sought elsewhere. Women in whose neurosis a fear of castration is most prominent usually are greatly alarmed by the sight of open wounds. A persistent and recurrent theme in their dreams and fantasies is that they must experience some horror, undergo bloody injuries, frightful mutilations, and the like. With monotonous regularity, analysis demonstrates that these ideas are "revised versions" of fantasies, whose origins can be traced back to the onset of menstruation, and even further back, to the time of infantile sexual florescence. The genital source of these ideas is therefore beyond question, their interpretation as "displaced fears of castration" legitimated, and again we encounter the problem of fear of castration in women.

Analytic literature has given most prominence to the self-punitive intention in these fantasies and has presumed that they originate from the sense of guilt for infantile masturbation. It is to the credit of Helene Deutsch[6] that she exposed the inadequacy of this formulation. "Punishment", she believes, is merely a secondary theme: the true source of these fantasies is the demands made by the instinct of masochism, which according to her views finds its place in female sexuality as far back as infancy, and from that time on remains included as one of its components. My observations had led me to a conception, which, in its interpretation of castration fantasies, coincides with Deutsch's view, but in other particulars I see the matter differently; perhaps because Deutsch does not go into the problem of castration fear, and does not sufficiently distinguish between the pathological and the normal.

In studying castration fantasies, we may consider one fact as assured. It is impossible for a little girl to get the idea that she is castrated until she knows that her body lacks a penis. This knowledge she can gain only by comparing herself with a boy. Before the discovery of the penis, there can be no castration fantasies. No girl can avoid making this discovery, but not all girls become plagued afterwards by castration fantasies. The persistence of these fantasies, which leads to such serious consequences, must be determined by special conditions. After pursuing many false leads, I was able to ascertain the salient precipitating factor: the anatomical experience was for these girls a psychic trauma. On perceiving the penis they lost self-esteem, suffered a severe emotional upset—and the sanguinary fantasies of castration appeared as a consequence of this narcissistic shock.

A process of this sort is, to be sure, not open to direct observation. I therefore chose an indirect approach. Other, more innocuous experiences that astonish children or bring them disillusion are more readily accessible to observation. I watched the children's reactions to these experiences attentively and united the impressions thus obtained through empathy with what I had concluded from the analysis of adult women. From this we may sketch the course of events in the inferred incident:—

The little girl suddenly catches sight of a penis. She is startled and fascinated. (Later on, in her neurosis the impression made by this initial encounter will be repeated again and again as terror, when a snake, mouse, or other "penis symbol", unexpectedly makes its appearance.) Her eyes are pinioned to the penis, and her field of vision restricted to this one object of perception. (This is probably the origin of the concentric restriction of the visual field, one of the "stigmata" of which so much was made in pre-psychoanalytic days, as a diagnostic point in hysteria.*) From her emotional chaos emerges the strident desire: "I want it!" which is followed immediately in fantasy by "I have it". Then comes the humiliating reflection, "But I haven't";—this knowledge produces severe psychic pain, and terminates in something like a paralysis of feeling.

The narcissistic shock at once inhibits the girl's actively directed desire for gratification, which up to this time was discharged in masturbation. But the intense mental pain which she experienced excited her sexually and supplied her with a "substitutive gratification". This emotional experience teaches her that she may obtain a new pleasure in place of the one that was destroyed by the traumatic event—passive pleasure in pain. A period of onanism ensues, in which the imagination dwells on sufferings. She remembers previous painful experiences, impressions of the "primal scene"—among these, possibly, the memory of a shadowy, at that time unintelligible, view of the penis. As a focal point for these fantasies, there is always to be found the idea of her own bloody, injured (mutilated) genital organ; the discovery of this "wound" stirred up the first critical pleasure in pain. The narcissistic wound aches, but in its own way the ache can be desirable.

The time at which the penis is discovered is obviously not a matter of indifference. If the event occurs during a period of genital latency, it is probably elaborated differently. But if it occurs at a time when the girl is masturbating, it is impossible for her to avoid being affected traumatically. We relate this masturbation to the "phallic phase", but it should be considered that this designation is not free from objections from the subjective

---

* This notion was substantiated in all particulars by a case presented by Dr. Walter Briehl, in one of my Technical Seminars held at the New York Psychoanalytic Institute. The patient had a classical concentric restriction of vision; and an obsessive impulse to stare at the penis of every man she met. Her fixation on the trauma of the infantile observation of the penis was proved by many other symptoms.

standpoint of the girl herself. Before discovering the existence of the penis, she could not endow the antithesis, man—woman, with a genital meaning. Similarly she lacked any idea of the dual erotogenic make-up of her genital area, no matter whether she masturbated using her clitoris or her vagina. It seems, therefore, more cautious to designate this level of the girl's psycho-sexual development, the "amorphous genital phase of the ego". Only after the anatomical experience and because of it, is the girl drastically coerced into distinguishing those who have a penis (male) from those who have none (female). For she then sees that at the same location on the body where she obtains so much pleasure, another child is much better equipped than herself. Her primitive, concrete mode of thinking leads her to the (false) conclusion that the boy's larger instrument must provide him with more and better pleasure. Her offended self-esteem provokes her to rumi-nate on her disadvantage. "I am wounded. . . . It must have been cut off . . . while I slept." She comes to the painful fantasies of castration, which will then be utilized by her blighted desire for pleasure to give her pleasure in suffering.

The traumatic discovery of the penis thus results in an abrupt demolition of the "amorphous genital phase of the ego", and in an urgent necessity for the girl to build up too soon and too precipitately, a henceforth sexually differentiated, "female" genital position. For this construction, however, her sexual constitution furnishes her as building material only the capacity of the organism, in an emergency—when it is impeded in its active pleasur-able activities, that is—to obtain pleasure from painful excitement and to bring about for this reason the very sufferings that are ordinarily avoided: in other words, what Freud refers to as "erotogenic masochism".[8] The new genital position that is built from this raw material is pleasure in being, or getting one's self, castrated. In this phrase we recognize the initial idea-tional content of "feminine masochism", as described by Freud.

We revert here to emphasize the crucial rôle played in this development by the masturbatory activity of the "amorphous genital phase". The striking frequency with which the discovery of the penis coincides with this masturbation is not a matter of chance. To begin with, the little girl may frequently miss discovering the penis, even though it may be exposed to her view. A "discovery" consists in a differential perception and an elabo-ration by thought (an assimilation) of the new ideational content obtained through the differentiation. The girl can discover the penis, then, only after she is prepared, and has an impulse to make the discovery. Such pre-paredness is primarily brought about or favored by her masturbatory ac-tivities in her own genital area. If she happens to see the penis, when she is at a certain stage of maturity, she may naturally discover it for other reasons than those connected with genital pleasure. But, in that case, with what different results! She does not then experience a genital-narcissistic, but a narcissistic blow. That is, she does indeed feel that she is "short", but not that she is short by *that* instrument of pleasure; there is lacking any overestimation of the penis, as a superior instrument of pleasure; there is lacking the (genital) instinctual energy that propels the narcissistic rumination, and with this too the degeneration of this rumination into genital masochism. We recognize here a determinant of the development to normality: the penis must be discovered, not in the "phase of amorphous genitality"—a phase of genital activity, that is—but in a phase of genital latency. For a pathological development, then, it is quite certainly the instinctual activity of the "amorphous genital phase" that, after the penis is discovered, compels the immediate, new genital orientation; the desire for genital pleasure kept alive through masturbation is subsequently continued perforce in the pain-pleasure activity of genital masochism.

But from this newly found source of pleasure, masturbatory revery is never able to extract an adequate gratification, even though it be carried to the point of exhaustion. It is easy to see why. The girl was made a woman by an experience that profoundly offended her self-love. This antecedent history burdens female genitality with a "narcissistic dependency" unknown in the genitality of the male. Subsequently, female genitality, in order to be considered truly satisfying, must include a reparation for this narcissistic blow. Genital masochism does not fulfil this requirement. On the contrary, it aggravates the narcissistic discomfort of the ego, which is mindful of the pleasure principle and desires not pleasure in pain, but pleasure without pain. It is now obvious that the appearance of genital masochism in the ego is not a stage of normal development, but the momentous beginning of a pathological—a masochistically deformed—femininity.

The excesses of painful pleasure endanger self-preservation and drive the ego into despair. Once its tolerance is exhausted, the ego adopts radical protective measures. Having had enough of torture, it now resuscitates its downtrodden narcissism. The ego suppresses the genital masochistic impulses, represses all of the bloody fantasies, and hallucinating, endows itself with an illusory penis. But, one may well ask in astonishment, how can so overwhelming a psychic alteration be produced? The simple answer is: in sleep, by a dream. This dream, in which the tortured mind of the child finally finds peace, must result in a persistent sense of reality; for the dream is based on a real fact, the observation of a penis. The girl dreams that she has a penis on her body and subsequently, in waking life, she is held in the spell of this illusion. Later, as we have seen, she will be compelled to convert this hallucinatory penis into a conversion symptom.

It may be interesting to give an example of the way in which this childhood event is repeated during an analysis in a patient's dream.

She dreamed: "I see a crippled child, and then another child. The latter child turns into Al Smith, has a derby hat, and mounts a fiery steed." The patient begins her associations to the dream with a remark that tells the whole story: "I am the child who turns into Al Smith." When I explained the phallic significance of the derby hat, she laughed heartily and exclaimed: "Of course! Al Smith built the Empire State Building, with the highest tower in the world." The unmistakable phallic architecture of this building with its glans-shaped cupola (derby hat) has not passed unrecognized in popular humor. It has been called "Al Smith's latest erection".—The crippled child, who also represents the dreamer, reminds her of the sufferings of the crippled child in Joseph Roth's novel, *Job*. From this she proceeds to associations concerning gloomy incidents of her own childhood.—The dream was a reaction to a vigorous but unhappy attempt on the patient's part to indulge in, and gain pleasure from sexual intercourse. It represents her flight from her masochistically deformed femininity ("cripple") into phallic masculinity, making use of the most extravagant symbolism.

We are now able to understand the great amount of affect with which the illusory penis is invested. The illusory penis is not a simple product of penis envy, but a *narcissistic reaction formation* of the ego, its bulwark against repressed genital masochistic impulses, and it must be strong enough to resist the attack of these forces. Thus, the economic problem in women's fear of castration is solved: it is a fear that the repressed genital masochism will return from repression. It is not the signal of an external danger, but of danger from the genital masochistic instinct.

Let us dwell somewhat on the situation produced for the girl's instinctual life by the accession of a hallucinatory penis. Her previous desire for genital pleasure, which was not guided by any idea of sexual differences, is now divided into two sexually differentiated tendencies, but for both the path of discharge is blocked. Her genital masochism must be repressed, as offensive. And her genital masculinity is useless, for she must avoid the site where she has placed her illusory penis, to preserve her illusion. Her masochistic femininity comes to naught because of the pleasure principle, her phallic masculinity because of the anatomical facts. The ego's narcissistic wound is now healed; the girl, as I should like to put it, has made her "autoplastic (phallic) complementation",* but her genital impulses have been sacrificed to her narcissistic interests. In consequence, the ego fumbles with both inadequate genital strivings and cannot acquire an orientation to genitality congruous with the genital organ. It may be that

---

* Autoplastic (phallic) complementation = *autoplastische (phallische) Komplettierung*. Tr.

clinical data which radiate from this situation led Ernest Jones[7] to the idea of aphanisis.

Critical compunction leads us to consider one point as yet untouched in this essay. It was obviously advisable to begin our study of the fear of castration by considering its narcissistic determination. Now it may be said that we have let ourselves be riveted to this aspect and have ignored the relation between the fear and the girl's emotional attitude to the members of her family,—to her desires, joys, and disappointments. This is a fair objection, but in defense it must be pointed out that the onesidedness was deliberate and unavoidable. Whoever wishes to find out how a complicated network is made must first single out the individual threads. Here too, to achieve a useful synthesis, we must consistently follow all points of view through the material, one at a time. Nevertheless it is true that we should be cautious and from time to time stop and see if some nodal point has not been overlooked. We may do so now by asking, who is the object of the sensual desire that finds an outlet in the masochistic masturbation. I have already brought out that this masturbation is predominantly mental* and have referred to its relation to the primal scene. Yet this does not imply that the girl's masturbation is caused by a desire for her father and an identification with her mother. This conjecture would be as incorrect as if the rôles were assigned conversely. The masturbation is not due to a sensual desire for anyone, but to the narcissistic distress of the little girl, and is *par excellence* autoerotic. For during this period, we find that she is turned in on herself, isolated, and secluded. To be sure, she is ready to accept (as if unaware) a great deal of tenderness from the environment, but she has no impulse to return it. In her genital masochistic fantasies, it is more important to her that she should be suffering, than that any special person should have made her suffer. She now has an "anatomic depression" (*anatomische Verstimmung*),† as we may designate it, which later on in her neurosis will be repeated as "menstrual depressions". Concomitant with her autoplastic (phallic) complementation, her mood changes into a sort of forced gaiety; she quits masturbating, as we have seen, and now more than ever, for a long time will not have any expectation of sensual love.

---

* The genital masochistic fantasies are often accompanied by typical, aberrantly genital masochistic activities, such as nail-biting, tearing out the hair, etc.

† Abraham knew of the existence of an early depression of this type, and described it as "primal depression" (*Urverstimmung*).[2] He also recognized that this depression was due to an estrangement from both parents. We may add that this twofold estrangement in the "anatomical depression" is an outcome of the girl's anatomical experience, which at one blow turns her love from the persons about her back to herself. The depression is of the severe type that degenerates into overt masochistic gratification.

Our reference to the parents reminds us to add another detail, although its significance will not be discussed here. To begin with, the repetitive dreams show that the girl acquires the illusory penis from her father or brother. (As in the dream reported above.) This is so intelligible that it would seem strange to question its being elementary. Yet in another connection, while studying the cyclothymic phenomena, I discovered that the father's appearance in the ideas relating to the illusory penis is secondary, and occurs only after the girl has experienced a momentous disappointment. In the original form of the fantasy, the girl gets her penis from the mother; and to do this she devours the breast! One's amazement disappears with the reflection that at this age, it is a matter of course that the mother is the source on which to draw for all that is desirable and worth having. To whom else should the child turn for a remedy of this deficiency? Simple children's nurses show great emotional knowledge when they tell children not to swallow the seed when they eat fruit, or a tree will grow out of their stomach. That fruit is symbolic of the breasts has been known for a long while by psychoanalysts.

We may now sum up our theory in a brief formula:

"Anatomical experience $\rightarrow$ Extinction of the amorphous genital phase of the ego $\rightarrow$ Domination of the ego by genital masochism $\rightleftarrows$ Narcissistic defense reaction of the ego: phallic complementation $\rightarrow$ Fear of castration in the ego, as a signal of danger from genital masochism."

III

The Modifications of Castration Fear

Castration anxiety in women is the product of a serious disorder, which arose in the infantile developmental phase of genitality. Unless a process of restitution intervenes during the following years, the deformity suffered will result in a permanent impairment of the female sexual function. The repression of genital masochism prevents the acquisition of the normal female genital attitude; the genital impulse cannot find its proper psychic expression. Its energy is divided between two mutually opposed strivings: the genital masochistic, and the illusory phallic. The fear of castration will persist as an infallible sign of this unfortunate course. It will be encountered later as the central pathological phenomenon in the neurosis of the mature woman. No matter how confusing the clinical picture presented to us by a neurosis in a woman, it is always possible, after some effort, to separate out of its complexity the following simple situation:

From puberty on, the genital impulse, reënforced in its somatic source, has been more and more insistent upon being gratified; and the girl's standards were formed under pressure of a society that expects her to fulfil her feminine destiny. The young woman despairingly attempts to adapt herself to this prescribed rôle, or at least to find a solution that will be an acceptable compromise, but, again and again, she finds it impossible. We now easily understand why she fails. For that which is being thrust upon her from within as her "female" sexual desire is really a repellent demand that she deliver herself over to excruciating, bloody tortures, in order to enjoy the pleasure of her own pain. Her ego reacts to this suggestion with a fear of castration and strengthens the investment of the illusory penis, which at this time is located where the ego most fears that the genital masochism will burst forth. At each post of danger an illusory penis (a masculine attitude) is stationed as a sentry.* The spontaneous attacks by the genital impulse, or the timid attempts of the ego to try out its femininity, immediately precipitate fresh anxiety. The result is an interminable effort on the ego's part to come to some terms with the genital masochistic instinctual danger indicated by the fear of castration. For this purpose a few psychic mechanisms, with which we are sufficiently familiar, are brought into play. The ego relies upon one or another of these procedures, and combines them or elaborates them in lengthy undertakings, during the course of which the same situations come to be repeated. The ego engages in the struggle at many different points, but always with the same unattainable goal: to find some protective "sanctuary" in itself, removed from the jurisdiction of its genital masochism, where it may find freedom from its consuming, impending fear, and peace in a modest pleasure.

---

* For example, in the dream reported on a previous page, each single phallic symbol represents a defense against a particular masochistic attitude. The "fiery steed" is the counterpart of the dreamer's masochistic masturbation fantasy of the sufferings of a horse, which has persisted unchanged since childhood, for which she took the ideas from the story of *Black Beauty*. The "derby hat" hints at her severe masochistic intellectual inhibitions, against which she was constantly trying to defend herself by outbursts of masculine intellectuality. (Cf. the discussion of "spurious feeble-mindedness" below.) Her identification with her father (the "Governor"), who leads his life more or less autocratically isolated from his family, denies the dreamer's intense masochistic fixation to her mother. The "Empire State Building" is, in the latent material of the dream, a symbol of impudent phallic exhibitionism, which takes the place of the earlier, bashfully anxious concealment of her phallic deficiency. This anxious self-concealment and the self-exposure are both represented in the dreamer's life by a number of extremely characteristic manifestations, which cannot be reported here. I may assure the reader that this phallic dream in its "choice of symbols" reveals all the crucial masochistic tendencies that have gone to form the dreamer's life.

To demonstrate the soundness of this theory, let us turn our attention to the neurotic mechanisms referred to above.

To begin with, let us be quite clear as to the "displacement" or "modification" of castration fear, mentioned so often in these pages. We must therefore ask several questions: how can we characterize this process more accurately?—in what way does masochism participate in it?—and in what way does the ego, which experiences the fear and heeds it as a warning participate? As a starting point for this exposition we may use the patients' fear of ordinary commonplace injuries. The thing that is feared here by the ego and considered a danger—physical or mental injury—is precisely what the genital masochism displaced from its original field of operations secretly desires. Genital masochism craves physical or mental pain, so that it may extract pleasure from the painful stimulation. Each apprehension of the ego conceals a latent, synonymous, intention to obtain satisfaction on the part of masochism. Essentially, therefore, what the ego fears (and quite justifiably) are the wishes of its own repressed genital masochism; as if it were aware of what was being planned within itself against its own welfare. It is hard, however, to grant that the ego has such insight, if, in the analytic hour, one sees how violently patients reject this insight when it is proffered them. But there is no need to enter into questionable hypotheses. Careful observation shows clearly the process that takes place in the ego: the ego's sensitiveness, and corresponding alertness, to pain is remarkably increased by the pressure of masochism. As the ego wishes to protect itself from masochistic experiences, it is forced to scour the field of its activities to find the most remote possibility of pain. With this—though completely unaware of what it is doing—it performs an excellent reconnoitering service for its masochism. For masochism seizes upon the new potentialities for suffering that the ego has made visible, and henceforth exerts a pressure towards their realization. The ego perceives the masochistic investment as an increase in internal tension, and the situation into which masochism is trying to bring it inspires it with fear.* The ego's attention is diverted entirely from the processes within itself and to the environment, where it

---

* In childhood and often enough later on also, the trouble of discovering new possibilities of "pain" for the masochistically sensitized ego, is taken over by other persons (parents, superiors, friends). It is instructive to compare the attitude of this ego with that of the normal ego. The healthy child is often given the idea of a new possibility of *pleasure* by some ineptly imparted warning on the part of its upbringer, which he then quickly tries out. The healthy ego, later in life, too, scents a secret pleasure behind every warning (or prohibition) that proceeds from authority, a pleasure that shall be withheld only from it. It reacts, consistently, with a *temptation to rebel*. The masochistically prepossessed ego has forfeited this healthy sagacity in regard to possibilities of pleasure. The warning (or prohibition) induces only the idea of a new possibility of *"pain"*; the ego is *masochistically tempted*; it represses the temptation and reacts with fear (anxiety).

seeks and finds the reason for its fears. This articulation with reality conceals the masochistic determination of the fear.

We are now equipped to scrutinize individually the modifications and displacements of the fear of castration. The most important of these originate in the great biological events in female sexual life. The ego, with its wits sharpened by bad masochistic experiences, has to deny that the initial menstruation is a masochistic gratification, and declare that the haemorrhage resulted from an act of violence, of which it was somehow the victim,—during sleep. This interpretation, which the girl spins out in dreams and reveries, follows the trail of the idea that she had once experienced a similar act of violence, castration. Here genital masochism acquires the second of its ideational contents: the wish to be violated. The ego's reaction to this is a modification of the fear of being castrated into a fear of being violated. The same reactions ensue if the girl's imagination has dealt with the fact of menstruation before she herself began to menstruate; her personal experience then merely reënforces these reactions. The masochistically sensitized ego handles the problem of childbirth in a similar way: again a part of her body is to be torn away. This then becomes the third idea in genital masochism: the wish to be delivered of the foetus through violence. The corresponding modification of the fear of castration is the fear of childbirth.

We have thus all three manifestations of genital masochism, which Freud described as "feminine masochism", and which Helene Deutsch has considered the "masochistic triad" of normal female sexual life—the three wishes for pleasurable pain: to be castrated, to be violated, and to be forced to deliver the child. We see that this masochistic triad expresses the aims and wishes of a pathologically distorted, masochistically deformed femininity,—against which the ego in alarm defends itself by a correlated triad of fears: a fear of castration, a fear of being violated, and a fear of childbirth. The painful pleasure in childbirth is not then, as Helene Deutsch and Georg Groddeck have supposed, the "orgasm" of *the* woman, but, at most, the sexual fulfilment of the genitally masochistic woman. The ego's fear follows after the genital masochism, when the latter penetrates to new secondary positions, and a number of further modifications proceed from the triad of fears. The fear of being violated persists with only slight modification as a fear of defloration, or as fear of sexual intercourse in general. Fear of delivering a child is intensified into a fear of dying; of which the text might read, "I have to die while in travail". From the original genital site, these fears spread to include other types of violation, coercion, injury, and so on. The ego's original reaction formation against genital masochism, the narcissistic illusory penis, persists during all of this pathological evolution, and is observable by the analyst as the location at which the ego's anxiety is ready to appear. To another reaction formation, which according to my findings has been formed in the ego and inherits partly or entirely the narcissistic investment of the illusory penis, I have given the name of "illusory foetus". The recognition of this fantasy renders accessible to our understanding the symptomatology of the unconscious pregnancy fantasies, which is as rich in clinical manifestations as in surprises. Since I am interested here in presenting the primary dynamics of the neurosis, in what follows I intentionally neglect these complications, and consequently the whole topic of "the child". They will be made the subject of another essay.

IV

Morphogenesis in the Neuroses

This survey of the transformations of the fear of castration strengthens our view of the attitude of the ego. Whenever the ego should be perceiving the masochistic instinctual danger, it discovers instead an external one and believes that this is the one it fears. Consistently it then concentrates its efforts on the task of protecting itself against the supposedly external danger. The central "source of danger" in the life of the masochistic woman is the man; the line of defense in her neurosis will be toward him.

The ego that is or supposes itself to be in danger, has three types of defensive means at its disposal:—(1) flight, (2) combat, and (3) the choice of the "lesser evil".

Accordingly, whichever of these three methods may be adopted by the neurosis, for each there results a corresponding special nosological type, or a special type of character, which may be found in life sometimes in pure culture, but more frequently in different transitional or combined forms. Here we may profitably limit our attention to those types that are best known to the analyst from his everyday practice or from the literature. It will be shown how if our point of view is assumed, the psychic structure of these types is illuminated, and how we can proceed from hesitant explanations, or no explanations, to satisfactory interpretations, and beyond this arrive at a unitary system of classification comprising the entire field. Since it is our intention merely to present a demonstration, we shall not attempt monographic comprehensiveness. The material has also been limited by our excluding the topic of "the child".

1. Flight

Let us begin with a consideration of the mechanisms of flight.

(a) The extreme result of flight from men is female *homosexuality*. After an initial period of overdone gushing or passionate tenderness, it regularly finds its way to clitoris pleasure. There are two reasons for the gratification: the successful avoidance of the dangerous man and the "realizing" of the masculinity inaugurated by the illusory penis. The neurotic disturbance peculiar to female homosexuality is a sense of guilt, the avowed source of which is the perversion itself with its attendant exclusion from the group. From this arises the tendency of homosexual women to strengthen their position by forming a group. This sense of guilt has as its roots a tormenting sense of inferiority, an uneasiness that one will be found inadequate, a fear of being exposed as ridiculous. The secret content of this fear is a fear of having the lack of a penis made public, which then would be immediately exploited by their genital masochism. Accordingly fear of exposure is a modified fear of castration, the persistence of which into the phallic sexual organization proves that this solution cannot free women from the pressure of their genital masochism.

(b) Another type of flight from the man is less conspicuous overtly. I refer to *frigidity*. Here the woman is willing to enter a sexual relationship with a man, but the relationship is without meaning. She offers him her genital organ, but retreats from it herself. In intercourse the organ is nonexistent for her, is consequently not excitable, and provides neither pleasure nor pain. If the genital retains or resurrects its capacity to feel pain, the woman begins to use all measures at her disposal—including hysterical attacks, vaginism, and the like—to resist sexual intercourse. The frigid woman then obtains a substitute gratification from forced intellectual, professional, social, or domestic activities, or from some other source. The sublimation of masculinity in mental work is the solution that is coming to be more and more preferred nowadays. In this work, the mentally masculinized woman again meets her enemy, man, whom she evaded sexually. The gnawing sense of insecurity, the eternal fear of being exposed to ridicule, which arises in the intellectual or professional field, comes from a fear of having her phallic deficiency made apparent, and hence from a fear of her genital masochism. Joan Riviere[18] has very ably shown that such women frequently adopt a "masquerade" of womanliness to hide their masculinity. They ingratiate themselves because of their charm and then emasculate men on a mental plane. This, to be sure, is already an example of "combat", and might be included in the section dealing with that technique.

The impulsion to reënforce the phallic position by masculinizing the intellect may make its appearance, in gifted girls especially, during the school years, and even this early, fail because of a great variety of emotional conflicts. Puberty sets a severe test. The early defeat of this effort may have very serious sequelae. As usual, if the illusory penis is destroyed, the position that it was designed to protect becomes a prey to masochism. Masochism can then occupy it. The girl begins to act as though she were stupid, through defiance. From the original site of the conflict, the process spreads first to one point, and then another, until it terminates as a chronic masochistic impairment of the intellectual functions, and under particularly unpropitious conditions, as a *spurious feeble-mindedness*.[4] In all cases of this type that I have had a chance to observe, the patient as a child was originally above the average in intelligence. Though an apparent paradox, it is none the less true that the talented child is the very one that is most exposed, in the intellectual field, to defeats which the stupid child does not risk. Experiences of this sort that encourage masochism are then of necessity followed by an attempt to utilize the intellectual ability as a phallic means of defense, and after this measure fails, by a masochistic paralysis of the intellect.

(c) Women with masculine ambitions often pursue another policy in order to avoid the dreaded unmasking of their "incapacity" (their lack of a penis). They withdraw from competition with men and are culturally active in some typically feminine field of endeavor. In this field, they behave more like a man than the men do. This type of avoidance has an interesting infantile history. The little girl, protecting her illusory penis from discovery, turns her interest from the genital region and ceases to masturbate. But this is not sufficient, for she incurs the same danger whenever she urinates. She does not hesitate to suppress her desire to urinate, and often brings on a stubborn, occasionally alarming, *retention of urine*. If, finally, she accedes to the impulse, she urinates like a boy. She may also elect to transport her device into her sleep, where she can urinate with her illusory penis (*nocturnal enuresis*). I suspect that this remarkable accomplishment—urinating with an illusory penis—may determine a subsequent tendency in our little heroine to indulge in *boasting* and *fantastic lying*; to the extent to which she develops a reactive compulsion neurosis, she will deny this past by *fanatic truthfulness*.

(d) Infantile reluctance to empty the bladder is also at the root of another conversion symptom, which may be continued in a slightly modified way into maturity. I refer to *blushing*, and its accompaniment, the fear of blushing, or *erythrophobia*, so-called. The blush exhibits to us the result of an unsuccessful flight. "If I should urinate now," the child thinks, when the urge is present, "all would be known." This idea is already a masochistic one; the faltering ego must consequently submit to being publicly humiliated by genital masochism. The girl blushes and thus involuntarily confesses that she has no penis. It is correct to say that her suppressed urethral erotic excitement literally goes to her head, there to produce as a consolation something resembling an erection. But this interpretation does not completely elucidate the blushing; for example, a severe headache may also appear—which is often enough the case. The concentration of excitement upon the exposed face indicates that the process does not end in a successful phallic reaction formation, but in the triumph of masochism. The fear of blushing in erythrophobia is accordingly an unconcealed fear of castration. Subsequently, in the dynamics of blushing and erythrophobia, genital excitement takes the place of the urethral variety. The intention was to suppress genital excitement because of its masochistic debasement, but masochism, gaining the upper hand, by means of the woman's self-betraying, erotically exaggerated modesty, is all the more able to deliver over this fearful fugitive to the assaults of men.*

In several genitally masochistic women, I have observed for a long time that they preferably wear *red clothes* or red articles of clothing (hats, ties, belts, handbags, etc.) while they are menstruating. If one draws their attention to this fact, they are at first surprised or amused or try to contradict it, but finally all admit that they were not aware of their habit. That

---

* To judge from a few unfortunately incomplete observations, the obscure condition of *psoriasis*, which from the psychological angle is to be considered a permanent blush, has the same masochistic instinctual basis. For a long while I have endeavored to ascertain the libidinal qualities of the body surface,—that is, of the skin. More than ten years ago there occurred to me the idea (expressed only privately) that we might assume as the earliest phase of libidinal organization, a tactile phase, and relying upon phylogenetic considerations, that we might suppose this to occur in prenatal existence. But I soon abandoned this idea, since it was wholly unproductive. I think now that I can defend my opinion that the skin is not only the narcissistic rind of the ego, but at the same time and completely antithetically, also an exquisite settlement-area for masochism. The skin takes a large part in the protection against stimuli (*Reizschutz* of Freud); because of its exposed position it is not only subjected to the most various insults—thermal, chemical, mechanical, etc.—but it is at the same time the place where the first defensive reparative reactions of the organism run their course. The two processes, injury and repair, are alike constantly associated with pain, which masochism can readily utilize as pleasure in suffering. There is thus formed an intimate connection between the cutaneous surface and masochism, of which the disposition may be traced back into the obscure phylogenetic past. (In this type of problem one must not lose sight of phylogenesis.) It would not be in the least miraculous, then, if relations of this sort were at work in the psychopathology of skin diseases, and of the major infectious exanthematous diseases (including syphilis).—From this angle, we may also interpret the libidinal dynamics of *tender stroking*, which is of so much importance in the love life of the masochistic woman. Stroking attains its erotic aim by evoking playfully for the person stroked masochistic instinctual danger, and then giving her all the more delight because of the totally painless nature of the proffered gratification. This is a splendid maneuver for the benefit of the narcissistic ego: the ego is permitted repeatedly to enjoy a triumph of the pleasure principle over genital masochistic temptation. The gratification obtained will naturally be in proportion to the genital masochistic instinctual danger.

this is a copy of blushing, is unconsciously planned as a provocation, and originates in the sexually exciting "castration experience" is self-evident.

(*e*) Considered as a flight from genitality, frigidity is a success: genital masochism cannot assert itself in the genital area that the ego has deserted. (Yet, such happenings as childbirth, venereal infections and the like may give fresh opportunities.) Genital masochism then finds a way to build a covert ideational bridge between the no longer realizable, damaging genital situation and some other, ordinarily innocuous and commonplace life situation. Such bridges are formed as a rule in childhood and remain potentially ready for use. Furthermore, the ego, with its equivocal anxious-sensual alertness to anything and everything that might injure it, always gives genital masochism the right cue. The previously harmless situation then has a sexual—that is to say, a genital masochistic significance. As soon as the ego approaches the genito-masochistically exciting situation, it is attacked by fear; the patient takes to her heels and for the future avoids this situation as a danger. She then suffers from a *hysterical situational phobia*. The flight, in the phobia, repeats the flight from the genital at the new position that the displaced genital masochism has brought into relation with genitality.

A few examples will illustrate this analysis: We may begin with the morbid *fear of high places*. Freud with a terse remark indicated the origin of this phobia in a fear of feminine masochistic temptation.[9] It may be added in corroboration that the masochistic temptation here is to throw oneself into the depths, symbolic of a self-inflicted damaging parturition (cf. German *Niederkommen*), and the ego's fear is an intensified fear of childbirth, that is, a fear of dying. The numerous morbid *fears of reptiles and small animals* refer back to the first appearance of a "snake"—the first acquaintance with the penis. The girl's reaction to that experience was masochistic masturbation. The reappearance of the "snake" is an incitement to masturbate masochistically—and later on to indulge in masochistic coitus. The fear of the terrified, recoiling ego has the hidden meaning of a fear of being violated. In the various morbid *fears of traveling* (in trains, automobiles, etc.) a somatic factor enters. The rocking and shaking excites masochistically sensitized persons in a genital masochistic way. The somatic agitation stimulates the repressed genital masochism and the corresponding fear of the ego. The patient who innocently details her apprehensions about a journey, is giving an accurate description of the latent genital masochistic desires aroused by the projected journey. Psychoanalysis then shows that the masochistic elaboration of the traveling links it with the important genital masochistic experiences of childhood,—the primal scene, birth of another child, etc. Many kinds of danger may be encountered while on a journey, and accordingly there is hardly a single variety of castration fear that may not be manifested as a fear of traveling: fear of collisions, of being mutilated, of being drugged and robbed, of being raped, of being killed,—in former bedwetters, a fear of being set afire or burnt, and so on.

Agoraphobia, the morbid fear of going out on to the street, has been dealt with repeatedly by analytic writers. Alexander recognized correctly that the essential danger on the streets is a covert temptation to be a prostitute.[3] Deutsch[5] later convincingly demonstrated that masochism played a great part in this illness. She did not, however, relate this masochism to genitality and narcissism, but to aggression, and thus narrowly missed the explanation to which we hold. It is quite evident that prostitution is a desired aim of genital masochism. It combines sexual gratification with a moral humiliation that the ego wants as little as physical damage. Furthermore, the latent fantasy of being a prostitute is not the sole masochistic ideational content, and surely not the original content, in agoraphobia. In my experience, the crucial fixation in this illness takes place at the primal scene, impressions of which, after the discovery of the penis, stimulated masochistic masturbation. To what extent this fixation of the primal scene depends upon the recurrent opportunity then to observe the penis, I shall not venture to decide. At any rate, the danger exists subsequently that a repetition of the coitus observation will immediately activate the urge to masturbate masochistically. To the observation of sexual intercourse, the ego reacts with a specific sensitiveness, which it later transfers to street traffic. This process of displacement may rest upon verbal associations (as in German, where *Verkehr* means intercourse and traffic), or may utilize the identity of certain perceptual elements ("motion", "noise"). The situation of being on the street activates the idea of parental coitus, which then stimulates the desire to masturbate masochistically, or later to have masochistic sexual relations. The ego's response is a fear of castration, the patient flees in despair and in consequence refuses to go on the street. This comprises the phobic mechanism in the restricted sense of the term. To go out with a companion, whose presence protects the patient from the fear, is then an act of prevention. It is true that the patient here flees from genital masochistic temptation to the protective guardianship of a trusted person. In certain cases in my experience, however, there was an additional secret significance in this symptom. If the girl takes her mother (or later a substitute for the mother) with her, the parents are separated, and nothing can go on between them. Then the symptom is no longer a flight but a "preventive counter-attack", and the aggression here is not one of the determinants of the pathogenic conflict, but one of its results. Many clinical histories contain a variation of this symptom—brought to our attention by Deutsch—that the girl is attacked by fear if she remains at home, while her mother has gone out. It then appears as though she were identifying herself with her mother, who is on the streets, and were vicariously feeling the appropriate fear. In point of fact the matter is simpler than that. The girl has become suspicious that when her mother goes out alone she meets a lover. So, although the girl stays at home, she is beset by the same sexual impression that precipitated her genital masochistic excitement; to be alone increases the temptation to masturbate and with it the fear. Her extreme, conscious or unconscious resentment of her mother is therefore not the cause but the result of her fear—that is, of her genital masochistic excitability.

Even this small selection of illustrations proves how numerous are the mechanisms of displacement in the phobias. They are by no means all of them correctly comprehended, but with our knowledge of the essential structure of phobias it can hardly be the case that any greater obstacle is placed in the way of their evocation. The problem is always the same: From the phobic situation we must dissect out that infantile experience, which compulsorily precipitates the patient into genital masochistic excitement. In the illustrations given, this specific experience was: the (re)appearance of the wound (the deep place), the (re)appearance of the penis, the mechanical shaking of passive motion, and the (repetition of the) observation of coitus. Obviously, through infantile fixations genital masochism acquires this specific sensitiveness to a particular excitation, which then determines the "selection of the situation" in the "situational phobia".

The Problem of Fear (Anxiety)—The true problem of phobias arises elsewhere. Freud has taught us that fear is a signal of danger; objective fear, so-called, heralds the presence of an external (objective) danger, neurotic fear the presence of an (unknown) instinctual danger.[9] From this foundation we have built up our own views and shown that castration fear in women is the signal of the instinctual danger emanating from genital masochism. Our whole study stands or falls on this point. The phobias—and other types of anxiety hysteria without phobic mechanisms—present the most tempestuous manifestations of fear, culminating in the great hysterical anxiety attack, which may overpower the patient for hours or days, and which so often proves to be refractory to any phobic device. These facts do not conform with the theory of anxiety as a danger signal. Can it be that our theory fails us in the very situation where fear completely dominates the clinical picture? This we cannot believe, for it is too firmly grounded in the facts; so that there must be a gap in our knowledge of anxiety phenomena. The great advance made by Freud's theory of anxiety was the introduction into the problem of the danger situation. The new productive mode of approach nevertheless compelled him to assume that the ego itself manufactured the fear. This is a difficult theoretical position to maintain, for introspection contradicts it. Linguistic usage also assigns an active rôle to anxiety and a passive one to the ego. We describe the experiencing of fear or anxiety in terms that emphasize their originally ego-alien quality: we are beset, attacked, overcome, overwhelmed, or shaken by fear or anxiety. It could also not be determined how the ego was supposed to make the fear, whether through "fermentation of the libido", or in some other way. Here then is the gap. A discussion of the problem of fear (anxiety) is not to be avoided.

Let us preserve our clinical point of view and inquire, by what means the anxiety operates as a signal. Unquestionably by means of a momentary constriction of breathing, that is, by means of a minimal transient paralysis, on which there follows an immediate remedial acceleration of the heartbeat. We may without harm ignore the accessory content of the anxiety picture; the nucleus of the experience of fear (anxiety) is the paralysis, and this can be brought about only by masochism. The narcissistic ego, which ordinarily does not wish to have anything to do with masochism, in this instance for a moment gives its archenemy a free hand, to be used as an instrument for the ego's own preservation. Masochism inflicts a trifling injury (the momentary paralysis) upon the ego's own body, which advises the ego of the approach of danger. Freud made the ingenious suggestion that fear (anxiety) anticipates an impending injury in miniature; but this mechanism could not be demonstrated by referring it to the anxiety at birth; insight into the masochistic nature of fear throws light upon it. The ego is obedient to the warning given it by masochism. It sharpens its attention (as Freud describes it) and awaits the danger in complete readiness for action (defense). In the case of neurotic fear, fear of castration, the signaling operations are even simpler. The source of danger, from which the threatened injury alone can emanate, is masochism itself, and the fear signal is a genuine sample of what confronts the ego. The ego's ignorance in regard to this internal source of danger accounts for the inappropriateness of its ensuing behavior. It behaves consistently enough from its own point of view, for it directs the attention aroused by the signal to the environment. Up to this point, the phenomenon of fear is nothing else than a remarkable biological signal service. But even in the less severe cases of anxiety attack, it may be seen that this useful function begins to fail, and that it completely collapses in the more severe anxiety attacks. The ego here loses its power over masochism, which it wished to put to use for its own purposes. Masochism penetrates deeply into the vital motor sphere of the ego and germinating there, brings forth the paralyzing effects, which become so intense and embracing that they make the ego, to the detriment of its own preservation, for a time incapable of action (defense). The anxiety attack is an explosive discharge of masochism in the field of the ego's psychosomatic functioning. This anxiety is no longer a utility, a signal, but a severe symptom of illness. The ego can no longer prevent the masochistic self-harming tendency, which craves pleasure from suffering, from producing suffering. But the ego's opposition spoils the pleasure. When masochism invades the ego, no matter whether as an anxiety attack or otherwise, the ego at first finds only suffering without pleasure. Only after the ego has become adapted to the anxiety attacks—or enforced masochistic experiences of other kinds—can it turn the masochistic experience into pleasure-pain; in this case, "pleasurable fear" or "anxious pleasure".

The hysterical anxiety attack depends upon a deepseated disorder of the sexual function, which is removed from the ego's field of authority. What is the case in the anxiety symptoms that appear in the "actual neuroses", from the study of which Freud came to the unique and productive conclusion that anxiety is due to accumulated genital excitement? Here the individual's sexual organization is functionally efficient, intrinsically, but is abusively utilized by the ego. In my opinion, we have only to insert the link "masochism" into Freud's classical description to explain this. The ego's abuse of its sexuality consists in its permitting the excitation of the genital but then suppressing the excitement, or rather preventing its complete fruition and discharge. Inhibition of a pleasure-giving activity is always reacted to by an unleashing of masochism. The greater the tension that remains after the frustration of an act of pleasure, the speedier and the more uncontrollably will the thwarted desire for pleasure throw itself into the exploitation of suffering for pleasure. An ego that is being checked in the genital act (left in the lurch by the sexual partner) is immediately attacked by genital masochism. In the actual neurosis, therefore, the suppressed genital excitement is not directly transformed into anxiety (fear), but into genital masochism; then, the no longer restrainable genital masochistic excitement is discharged as anxiety. The *Aktualneurose* is well named, for the *"aktual"* origin of this anxiety, (i.e., its origin in the immediate situation) is incontestable. In this way, some of the obscurities in regard to anxiety, which have troubled us for a long while, are satisfactorily dispelled. And the anxiety attack, which threatened to overthrow our theory, now becomes its strongest support.

Here we may venture a "bioanalytic" speculation, in Ferenczi's sense, in regard to the phylogenesis of the signaling device, fear (anxiety). We may begin with the primitive living creature, which has not developed such a danger signal and is therefore often in jeopardy of being injured. Each wound restricts the animal's freedom of motion, lessens or frustrates his pleasure-giving acts, and thus compels the pleasure function to turn to pain-pleasure. In other words, the wound is elaborated masochistically by the ego. This is the state of affairs that we were able to study thoroughly in the case of the little girl, in her response to the anatomical experience. To be sure, the animal is responding to a physical injury and the girl to a mental one. But both alike are insults to self-love, narcissistic injuries. No one can be sure that it is not the injury to the animal's narcissism, which accompanies the bodily injury, that initiates the masochistic reaction. If this is true there would be even less disparity between the two cases. Within the limits of a bioanalytic speculation, such a similarity is sufficient to permit the analogy. As we have seen, each reawakening of that wounding impression evokes in the girl an intractable masochistic excitement. The phobic anxiety attack, in which, according to our views, this reaction continues to exist, attests its violence and perseverance. May it not be assumed that the masochistically sensitized animal, too, responds to a new danger of injury with a masochistic paralytic attack—with a kind of hypnotic fascination?* The ego combats these attacks of masochistic paralysis, and learns, in the course of countless generations, to moderate their intensity and duration, until they appear only as a trace. With this the gradual transformation of the injurious paralyzing process into a useful danger-signaling device is complete. The way in which this danger signal is first created, and what modifications it undergoes before it assumes the form of the affect, fear, are problems of which the biologist must supply the solution. Our psychoanalytic study permits him to anticipate that the danger signal from the start would be a transient *paralytic process*, which attacks a *vital* bodily function, and which is due to the energy of the *masochistic* instinct within the organism. Possibly the function attacked by masochism is, in each case, respiration. But one must be wary of any such suggestions; we do not even know, for example, what relationship there may be between the masochistic anxiety attack and the organic disturbance of cardiac function in angina pectoris. For the time being, "bioanalysis" suggests the theory that anxiety (fear) is not produced by the ego, but is only a product domesticated by the ego. We are inevitably reminded of the wise peasant, who succeeded in curing all but a tiny trace of the rheumatism that had tormented him; but this little trace he preserved, so that he might always be apprized in time of the approach of bad weather.

2. Combat

Entirely different symptomatic pictures are formed by a second variety of defense, which we may call: combat. Its most efficient means is, prefer-

---

* Compare with this the "feigned death" of animals in danger ("playing 'possum"). According to our view, the animal does not feign death but is paralyzed by an attack of masochism. The dubious value for self-defense of this apparent death is a "secondary gain from illness".

ably, preventive counter-attack; and its objectives are, incapacitation and revenge.

(a) Thus we have the woman who intimidates a man, who marries a weakling, puts an end to his potency, and holds him responsible for her unhappiness. This "masculine sadistic" attitude gives her a chance to deny and keep down her own genital masochistic tendencies. Since Abraham's brilliant observations, the "castrative woman" is perhaps the best-known type analytically; as will be remembered, he used the designation, "revenge type". In the connections we are considering, I must regard protection from the enemy, or his incapacitation for combat, as the primary intention of this attitude. It becomes vindictiveness as a rule in relation-to the first man who accomplishes her defloration. Premarital defloration rites and customs, found among many primitive peoples and even among the peoples of classical antiquity, are to be accounted for, according to Freud's well-known interpretation, by this fact.[12]

(b) The woman's combative pleasure, which is inaugurated by her effort to protect her genital, is differentiated in several ways. It appears as a pleasure in stealing, in *cleptomania*; and in the so-called *"vampire"*, as a pleasure in exploitation.

The true cleptomaniac—who must not be confused with occasional thieves who sham cleptomania—commits her theft while in a state of extreme genital masochistic excitement, and endows the object stolen—in reality usually worthless to her—with great emotional values. She is acquiring a penis, in order to strengthen her tottering phallic position.* This desperate step of the ego is always preceded by a severe genital masochistic temptation, started by a threat to the illusory penis; this point can be clarified only by a consideration of the anal fate of diverted genital masochism, which we cannot give in detail here. The obvious points are that the woman's retention of this illusory penis is soon marred by castration fear, which she experiences as a well-founded "fear of the consequences". The forces involved are too unequal; of these, genital masochism is the stronger. The woman soon flings away what she has stolen, betrays herself, and in the end satisfies her masochism, in prison. The masochism is now acknowledged as being the ego's, because it can be cloaked under the moralizing motivation of "atonement".†

The "vamp" is assuredly no baseless invention of the moving picture industry, however much her popularity may be due to this source. I have

---

* The first analytic elucidation of cleptomania we owe to Elisabeth Révész. As early as 1919, on the basis of a case analyzed in masterly fashion, and reported before the Hungarian Psychoanalytic Society (but not published), she showed that the impulsive act of the cleptomaniac represents the concealed theft of a penis (or child).

† Cf., below, the remarks on "moralizing genital masochism".

never analyzed a professional "vamp", but, in compensation, some ama-
teurs. It was not surprising to learn that their vampiric behavior was
fundamentally designed to capture a penis. The financial trophy (money =
penis) clinches the fact for the woman that she has conquered the enemy
and appropriated his power. It is certain now, she feels, that *she* has the
penis and no harm can befall her. A rascal then appears on the scene (in
the film, the criminal whom the heroine loves and wishes to rescue) and he
despoils her. Genital masochism is not to be avoided even on this by-path.

Thus far no light has been thrown on the name "vampire", applied to
this type of woman in common parlance.* It is an obvious fact that these
women figuratively "suck" men dry, that they make men infatuated with
them by using the most childish tricks and flatteries,—very much those
that children are accustomed to use with their mothers. This would be an
example of the fact, to which the most recent analytic literature has
ascribed so much importance, that the woman brings into her later relationship with a man attitudes that began in her early infantile relationship
with her *mother*.† However, I do not share the view of those writers that
the little girl at first feels as a boy does, directing her "phallic" genital
impulses to her mother, and passing through a "negative oedipus complex"
in a genital sense before she begins her female genital career. The little girl
at first does not attach any genital ideas to the fact that she belongs to the
female sex; there are no sexually differentiated ideas or desires behind her
early masturbation; she knows that she gets pleasure at this part of the
body, and she may weave all kinds of ideas into this pleasure,—but that
is all. It is the discovery of a penis that raises the veil covering the difference between the sexes; she then learns that she is "castrated", and develops the wish to be the possessor of a penis, a boy. Up to this time, she
was attached to her mother "pregenitally"; she now turns tempestuously
to her mother with a "genital"-need: she hopes through her help to (re)-
acquire a penis. It had so often been told her that if she wished to grow,
she must eat; and that she obtained her first nourishment from her mother's
breast. Now again, she wishes to nurse at her mother's breast, indeed
devour the whole breast, only so that a penis will grow on her after that,—
which happens, too, in a dream. This is the secret of the art that the vampire
applies with men.

The Oedipus Complex—The views current in the most recent psychoanalytic literature, referred to above, lead me to an exposition that I should
not otherwise have presented in this essay. By means of a fragment of an
analysis, I should like to demonstrate the way in which the girl's problem

* I wish to thank Dr. Bertram D. Lewin for the suggestion that the designation
(popularly shortened to "vamp") originated in Kipling's poem, "The Vampire".

† See Freud[10], and the papers of Jeanne Lampl de Groot and others cited there.

concerning the possession of a penis finds its entrance into her relationship with the parents, the alterations it brings about in these, and the modifications it undergoes itself in so doing:

The patient narrates the following dream:

"I was with my mother in a room. I got into bed with her and had intercourse with her. I believe I was on top and she beneath me, for I could observe her facial expression very well. I felt very well satisfied but did not have any genital sensations. Mother too was satisfied; she made a puzzled and sheepish face. I walked up and down in the room afterwards and became stricken with a bad sense of guilt. 'Terrible', I thought, 'I shall have to tell you [the analyst] this.' I became enraged with mother: Why had she suppressed me so much? It's all her fault!"

Then the patient added: "I don't know whether these last thoughts didn't come only when I awoke. I am very much perturbed by the dream. I don't trust myself to meet mother."

Her first associations were: "Yesterday while I was out, my mother came to see the children. She busied herself with a plant that I have in a dish. She told the maid that she had poured in water, for otherwise the plant would have died. This made me lose my composure completely. My mother and brother were at my home for dinner. Mother talked a great deal and made many remarks that I had to think were meant for me. I was intimidated and much agitated. I don't understand how I could dream such a thing after that.—Perhaps I wished to console mother because she is a widow and hasn't any husband."

The analytic situation: The patient is at the apex of her sensual transference. She is quite hurt by the failure of her courtship, depressed, but takes herself in hand.

With the aid of other material brought to light by the patient's analysis, the following interpretation and reconstruction could be made:—

The patient had first discovered the penis on this brother. She then took refuge in the hope that her mother would see to it that she would grow a penis. This appears to have taken place in her dreams, but she could not maintain her dream illusion. Her mother had not, therefore, worried about her daughter's desired penis, and to make matters worse is now giving her attention to that stupid plant and worrying whether it will wither. Our theory permits us to surmise that when the girl's hope of obtaining an illusory penis collapsed originally, there followed an eruption of genital masochism. This surmise could be confirmed only indirectly. Later in life it happened that she three times developed a *pollakiuria* that lasted for weeks. Each time there were no explanatory organic findings. She had no physical complaints, either, but merely was compelled to urinate at brief intervals and felt irked and humiliated because of this. The illnesses appeared immediately after her first menstrual flow, and *after* her two children were born. All three precipitating events destroyed her illusory penis, and the genital masochism that emerged was not discharged, as might have been anticipated, in masochistic masturbation, but in *masochistic* polla-kiuria. At these times, she was not able to urinate properly, to "water", and now her mother comes along and takes her place in watering the plant. Why this trifling act should have so excited the patient is now clear. Her mother's action hit her in a tender spot in two ways. Then at dinner she had had the impression that her mother preferred her brother to her. This oversensi-tiveness and intense emotional reaction betray that the patient was "reliv-ing" a critical event of her own childhood; at one time, she must have regarded it as hostile on the part of the mother, that the mother neglected to fulfil her expectations of having a penis. She turned away from the mother in bitterness (this is unquestionable) and probably immediately turned to her father with the hope that he would arrange for her to grow a penis. At any rate, the disappointment she felt with her mother pulled her out of her ruminations and incited her to make sexual investigations. They were not unsuccessful; she discovered or understood suddenly what it was that took place between mother and father (the primal scene). It came as a revelation to her that only her father had a penis,—and that mother had none. This knowledge acted as a tonic to her narcissism and restored her self-confidence. For she saw that she need no longer inflict suffering upon herself through painful fantasies, because of her defect; she could now look down upon her mother with contempt mitigated by pity. She could re-nounce her wish to have a penis herself but instead she wished to have father's penis—that is, what the mother has. The discovery of her own phallic deficiency had made her into a masochistic woman, and driven her to phallic complementation. The discovery of her mother's lack made her into a true woman and inaugurated her normal oedipal desires for her father. A process of this type may be called a "remedial developmental step". The expectation that the father would respond to her advances by turning to her with his penis, subsequently ended in painful disappoint-ment. This expectation and this disappointment the patient now repeats in her transference.

Here we see the application of the two precipitants of the dream. The patient's analysis was provoking her to relive her old disappointment in her father; in addition, an accidental occurrence reactivated the even older offense she had suffered from her mother. The dream then shows the way in which she can put an end to this situation. She kills her father, appropriates his penis, becomes a man and—cohabits with his "widow". Hence the fear, in the dream, of confessing to the analyst what she is doing to her father (or would like to do to the analyst). Her revenge on her father leaves nothing to be desired. But at the same time she also revenges herself on her mother: the mother did not favor her with a penis and mocked at her deficiency; now she has been a success and has a penis, and she goes and gratifies—her mother. The daughter's magnanimity makes the mother—whose lack of a penis is thus brought home to her—look "puzzled and sheepish". This is, to be sure, a refined form of revenge. Obviously the old tender affection for the mother has tamed the aggression to her; so that it is the girl's conceit that triumphs in the revenge. The dream process compellingly takes one back to the patient's childhood and makes one believe that he has eavesdropped on the excited girl while she fantasied: "Just wait, you bad father, I'll kill you and take your penis, and then I'll be a man. And you, you bad mother, you shall see then, when I get the penis, how *I* will behave with you." This infantile fantasy is the basis of the dream.

The girl's phallic sexual act is now adequately explained. This coitus fantasy does not satisfy her genital impulse, but her narcissistic conceit and vindictiveness. The patient's spontaneous remark that she is given satisfaction (redress) in the dream, but feels no trace of a genital sensation, is based upon accurate self-observation. Her narcissistic vindictive impulses arose for genital reasons, and hence are executed with the (narcissistic) sexual weapon. The sense of triumph, moreover, is soon at an end. Only too quickly does the dreamer begin to be afraid of her own godlike state. The sense of guilt that overtakes her on awakening already announces the resurgence of masochism. The narcissistic counter-post must as rapidly as possible be fortified by the release of an energetic aggression. And this occurs, too; the woman protects herself—still half asleep—from the imminent masochistic self-reproach by means of her reproach to her mother: "It's all your fault." Then throughout the day she becomes more depressed, more masochistic even than before. The satisfaction in the dream was a rich pyrotechnic display, which beautified the tortured woman's sleep, and illuminated the path into the depths for her analysis.

The many hints in the dream of an infantile observation of coitus may be passed by without discussion. It must be remarked, however, that in her analysis before she had this dream, she had never spoken of the fact that her mother was at one time involved in the fate of her wish for a penis. It is evident that the accidental episode with the plant first brought up the material out of repression; for this reason too the infantile documentation was sketchy.

Discussion: The "remedial" development recorded here is not identical with the normal one; it remains undermined by genital masochism. To disappointments that take place after the girl has just reached this "normal" attitude, as we see here, she can only too easily react with a regression to genital masochism and the illusion of phallic masculinity. I have been successful in obtaining an insight into some varieties of remedial (and normal) development. For the time, I should like to limit my account by bringing into relief those points in the process recorded above that remain constant in all varieties.

The girl's genital interest, properly speaking, commences with the discovery of the penis, as a narcissistic problem concerning the organ. The advance to a need for a genital object, which is expressed in fantasies of coitus, can only come into effect if the girl makes a second discovery—namely, that there is such a thing as coitus, an activity that depends on the difference between the genitalia of the two sexes. Conceivably, the girl may make both discoveries—of the organ, and of the function—at the same time. This, however, is not in accord with my experience. It often happens that coitus is observed before the penis is discovered, but then the little girl simply does not understand that what she is observing is a genital process, and she puts some other interpretation upon it. The accurate observation of a penis, that is, the discovery of the penis, first equips her intellectually to construe (approximately) correctly that which she has experienced or will experience. The girl's desire for coitus is thus inaugurated and made possible by the information that only her father has a penis, and not she herself or her mother. From this it follows that the first wish for coitus is for coitus with her father. From this normal genital orientation, disappointments (fear of castration) may throw her back to the previous stage of the illusory penis. This is not in that case the old illusory penis: the girl introduces into her illusion the phallic impulse to have coitus (with an object) that she has learned from her father. Thus the girl acquires her phallic impetus to coitus, with which she turns to her mother. All attempts to place a different construction on the dynamics of this development lead to inconsistencies and in the end founder upon the more delicate details in the material.

It remains to the credit of Jeanne Lampl de Groot, that she pointed out the occurrence in girls of fantasies of phallic coitus with the mother, but their interpretation and setting should be dealt with in a different way. The suggestion, made by several persons, that the girl carries a genital desire into the original relationship with her mother, is correct; but what she desires from the mother is merely the correction of her organ defect, that is, a penis. The negative oedipus complex is, then, a secondary formation, the reaction to the breakdown of the genital relationship to the father. It must also be explained that the girl's negative oedipus complex, except for its designation, which is fixed through our scientific tradition, has little in common with the positive oedipus complex of the boy. The boy hates his father because he is afraid his father will take his penis from him. The girl hates her father because she is afraid he will not give her his penis. And of the boy's native genital desire for his mother, the girl shows nothing. Her phallic fantasy of coitus with her mother is a blow aimed at her mother, which gratifies her own narcissistic conceit and vindictiveness, but which does not gratify her sensual love. Only later, after puberty in some women, is this fantasy given a sensual meaning and serves than as a base on which to erect a homosexual attitude.

A closing remark will return us to the vampire, of whom one trait remained obscure. The sucking at the mother's breast, from which the girl at one time expected to grow a penis, was a procedure born of trust in the mother. Only after she then experienced *disappointment*, was there produced the vindictive appetite for exploiting, which the woman who has become a "vamp" satiates on men.

(c) Genital masochism, repelled so competently by the reaction formation, "castrative woman", finds a good place of refuge in anality. Its vicissitudes there are too manifold for detailed treatment here. I shall mention only the basic position of the aberrant genital masochism in the anal region. I refer to the desire for the pleasure to be obtained from painful and bloody evacuation. The retention of faecal masses, which results from this purpose, is given further support by the ego, because of its totally misguided defensive strategy. Against direct onslaughts of masochism, the ego has no other means of defense then to set up its narcissistic reaction, the illusory penis, in the danger zone. So, the ego is investing an anal penis to protect itself from anal masochism! Hence, both processes, the combated masochism and the narcissistic defensive action of the ego, work together towards the same end: the retention of faeces, which explains the peculiar obstinacy of this symptom. Only after persons in the environment have intervened (as they always do in the case of children) with local measures to relieve the chronic constipation, can the ego's defenses be turned against an attack that threatens from without. It awaits the impending intestinal irrigations with great (castration) fear and attempts to prevent them by every means possible. After that, it reacts with an outburst of rage and develops a deep-seated tendency to inflict revenge on the person who has perpetrated the "assault".

(d) In this conjoint secondary attitude—pleasure in aggression directed outward, and masochistic gratification from processes within the body— the conflict that the woman wages with her genital masochism has been forced down to the province of the anal and sadistic impulses. Against the nascent refreshing here of early infantile instinctual aims, especially the heightening of destructive tendencies to a murderous pitch, the ego must soon intervene. It acts through fear of conscience; which means here, fear of punishment, fear of masochistic exploitation of the punishment, fear of castration. If the ego fails in its defensive effort, the combat—the same combat—continues in the more elevated region of the *compulsion neurosis*. To broach the discussion of this gigantic field here would be rash. I merely wish to indicate the road that leads from masochistically deformed genitality to the compulsion neurosis.

3. The Choice of the Lesser Evil

The third variety of defense, the choice of the lesser evil, is the gravest; its discussion leads us into an obscure, almost unexplored field.

If the ego can neither flee nor offer combat, it itself brings about the threatened harm or meets it half way. It takes this desperate step in the hope of lessening the damage it must incur, or in the hope of preventing a greater evil. Freud called our attention to this type of behavior on the part of the ego, in his interpretation of the phenomenon of anxiety (fear)[9]; its appearance in the process that gives form to the neuroses has as yet not been described. The choice of the lesser evil is as a rule preceded by menacing signs. The process is initiated by the mortification of self-esteem. The patient loses a modest potentiality for gratification, which she still possessed. Concealed beneath this is an injury to her illusory penis, or, even more clearly, an unavertable (sexual) event is approaching, in the patient's life, that she perceives as a violation. Her genital masochism is stimulated and goes into action. Wild apprehensions and terrifying fantasies occupy more and more place in the patient's living. The internal tension grows to an insupportable degree and robs her of the last remnant of her peace. In this state of exalted depression, the impulsive action takes place, by means of which the woman injures herself or gets herself injured. In comparison to the terrors, which she dreads as inevitable, what she does or gets done to herself appears to be a real deliverance. Beneath this rationalistic attitude of the ego may be recognized, as its prototype, that early genital-narcissistic injury which in its time terminated in the self-inflicted injury of masochistic masturbation. It is characteristic of the choice of the lesser evil, that the patient *always* carries out the desperate action while in a sort of self-stupefaction. The ego is blind to the harm it inflicts, or permits to be inflicted, upon itself; or it deceives itself as to the meaning and extent of what it is doing by all kinds of rationalizations. This attitude of the ego does not simplify our assessment of the situation. Especially in cases that terminate in extreme self-injury, one would hesitate to ascribe to the ego any attempt at deliberative reflection. The situation can be more satisfactorily described then as an eruption of genital masochistic desires; the ego, overwhelmed, surrenders to the masochism, and in its weakness must be content to pursue an ostrich policy in regard to its own unwilled doings or inactions. These two formulations differ only in respect of an ego-psychological nuance; they agree in attributing the formation of symptoms to the victory of genital masochism over the ego.

The choice of the lesser evil produces not alone tempestuous individual incidents in a neurosis, but developments that take a chronic course as well. The patient's self-esteem gradually declines as the result of a series of narcissistic insults; the sensitive spot, at which she is hurt each time, is her phallic reaction formation, which stands guard in the ego, against genital masochism. In accordance with this, the ego's conquest by masochism proceeds in the form of a peaceful penetration; the patient again and again chooses the lesser of the evils, and her life becomes increasingly a renunciation.

(a) The first opportunity for the choice of the lesser evil is in *self-defloration*. This happening is usually due to roughly executed (post-pubertal) masochistic masturbation. Recently [and I may refer to the series reported by Joan Riviere[18]] an increasing number of cases has been encountered in which women use a surgeon to perform the defloration for them before they are married. This may, of course, be undertaken for a second reason—namely, to spare their future husband the defloration, and themselves the resulting vindictive hostility, in order to facilitate their subsequent living with him in a desexualized sexual relationship. The present day neurosis thus arrives at the above-mentioned rite of our ancestors.

(b) Another method which genital masochism drives the ego to use operates with more cruel measures. Girls who have repeatedly rejected decent suitors because of a fear of castration, or to conceal this fear have always chosen to love where it was obvious from the beginning that nothing would come of it, may in the end have themselves deflorated by the first chance person who happens to be available. The event takes place ordinarily while the girl is drunk and only too often under particularly humiliating circumstances. Clinically, as we know, the most salient theme in this "throwing herself away" is an avoidance of committing incest with her father, or rather, a revenge on her father, which might be phrased as follows: "If it is not father, then it may well be anybody." But it is only in the choice of the lesser evil—in the ascendancy of masochism—that we can find the explanation of the offensive self-injuries which enter into this reaction of the woman to her unresolved father attachment. The most extreme achievement in the way of genital masochistic self-debasement is prostitution, fantasied or real.

(c) Equally serious in effect are those injuries which women driven by genital masochism inflict upon themselves extragenitally. I am acquainted with cases in which a woman's heroic determination to allow a man to approach her sexually continually miscarried because of her unconquerable fear of castration; after each failure, she promptly met with some accident or provoked an unprofitable surgical operation. In the severest cases, there follow frank or covert suicidal attempts, until in the end one attempt succeeds.

(*d*) If the ego successfully diverts this overpowering masochism from the physical, sexual sphere to that of general behavior, it can give recognition to the unavoidable self-injury in the form of psychic suffering. The ego accepts the suffering as its own because of the allegation that it comes from the performance of a duty. This is the attitude of *"moralizing genital masochism"*.[5] The women now satiates her masochism, from which anxiety no longer protects her, using her husband and children, as a *"mater dolorosa"*. She has exchanged her lot, to suffer in the genital rôle, for the lot of more general suffering in the rôle of wife and mother. However, here too, the ego's endurance is more strictly limited by the pleasure principle than one would at first suppose; it soon rebels against excessive impositions of suffering. The mater dolorosa—perpetually anxious about her husband and children—then begins to direct their lives through "protective measures" and "care", which are of no practical value but torture the persons thus "protected". With the pretext of fulfilling sacred obligations, she now revenges herself for her suffering upon her husband and children.[6] And if anyone ventures to remonstrate, her sense of guilt causes her to collapse. "But all I want is your welfare", she will say. Not only sexuality, but morality as well, fares badly if it comes into the bondage of masochism.

(*e*) The ego may accept genital masochism as an overt *sexual perversion*. This end is usually due to a clever seducer, one who is capable of giving women who have become frigid—because they repressed their masochistically distorted genitality—a chance to "enjoy" the sexual act.

The conflict started in the ego by the anatomical problem is rekindled with the emergence of the problem of "the child". With this, as I hope to show later, there is an opportunity for sexual development to find its way back to the normal channel. Otherwise, symptoms crop out, which to be sure have their own clinical imprint, but which are sustained by the same forces that were inaugurated by the original conflict concerning the organ.

V

Conclusions

The clinical pictures sketched are intended as evidence that the morphogenesis of the neuroses makes use of a few stereotyped mechanisms, and depends on a constant relation between genital masochism, ego, and fear of castration, which in turn depends upon a tragic dilemma of the ego that is occupied in finding its sex. It was possible to make brief references only to the way in which the girl interjects her "sexual dilemma", or rather, the misguided efforts that this gives rise to, into all the emotional contacts that she makes with her environment. In my opinion, it is only because of this ominous and excessive burden that the early infantile relationship with the parents—with the material for conflict that it includes, material long recognized as inevitable and ubiquitous—attains its outstanding pathogenetic rôle in the etiology of the neuroses. The same legacy is transferred to the relationships with persons that are entered into later in life by women, in which they follow infantile patterns. Whether boys too encounter a kind of "sexual dilemma of the ego", or in what way the danger from the masochistic genital instinct appears in them, which then would determine the pathogenicity of the oedipus conflicts and hence their health or neurosis, is a question that I shall take up in another essay.[17] It cannot be assumed that the part, recognized here, that genital masochism and fear play in the neurosis of women, is limited to the female sex. For the present, we may say that we now have a better comprehension of how a neurosis is formed in women.

A contrast of normality and neurosis will aid us to recapitulate our results. The functionally efficient genital organization of an adult person is composed of two elements:—first, of the given somatic apparatus, which by a particular instinctual stress indicates its existence to the ego and commends itself for use; and second, of the ego's readiness and capacity to make use of the opportunity for pleasure thus proffered. The ego's "genital willingness" is not inborn in the same sense as the somatic apparatus. Like many other biologically required orientations, this must be acquired during the long period of the ego's infantile development. Some external influences are conducive to the ego's realization of this goal, while many others—restrictions imposed by civilization—are adverse to it. A further difficulty is determined by the plan of biological development itself. At first the contributions of pleasure received from the activities of organs other than the genital make up the bulk of the organism's pleasure-receipts; it is only at a more advanced stage in the evolution of the pleasure function that genital activity becomes by far the richest source of pleasure. The process of construction of the pleasure organization may be disturbed for external or internal reasons; disturbances of this kind do not, to be sure, diminish the vigor of the genital instinct, but nevertheless surely distort its psychic expression, obscure the indications for pleasure, and divert the ego's search for pleasure to other organ activities. In the neurotic woman, infantile sexual development has failed in its purpose of providing the ego with a functionally efficient genital organization. The precocious appearance of the genital instinct, the immaturity of the ego, which is still in the process of developing, and an experience—under these circumstances a shattering experience—result in the deformation of her genital instinct into genital masochism. The ego in alarm at these instinctual demands tries to find refuge in phallic complementation, and attempts to introduce better adapted genital aims, in accord with its possession of the fictive organ. The "female orientation", degraded to genital masochism, had to be repressed, since it was incompatible with the ego; the "male orientation" founded on the illusory penis collapses because it is incompatible with the genital organ. The impulses brought into the psyche from its organic source by the genital instinct, now are drained into masochism and increase its pressure on the the ego. The two-fold erotogenic division of the female genital organ enables the ego to intercept some of the organic force of the instinct to utilize in its phallic orientation and to discharge it in affranchised clitoris pleasure; but this rarely redresses matters. The stronger instinctual energy is firmly attached to the suppressed genital masochism, of which the ego must constantly dread an outbreak; the ego, harassed, cleaves to its fictive possession of a penis and thus provides its fear with the psychic characteristics of a fear of castration. The force of the genital instinct, periodically renewed by its organic sources, and, on the other hand, the social pressure of her environment then coerce the woman into fighting for or against impulses, which so to say waylay her from ambush, without any clue as to what determines them. These struggles, including the oft-repeated attempt to arrive at the sexuality organically prescribed for women, form the nucleus of the woman's neurosis. And the often so remote pathological productions, which apparently are not at all connected with genitality, are only metastases from this lesion.* To put it differently: the basic phenomenon of a neurosis is the deformation of the ego-inherent genital impulse into ego-adverse genital masochism; its essential principle lies in the ineluctable encounter of the ego with the danger of suffering (or death) created by life-destructive masochism; its richness in symptoms is due to the multiplicity of the (ortho- and hetero-topic) effects of genital masochism and the multiplicity of the corresponding defensive (adaptive) measures of the ego. As long as the ego, by persisting in its repressions, is deprived of the true guiding points of inner orientation and steers with an untrue compass, its efforts are necessarily unavailing. What does succeed in the neurosis is after all only masochistically travestied womanliness, or its counterpart, the ego's biologically wrong solution, arising from perplexity: the illusory penis.

---

* The central significance of the genital disorder in the origin of the neurosis is emphasized by Wilhelm Reich.

References

1 ABRAHAM, K.: Manifestations of the Female Castration Complex. *Internat. J. Psycho-Analysis, 3.* (Reprinted in *Selected Papers of K. Abraham.* London, Institute of Psycho-Analysis and Hogarth Press).

2 ——: A Short Study of Libido. *Selected Papers of Karl Abraham.* London, Hogarth.

3 ALEXANDER, F.: The Psychoanalysis of the Total Personality. *Nervous and Mental Disease Monograph* No. 52.

4 BORNSTEIN, B.: Zur Psychogenese der Pseudodebilität. *Int. Ztschr. f. Psychoanal., 16,* 1930.

5 DEUTSCH, H.: The Genesis of Agoraphobia. *Internat. J. Psycho-Analysis, 10,* 1929.

6 ——: The Significance of Masochism in the Mental Life of Women. *Internat. J. Psycho-Analysis, 11,* 1930.

7 JONES, E.: The Early Development of Female Sexuality. *Internat. J. Psycho-Analysis, 8,* 1927.

8 FREUD, S.: The Economic Problem in Masochism. *Collected Papers, 2.* London, 1924.

9 ——: Hemmung, Symptom und Angst. *Ges. Schr.* XI.

10 ——: *New Introductory Lectures on Psychoanalysis.* New York, W. W. Norton, 1933.

11 ——: Some Psychological Consequences of the Anatomical Differences between the Sexes. *Internat. J. Psycho-Analysis, 8,* 1927.

12 ——: The Taboo of Virginity. *Collected Papers, 4.*

13 HÁRNIK, E. J.: The Various Developments Undergone by Narcissism in Men and Women. *Internat. J. Psycho-Analysis, 5,* 1924.

14 HORNEY, KAREN: On the Genesis of the Castration Complex in Women. *Internat. J. Psycho-Analysis, 5,* 1924.

15 LEWIN, B. D.: The Body as Phallus. *Psychoanal. Quart., 2,* 1933.

16 RADO, S.: An Anxious Mother. *Internat. J. Psycho-Analysis, 9,* 1928.

17 ——: The Psychoanalysis of Pharmacothymia. *Psychoanal. Quart., 2,* 1933.

18 RIVIERE, J.: Womanliness as a Masquerade. *Internat. J. Psycho-Analysis, 10,* 1929.

19 VAN OPHUIJSEN, H.: Contributions to the Masculinity Complex of Women. *Internat. J. Psycho-Analysis, 5,* 1924.

Psychoanalysis and Psychiatry*

The material studied by the psychoanalyst emanates from his patient and is biographical in kind. This material comprises as its very essence an abundance of data such as are otherwise inaccessible to investigation. The patient under examination either is unaware of these data, though they are deposited in his mind, or he is disinclined to confess them. They are brought to light, and their overwhelming significance for the scientific study of the individual clearly revealed, through the special situation designed for the patient by the analyst. In this situation, technically known as the 'analytic situation', the patient is given the opportunity of developing his confidence, his feeling of trust, to the full; he is enabled gradually to remove the mask which every individual is compelled to wear in social life, and ultimately to lift that inner mask behind which every individual keeps hidden from himself what he does not desire to know about himself. The patient accomplishes this self-unmasking by the technical means of 'free association'. His compliance with this procedure is enforced by the pressure of his sickness, by his desire for recovery. But sooner or later, inevitably, the analytic situation changes its aspect. The patient turns uncompliant; he engages in a display of varying emotions; he behaves as if pulled hither and yon by one or another acute conflict; finally one sees he has become emotionally involved with the analyst himself in some personal way. The deciphering of this surprising phenomenon called 'transference' remains Freud's greatest methodological discovery. What happens is this: The patient has been asked by the analyst to give free rein to his thoughts and feelings. He does so, and in doing so he progressively abandons the higher intellectual controls characteristic of maturity and thus revives that primitive childhood state of mind in which such controls are lacking. In consequence, he comes to feel increasingly helpless and dependent; he feels the need of parents to rely on, precisely as he did in early life. He now seizes upon the analyst and installs him, quite automatically, in the place of his parents, thus reviving, and transferring to the analyst, all the feelings

* Under the assigned title of 'The Material as it Organizes Itself with the Psychoanalyst', the present paper formed part of a Symposium conducted by Adolf Meyer of Baltimore upon 'The Material dealt with as Personalty-function by the various Workers in the Field of Psychiatry', which was held at the Ninety-first Annual Meeting of the American Psychiatric Association at Washington, D.C., May 14, 1935. First published in *American Journal of Psychiatry*, *92*, 297–300, 1935.

and thoughts originally related to his parents. Naturally, the very presence of such a suitable substitute for the parents as the analyst has been facilitating his submersion in uncontrolled thought.

It has to be emphasized that the whole period of childhood is dominated by the biological phenomenon which is called in animals 'care of the young', in human beings, 'care of the infant' or 'care of the child'. The child, helpless as it is, is dependent for its very survival upon the ministrations of its parents. Owing to this fact, the child's ego is able to indulge in a mode of functioning which is profoundly different from the self-sustaining regime of the mature ego. It is this archaic system of functioning, wholly conditional upon external support, that the ego of the patient tends to reinstate in the transference. The analytic transference, though in itself a kind of artifact, truly rests upon deep and genuine biological foundations.

By exploring the analytic situation, especially the transference, the psychoanalyst carries out a work comparable to that done by the palæontologist: his work uncovers beyond a doubt the most ancient and deeply buried material of the human mind. The present significance of this material from the past is two-fold: first, we encounter in it that raw material out of which the influences of life have moulded the mature shape of the personality; second, as Freud and his co-workers have demonstrated in forty years of research, psychoneuroses—i.e. such nervous disturbances as are not due to a lesion of the brain—can only be explained in terms of a partial recrudescence of the infantile mind. In every neurosis we see mental processes regressively assuming infantile forms and contents, and observe the efforts of the otherwise integrated ego to fit these strange and obviously self-injurious elements into its organization.

It is, of course, the neurotic process that brings about the regressive changes in the patient's mind; the transference merely exposes and re-models them. Hence, the unique therapeutic value of the transference, which through its action assimilates the neurosis to the analytic situation. Thus the analyst comes to gain control over those complicated systems of self-injury which we term neurosis; gradually he extricates the forces of the ego from their neurotic entanglements and furthers their tentative employment in more appropriate activities, until ultimately he is able to reconcile the patient to the joys and sorrows of realistic functioning.

Needless to say, the task of rendering analytic material accessible, and of utilizing it for therapeutic purposes, requires a rather lengthy period of time and can only be accomplished by workers who are skilful and properly trained in the analytic field.

To sum up: Psychoanalysis deals with such personality material as the patient is capable of expressing or exhibiting under the favouring conditions of the analytic situation. This material is of a very intimate nature, mirrors the basic impulses and emotions of love, self-love, hatred and fear, and is, in the main, such as ordinarily remains hidden or unconscious. The 'via regia' to its disclosure is, I would add, the study of the dream-life of the patient.

That organized body of scientific thought which psychoanalysis has evolved from the study of its material is distinguished by two features:

The first of these is its consistent biological orientation. Looking upon mental life as the activity of a 'mental apparatus' operated by 'instinctual forces' of bodily origin, psychoanalytic theory has adopted the basic biological conceptions of living structure and dynamic functioning. Furthermore, with regard to both the structure and functioning of the mind, it has adopted from biology the genetic principle. Because of this biological orientation, psychoanalysis is ready for co-operation with somatically oriented personality research. Among the questions which stand in urgent need of such conjoint study are, to mention but three or four, that of the somatic origin of instinctual forces, of the bodily changes brought about by mental and particularly by emotional processes, of the effect of certain bodily changes upon the mind, etc.

The second and intrinsically psychological feature of psychoanalytic thought is its teleological frame of reference. Psychoanalysis has here added to the study of the utility or expediency of functions the systematic study of their pleasure and pain effects, and has thereby established the outstanding significance of the pleasure-pain balance in the mental economy; hence the stress it is compelled to lay upon sexuality. In fact, it studies both these aspects of functioning with the express ultimate purpose of improving the efficiency of the mind—in other words, of increasing the individual's capacity for enjoyment and active achievement in life. Were I to designate in one sentence the contribution made by psychoanalysis to psychiatry, I would say this: More than any other branch of personality research, psychoanalysis has advanced the psychiatrist towards the attainment of his foremost goal, that of being the *efficiency engineer of the human mind*. It has done so despite the fact that it has not as yet been in a position to embark upon the study of the psychoses on more than a very restricted scale. To place competent psychoanalytic research workers into our mental hospitals is the task of the immediate future.

Scientific Aspects of Training in Psychoanalysis[*]

Building upon the pioneer achievements of the European psychoanalytic organizations, the New York Psychoanalytic Society established the New York Psychoanalytic Institute in 1931. On a previous occasion the present writer reviewed these developments and described the scope, functions and future plans of this Institute. Foremost among these plans was the hope to establish in our Institute a small mental hospital for psychotic in-patients and a department for neurotic out-patients that would serve the purposes both of teaching and of research. For lack of funds these key projects have not yet been accomplished. They remain a challenge to those who wish to promote teaching and research in psychoanalysis as a means of alleviating man's suffering from mental illness.

Within its present range of activities, that is, in the field of teaching, the Institute has met its obligations fully. The administrative and statistical aspects of its activities are presented elsewhere in this report; but more important than its growth in size is the fact that this growth has occurred without sacrificing high standards. The Institute has steadily raised both its entrance requirements and the exactions of its curriculum to a point which in some respects is higher than has been attempted before. With the collaboration of the other psychoanalytic institutes in the United States, minimal requirements such as ours will now be made effective on a national scale. Owing to the fact that in recent years some of the older centers of psychoanalytic scholarship in Europe have been hit hard by world events, this vigorous advance of psychoanalytic learning in America has added significance; work in psychoanalysis goes on in undisturbed continuity although the geography of psychoanalysis has changed.

Educational formulas are worth precisely as much as are the results they achieve. The formula exists on paper. The results walk around in life and have their ultimate effect on the lives of others. This is reason enough to subject the results of our own system of training to critical scrutiny.

The basic structure of our system of training has taken shape gradually over the last fifteen to twenty years. During this entire period the present writer has been active in teaching both abroad and here. This has given him

---

[*] First published by the New York Psychoanalytic Institute, in *Report for the Academic Years 1934–1937*.

an opportunity, therefore, to observe the work and the methods of many teachers, the immediate results accomplished and the more remote effects in the lives and scientific activities of many students. These observations have convinced him that basically our system of teaching is sound and efficacious. It gives the student a better knowledge of himself and an increased degree of self-direction; it familiarizes him with the intimate clinical complexities of the neuroses and with the means of understanding them analytically; and it gives him a working knowledge of the technique of treatment. In short, it provides him with the equipment to become a competent practitioner in the analytic field. How much that means may best be estimated by comparing a trained analyst with a physician who gathers his knowledge of psychoanalysis from books alone. Such a self-styled analyst is, as a rule, involved in a hopeless struggle with the theoretical concepts of psychoanalysis; and the difficulties which he encounters when he undertakes to give psychoanalytic treatment are even more insurmountable. It is fortunate indeed if he discovers in time that such knowledge of psychoanalysis as he possesses is a limitation rather than a resource.

These are the virtues of the accepted system of training but we must also examine its shortcomings. Analytic training has been deeply rooted in an old educational tradition. It has tended to patronize and to overawe the student rather than to foster his intellectual independence. It has not appealed sufficiently to his critical faculties; it has not impressed upon him the fact that only by means of his own independent thinking can he properly assimilate what he is taught. This attitude is especially undesirable in a science that deals with the interpretation of the unconscious. To be sure, it is a basic function of training to disclose to the student his own internal difficulties and the influence his unconscious preoccupations have upon his intellect; yet, he must not be made to feel that his teachers do not even recognize scientific doubt as objectively justified, and that they will, therefore, consider every scientific question he might raise merely as a manifestation of his "resistance". That training is a failure which accomplishes no more than to make the student believe that his role is blind belief. The student should be helped to derive true intellectual enjoyment from the precious knowledge handed down to him; but he should be helped to form an objective conviction of the validity of this knowledge. Short of this, the student has at best been indoctrinated, not educated.

Perhaps some analysts will try to justify this very procedure. They may warn us not to lose sight of the peculiarities of psychoanalysis and not to forget the lessons of its past. They might feel that we have been troubled by too much independence of thought rather than too little, and by too little discipline; and as evidence they will point to the deplorable schisms which have confused the history of psychoanalysis. They will argue that it has been a natural and necessary reaction to these schisms to tighten the discipline in teaching. Hence, lest schisms occur again, the teaching in psychoanalysis must always remain as rigid as it now is.

Like all fear, however, this fear is a poor counselor. Rather should we ask why the development of psychoanalysis has repeatedly been disturbed by schisms and why such disturbances do not occur in physics, chemistry or general medicine. The incident of schisms is a symptom; we must suspect that something is wrong in the science itself that produces this symptom.

Every empirical science has two components. Of these one is the body of factual findings; the other, the body of assumptions. Their mutual position within the whole structure is defined by the very nature of science; the body of factual findings must carry the body of assumptions. This, of course, is possible only if a sound proportion is maintained between the two bodies. If this relationship is disturbed and the weight of assumptions exceeds the strength of the facts, then the body of facts will no longer be able to carry the load. Instead, the hypertrophied body of assumptions will come more and more to rest on the shoulders of an authority. What follows then is no longer within the province of reality-testing; controversies can no longer be settled by searching for decisive facts or by increasing the accuracy of observations. Science has been moved from a factual base into the realm of opinion, and in this realm scientific controversies are reduced to a personal struggle between authorities. Competing authorities do not like to dwell under the same roof. One of them has to get out. And when he does, he founds a school of his own in which he can be just as authoritarian as is his opponent in the school which he left.

Therefore, if there is a danger of schisms in psychoanalysis, this danger cannot be averted by making training dogmatically rigid. For this attitude works precisely in the opposite direction. It aggravates the condition of which schisms are merely a symptom. Ultimately it leads to scientific deterioration.

Years ago this state of affairs seemed clear to the present writer who tried quietly to alter his own methods of teaching accordingly. He proceeded in this way because he felt that he should offer criticism only when he was in the position to suggest improvements that had passed the test of experience. His goal was to present psychoanalysis to students as an empirical, clinical science—not as an authoritarian, theoretical doctrine. This meant hard work both for the teacher and for the students; for they had to give up the narcotizing satisfaction inherent in any authoritarian system. It is wonderful to identify oneself with the great, to memorize and recite their teachings and to feel that every word is true forever. It is somewhat less comfortable to sit down and to study the development of psychoanalysis in an objective and critical spirit.

In the course of such study an effort was made clearly to segregate the proven facts from the working assumptions, and these from the assumptions of the second order that were needed to explain the assumptions of the first order, and so on. It became evident that the accepted language of psychoanalysis is not altogether suited for the clear differentiation of facts from theories. As a rule, even the factual statements of psychoanalysis are couched in abstract and theoretical language, the vocabulary of which reflects various stages of theoretical development. Some of the technical terms had no precisely defined meaning even at the outset. Often they have subsequently been used in such a manner as to include in their scope every new finding. As the years pass, more and more factual references are packed into the same terms, so extending their range and so multiplying their meanings that it becomes difficult for a newcomer to see whether or not they mean anything at all. Older analysts have acquired a unique skill in understanding each other in spite of, and not by virtue of, this language.

Yet there is nothing in the nature of the subject matter of psychoanalysis that requires treatment so different from the routine methods of science. An attempt to reduce our concepts to factual language sufficiently descriptive and specific to meet the needs of actual observation has proved a success. Any such language of facts reveals a truly impressive amount of objective knowledge hitherto obscured under our abstractions and brings this knowledge within easier reach of the student, helping him to recognize these facts as they turn up in his own experience, and giving him a real opportunity to check up on them. The improvement in teaching which this simple change in and of itself has brought about can hardly be exaggerated.

Moreover, much had to be done to revise our theories as well. This was an educational necessity not to be postponed any longer. The students' attention was directed to those theories which bore on clinical subjects. The meaning and validity of these theories were specified in terms of the phenomena they actually cover. On the other hand, superlatively abstract and general formulas had to be entirely excluded from the discussion of clinical problems. Such speculations admittedly reach out into spheres which are not only beyond the range of direct analytic observation but also outside the legitimate limits of inferential interpretation. *They can neither be verified nor refuted by empirical analytic methods.* When such speculations are used as though they had clinical significance and are applied to directly observed events, the result is verbal dialectics and not scientific penetration. The student uses the patient to understand the theory and not the theory to understand the patient; and such a patient, too, will end by "understanding" the theory but not himself. Teaching experience demonstrates that while such speculations offer an outlook upon life fascinating from the psychocentric viewpoint, they are nonetheless too remote to be useful in the narrower field of psychopathology. The theories needed by the physician for the control of clinical conditions must remain close to clinical observation. And they must use our established biological knowledge of man as their ultimate frame of reference. Either we understand mental processes as functions of the human organism or we of necessity interpret them away from the human organism—as has been done in bygone days. In our teaching we recognized these principles and unhesitatingly reorganized our clinical knowledge to meet urgent medical responsibilities. I believe that in this process of medical revision not an iota of analytic insight was lost and some new analytic insight was gained.

The response of our students to such work as this has been excellent. They saw the complexities of analysis in a brighter light, derived much needed encouragement from their better understanding and actually increased both their scholastic and their therapeutic skill.

The psychological findings of psychoanalysis may be profitably applied to any field of study which has a psychological frontier. Since we have considered it imperative to teach psychoanalysis as an autonomous branch of medicine, we must recognize that in turn these applications of psychoanalysis to non-medical subjects are also autonomous. Clearly, medical psychoanalysis and applied psychoanalysis are not one and the same science. The opportunities for direct observation, the accuracy and completeness of data attainable are much greater in the native medical domain of psychoanalysis than they are in any of its applied fields. Owing to the individual character of the subjects concerned, applied psychoanalysis must be satisfied with cruder methods and less reliable results. These inescapably lower standards of scientific procedure must not be transplanted into medical psychoanalysis. An analytic speculation which might be brilliant in comparative mythology would be unsatisfactory if employed in the study of a clinical problem. Therefore, although we urge our students to acquaint themselves with the non-medical applications of psychoanalysis, we train them to be aware of the differences in method.

Let us stop again to consider our conclusion: that it is an inescapable necessity to invade the magnificent edifice of psychoanalytic theories and, disregarding their beauty as a whole, reduce them to their factual and heuristic content. In stating this position, it is a privilege to listen to the opinion of a distinguished expert. In an address delivered in Vienna on the eve of Freud's eightieth birthday, Dr. Ernest Jones of London, the present head of the International Psychoanalytical Association, made the following statement:

"In the field of Theory, on the other hand [in contradistinction to technique], I am inclined to anticipate very considerable changes in the course of the next twenty years or so. The scaffolding, as he modestly called it, that Freud has erected, has stood much rough weather extraordinarily well, though he has had to repair and strengthen it from time to time. But it would be counter to all our knowledge of the history and essential nature of science to suppose that it will not be extensively modified with the passage of time. The preconceptions from the world of contemporary scientific thought with which Freud approached his studies had a visible influence on his theoretical structure, and they necessarily bear the mark of a given period. We must expect that other workers, schooled by different disciplines than his, will be able to effect fresh orientations, to formulate fresh correlations. In spite of our natural piety we must brace ourselves to welcome such changes, fortifying ourselves with the reflection that to face new truth and to hold truth above all other considerations has been Freud's greatest lesson to us and his most precious legacy to psychological science."[1]

At the time when Dr. Jones' address was delivered and printed, our work at the New York Psychoanalytic Institute was in full swing. Dr. Jones' view of the future of psychoanalysis, lucid and realistic as his opinions always are, gave us much reassurance and much encouragement.

Freud's work as it stands is preserved for eternity. In its infinite richness of detail it is a classic of science; in its monumentality a great work of art. No student could think of becoming a psychoanalyst without a penetrating study of Freud's own writings. This study is an experience in itself, incommensurable with anything that systematic instruction offers. We aid the student in this study. We teach him to see the canyons as well as the peaks in the work of the creative genius; and we also teach him to see that the humbler mind must not proceed in science without the safeguards of methodological precision.

Since our students are all graduates of universities, our psychoanalytic institutes are in their formal status teaching institutions of the highest order. Our foremost duty towards our students is to fortify and refine their own scientific judgment, upon which the value of their future work in science and practice depends. If, instead, we would paralyze our students' critical judgment and thus make them dependent upon authority, we would seriously hurt their professional interests as well as the interests of the science they are expected to serve. Psychoanalysis makes high demands upon the intelligence and productive ability of the student. Students who are incapable of dispensing with the crutch of indoctrination would better be advised to turn their backs upon psychoanalytic work: their opportunities lie in other fields which offer them methods more standardized and stereotyped than are the methods of psychoanalysis today.

Only men who are capable of facing facts fearlessly can be good scientists and good physicians. To help physicians to become good scientists and practitioners in the field of psychoanalysis is the educational aim of this Institute.

REFERENCES

[1] JONES, E.: The Future of Psycho-Analysis. *Internat. J. Psycho-Analysis, 17,* 1936.

Developments in the Psychoanalytic Conception and Treatment of the Neuroses*

During the past few years we have witnessed rapid progress in general medicine culminating in the recent advances in the chemotherapy of infectious diseases. In view of this bright picture in our neighbor's field it is fitting to ask ourselves whether we too are in a position to report improvements. The purpose of my paper is to show that we are, although in our field developments have been slower and less spectacular.

Although mental healing is the oldest kind of healing, scientific psychotherapy is a very young branch of medicine. It was only some forty years ago that Freud laid its foundations by the discovery of a method for the penetrating psychological investigation of mental life. The essence of this method was, and still is, to maintain a special kind of psychological contact with the patient over an extended period and by certain technical means enable him to unfold himself mentally before the eyes of the physician. This procedure of prolonged observation however was more than a method of investigation. It appeared itself to have a therapeutic effect which could be directed and intensified by skillful influence. In medical practice it has been employed ever since that time for its value as a means of treatment.

Freud summed up the early results of his psychoanalytic studies in two closely interrelated formulations based on the hypothesis of instinctual drives. According to the first formulation, neurotic symptoms are due to the repression of instinctual drives during the period of childhood; the drives thus repressed are excluded from normal development yet they remain powerful and produce the derivative manifestations which we encounter as symptoms. The second formulation stated that the psychoanalytic procedure remedies the symptoms by inducing the patient to overcome his resistances—the repressing forces in his mind—thus allowing the repressed pathogenic unconscious in him to become conscious again. In spite of the many complicated details that were later added, these twin formula-

* Read before the Section on Neurology and Psychiatry of the New York Academy of Medicine, May 1939, and at the joint meeting of the American Psychoanalytic and American Psychiatric Associations, Chicago, May 1939. First published in *The Psychoanalytic Quarterly*, 8: 427–437, 1939.

tions have remained the foundation upon which psychoanalytic work has been carried out.

In accord with these formulations the practicing analyst focused his attention upon the abundant fantasy productions of the patient. These fantasies were seen as forming the mental background of his neurotic symptoms and behavior; they were considered the flagrant manifestations of his hitherto repressed and unconscious drives. Their production was therefore encouraged. The analytic procedure was to retrace these fantasies to early infantile experiences of the patient. As a rule he could be shown that in his fantasies and symptoms he had revived and repeated his remote past and was reverting to the primitive instinctual gratifications of that time. Sometimes tangible improvements followed this type of analytic work; in other cases no improvement was forthcoming. It was then disquieting to find that neurotic fantasies and symptoms are like the heads of the fabled hydra any of which when cut off was replaced by two others unless a fire brand were used to scorch the growth. Unfortunately we had no formula for such cauterization.

The capriciousness of our therapeutic results puzzled us. It required years of clinical study and the repeated revision of our working assumptions to bring us closer to a solution. The first move in these developments was made by Freud. In his book *Hemmung, Symptom und Angst*, published in 1926, he reëxamined his theory of the pathogenesis of the neuroses.[2] Here he reversed his previous conception that the repression of instinctual drives leads to anxiety, holding that on the contrary anxiety leads to the repression of instinctual drives. He came to the conclusion that *anxiety* was the decisive factor in the causation of the neuroses. In his own words: 'Whence springs the preference over all other affects which the affect of anxiety seems to enjoy in *alone evoking reactions which we distinguish from others as abnormal* and which in their inexpediency obstruct the stream of life?'

From this recognition of the dominant rôle played by anxiety in the pathology of the neuroses Freud, astonishingly, drew no conclusions for the technique of treatment. Other authors, especially Ferenczi and Wilhelm Reich, attempted to do so during the ensuing years but without conclusive results. My own therapeutic efforts gradually led me to realize that we had reached a stage of development when our understanding of the etiology and treatment of the neuroses was hindered rather than aided by the theory of instincts itself. This theory was repeatedly modified by Freud, each time becoming more speculative, more general and remote. Although captivated by the philosophical implications of this theory, Freud was aware of its scientific shortcomings. He wrote in 1933: 'The theory of instincts is, as it were, our mythology. The instincts are mythical beings, superb in their indefiniteness.'³ Obviously this hypothesis, though of great heuristic value in the early development of psychoanalysis, has outlived its usefulness. If Freud's discoveries were to bear new fruits by stimulating further scientific inquiry, it was necessary to segregate the factual findings of psychoanalysis from its metaphysical elements and to build some other frame of reference that would rest on our established biological knowledge of man and suit our medical needs.

We attempted to meet this need by describing the actually observable dynamics of the mind in terms of integrative ego functioning or to introduce a convenient designation, in terms of an *egology*.* This egological concept has gradually evolved from a theoretical position first stated in 1927 and further elaborated in 1933.⁴ It has enabled us to look upon the neuroses as disorders of integrative ego functioning and thus to study and describe them in terms of an *ego pathology*. The results of our attempt have been presented elsewhere⁵ and will be published. Here I shall merely indicate the few points needed to clarify the problem of treatment.

The first task was to learn more about anxiety, and also to arrive at a closer definition of our terms, making a sharp distinction between the affect of anxiety and the state of fear or apprehension. Fear (apprehension) is marked by a highly intellectual content, a specific feeling tone, and the absence of peripheral motor manifestations. Hence fear (apprehension) is not an affect but a predominantly intellectual state of mind.† Its general characteristic is alertness to danger; egological analysis however reveals its essential substance to be *anticipation of pain from impending injury*. Pain and injury must of course be understood to include purely mental as well as physical experiences. In anxiety, on the other hand, the intellectual element is negligible, though it too is perceived as a specific feeling (related to fear). The decisive component from which it derives its character as an affect is its specific peripheral motor manifestations centered around a sudden and transitory impediment of breathing.

The outstanding fact in regard to fear and anxiety as well as pain is that they are the key devices of a safety function of the ego which I propose to call *emergency control*.¹ These devices act on the ego in a definite way; they prompt it reactively to *emergency measures*, such as quick emergency moves, elaborate emergency fortifications and finally reparative adjustments. Here I shall mention only the emergency moves. They are: the outward operations of flight or evasion; the release of anger or rage

---

* Integrative ego functioning is of course the integrative functioning of the 'total personality'. The latter term is avoided because of the somewhat metaphysical content that it has been made to represent.

† In the sense of the definition advanced in the text the term 'fear' is the exact equivalent of the German *Befürchtung*.

resulting in the outward operations of combat; the purely intellectual move of 'choosing the lesser evil'; and last, the inward inhibitory impulses, the operations of self-control. The latter restrains the ego in cases where it would otherwise expose itself to emergencies and must therefore be considered the prophylactic branch of emergency control. All this is readily observed in the normal ego.

Anxiety is a reflex-like response. We may refer to it as the *anxiety reflex*. The ways in which this reflex is elicited in the newly born infant are obscure but we see that it undergoes a definite development in early childhood. This development falls into two stages. In the first, experience and training tend to condition it to become responsive only to sense perceptions which truly indicate that the ego is exposed to injury, in other words that there exists a state of actual emergency. With this process of early conditioning an attempt is made to enable the anxiety reflex, inherited from our subhuman ancestors, to serve as a device of emergency control under the conditions of civilization. The control then to be fully adequate should function according to the following pattern: sense perceptions truly representative of emergency (of impending injury) reflexly evoke anxiety whose action in turn prompts the ego to reactive emergency measures.

This aim however can only be realized in the second stage when the development of the child permits the fuller enlistment for this purpose of its intellectual function. The anxiety reflex is then gradually transformed into and superseded by the higher *fear reflex*. The vital point in this change is the *anxiety affect;* whereas its feeling tone remains unchanged, its motor elements are replaced by the intellectual components characteristic of fear. Upon completion of this metamorphosis then, the devices of emergency control, originally pain and anxiety, have become pain and fear. With the evolution of fear anxiety has withered away.

It is a symptom of abnormal development if the evolution of the fear reflex from the anxiety reflex is not a full transformation but merely a branching out. Though the fear reflex develops, the anxiety reflex also persists and far from dwindling away, shows signs of increasing strength. Its reflex excitability increases; its affect manifestations expand. If elicited, the reflex no longer manifests itself as a *flash* of anxiety but as an *attack* of anxiety. The former served as a stimulant to useful action; the anxiety attack, on the contrary, has a paralyzing effect on the ego, sometimes to the point of complete incapacitation. Previously a serviceable device of emergency control, the anxiety reflex has by its survival and hypertrophy become a menace to the ego.

Henceforth the ego will be subject to attacks of anxiety. These attacks seem to occur first as an added affect manifestation in real emergencies where the normal child would respond only with fear. Later however, they arise independently of such occasions. Our investigations have recently begun to shed light on the chain of internal events responsible for this momentous change, events which of course remain hidden from the ego itself.

After experiencing a few anxiety attacks the ego begins to dread their recurrence. In its desperate efforts to prevent them it has only the intellectual resources of fear at its disposal. For want of better insight the ego will trace its attacks of anxiety to imagined causes and henceforth will be afraid of these. In other words, it now dramatizes anxiety in terms of morbid fears. During the further course of childhood development both the anxiety attacks and the morbid fears sustained by them may subside. It is then in typical situations in the period of puberty and later in maturity that they recur. Though the content of the morbid fears is now colored by contemporary elements, they are easily revealed as revivals of the fears formed in childhood.

The significance of the morbid fears can hardly be over-rated; it becomes apparent when one realizes that the ego reacts to them in essentially the same way as to ordinary fear. Under their pressure the ego though actually in no danger, fights, retreats, fortifies and readjusts itself, exhausting itself in superfluous emergency measures. These measures are the decisive factors in the development of the neuroses. They carry the disturbance set up by the anxiety attacks into the individual functions of the ego. The manifold details of these measures have been gradually disclosed by the minute analysis of a large variety of cases. Clinical findings have demonstrated the validity of the following conception: *neurosis is ego functioning altered by faulty measures of emergency control.* In the pathogenesis of neurosis the first observable event is a disturbance in the development of the fear reflex resulting in the survival of the anxiety reflex and the expansion of its affect manifestations to attacks; in the effort to control anxiety attacks the ego generates morbid fears and is then pushed by these into faulty emergency measures which invade and upset any or all of its functions.

The ego however is unconscious of the true meaning and source of its neurotic manifestations. Such a striking lack of self-awareness may seem astonishing. However closer observation reveals that the normal ego behaves in a similar fashion in regard to its realistic fears. Its behavior may be definitely motivated by fear of which it neither is nor dares to be conscious. One is forced to realize that it is precisely because of their intimidating humiliating side effects that the ego shies from a consciousness of its fears, though wholly under their domination. It is no longer surprising then that it should be unaware of the nature of the complicated operations deriving from this unrecognized source.

The neurotic ego is thus driven by its morbid fears blindly to carry out unnecessary emergency measures which reduce both the range and the efficiency of its functioning. The damage is particularly serious if the disturbing influences of morbid self-control invade the delicate physiological mechanism of organ functions, depriving the ego of its due command of the organs. This is notably the case in disturbances of the genital function, an element rarely absent in any neurosis. Though the development of this function is completed only in puberty, its finer coördinations are unbalanced under the impact of anxiety in early childhood. Also to be emphasized as another fairly constant feature in the neuroses is one that has not been given the attention to which it is entitled by its practical importance. I am referring to the disturbances of the group membership functions of the ego which include the individual's capacity for and way of doing his share of work in the community, and his handling of the competitive aspects of life. Since our knowledge of these functions themselves is incomplete, their disturbances are as yet somewhat obscure; but here too our approach has led to clarification.

Strangest of all however, are those actions of the neurotic ego which are obviously self-injurious. We have gradually come to understand these phenomena as the outcome of morbid fears under whose pressure the ego often brings down on itself the very injury which formed the imaginary object of its fear. A woman has a wholly unwarranted fear of being slighted and ignored; unwittingly she displays a resentful attitude which will lead to her being avoided in fact. The morbid fear of being persecuted drives many into actions that bring about their actual persecution. The sexual life of neurotics is full of self-injuries inflicted in this way. Once an ego has come to the point of coping with its anxiety by producing and sustaining morbid fears, the consequences are far-reaching indeed. Yet this mechanism alone far from explains all the spectacular self-injuries involved in the neuroses. Further insight into them was gained with the realization that emergency control is integrated on three hierarchic levels. On the highest, the intellectual level, its device is fear; on the next, the subintellectual or affectomotor level, its device is anxiety; and on the lowest, subaffect level its device is pain. These superimposed levels of integration possibly reflect the course of phylogenetic development. Fear is anticipation of pain, eliciting efforts to avert the impending injury. The flash of anxiety is a cruder device for the same purpose. On the lowest level of organization pain cannot yet be foreseen and thus averted, but must none the less be dealt with when it occurs. Control of pain is therefore directed toward eliminating the source of suffering, if necessary even by the sacrifice of a part of one's own body. Such conduct reveals a principle ingrained in the organization of all animals, including man. In the phylogenetic scale of increasing differentiation and complexity of organization there gradually become apparent many reflexes designed to eliminate pain-causing agents from the surface or inside of the body. The scratch reflex, the shedding of tears, sneezing, coughing, spitting, vomiting, colic bowel movement are but a few well-known instances of this principle of pain control in our bodily organization. This principle I have called the *riddance principle*, and its physiological embodiments the *riddance reflexes*. Reverting to the voluntary operations of ego functioning, we may observe in ourselves an impulse to tear away an intolerably aching portion of the body: a tooth, an ear, a finger, etc.

The decisive step came with the recognition that the same basic riddance principle governs the ego's attitude toward *mental* pain, toward the torment caused by its morbid fears and anxieties. For example: when the morbid fears responsible for sexual incapacitation have become intolerable, the individual develops the impulse to rid himself of this organ which appears to be the cause of his distress. Such primeval impulses of emergency control are checked by the intellectual realization that their pursuit would harm rather than benefit the ego, or more frequently these impulses are automatically repressed. In the latter case no less than in the former is the effect upon the ego tremendous. The ego cannot escape a faint awareness of being impelled toward the very injuries it dreads, and its fears feed and grow on this awareness. A vicious circle is then established: the fears thus intensified reflexly turn back on and stimulate the deep-seated riddance impulses which in turn magnify the severity and painfulness of the fears. Once this mechanism has been set in motion, the outlook for the further course of the neurosis is indeed alarming. The patient moves from defeat to defeat. In other cases, in psychoses or under morbid excitement, he loses his controlling insight and in a paroxysm of riddance, actually inflicts self-injury in order to end the insupportably painful tension of anticipation.[6] In some cases, driven to end the tension, the patient brings about a situation in which he is inevitably injured by others. A refined technique of achieving this is to lure the surgeon into the performance of unnecessary operations.

It was the disclosure of the riddance principle that finally led me to feel that the attempt to understand the neuroses in egological terms of emergency control was fully justified and offered a promising approach. It was a great satisfaction to me to be able to demonstrate in a crucial problem of psychopathology that voluntary operations of integrative ego functioning are governed by the same principles embodied in the ego's reflex organization.

Leaving many important points untouched, we must now return to the problem of neurotic fantasies. Whereas until now we have been concerned mainly with the devices of emergency control and the corresponding emergency moves, in dealing with neurotic fantasies we touch on those other elements of emergency control that we have called fortifications and reparative adjustments. We regard these fantasies as illusory operations acting vicariously for inhibited normal operations. The greater the pleasure deficiency of the functionally crippled ego, the greater its tendency to indulge in wishful fantasies. This is but one instance of the ego's effort to increase its working equipment by the revival of the magic operations of childhood, a morbid act of fortification that takes place on a large scale in every neurosis. Yet these illusory operations are themselves not immune from the inhibitory action of morbid fear and anxiety, and the ego is therefore obliged even here to retreat and make its reparative adjustments.

We need not go further into these details. The point to be stressed here is that neurotic fantasies are vicarious operations. Our first task then is to retrace them to the operations one would find in their place had the ego remained normal and to use them as in indication of the forces interfering with the ego's normal functioning. The same is true in regard to the other symptoms which owe their existence to the reparative efforts of the neurotic ego to open up inferior sources of pleasure and profit as a compensation. In this procedure, instead of allowing ourselves to be sidetracked to the secondary consequences of the disturbance we use the fantasies and symptoms together with other data to direct attention to those focal points where the chain of pathological events actually originates. We can restore to normality functions damaged by anxiety only by removing the obstacle of anxiety from their range. This implies incessant study of the disturbed functions themselves rather than of the functions that have come to act vicariously for them, and the careful disclosure of the manifold damage done to their structure by anxiety. Gradually unfolding the patient's life history in terms of his intimidation we arrive inescapably at his early childhood when the first impact of anxiety on functions not yet fully developed laid the foundations for their future disturbances.

This reorientation of therapeutic work unfortunately does not lessen the time needed for treatment, and demands if possible even keener penetration than before into the patient's present and past, but it does reward us with a greater measure of success.

I have been able to present only a fragmentary picture of developments in our field. Foremost among the many other subjects that are ready to be reported is the better understanding, in the light of integrative ego functioning, of the phenomenon known as transference and the utilization of this insight in the technique of treatment. The discussion of these subjects however must await another occasion.

138 PSYCHOANALYSIS OF BEHAVIOR

REFERENCES

1 CANNON, WALTER B.: *Bodily Changes in Pain, Hunger, Fear and Rage*. New York: Appleton-Century, 1934.
2 FREUD, S.: Hemmung, Symptom und Angst. *Ges. Schr.* XI, authorized trans.: *The Problem of Anxiety*. New York, Norton, 1936.
3 —— *New Introductory Lectures on Psychoanalysis*. New York: Norton, 1933.
4 RADO, SANDOR: An Anxious Mother: A Contribution to the Analysis of the Ego. *Int. Ztschr. f. Psychoanal.*, *13*, 1927; trans. *Internat. J. Psycho-Analysis*, *9*, 1928.
—— Fear of Castration in Women. *Psychoanal. Quart.*, *2:* 425, 1933.
5 —— Lectures at the New York Psychoanalytic Institute from 1936 to 1939.
6 —— The Psychoanalysis of Pharmacothymia (Drug Addiction). *Psychoanal. Quart.*, *2:* 1, 1933.

A Critical Examination of the Concept of Bisexuality*

Historical Survey

Man and woman were once a single being. This entity was cut in two by an angry god, and ever since the halves have reached toward one another in love, out of a longing to restore their original state. So the story runs in Plato's "Banquet." Traces of it have been found, however, in older sources including the Upanishads and the Old Testament, proving that Plato's fanciful conception was based upon a far more ancient myth[4, 18, 19].

This myth represents one of man's earliest intellectual approaches to the puzzle of the existence of two sexes. It offers a simple solution to this problem by creating an opposite concept, that is, the idea that man was formerly bisexual. To the primitive mind, however, this means that he still is. Consequently the myth is curiously equivocal, and manages to convey the exact opposite of the fact that it so ingeniously explains. It is as if the myth read: "I will tell you why there are two sexes. The truth is that they are one. Properly speaking we are all bisexual."

It is clear that ancient man must have had strong motives for denying the differences between sexes. He may have found support for his comforting solution in the occurrence of hermaphrodites. The two other elements of the myth are traceable to simple and profound human experiences. The image of violent separation is reminiscent of the event of childbirth, culminating in the cutting of the umbilical cord, while the concluding idea of a partial reunion brings to mind the pattern of the mother holding the child in her arms.

The conception of bisexuality was sanctioned by religious authority. Embodied in a system of belief, the idea had the power to eclipse the facts. Certain Egyptian gods were notoriously bisexual and Hermaphroditus, a favorite Greek god and highly popular subject for painting and sculpture, still carried an implication of deity in the Roman Empire. The advent of Christianity wiped out the religious significance of this foremost symbol of

* Read at the ninety-sixth annual meeting of The American Psychiatric Association, Cincinnati, Ohio, May 20–24, 1940, before the joint session with the American Psychoanalytic Association. First published in *Psychosomatic Medicine, 2:* 459–467, 1940.

bisexuality, but the idea itself remained, to be revived in less spectacular form throughout the ages. Nor was its diffusion by any means limited to cultures touched by the heritage of the classical world. Anthropologists have found it to play a vital rôle in the cults, customs and folklore of primitive societies of our time, the Dutch Catholic missionary and anthropologist, J. Winthuis, even making it the title and central theme of his book "Das Zweigeschlechterwesen"[18]. To what can we attribute the extraordinary range and tenacity of this myth? This question, involving as it does the history of civilization, obviously reaches beyond the province of psychoanalysis. We have, however, an experimental approach to the problem. Through the analytic study of children and neurotics we are familiar with the emotional conflicts associated with the discovery of the differences between the sexes. Since many of these reactions are elementary, it is reasonable to assume that they are also ubiquitous and that they are a part of the aboriginal matter from which the concept of bisexuality has arisen.

These scanty references may suffice to show that the idea of bisexuality far antedates the scientific era and owes its origin to primeval, emotional needs of animistic man. It is important to bear this in mind in our examination of the part played by the same concept in modern science.

In about the middle of the 19th century it was discovered that the urogenital systems of the two sexes derive from a common embryonic origin. The question of whether this uranlage should be considered neutral or hermaphroditic was at first a subject of debate. When it was found to contain cellular material of both gonads (Wittich, 1853; Waldeyer, 1870) it was definitely labeled hermaphroditic[16]. This unfortunate appellation of an undeveloped embryonic structure marked an historical turning point, as it opened the door to indiscriminate speculations on man's bisexuality. These speculations, resting on generalizations drawn from biological findings in lower animals, seemed to offer at last what appeared to be a scientific basis for the explanation of homosexuality and it was because of medical interest in this subject that the concept of bisexuality found its way into psychiatry. The first attempts in this direction were made by Kiernan (1884, 1888), Frank Lydston (1889, 1892), and the Frenchman Chevalier (1893). The writings of these men stimulated the Viennese psychiatrist v. Krafft-Ebing to expound the neuropsychological aspects of bisexuality in the following theory: since the peripheral part of the sexual apparatus is of bisexual predisposition, this must be true of the central part as well. Thus one must assume that the cerebrum contains male and female centers whose antagonistic action and relative strength determine the individual's sex behavior. Homosexuality results from the victory of the wrong center. v. Krafft-Ebing realized that hermaphroditic developmental abnormalities of the genitals and homosexuality are rarely associated. So he went on to the further assumption that the central part of the sex system is autonomous and therefore independently subject to developmental disturbances. Not a trace of neurological evidence was then or is now available to give credence to v. Krafft-Ebing's chain of hypotheses.

From 1896 on v. Krafft-Ebing's views on bisexuality were included in his "Psychopathia Sexualis" and thus gave the first impetus to the vogue which the concept has enjoyed even to the present time[15]. Two other writers during the 1890's also contributed to its popularity: Havelock Ellis embraced the idea in his eclectic tenets, and Magnus Hirschfeld, who engaged in a lifelong defense of homosexuals against the harshness of a mediaeval law, became a devoted partisan of the concept of bisexuality[3, 9]. The latter gave a new slant to the subject implicit in his view of homosexuality as an inborn characteristic brought about by a specific proportion of male and female substances in the hereditary composition of the brain. This version places the burden of proof primarily on the shoulders of geneticists, who, however, have not yet fulfilled this obligation.

In 1905 Freud published his "Contributions to the Theory of Sex"[5]. Here he followed the lead of v. Krafft-Ebing in applying the notion of bisexuality to the central as well as to the peripheral part of the sex apparatus. However, he was aware of the futility of ascribing to the brain hypothetical properties and functions not yet ascertainable by neurological research, and claimed that the central manifestations of sex, i.e., psychosexuality, must be studied by psychological means. This was in line with his general attitude in regard to all the psychologically accessible functions of the brain and it was precisely for this purpose that he had evolved the method of psychoanalysis. In the desire to remain free and unbiased in the evaluation of his findings, Freud intentionally kept himself apart from the other medical sciences. He was obliged however to use as points of orientation a few of the basic assumptions of biology, and it was as one of these that he introduced into psychoanalysis the concept of bisexuality. This borrowed concept, formulated as a general characteristic of every human individual, came to play so important a rôle in psychoanalytic theory that younger men in the field dealt with it, not as a postulate or convenient frame of reference for interpretation, but as an established fact. Freud himself had no pretentions on this score: as recently as 1933 he reiterated that he had merely "carried over the notion of bisexuality into mental life"[6]; he spoke significantly of "constitutional bisexuality," and as he of course always maintained that constitutional factors were beyond the reach of psychoanalytic investigation, the phrase explicitly disclaims for psychoanalysis all responsibility as to the validity of the assumption. Psychological data alone have never been, and could not be, conclusive in this respect. If the hypothesis were abandoned in the field of biology from which it had been taken, the data accumulated by psychoanalysis would have to be reinterpreted. In any case verification rested, and quite rightly, with biology.

This state of affairs is somewhat disconcerting to a psychoanalyst, as grave doubts have arisen as to the psychological value of this concept, doubts substantiated by certain observations made in its application to medical practice. The analyst therefore has an urgent theoretical and practical motive to seek clarification of this subject, and for this he must turn to a field other than his own.

Sex and Bisexuality in Contemporary Biology

We shall now glance briefly at the actual status of the idea of bisexuality in the biological field[19, 1, 14, 2, 17, 7, 8, 11]. What has happened to this idea since its first appearance as a scientific generalization? On examination one finds that a truly enormous amount of relevant data has been assembled, leading to new formulations and terminology, and that as a result the old speculative notion of bisexuality is in the process of withering away. These developments are due not only to the greater body of available facts, but also to an increasingly scientific attitude, less animistic, dedicated to a finer logical precision, and coinciding with a definite shift of emphasis from the morphological to the functional point of view. This trend is clearly indicated by Frank R. Lillie in the following passages[19]:

"There is no such biological entity as sex. What exists in nature is a dimorphism within species into male and female individuals, which differ in respect to contrasting characters; it is merely a name for our total impression of the differences. It is difficult to divest ourselves of the prescientific anthropomorphism which assigned phenomena to the control of personal agencies, and we have been particularly slow in the field of the scientific study of sex characteristics in divesting ourselves not only of the terminology but also of the influence of such ideas. . . . Sex of the gametes and sex in bodily structure or expression are two radically different things. The failure to recognize this elementary principle is responsible for much unsound generalization."

From the biologist we learn that sex in the gametes refers to their differentiation in form and function relevant to their reciprocal action of fertilization. In the somata, carriers of the gametes, sex referes to their differentiation in form and function relevant to or associated with 1) their reciprocal action of ensuring proper functioning of the gametes, and 2) the development of the embryo, giving birth to and caring for the child. If we put these two references together, we see that sex in its entirety refers to the differentiation in the individuals as regards their contrarelated action systems of reproduction. Taking these considerations now in reverse order, we start from the fact that in so far as concerns their reproductive action systems, individuals are of two contrarelated types. It is precisely this differentiation that constitutes the character of the sexes. Each of the two systems may be dissected into a multitude of structures, substances and functions, of which it is composed. The sex aspect of every one of these constituent parts is derived from the fact of its participation in the system as a whole.

From this definition of sex it follows that it is not permissible to single out any one element no matter how conspicuous, such as the gonad, and make it the sole criterion of sex. To attempt to determine "maleness" or "femaleness" by the relative percentage of male and female hormones in blood or urine is obviously to carry this error to an extreme. Sex can be determined only by the character of the reproductive action system *as a whole*. The human being is not a bundle of cells or tissues but a complex biological system, in which new system properties appear on every hierarchic level of integration. And sex is not a small bundle of cells and tissues within a larger one, but a component system of the total system: the individual. The relative significance of the various elements in each of the two sex systems has still to be established. The usual distinction between primary, accessory and secondary sex characteristics is one-sided and inconsistent, and misleading when applied in medical practice. This is a problem to be approached from different theoretical and practical angles and to which there is accordingly more than one solution.

Reproductive activity of course presupposes reproductive maturity. What then is sex, in terms of this biological conception, in the infant, the embryo, the zygote? The answer is obvious: differential development, directed toward the construction and perfection of the reproductive system. At this point, however, the picture becomes more complicated. Biologists today agree in the assumption that every zygote has the intrinsic capacity to give rise to an individual with either a male or a female reproductive system. The developmental process is shunted into one or the other direction by the successive action of determining factors such as genes and endocrine substances. It may even happen, as demonstrated in animal experiments, that the initial direction is reversed by the action of a later determinant. Also important is the fact that although by its gene composition the zygote is already earmarked for one sex, the traceable developmental process is at first identical for both sexes; and even when visible differentiation begins there may still appear two sets of discrete primordia for some parts of the genital apparatus, as if a choice of direction still remained. Thereafter, one set of primordia develops further while the other degenerates, regresses, or remains in a rudimentary state. In accord with these facts the zygote as well as the early embryonic stages are no longer referred to as bisexual, but are said, more accurately, to possess bipotentiality of differentiation. Under normal developmental conditions, as differentiation proceeds and one type of reproductive action system grows to completion, the original bipotentiality ceases to have any real significance. It is true that in some classes of mollusks, such as oysters, certain gastropoda and pteropoda, every individual has as standard equipment two complete reproductive systems, one male, one female, and actually engages in fertilization in both ways. The individuals of these species are truly hermaphroditic, *i.e.*, bisexual in the only legitimate sense of this term. However, from the existence of species so organized nothing whatsoever may be deduced in regard to the organization of the human species or of the higher vertebrates in general. The standard developmental pattern of our species provides for each individual only one reproductive action system. The two inherent potentialities of the zygote are thereby mutually exclusive.

In humans the complicated embryological past of the reproductive system has no detectable influence on the efficient reproductive functioning of the normal individual. It can, however, play a part in disturbances of embryonic development or later in the life cycle. Embryonic differentiation of the reproductive system may be hampered by abnormally changed genes or hormonal or other factors, which foster a rival development on the part of the contrasting set of discrete primordia. The stimulation of tissues which produce hormones of the opposite sex is an important element in these disturbances. The result is anatomic malformation ranging from a marginal inconsistency in the ultimate differentiation of the sex system to a bizarre fusion and confusion of parts and characteristics of both systems. In such individuals the capacity of reproductive functioning is often hindered or lacking; they are sexually crippled, but obviously not bisexual. Derangement of a normally built sex system in later life may be observed in the female. Certain tumors of the ovarian medulla, of the adrenal cortex or of the pituitary entail an excessive output of male sex hormones that rouse the male embryonic rudiments to belated developmental activities. As in the case of embryonic malformations, this conflicting growth impedes or destroys one form of reproductive functioning while creating no new capacity to function in the opposite way. Similar changes can also be brought about artificially in animal experiments in so-called sex reversal. With or without removal of the animal's own sex hormone-producing tissues, hormones of the opposite sex are injected at various stages of embryonic development or later. Although in mammalia this has resulted only in the derangement of the established sex system, in lower species complete and successful reversal has been obtained. Partial reversal means that the individual is sexually incapacitated; in complete reversal the sex is changed but there is still only one.

To sum up this biological survey: using the term bisexuality in the only sense in which it is biologically legitimate, there is no such thing as bisexuality either in man or in any other of the higher vertebrates. In the final shaping of the normal individual, the double embryological origin of the genital system does not result in any physiological duality of reproductive functioning. This double origin is of significance only in developmental disturbances and reversals resulting in an admixture of structural characteristics of the opposite sex and thus recognizable as inconsistencies of sex differentiation. In such abnormally built individuals reproductive activity may be impaired or impossible, but the presence in their genital structure of fragments of the opposite sex does not confer upon them the reproductive capacity of that sex.

The Problem in Psychoanalysis

Reverting to the psychological study of reproductive activity we are at once struck by the element of pleasure, a feature that necessarily eludes the physical methods of the biologist and which seems at first to lead us into another world. Must we now abandon the dictum of biology, that sex is a matter of the reproductive action system? Let us glance briefly at the decisive psychological facts. It is man's practice to engage in genital activity regardless of reproductive intent. He may even abandon any possibility of reproduction by evading in this pursuit the genital organ of the opposite sex. But how then is the pleasure yield of genital activity obtained? What is its nature? It is, of course, orgasm, a reflex effect of the reproductive action system. Having so identified genital pleasure, we see that it is precisely the orgasm element of the reproductive system that forms the basis of the genital pleasure function. Orgasm is a pivotal point, being also the point of insemination. Considering the enormous variety of man's sex practices it seems at first incredible, but on second thought quite natural, that they can all be reduced to a simple formula: in deviating from the standard pattern of genital activity man derives excitation from stimulating the sensitive spots available in his mind and body; he may even be driven to seek excitation by dramatizing himself in terms of the opposite sex; yet all this preparatory excitation culminates in genital excitation and is discharged by way of the orgasm reflex. To repeat: the common denominator in all clinical pictures of genital psychopathology is that they represent abnormal conditions of *stimulation*; yet all the stimulation derived from whatever sources, and by whatever means, acts upon a single physiological pleasure-effector, the orgasm reflex. This reflex partakes of the differentiation of the two reproductive action systems, for it involves different anatomic structures and performs different mechanical duties in each. Physiologically, genital pleasure activity in an individual with male organs is always male, and the same applies to the female. Whatever man does or fancies, it is just as impossible for him to get out of the confines of his biological sex as to get out of his skin.

At this point there of course arises the question of the extra-genital pleasure functions, discovered and explored by psychoanalysis: oral, anal, tactile, etc. These are rooted not in the reproductive system but in the alimentary or some other basic biological system. They interact and combine with one another and with the genital pleasure function to make up the individual's entire *pleasure organization*. The latter is obviously neither sexual nor non-sexual, but an entity of a new order, brought about by integration on a higher level. It undergoes typical changes during the life cycle and is characterized at every stage by a measure of functional flexibility, working in the service of one and then another of the underlying biological systems. If pathologically disturbed it of course hampers rather than benefits the utility function of the system involved. This pleasure organization requires a term that reflects its biological nature and avoids confusion between the superior entity and its component parts. The identification of pleasure and sex made by classical psychoanalysis is at any rate biologically untenable; though originally a dynamic source of inspiration and unparalleled in popular appeal, it led eventually to hopeless confusion and doomed the psychoanalytic study of sex to scientific frustration.

Thus the biological status of the genital pleasure function, heretofore wrapped in ambiguities, is definitely established: inseparable from the reproductive action system, it is also integrated on a higher level into the pleasure organization in the individual.

This clarification was a prerequisite to any examination of the use that has been made of the concept of bisexuality in psychoanalysis. Essentially the procedure has been as follows: Certain types of behavior, or attitudes, or even mere phantasies have been interpreted in the male as "feminine," and analogously with the female, and taken as manifestations of the individual's "negative Oedipus complex" or "homosexual component." Such a component has been assumed, on the basis of the concept of bisexuality, to be present in every individual. It is not pleasant to have to admit that a closer scrutiny reveals no less than six major flaws in this procedure.

1) The designation of masculine or feminine can be made with reasonable certainty only in the case of a relatively small group of phantasies referring either to the individual's possession of one or the other type of genital equipment, or to impregnation, pregnancy or childbirth. Where no pos-

session or reproductive use of genital equipment is implied, as is the case in the vast majority of phantasies, attitudes and types of behavior, such a designation, though perpetuated by convention and routine, has rested on purely arbitrary grounds. Freud was always aware of this stumbling-block and in 1905 suggested as the psychological definition of male or female the pursuit of active or passive goals. However in 1933 he was forced to retract this suggestion and to admit the futility of any such attempt[5, 6].

2) In diagnosing psychic manifestations as masculine or feminine no distinction has been made between adults and the youngest children, in total disregard of the differences in information and intellectual maturity. A phantasy whose content is unquestionably male or female in an adult, might in a child reflect nothing but complete ignorance or deliberate misinformation. The inheritance of knowledge and ideas, first envisaged by Plato and lately revived in psychoanalysis, must obviously be left out of consideration in the absence of any factual basis for such a claim.

3) Equally unwarranted is the idea that these so-called masculine and feminine manifestations are the direct expression of a constitutional component of the opposite sex. It is well known that phantasies draw their content from experience and therefore to a large extent reflect environmental influences, but this has been lost sight of in the field of sex. A phantasy, even though influential in attitude or behavior, may or may not be the expression of a particular constitutional component. Inspired by birds, man has dreamed for millennia of flying under his own power, but no one has ever suggested that this implied a flying component or predisposition in his constitution. It is also noteworthy that pure phantasies devoid of any driving force and behavior indicative of a strong motor urge have been considered equally representative of a constitutional component.

4) The constitutional component itself has been a subject of further ambiguity and error. In general theoretical formulations as well as in practice it is indiscriminately referred to either as a homosexual component, or as the female component in the male and the male component in the female. This is all the more remarkable as it is a matter of general knowledge that in some forms of homosexuality behavior is in no way related to the behavior pattern of the opposite sex. Obviously no knowledge is immune to the truly narcotic effect of an appealing generalization.

5) Even aside from this confusion, the term homosexual has been so stretched as to become almost meaningless. Any relationships between two individuals of the same sex, domination, submission, competitive struggle or friendly cooperation, have readily been interpreted as manifestations of "unconscious homosexuality," regardless of whether or not they have any conscious or unconscious bearing on the patient's sexual life. We have

already seen the inconsistency and inaccuracy of the term sex as used in psychoanalysis; the term homosexuality has been even more grossly misapplied.

6) The assumption of a "homosexual" or "opposite sex" component in the constitution has not served as a challenge to discover what such a component might actually consist of, and in what specific ways, if at all, it influences man's sexual behavior. On the contrary, it has been relied on as if it were the outcome of research which in reality has never been made or even attempted.

It should now be apparent that the vague notion of biological bisexuality, and the incredibly loose manner in which it has been used in psychoanalysis have had deplorable consequences. It has acted like a will-o'-the-wisp, always and everywhere luring our attention so that it was impossible to see where the real problem lay. And it has gravely detracted from the benefits to be derived from the unique method of research possessed by psychoanalysis. This could not but have the effect of lowering our therapeutic efficiency. The idea that he is up against a homosexual component in his constitution has often produced in a patient needless discouragement or panic, if not more serious complications.

Free from the preconception of bisexuality, we must of course take new and more reliable bearings in the field of genital psychopathology. The position outlined above on biological grounds then inevitably becomes our point of departure. The basic problem, to state it briefly, is to determine the factors that cause the individual to apply aberrant forms of stimulation to his standard genital equipment. Following up this line of inquiry, we find that the chief causal factor is the affect of anxiety, which inhibits standard stimulation and compels the "ego action system in the individual" to bring forth an altered scheme of stimulation as a "reparative adjustment"[12, 13]. Both the inhibitory and the reparative processes begin far back in early childhood, leading up to the picture which we encounter in the adult. The reparative adjustment may allow the individual several alternatives of morbid stimulation, or may take the form of a rigid and inexorable pattern on which he depends for gratification. This approach, of which we can give here only the barest suggestion, has in practice unfolded a wealth of clinical details leading to a theory that is free of inconsistency and that serves as a reliable guide to treatment.

It also demands a change in outlook toward the underlying problem of constitution. If we assume, as we must, that constitutional factors may have an influence on morbid sex developments, we are now justified in considering this influence to be of two kinds: one preparing the ground for the inhibitory action of anxiety, the other modulating the course of the reparative adjustment. In considering the factors so involved we must not overlook the possibility of general, *i.e.*, non-sexual factors, as well as innate defects of the sexual action system of as yet unknown character. It is well to recall, lest we underestimate this eventuality, that we are still in the dark even as regards the physiological mechanism of such an elementary phenomenon as sexual attraction. Still another possibility is of course the presence of elements of the action system of the opposite sex such as reflexes, or rather chains of reflexes, susceptible to resuscitation by hormones or other agents[20]. However, not until somatic research has disclosed such elements shall we be able to determine by psychological methods their rôle in shaping morbid sex behavior. Meanwhile unbiased psychological analysis can offer invaluable clues to the somatic investigator in his search for predisposing somatic factors. Any such contribution was obviously out of the question as long as we employed fictitious constitutional factors as a means of psychological explanation. This methodological error not only trapped us in a vicious circle, but also deprived somatic research of a lead not obtainable elsewhere.

In conclusion it is imperative to supplant the deceptive concept of bisexuality with a psychological theory based on firmer biological foundations. Reconstructive work of this nature is more than an invitation; it is a scientific obligation for psychoanalysis. It is also an obligation to the founder of our science, Sigmund Freud, who left us not a creed but an instrument of research.

REFERENCES

[1] ALLAN, EDGAR (Ed.): *Sex and Internal Secretions*. Baltimore, 1939.

[2] BARD, PHILIP: The Hypothalamus and Sexual Behavior. *Res. Publ., A. Nerv. & Ment. Dis.*, Vol. XX.

[3] ELLIS, HAVELOCK: Sexual Inversion. *Studies in the Psychology of Sex*. New York, Random House.

[4] FREUD, S.: *Beyond the Pleasure Principle*. London, 1922.

[5] ——: Three Contributions to the Theory of Sex: *The Basic Writings of Sigmund Freud*. Modern Library.

[6] ——: *New Introductory Lectures on Psycho-Analysis*. New York, Norton, 1933.

[7] HARTMANN, MAX.: *Allgemeine Biologie*. Jena, 1933.

[8] ——: *Geschlecht und Geschlechtsbestimmung im Tier- und Pflanzenreich*. Berlin, 1939.

[9] HIRSCHFELD, MAGNUS: *Die Homosexualität des Mannes und des Weibes*. Berlin, 1922.

[10] LILLIE, F. R.: General Biological Introduction. *Sex and Internal Secretions* (E. Allan, ed.). Baltimore, 1931.

[11] MEISENHEIMER, JOHANNES: *Geschlecht und Geschlechter im Tierreich*. Jena, 1921.

[12] RADO, SANDOR: Developments in the Psychoanalytic Conception and Treatment of the Neuroses. *Psychoanal. Quart.*, 8: 427–437, 1939.

[13] ——: Lectures at the New York Psychoanalytic Institute from 1936 to 1940.

[14] STEINACH, EUGEN: *Sex and Life*. New York, 1940.

[15] v. KRAFFT-EBING: *Psychopathia Sexualis*. New York, 1931.
[16] WALDEYER, WILHELM: *Eierstock und Ei. Ein Beitrag zur Anatomie und Entwicklungsgeschichte der Sexualorgane*. Leipzig, 1870.
[17] WEISS, PAUL: *Principles of Development*. New York.
[18] WINTHUIS, J.: *Des Zweigeschlechterwesen*. Leipzig, 1928.
[19] YOUNG, HUGH HAMPTON: *Genital Abnormalities, Hermaphroditism and Related Adrenal Diseases*. Baltimore, 1937.
[20] YOUNG, WILLIAM C. AND RUNDLETT, BREWSTER: The Hormonal Induction of Homosexual Behavior in the Spayed Female Guinea Pig. *Psychosom. Med. 1:* 449–460 1939

The Relationship of Patient to Therapist*

In a psychoanalytic treatment, the patient's attitude toward his physician is either realistic or neurotic. The patient's realistic attitude is characterized by insight into his illness, genuine desire for recovery, confidence in the physician, and cooperative behavior. He acts like an intelligent human being who wants to be cured of an illness.

The patient with a fully realistic attitude is encountered none too frequently. Even when he starts with a realistic attitude he cannot retain it. Inevitably he shifts into a neurotic one, characterized by his involvement with the physician and distinguished by the irrational, regressive, and affective features of this involvement.

In essence, the patient then regards the physician as an omnipotent deity whose role is solely to function for the patient's benefit. This adult version of the infantile egocentric concept of life is not necessarily expressed by the patient, but is readily inferred from his behavior during treatment. Its most outspoken form is the patient's craving to be loved by the physician and receive from him the proof of his love: fulfillment of every longing, including sexual gratification.

The more intense the patient's unconscious preoccupation with the idea of the doctor's magic, the less he will do for himself. When his high expectations are disappointed, he feels frustrated and rejected. Schematically, the patient then responds either with anxiety or rage, and the consequences depend on which reaction holds sway. If anxiety prevails, then a submissive, ingratiating attitude results. The patient tries to court the physician's favor, to get into his good graces by displaying virtue. Also he resorts to an expiatory attitude, hoping to ingratiate himself by penitence for his sins. When carried to an extreme, this attitude results in a state of "quasi-hypnotic bondage." If the patient's reaction to frustration is predominantly rage, he becomes assertive, pugnacious, resentful. His aggressive responses are coercive, aiming to force the analyst to be good to him, or vindictive, taking the form either of revenge or breaking the analysis.

The patient's neurotic involvement with the analyst is technically known

* Abstract of a discussion at the June, 1941 meeting of the New York Regional Division of the American Orthopsychiatric Association. First published in *American Journal of Orthopsychiatry, 12:* 542, 1942.

as his "transference neurosis." Altogether it mirrors his childhood behavior toward his parents and stems from the child's earliest and most fundamental illusion that the parents are merely tools of his own omnipotence. The therapeutic task is promptly to extricate the patient from his recurring involvements with the analyst. Correcting his neurotic behavior toward the analyst is a prerequisite to correcting it toward the rest of the world, for the latter goal is attainable only if he is realistic in regard to the physician and the treatment. Departure from this technique leads to short-lived "transference improvements."

There is a decisive difference in the "transference neurosis" of adults and of children. In the child, lust for omnipotence and the ensuing struggle with a parental world are not anachronistic but timely occurrences consistent with his developmental stage. In a measure dependent upon his age, it is for him "realistic" to be involved with the physician. Hence, the adult's formula does not apply to the child. His attitude toward the psychotherapist requires special investigation and is obviously complicated by the problems of immaturity and growth.

Pathodynamics and Treatment of Traumatic War Neurosis (Traumatophobia)*

INCIDENCE IN WORLD WAR I

During the first World War attention was focussed for the first time on the illness known either as "shell-shock" or "traumatic neurosis," the clinical entity previously described by H. Oppenheim as an aftermath of peacetime accidents. The disease proved a serious form of military casualty, the victim's appearance alone often being such as to threaten the morale of the troops. Under the pressure of military needs treatment was improvised to restore the men as quickly as possible to combat duty. Most of them relapsed, however, as soon as they reached the front, had to be sent back to hospitals, and after the war were turned over in vast numbers to the veterans' services. More sensitive than other casualties to the idea of compensation, they put up a notorious resistance against readjustment to civilian life. In countries without a solvent treasury they were said to have made good recoveries or at least to have lost their more conspicuous symptoms.

FROM THE "ORGANIC" TO THE "PSYCHOGENIC" POINT OF VIEW

Since the early days of the last war considerable progress has been made in the knowledge of this illness. We shall briefly survey this development[1-12, 14, 15].

The symptoms of traumatic neurosis were originally attributed to "microstructural" or "molecular" changes in the nervous system. This explanation, though widely accepted at the time, was neither verifiable nor helpful.

The war cases, incomprehensible by the current theories, forced an acceptance of concepts introduced long before by Freud, and a growing recognition of psychoanalysis as a means of exploring nervous disturbances not associated with anatomic lesions. The pattern was seen to consist of a conflict between military duty and self-preservation, with an ensuing "flight

* Read at the 98th annual meeting of the American Psychiatric Association, Boston, May 18–22, 1942, before the joint session with the American Psychoanalytic Association. First published in *Psychosomatic Medicine, 4:* 362–368, 1942.

into illness," "fixation on the trauma," and a "secondary gain from illness" in terms of pension. The clinical picture was then recognized as including elements of hysteria, anxiety neurosis, phobic reactions, also a relapse to the crude forms of childish egotism, loss of sexual potency, etc. The excellent chapter on war neuroses in the official publication, "The Medical Department of the United States Army in the World War"[15], clearly reflects this change from the "organic" to the "psychogenic" point of view.

The cost of this progress was a misuse of the new terms by writers only superficially acquainted with psychoanalysis, who took such phrases as "unconscious motivation" to refer to deliberate intent on the part of the patient, rather than to automatic biological reactions not subject to his control. This misinterpretation lent support to the frequently heard charge of malingering, leading to futile disciplinary measures and needless cruelty. Another unfortunate by-product was the assumption that since war neuroses show the same fundamental mechanism as peacetime neuroses, knowledge of the latter was sufficient for dealing with them, whereas in fact the war neuroses are marked by unique characteristics and present special military problems. Confusion also arose from the tendency to refer to all war cases, whether traumatic or not as "war neuroses," with the result that the peculiarities of the traumatic group were in danger of being obscured.

Freud himself saw no war casualties, yet he made important theoretical suggestions concerning war neuroses, pointing out that, whereas peacetime neuroses are characterized by a conflict between the ego and the repressed forces of the libido, in war neuroses the struggle is directed against the hostile forces of the external world[5]. His distinct explanation of the traumatic neurosis derived from a consideration of the protective devices whereby the organism wards off undue stimulation. Freud concluded that in the traumatic experience these defenses are ruptured, exposing the mental apparatus to overwhelming excitation. This excitation is then discharged in anxiety attacks so urgent as to burst out even in dreams, which lose their wish-fulfilling function and can no longer insure sleep[4]. This analysis of Freud's was the first to present such a picture of traumatic damage to component parts of the mental organization, with an ensuing collapse of basic psychophysiological functions.

More recently Abram Kardiner[3], following along the new line of inquiry suggested by Freud's ideas, undertook a comprehensive study of traumatic neurosis in a veterans' hospital and published the most valuable contribution yet made to our knowledge of this illness. Kardiner found that all chronic cases, however diverse, are characterized by the following invariable features: irritability; proclivity to explosively aggressive reactions; stereotype dream life marked by endless recreations of the war scenes, frustrations or threats of annihilation; a lowering and lessening of exterofective personality functions; a change in the patient's conception of himself and of the world; a craving for compensation; and a "traumatic" war experience as the origin of all these morbid developments. Kardiner interprets pathogenic trauma as a sudden loss of all effective control over the situation, which wreaks lasting damage on the patient's adaptive capacity, his perceptive, coordinative and manipulative skills, and instills in him a feeling of helplessness. The outer world then changes for him "from a friendly to a hostile place." There follows a continual and often fruitless struggle to recapture the tools of mastery that have been lost through the trauma, and in serious cases a final acceptance of defeat.

The "Pathodynamic" Point of View

Reports from the Second World War have so far thrown little new light on this illness. Further clarification should however be facilitated by the fact that we have gradually freed ourselves of the obligation to classify an illness as either "psychic" or "physical." It is now recognized that these terms characterize not the disease but the methods of the investigator, and that every illness must be explored by both psychological and physical tools, and the findings synchronized and cross-interpreted. Two languages are involved, one based on *introspection*, the other on *inspection*: the difficulty and the challenge is to use both of these for the achievement of a unified insight. Applying this principle to traumatic neurosis, we have attempted here to align both the psychological and the physiological factors of the illness into a coherent picture of its pathodynamics, as a guide in prevention and treatment. The study is based on personal observations in the last war, the resources of literature and recent insight gained from the consideration of ordinary neuroses[13].

Chronological Pathodynamics

We have divided the chronology of the disease into four periods: 1. pretraumatic, 2. traumatic, 3. early post-traumatic, and 4. late post-traumatic.

1. Pre-traumatic period

In facing the novelties and dangers of military life the soldier is provided with various psychic resources, notably his sense of duty, which is backed by his desire for self-respect and the regard of his fellow soldiers, superior officers and home relations, and heightened by the fear of punishment and disgrace. Compliance with the demands of conscience brings a sense of stature and social security. This moral force, originating as it does in the situation of the helpless child, dependent for its very survival upon the love of its parents, may be so powerful as to vastly increase the soldier's strength and endurance. His capacities may be further stimulated by an ambition, rooted in early sibling rivalry, to be distinguished and thereby achieve still greater stature. In some cases a powerful factor is the escape offered from the failures and frustrations, neurotic or otherwise, of civilian life. Feeling himself transposed as by magic into another life, the individual may become intoxicated with a determination to make good this time. The soldier is also fortified by the satisfactions contingent on his new life, the pleasures of comradeship, mass action, freedom from his usual responsibilities and so on.

However, these guards against psychological collapse are counteracted, first, by the general upheaval of the soldier's life. He has been taken away from his family, occupation and social relations, into a highly organized group imposing new goals and new forms of discipline. He is constantly subjected to unwonted strains, responsibilities and physical exertions. In actual combat he must perform the special feat of overcoming both suffering and the thought of death, and this psychological struggle takes place in an organism progressively weakened by fatigue, dirt, hunger, thirst, exposure to the elements, sexual deprivation. To understand the precise nature of the struggle and the factors determining its outcome we must take a closer view of the mental organization.

The personality function most directly involved in the struggle is *emergency control*[13]. This control concerns injury, the essence of all emergency. On the lowest personality level its key device is bodily pain, a response that comes *after* the injury. On the next or affect level the key devices are the affects of anxiety and rage, anticipatory responses to *impending* injury. The highest is the intellectual level with the devices of anxious and angry apprehension of *future* injury. These devices, which may be set in action by either mental or bodily injury, in turn elicit "riddance reflexes" as well as personality operations designed to end or forestall pain by escape from the danger zone, or to remove the threat by attack on its source. Thus we see first, that pain, anxiety, and rage, far from being isolated events in mental life, are component parts of a highly organized function, and secondly, that in spite of its complexity this function is built on the same principle as the elementary reflex. It is set in action by certain stimuli and leads through a chain of regulatory responses to the appropriate motor behavior.

In battle, where the threat of injury is both immediate and general, the whole elaborate machinery of emergency control will obviously set to work to remove the individual from danger. It produces anxiety or rage, or both, and these affects impel him either to flight or to blind attack, perhaps even on his comrades and superiors. But these impulses are in direct conflict with his sense of duty, which requires that he remain calm and attend only to his specific military tasks.

By far the most efficient technique at the soldier's disposal in resolving this conflict is completely to ignore the dangers surrounding him as though disregarding his own life, and thus stop the entire working of emergency control. Transformed from a sensitive man into an insensitive technician of war, he then interprets combat not as a continued threat of injuries but as a sequence of operational demands to be responded to by precise military performances. He is able to take this remarkable attitude because the situation touches off in the depths of his mind the eternal human illusion of one's own invulnerability and immortality. With his self-love thus powerfully protected he can afford to lose his identity in the military unit, can give himself entirely to the job in hand and may even perform deeds of heroism. In assuming this attitude he is therefore doing the greatest possible service both to his country and to himself.

In the man who cannot achieve this disregard of danger, the devices of emergency control are left wide open to the onslaught of excitatory stimulation, and unless inhibited will lead inevitably to the motor impulses of flight or mad attack. He is obliged to curb these impulses, and since this will be impossible if he permits his emergency control to throw him into a constant state of anxiety or fits of rage, he must first of all try to prevent his anxiety and rage responses from rising in spite of continual stimulation. In other words: both the motor and the affect devices of his emergency control are now undergoing at the same time severe excitatory and still more severe inhibitory stimulation. We are speaking, then, not of the mere suppression of ideas, but of an interference with the individual's affect and motor systems so profound that its psychological consequences cannot be fully understood without reference to physiological data. It is in any case clear that this ever-increasing internal tension marks a crucial point in the preparation for breakdown.

An inevitable consequence of such failure to protect his emergency control is that the soldier becomes re-established as an individual, as against an integrated part of the military unit. His self-preoccupation thus lessens his military efficiency and by "psychic contagion" may affect that of his comrades as well.

The case histories and descriptions drawn from the last war by M. Culpin and others corroborate this theoretical reconstruction[10].

2. Traumatic period

In most cases the traumatic event acts only as the last straw. A variety of harassing experiences can serve this purpose. The story most commonly told by patients from the last war was of being buried or blown over by a shell and losing consciousness for some time, and it is unquestionable that some cases did involve a neuro-circulatory breakdown with loss of consciousness. The particular content of the critical incident often colored the ensuing symptomatology. However, as these incidents did not always involve a physical impact, it is clear that such impact could have had no specific role in the formation of the psychological trauma. We may therefore concentrate on the psychic factors responsible for the psychic trauma.

According to Kardiner's convincing analysis, psychic trauma is an abrupt and transitory stoppage in the individual's efficient personality operations, resulting in inability to meet the demands made on the personality by a new situation. This psychological reaction does occasionally appear in the wake of physical injury. More typical instances would be an hysterical fainting spell or paralyzing fright, or even the momentary mental paralysis of an incident of trivial embarrassment. The healthy reaction to an experience of the latter type is to make almost automatically immediate efforts to repair the failure. The example of the hysteric, however, introduces the element of desire to be overwhelmed by the situation so as to avoid coping with it, and also the tendency to shun that situation from then on. In this respect the soldier is in a similar situation. In incapacitation he finds relief from the mounting tension of his inhibited affects and motor impulses, especially if his disability can be made to last for the duration. The unconscious operations of his emergency control can therefore do nothing better at this juncture than to inhibit the very forces that would otherwise bring recovery, and thereby perpetuate the operational failure. Emergency control, whose further workings we shall discuss in relation to symptomatology, is thus using the "trauma" as a means of fulfilling its original purpose of removing the man from danger. It cannot be over-stressed that this inhibition of repair is an unconscious anxiety mechanism; while it is in force, the patient is unable to rid himself of a sense of helplessness and discouragement.

3. Early post-traumatic period

Whether or not the breakdown is followed by a brief period of apathy or stupor, there soon evolves a state of general excitement punctuated by outbursts of anxiety. A characteristic of some cases is that these attacks occur only in sleep, in the form of terrifying dreams accompanied by violent bodily expressions such as shouting and attempts to run. In general, the less the discharge of anxiety in the waking state, the greater the likelihood of there appearing shortly disturbances of the personality functions, concerned with exploring, planning and effecting, also of the physiological organ functions. Almost any function may be affected over the entire range of voluntary and autonomic control. It would be both needless and difficult to establish the statistical distribution of these various disorders; among the cases that I saw during the last war, the functions most commonly impaired were those of the extremities. The patient trembled from head to foot, was unable to stand or walk and could perform the simplest manipulative tasks only with great difficulty. In other cases there was paralysis of limbs, loss of voice, speech, vision, or hearing; psychic contagion was obviously a determining factor. Such symptoms were accompanied by marked sensitiveness, irritability, eruptions of rage, loss of sexual potency, and self-pampering behavior. In our special hospital we saw no cases involving internal organs such as peptic ulcers for these were kept in the medical wards, the neurotic aspect of their illness being still undiscovered at that time.

To understand the fundamental psychodynamics of this symptomatology we have only to remember the previous strain on both the affect and the outward executive apparatuses of emergency control. After the breakdown, the personality relaxes its efforts to quash the operations of emergency control, and from deadlock these systems now swing into a phase of overactivity. This shift calls for neuro-physiological explanation. Its psychological results are the resurgence of anxiety and rage and the impulses to act accordingly. Though the individual again tries to inhibit both the affects and the impulses, they remain active on the level of unconscious integration and break through in the form of symptoms.

The first unconscious idea inspired by anxiety is to offer glaring proof of the soldier's disability. This need gives rise to incoherent behavior fragments of symbolic value. "Look! I cannot stand, I cannot walk, I cannot use my hands, or see, or hear, or speak!" Naturally such language could be effective only as long as it remained incomprehensible to both patient and doctor and could be written down simply as enigmatic manifestations of an illness. Now that psychoanalytic knowledge has entered into common parlance, it is safe to predict that in the present war we shall see a decrease in this type of functional disturbance, and that the over-stimulated affects will instead express themselves through the internal organs, precipitating such illnesses as peptic ulcer and neurocirculatory asthenia. But these more serious interferences with physiological functions, though not hysterical in character, will serve the same purpose of bearing witness to the soldier's incapacitation. "Look! I cannot digest food; my heart is too weak to stand the strain." This psychological withdrawal of symptomatology from the outside to the inside of the body, i.e., the replacement of "hysterical" by "psycho-somatic" disorders, is thus a cultural phenomenon, already observed in peacetime practice.

Anxiety also perpetuates itself by creating the unconscious illusion that the patient is still in the thick of his critical experience. Thus he will have attacks of the same type of paresthesia of the legs that he had while standing for hours in the water, or reproduce some gesture of the arms by which he tried to defend himself against an exploding shell. Again he is quite unaware of the meaning of his symptoms.

The sex function, though not directly related to the emergency, has been particularly vulnerable to anxiety since childhood and cannot fail to be affected by this new upheaval; unconscious infantile fears of sexual incapacitation (loss of the genital organ) are now revived and cause an impairment of sexual potency.

Finally, as in any aberration of personality, there is the problem of self-esteem. Driven by anxiety into a state of submission, the patient tends to blame himself for his failure and runs the risk of serious depression. This situation in turn gives rise to a desire to retrieve his former stature, and to a group of symptoms that must be considered as efforts to this end.

The most primitive of these is self-centered and self-pampering behavior; like a small child, he now tries to prove his stature by showering affection on himself and so tacitly inviting his environment to do likewise. Another effort, self-assertive in character, springs from his pent-up rage, manifesting itself in irascibility, tantrums and general resentment which serves to shift the blame from himself to others; officers, doctors, relatives, and society at large.

This wide array of disturbances created by the overactive state of emergency control finds its central psychological representation in the dread of being exposed to further injury or death. The vague idea of future harm takes shape in the patient's mind as the hurt already suffered, and thus his dread of injury becomes a dread of the recurrence of that particular experience. This may be termed the traumatophobic factor in the illness.

4. Late post-traumatic period

After the war, the overactive components of emergency control that were constantly reinforced while the war was on may gradually calm down, and the symptomatology sustained by them will then disappear. However if the traumatophobic factor is too strong, the patient's fear of a recurrence of his injury will continue to dominate him and will prevent his resuming the activities of civilian life. The trauma, originally representative of the threats of war, now comes to stand for all prospective dangers. The whole psychology encountered in this late period of the illness may be summed up in one phrase: the personality under traumatophobic regime. As the human being does always in a state of helplessness, the patient now reverts to the technique of the infant and reaches out automatically for support. He wishes to be treated with the respect due to his sacrifice and to be compensated for the wrecking of his life. Ridden by his fear, he retreats more and more from the risks involved in any enterprise or pleasure, and dedicates himself to protection against imaginary menaces. Since it is precisely the traumatophobic factor that effects the transformation of this neurosis from a fear of war in particular to a fear of the responsibilities of life in general, the term most apt for this illness is *traumatophobia*. The fact that it carries the prospect of such far-reaching deterioration makes it one of the most malignant of war neuroses.

DIFFERENTIATION FROM OTHER NEUROSES

The symptoms of this illness are caused by an acute disturbance of emergency control and are psychologically organized around the traumatophobic factor. This simple characteristic differentiates traumatophobia both from the less highly organized war neuroses and from the neuroses of peacetime. However the clinical pictures produced by psychoneuroses invariably overlap and often interchange, so that we must not be tempted to deal with them as "entities" exactly marked off one from another. Many chronic peacetime neuroses, involving resignation to an attitude of submission, show developments that strikingly resemble those in chronic traumatophobias.

PREVENTION AND TREATMENT

The best method of prevention would be of course to eliminate potential traumatophobics beforehand, but this is unfortunately out of the question. We can weed out men obviously unfit for service because of psychosis or severe psychoneurosis, but the records show that victims of tramautophobia have often been excellent soldiers with an impeccable history of mental and physical health. These could be detected in advance only if some latent factor in the personality predisposed them to this type of breakdown. If our analysis is correct the decisive factor in the pathodynamics of the illness is the inhibition of "spontaneous" repair, that is, a shift from the activistic, enterprising attitude toward life to one of retreat, inertia and avoidance. Most, if not all, human beings contain the possibility of such a development, and it would be fruitless to try to tell beforehand how much strain they can stand before withdrawing to this last line of defense. It is therefore meaningless to speak of a special predisposition to traumatophobia.

This makes it all the more essential that psychiatrists should be at hand to give preventive treatment at every developmental stage of the illness. The most auspicious time for this treatment is at the first signs of approaching breakdown. After the collapse has occurred, the worst phases of the illness may still be avoided by the application of preventive treatment during the state of apathy or stupor, i.e., before the affect and motor systems swing into an over-active state. If this last chance of prevention is lost and the disease becomes fully developed, treatment should be applied as early as possible.

During the last war hypno-catharsis, a method originated by Breuer and Freud some fifty years ago, was used by Ernst Simmel and others for the treatment of acute cases, Simmel even providing the soldiers with a dummy on which to vent their aggression[5, 14]. Though momentarily successful, this method was not enough to forestall a relapse. However, there is reason to believe that if divorced from its underlying presupposition, which though brilliant at the time is no longer viable, its technique could be improved and made to yield much better results. In our hospital we resorted to the still older method of Charcot, re-introduced by Victor E. Gonda. Mild faradic current, producing neither unconsciousness nor convulsions, was used as the vehicle of suggestive influence. After the creation of a Lourdes-like atmosphere, actual treatment took no more than a minute. It was always successful and always followed by a relapse. This method too could be made helpful by a complete overhauling of its psychotherapeutic essentials. Such means however are incidental to the basic principle on which treatment in all stages must rest.

We can do no more than indicate the broadest outlines of this principle, as deduced from our analysis of the illness. The ideal result would be to induce the soldier to adopt the attitude described above as a shutting off of emergency control, an attitude taken spontaneously by his more fortunate companions. To achieve this we have first to undo the damage he has incurred by first exposing his emergency control to a barrage of stimulation, and then trying in vain to suppress the ensuing affect and motor impulses of this control. Our first target is therefore his horrifying memories of the war, particularly of the culminating event if he has already passed the stage of breakdown. These for the most part have been automatically repressed because of their alarming effect; while awake the patient is now relatively safe from outbursts of anxiety and rage, and is instead in dread of a return of these memories. In sleep, when the repression is relaxed, they do return, producing spectacular dreams of agitation and terror. In cathartic treatment repression is similarly relaxed, with resulting outbursts of anxiety and rage; the inevitability of relapse after such treatment proves however that therapy cannot rest merely in the discharge of "strangulated affect." In my opinion the decisive factor to be introduced into the therapeutic procedure is the de-sensitization of the patient to all memories of the war, whether repressed or not. In other words: his war memories must be stripped of their power to perturb him again and again, and be turned instead into a source of repeated pride and satisfaction. Even if it be overdone, he must be brought to see the war as an adventure as well as a high collective enterprise, and himself as an object of envy to those not engaged in it. He must be made to think, not of his failure but of his endurance, so that he can say to himself: "What a guy you are. You went through all that and nothing happened to you, and the chances are that nothing will." An important aid in this process will be the use of medication to subdue the over-active affect and motor systems of emergency control. A further requirement is to set free the inhibited forces of repair and thereby restore the patient's lost ability to take pleasure in spontaneous activity and to enjoy initiative and enterprise of whatever kind. In short, the job in its essentials is to deflate his fears and inflate and reactivate his ego.

Needless to say, it would be useless if not detrimental to preach or prescribe such an attitude. It must be instilled into him by intricate means and success or failure will depend on the instruments used and the skill with which they are handled. Details of the therapeutic technique best suited to the various stages of the illness will have to be worked out through experience with the cases we must be prepared to see in the present war.

REFERENCES

[1] BRUN, R. (ZÜRICH): Die Neurosen nach Schädeltraumen. *Schweiz. Arch. Neurol. Psychiat.*, *41:* 269, 1938.

[2] DUNN, WILLIAM H.: War neuroses. *Psychol. Bull.*, *38:* 497, 1941.

[3] FETTERMAN, J.: Traumatic neuroses. *J. A. M. A.*, *91:* 315, 1928.

[4] FREUD, SIGMUND: *Beyond the pleasure principle.* International Psycho-Analytical Press, London and Vienna, 1922.

[5] FREUD, SIGMUND, FERENCZI, S., ABRAHAM, KARL, SIMMEL, ERNST, AND JONES, ERNEST: *Psychoanalysis and the war neuroses.* International Psycho-Analytical Press, London and New York, 1921.

[6] GILLESPIE, R. D.: *Psychological effects of war, on citizen and soldier.* New York, Norton, 1942.

[7] GOLDSTEIN, KURT: *The organism.* New York, American Book Company, 1939.

[8] KARDINER, ABRAM: *The traumatic neuroses of war.* Psychosom. Med. Monograph II–III, also New York, Paul Hoeber, 1941.

[9] MASKIN, MEYER: Psychodynamic aspects of the war neuroses, a survey of the literature. *Psychiatry, 4:* 97, 1941.

[10] MILLER, EMANUAL, AND OTHERS: *The neuroses in war.* London and New York, Macmillan, 1940.

[11] MYERS, CHARLES S.: *Shell shock in France 1914–1918.* Cambridge, University Press, 1940.

[12] OBERHOLZER, E.: Zur Differentialdiagnose psychischer Folgezustände nach Schä-

deltraumen mittels des Rohrschachschen Formdeutversuchs. *Z. ges. Neurol. Psychiat., 136:* 596, 1931.

[13] RADO, SANDOR: Developments in the psychoanalytic conception and treatment of the neuroses. *Psychoanal. Quart., 8:* 427, 1939.

[14] SIMMEL, ERNST: *Kriegsneurosen und "Psychisches Trauma."* Leipzig and Munich, Otto Nemnich, 1918.

[15] The Medical Department of the United States Army in the World War, Volume X, *Neuropsychiatry.* Government Printing Office, Washington, 1929.

Development of
Adaptational
Psychodynamics

Psychodynamics as a Basic Science*

The outstanding event in psychiatry is the rise to prominence of psychoanalysis. If World War I put psychoanalysis on the map, World War II demonstrated its indispensability. Despite this success, there is still much confusion about the nature of psychoanalysis and its relation to the other branches of knowledge. One psychologist, who may serve as an extreme example, recently denounced psychoanalysis as demonology and the practice of exorcism in modern guise.

To determine the scientific function of psychoanalysis we must consider the human individual as the object of medical inquiry.

Before psychoanalysis existed, medicine was limited to the *public* aspect of the organism; it used only physical methods, based on inspection. The psychoanalytic method rests on reported introspection; it brings the *private* aspect of life into the scope of medicine. Furthermore, the other methods of medicine are geared to examine the component parts of the organism, its cells, tissues, organs, and organ systems. They yield no more information on the behavior of the whole than can be surmised from the knowledge of the parts. Psychoanalysis is the only method by which medicine can reach the whole individual on the behavior level. This may sound surprising. As an integrated whole, the human organism is almost completely controlled by the central nervous system, preeminently the cerebral cortex. Then why is not neurophysiology the logical instrument for exploring human behavior?

Brief reflection shows that neurophysiology is a necessary but not a sufficient means to this end. The cortex in action is so completely unique in the universe that it is literally beyond comparison. It has what one may call *inward self-expression*, known to us directly in our conscious state. This private feature of the cortex in action, called psyche or mind, dominates behavior, because it *represents* to us the whole of reality. (To the solipsistic philosopher, *his* mind *is* the whole of reality.) Neurophysiology has no tools with which to grasp this inward self-expression of the cortex; it meets behavior on the physiological, not on the decisive psychological, level which is operationally defined by investigative methods of its own.

---

* Read before the twenty-third annual meeting of the American Orthopsychiatric Association, in New York, February 15, 1946, as part of a symposium on *Principles of Training: The Preparation of Psychiatrists for Practice, Teaching and Research*. First published in *American Journal of Orthopsychiatry, 16:* 405–409, 1946.

Nothing would aid our psychological analysis more than disclosure of the cortical mechanisms of behavior, but neurological work on this task is still in the preliminary stage. The present aim of neurophysiologists is to discover the functional design of the cortex. Almost as if it were a mosaic, they remove surgically or otherwise smaller or larger portions in order to find out, by way of exclusion, the contribution each portion makes toward the total function of the cortex. Brilliant work though this is, the major goal, that of tackling the performance of the cortex in its systemic integrity, is in the distant future. This is why one of our foremost experts, E. D. Adrian, cautioned us to expect but little understanding of human behavior from neurophysiology. The only promise he saw fit to make was that if we could breed a man with a brain twice its present size, such a creature would be unfathomably more intelligent than we are. Neurophysiology cannot explain human behavior. Psychoanalysis can.

Psychodynamics is the name for the theory which brings order into psychoanalytic observation and into the material of data ascertained by such observation. Psychodynamics represents the organized body of psychoanalytic findings, complemented by results obtained through other methods of research. Because of its singular value for the understanding of human behavior, psychodynamics must take its place in medicine as a basic science. Had we not been slow in bringing psychodynamics up-to-date, this might have happened long before.

When Freud began his work, the organism was considered an aggregate of cells, an object for dissection. Freud lost little by turning his back on medicine and developing theories of his own, founded on motivation. The idea of motive forces, like all dynamic thought, derives from the ancient animistic or demonic pattern. There is no alternative to this pattern; we cannot escape ourselves. Some three hundred years ago, physics was revitalized by a closely related proposition. This was to observe the *action* of force, shifting the emphasis from the old question "Why" to the new question "How." This in turn called for empirical investigation and, more than anything else, made physics the science it is today. Freud was headed in the right direction. He searched for the action of motive forces, for psychological mechanisms, which supply an answer to the question "How." This spirit imbued his entire early period (1890–1905), a period marked by the discovery of the lasting influence of infantile patterns and climaxing in his *Interpretation of Dreams* (1900), which he often referred to as his best.

Later Freud turned from the "How" back to the "Why." He then identified motive forces with the forces of instincts, and perfected his monumental *Theory of Instincts* ("Libido:" 1905–1919; "Eros and Death:" 1920–1939), which became the all-absorbing philosophical interest of his life.

In his own evaluation of this theory, Freud was divided against himself.

In a disarmingly self-critical vein he wrote (1933): "The theory of instincts is, as it were, our mythology. The instincts are mythical beings, superb in their indefiniteness." At the same time he clung to this myth with increasing tenacity. Freud accumulated an astounding amount of empirical knowledge. This knowledge, however, he systematized exclusively in terms of his theory of instincts. The influence of this theory was overwhelming. In psychoanalytic thinking, the "Why" swallowed the "How" almost completely.

Psychodynamics now has to revert to the early Freud, to his model investigations of the "How." To speculate on the nature and origin of instincts is the prerogative of the metaphysician who specializes in matters beyond the reach of scientific method. The investigator views the motive forces of behavior in the context of the operating organism in relation to its parts, environment, and history; his task, therefore, is to discover the mechanisms by which these forces operate. Self-sufficient interpretation thus must yield to an unbiased search for significant correlations and sequences. In no other way can psychodynamics guide the experimental analysis of animal behavior and obtain the full benefit of this promising new technique.

In the last fifteen or twenty years a development, inspired by the philosophy of Herbert Spencer, began with the neurological work of Hughlings Jackson, and continued with the psychobiological teachings of Adolph Meyer. It had a new start in animal biology and was consolidated through the pioneering methodological inquiry of J. H. Woodger. Its status was recently reviewed in a symposium of the University of Chicago (*Levels of Integration in Biological and Social Systems*, 1942). The new theory combines traditional analysis into component parts with analysis of relations, thus clarifying the notion of organization. It envisages hierarchic levels of integration, with emergent entities and laws on each superposed level. Its scope includes the cultural aspect of life.

This theory is the new biological foundation upon which to rebuild the structure of psychodynamics, with the point of view of adaptation and survival as the cornerstone, and W. B. Cannon's concept of emergency function as one of the main pillars. Very few workers are engaged in this resystematization of psychodynamics, and their work is carried out against stiff resistance. The fear prevails that unless the shafts of the Freudian mines are preserved untouched, the insights of psychoanalysis will "lose in depth." However, the history of science teaches a different lesson: by improving our means of reality testing, we can lose nothing but our illusions.

Every student of medicine should receive instruction in the elements of psychodynamics. For the psychodynamic factor, that is, the behavior of the whole, is a determinant in every disease and therapy, regardless of the organ system primarily affected. This is increasingly apparent in emotional behavior. Social life, the psychological impact of one individual upon the other, produces emotional stresses and strains that can interfere with healthy function in any part of the organism. Therefore, in time, every department of medicine will have to be behavior-conscious or, according to the current slogan, psychosomatic.

Physicians who plan to specialize in psychiatry should be expected to complete a course of graduate training in psychiatry. Such training should begin immediately after internship and should require about three years of full-time work. The curriculum should center around the study of psychodynamics. A basic course in the detailed psychodynamics of healthy, neurotic, and psychotic behavior should be followed by a course in the psychoanalytic techniques of investigation and treatment, including the reconstructive and briefer methods. This theoretical instruction should be closely allied with practical work on clinical material. From the outset, the student should have extensive contact with a variety of cases, ambulatory and hospitalized, he should participate in demonstrations and discussions and, under close supervision, carry out treatment of every type. Training based largely on the study of records was an expedient of psychoanalysis in exile, and can no longer be accepted as adequate.

The curriculum should include courses in the psychodynamics of growth and development, comparative analysis of cultures, experimental analysis of animal behavior, psycho-physiology, the psychodynamic aspect of bodily functions in health and disease (psychosomatics), related chapters of neurophysiology and neuropathology, and somatic methods of treatment and care employed in a modern psychiatric clinic. The graduate residency training offered by the new Psychoanalytic Clinic of Columbia University is a step toward the realization of this program.

In our view, psychoanalysis is no sub-specialty of psychiatry; it is an integral part of psychiatry itself. The physician specializing in psychiatry should be given the opportunity to absorb all available knowledge on the psyche, and the main body of this knowledge is psychodynamics and the techniques of psychoanalysis. The first step toward accomplishing this goal is to recognize that it is not unattainable; the second, to give preference to students who prepare to take up teaching and research in psychiatry as a career. The past separation of psychoanalysis from psychiatry was artificial and scientifically harmful to both. The sooner this unnatural condition disappears the better.

So far, no mention has been made of a complication in the study of psychodynamics. Psychodynamics requires a personal preparation by each student: he must first undergo a personal psychoanalysis. If this requirement is unique, so is psychodynamics as a science. The other sciences deal with things that can be put on display and pointed out. This cannot be done with things of the mind. When you say you are happy or afraid, I can understand what you mean only because on occasion I have felt this way myself and can recognize the identity. Without my own experience, I could not understand—and you could not explain—what you mean by happy and afraid. Quite unlike physical language, based on common sight, the language of our private worlds is based on identifiable insight. The student can learn what this psychological language refers to only through a psychological study of himself. Psychoanalysis penetrates into the unconscious reaches of the mind and increases greatly the range of inner awareness. The student must explore thoroughly this psychoanalytic range in himself, before he can venture to explore it in others. In his personal analysis, he is expected to improve his own adaptive efficiency and achieve a comparative understanding of himself as an individual and as a product of a given period and culture. The requirement that he undergo psychoanalysis is inescapable.

Psychodynamics will have to be taught to many people who have not been psychoanalyzed. In such cases, instruction should go only to the boundaries within which the unanalyzed mind can be made to feel at home. From psychodynamic instruction which he cannot assimilate, one is likely to emerge more confused than enlightened.

Under ideal conditions, every medical student would be psychoanalyzed, preferably during his (pre-medical) college years. But even today, to be psychoanalyzed is a *must* for those who plan to specialize in psychiatry.

Psychoanalytic therapy remains the fountainhead of psychodynamic knowledge, especially if comparative research is done on larger groups with the proper controls. If he has the proper command of the scientific method, the psychiatrist here has unrivalled investigative opportunities. This qualification is an art, best acquired by apprenticeship at such places of learning as have established it as a tradition.

Though psychodynamics is an offspring of medical inquiry, its realm of application by far exceeds the province of medicine. It includes all social sciences and services concerned with human relationships. Psychological techniques of some kind are used in all of these scientific and practical pursuits. Each field has developed techniques of its own, based, as a rule, on common sense plus a generous sprinkling of superstition. These techniques could be immeasurably improved by the addition of sound psychodynamic information. It is the psychiatrist's responsibility to act as teacher and advisor to each of these groups, supplying them with needed psychodynamic knowledge. Our mutual interchange with social workers is a model in this respect. Inroads have been made in maternal care, pastoral care, education, anthropology, sociology, criminology, industrial relations, etc.

Let us make no mistake, our opportunities are more impressive than our actual state of knowledge. To fulfill our obligations here as well as in medicine we must concentrate on fundamental research in psychodynamics and make this science the pivotal study in the training of psychiatrists.

Graduate Residency Training in Psychoanalytic Medicine*

I. THE HISTORY OF TRAINING IN PSYCHOANALYSIS

Upon his return from Paris in 1886, young Dr. Freud appeared before the Viennese Society of Physicians to report on his experience under the Master, Charcot, whom he had seen probe the puzzles of hysteria with the technique of hypnosis. In those days, the vanguard of the profession in Vienna believed in pathological anatomy; they disliked hysteria and thoroughly distrusted hypnosis. And so they resented seeing young Dr. Freud, a product of their own training and a promising neurologist, show himself, by their standards, to have no sense of scientific discrimination. And when Freud tried to discuss the incidence of hysteria in male patients, their indignation over such nonsense exploded in open censure.

This unfriendly reception destroyed Freud's standing as a *Privatdozent* at the medical school and forced him into scientific isolation. Save for his brief but decisive collaboration with Dr. Joseph Breuer, Freud's isolation lasted for nearly two decades. During the second half of this period, from 1895 to 1905, he published his fundamental papers on psychoanalysis. But the all-powerful academic circles of the Continent dismissed his work as concerned exclusively with such undignified matters as dreams and sex. And so, in those years of awe-inspiring productivity, Freud failed to attract a single student[1, 2].

The first physician to become a pupil of Freud's came to him as a psycho-analytic patient. From 1905 on, pupils began to arrive. Freud advised them to read his publications and learn the psychoanalytic technique by analyzing their own dreams. Such preparations admitted them to the private discussion group which gradually sprang up around him. This group became the nucleus of the International Psychoanalytic Association, organized in 1908 upon the initiative of the late Dr. Sandor Ferenczi of Budapest. Insofar as the personal analysis of healthy pupils was concerned, Freud wavered for quite a time, reiterating in 1914 his original position[1, 3, 4].

In the first World War, the remarkable contributions of psychoanalysis

* Read at the 103d annual meeting of The American Psychiatric Association, New York, N. Y., May 19–23, 1947. First published in *American Journal of Psychiatry*, *105:* 111–115, 1948.

173

to the understanding of the war neuroses aroused the scientific interest of many physicians. After the war they wanted to learn more about psychoanalysis. The experience of those years eventually convinced Freud and his closest pupils of the inadequacy of the early method of training. As a consequence, they established the rule, advocated at Zürich from the outset, that physicians desiring to practice psychoanalysis must first undergo psychoanalysis themselves[3]. Today, almost 30 years later, one may say that they appear to have used sound judgment in making this decision. To set it apart from the therapeutic analysis of patients, the personal analysis of students was called *Lehranalyse*—didactic analysis.

The first systematic course of training in psychoanalysis was organized in the early twenties at the Berlin Psychoanalytic Institute. This was the work of the late Dr. Max Eitingon, then president of the Berlin Institute; the late Dr. Karl Abraham, then president of the Berlin Psychoanalytic Society; the late Dr. Hanns Sachs; and Drs. Franz Alexander, Carl Müller Braunschweig, Karen Horney, Ernst Simmel, and myself, constituting the first faculty of the Institute[6].

The curriculum was divided into 3 parts: didactic analysis, theoretical instruction, and practical work. Didactic analysis was considered the very foundation of training. Theoretical instruction comprised the presentation of the subject matter in a system of courses, supported by an extensive reading of Freud's own writings. Practical work comprised the psychoanalytic treatment of two patients under supervision and the discussion of therapeutic problems in technical and case seminars.

Though the Berlin Institute maintained a small outpatient clinic, in the main it functioned as a night school. Completion of the entire course of training required 3 to 4 years. The Berlin Institute was very successful and attracted students from many lands. Freud was delighted with this Berlin development. In 1924, after Dr. Otto Rank's resignation, he appointed me editor of the two official journals of psychoanalysis—*Internationale Zeitschrift für Psychoanalyse*, and *Imago, Zeitschrift für Anwendung der Psychoanalyse auf die Natur und Geisteswissenschaften*—of which he himself was the director, thereby transferring the editorial office from Vienna to Berlin[5]. The new training centers that were opened subsequently in Budapest, London, Paris, and Vienna adopted the Berlin curriculum.

The first psychoanalytic institute in the United States was brought into being in 1931 in New York under the leadership of Dr. A. A. Brill and with the executive assistance of the late Dr. Monroe A. Meyer. Dr. Brill honored me with an invitation to organize the New York Institute on the Berlin model. This task was fulfilled over a period of years, in close collaboration with Dr. Abram Kardiner, first chairman of the Institute's educational committee, Dr. Bertram D. Lewin, president of the Institute after Dr.

Brill's retirement, and with the help of the late Dr. Dorian A. Feigenbaum, and Drs. George E. Daniels, Lawrence S. Kubie, David M. Levy, Sandor Lorand, Adolph Stern, and many other devoted members of the Institute, we added an innovation to the Berlin curriculum, making one year of intramural psychiatric experience a requisite of admission to psychoanalytic training[7]. Training centers that were opened later in Chicago, Boston, Washington-Baltimore, Topeka, and elsewhere followed closely the Berlin-New York curriculum but, with the exception of Chicago and Topeka, they had no outpatient clinics.

In 1938, the American Psychoanalytic Association adopted the Berlin-New York curriculum as its minimal standard of training. This was due chiefly to the efforts of Dr. Lawrence S. Kubie, then secretary of the Association, and Drs. Franz Alexander, Leo H. Bartemeier, George E. Daniels, Thomas M. French, Lewis B. Hill, M. Ralph Kaufman, Bertram D. Lewin, Karl A. Menninger, LeRoy M. A. Maeder, myself and others.

With the devastation of Europe in World War II, the initiative in psychoanalytic training and research shifted to the United States. In this country, psychoanalysis encountered less prejudice and developed more rapidly than in the old scientific centers of Europe. Though in some respects this unbroken progress surpassed Freud's own expectations, nonetheless it stopped short of his long-cherished hope that one day the medical schools would open their doors to psychoanalysis. Curiously enough, this almost happened in the early days. In 1906, Professor Eugen Bleuler and his associate Dr. C. G. Jung introduced psychoanalysis at the Zürich-Burghölzli Psychiatric Clinic. The beginnings of this experiment were so encouraging that Freud and his pupils elected Jung first president of the newly organized International Psychoanalytic Association and made him editor of the new *Jahrbuch*—Archives of Psychoanalysis. At that time everyone was persuaded that the Zürich-Burghölzli Clinic would become the first academic homestead of psychoanalysis. However, the secession of Jung in 1913 put an end to this dream.

Our own training institutes saved the art and science of psychoanalysis but they could offer no full compensation for its exclusion from the medical schools. More and more, this exclusion proved harmful to both sides.

II. The Establishment of the Psychoanalytic Clinic for Training and Research at Columbia University

Keenly aware of this state of affairs, Dr. Nolan D. C. Lewis, professor of psychiatry at Columbia University, and director of the New York State Psychiatric Institute and Hospital, himself a member of long standing in the American Psychoanalytic Association, evolved a comprehensive project for training in psychoanalysis. This project received added impetus from the far-sighted policy of Dr. Willard C. Rappleye, dean of the College of Physicians and Surgeons of the university. Dean Rappleye gave the proposal its final shape, providing for the complete integration of psychoanalytic training into the elaborate system of graduate medical education at the college. Acting on this proposal, in the autumn of 1944, the university established the Psychoanalytic Clinic for Training and Research as a part of the department of psychiatry.

The College of Physicians and Surgeons was well prepared to assume this responsibility. For a decade or more, Dr. Lewis, Dr. George E. Daniels, and others had infused undergraduate teaching in psychiatry with psychoanalytic principles; and in the postgraduate program of the college, year after year, Dr. Brill gave orientation courses in psychoanalysis. With the establishment of the new clinic, Drs. Daniels, Kardiner, Levy, and I were given the unique opportunity to work out in detail and put into operation, under the supervision of Dr. Lewis, a graduate psychoanalytic curriculum. In this task we were assisted by Drs. Nathan W. Ackerman, Robert C. Bak, and Viola W. Bernard, who soon joined our staff.

The psychoanalytic clinic has a therapeutic service for outpatients located in the clinic itself; therapeutic services for psychiatric inpatients, psychosomatic patients, and children, located in the New York State Psychiatric Institute and Hospital, the Vanderbilt Clinic, and the Babies Hospital; and has collaborative arrangements with basic science laboratories of the university, with the Manhattan State Hospital, and other hospitals.

The Columbia plan of graduate residency training in psychoanalytic medicine, based on these facilities, and now in operation for 3 academic years, may be outlined as follows:

Training requires 3 years of full-time graduate work. During the first and second years, the student's time is divided between work at the psychoanalytic clinic and work in a collaborating hospital. During the third year, the student's full time is spent in the psychoanalytic clinic. Through this arrangement, the Columbia plan combines complete training in psychoanalytic medicine, that is, in psychoanalysis and psychosomatics, with training in intramural psychiatry and in the related basic sciences.

This combined course of training is open to qualified physicians who have served one year of internship, satisfied the standards of the clinic with respect to scholastic attainment, integrity, and psychological aptitude, and completed their preparation for the course by having undergone psychoanalysis themselves, under a psychoanalyst accredited by the clinic. This conception of the student's personal analysis as an indispensable prerequisite, rather than a phase of graduate training, has many obvious advantages. However, as a purely transitional measure, students are temporarily being allowed to fulfill this requirement during the course of graduate training.

In his personal analysis, the student undertakes a penetrating psychological study of himself. He is expected to explore resolutely and thoroughly the unconscious reaches of his mind, trace his development back to the formative experiences of his childhood, and arrive at a better knowledge and realistic appraisal of himself as an individual and as a product of a given period and culture. He is expected to overcome his psychological difficulties, increase his self-direction and intellectual independence, and acquire a more mature outlook upon life.

It is not a function of personal analysis to train the student in psychoanalytic theory or technique. That is the function of his classroom and clinical work.

The program of theoretical instruction features psychodynamics as a basic science of human behavior. Though this science utilizes auxiliary methods, its solid mass derives from psychoanalytic inquiry. The first course in the program is a historical review of Freud's own writings. A full-year course in the psychodynamics of adapted and disordered (neurotic, psychopathic, psychotic) behavior includes the new material accumulated in recent decades through the general advance of science and thus undertakes the pressing task of currently revising and resystematizing the subject from the point of view of Freud's own objectives[8, 9]. Another full-year course is devoted to the far-flung field of psychosomatics, dealing with significant interrelations between behavior of the whole organism and disease processes in its component parts. One half-year course presents the investigative, and another half-year course the therapeutic techniques of psychoanalysis, graded according to duration, intensity, and point of attack of the therapeutic effort. Further courses deal with the psychodynamics of growth and development, treatment of children, experimental analysis of animal behavior, comparative analysis of cultures, methodology, and current literature.

Under the Columbia plan, the students receive psychoanalytic clinical instruction from the beginning parallel with the theoretical program. This is, indeed, one of the distinctive characteristics of the plan. Throughout the first year, in weekly demonstrations, patients are presented in person before the class. The purpose of these demonstrations is to introduce the students to the art of psychoanalytic observation and examination, and acquaint them with the clinical variety of cases by unfolding before them, in a comparative manner, the gross psychodynamics of every case. During the second and third years, the students engage in the psychoanalytic treatment of patients, under close supervision. They work with inpatients, outpatients, psychosomatic patients, and children, using full-fledged psychoanalytic technique and also lesser methods of limited scope. Throughout these years, in weekly clinical conferences, patients under treatment are presented in person for the discussion of the minute psychodynamics and of the technical problems of treatment. In addition, each student has week-by-week individual supervisory sessions and section supervision.

During the first 2 years, 3 mornings of the week are devoted to the psychoanalytic program. During the rest of the time, throughout these 2 years, the students work with ward patients in a collaborating psychiatric hospital.

To increase the value of this combined clinical experience still further, a supplementary program of theoretical courses was organized with the collaboration of Drs. Armando Ferraro, Franz J. Kallmann, and Paul H. Hoch of the department of psychiatry; Dr. Heinrich B. Waelsch of the department of biochemistry; and Dr. Harry Grundfest of the department of neurology. At the start of residency work in intramural psychiatry, a brief introductory course familiarizes the student with the principles and techniques of psychiatric examination. This is followed by a full-year course on the pathology of the psychoses and the techniques of intramural therapy, and by a course on neuropathology for psychiatrists. A full-year basic science course, devised for the needs of psychiatrists, combines selected chapters of genetics, general and chemical neurophysiology.

When students fulfill the requirements and pass a final examination, they receive a "Certificate of Training in Psychoanalytic Medicine" from Columbia University. Students who engage in original investigative work, submit a dissertation, and pass a supplementary examination in the related basic sciences receive in addition the advanced degree of Doctor of Medical Science from the university.

The Psychoanalytic Clinic for Training and Research is in the process of expansion. At present, it has a staff of 21 psychoanalysts to take charge of the personal analysis of students, and it has more competent applicants seeking training than it can accommodate.

It is hoped that, with the increasing recognition of psychodynamics as the basic science of psychiatry, other medical schools will undertake similar developments.

REFERENCES

[1] FREUD, S.: On the history of the psychoanalytic movement. *Collected Papers, 1.* London, Hogarth, 1924.
[2] ——: *Autobiography.* New York, Norton, 1935.

[3] ———: Recommendations for physicians on the psychoanalytic method of treatment. *Collected Papers, 2:* 329. London, Hogarth Press, 1924.

[4] ———: *General Introduction to Psychoanalysis.* New York, 1935.

[5] ———: Mitteilung des Herausgebers (Announcement by the Director). *Internat. Ztschr. f. Psychoanal., 10:* 273, 1924.

[6] RADO, SANDOR (Ed.). *Zehn Jahre Berliner Psychoanalytisches Institut* (Ten Years of the Berlin Psychoanalytic Institute). Internationaler Psychoanalytischer Verlag. Vienna, 1930.

[7] ———: The Institute in relation to psychoanalytic teaching and research. The New York Psychoanalytic Institute Report for the Academic Years 1931–1934.

[8] ———: Scientific aspects of training in psychoanalysis. The New York Psychoanalytic Institute Report for the Academic Years 1934–1937.

[9] ———: Psychodynamics as a basic science. *Am. J. Orthopsychiat., 16:* 405, 1946.

[10] Columbia University Bulletin of Information, 47th Series, No. 2, January 4, 1947. Faculty of Medicine. The Psychoanalytic Clinic for Training and Research. Graduate Training for Qualified Physicians 1947–48.

Mind, Unconscious Mind, and Brain*

One may conceive of the mind as the loudspeaker of the brain. This is a crude analogy because mind is not only a loudspeaker but also its own audience. However, even a crude analogy is better than none.

Awareness and Reporting

Looking at it in this light, consciousness is our awareness of the running report produced as its inward expression by the underlying nervous activity of the brain. The latter may be called the *reporting process*, and consciousness, the *awareness process*.

The Postulate of Spinoza

Almost 300 years ago Spinoza said: "The order and connection of ideas is the same as the order and connection of things."

Translating this into our language, we postulate that the awareness process is exactly synchronous and exactly congruent with the reporting process.

But the two processes are not identical. The awareness process is known by *introspection*, the reporting process by *inspection*; hence, operationally, the former is psychodynamic, the latter, physiologic.

Evolutionary View of Awareness and Reporting

In man, awareness and reporting are presumably functions of the cerebral cortex; in other species, presumably of the highest nervous structure attained by the species. These functions have been justifiably considered the trail-blazers of evolutionary encephalization.

In the organism awareness is the highest, and reporting the next-to-highest, level of central integration.

Nonreporting Nervous Activity

The cerebrum and the rest of the central nervous system buzz with activity at nonreporting levels. In view of the fact that such nonreporting

* First published in *Psychosomatic Medicine, 11:* 165–168, 1949. Revised, 1955.

nervous activity has by itself no effect upon consciousness, it is a purely physiologic activity. But this physiologic activity may be relayed to the reporting level, and thus eventuate in reporting and awareness. In reversed order awareness and reporting may elicit activity at nonreporting, purely physiologic, levels.

Psychoanalytic Exploration of Nonreporting Phases of the Goal Mechanism of Behavior

Since time immemorial human beings have sought to understand, predict, and influence each other's behavior in terms of motives. But this effort was hampered by the fact that the material of consciousness gives only a fragmentary picture of presumably motivated behavior. The gaps indicate that important phases of the presumed goal-mechanism occur at nonreporting levels and hence are purely physiologic.

In the last decade of the nineteenth century, Freud discovered that the psychodynamic meaning, i.e., motivational significance, of these nonreporting phases can be inferred from convergent contextual evidence gathered for the purpose by an investigative technic, which he devised and designated as the psychoanalytic method. And Freud demonstrated that this inferred meaning can be stated in terms of "unconscious" tension, "unconscious" hedonic sensation, "unconscious" emotion, "unconscious" thought, etc.

Freud used "latent," "hidden," and other cognate adjectives as equivalent to "unconscious." We suggest *nonreporting* be added to this list. Terms qualified by any one of these adjectives are extrapolated psychodynamic terms. Speaking, for instance, of an *unconscious* or *nonreporting desire*, the investigator refers to a missing causal agent, which his investigation shows to have acted as if it had been a *desire*, though in fact it was a purely physiologic event. Since the psychodynamic meaning of nonreporting nervous activity can be arrived at only by this process of psychodynamic inference, naturally it can be expressed only in an extrapolated language of psychodynamics.

To the emotionally inspired imagination, unconscious mind appears like a department of mind working "below," or "outside" awareness; as it were, like another, mysterious mind, a thing in itself. Freud adopted this metaphysical conception of unconscious mind, basing it admittedly upon Kant's philosophy of *Ding an sich* (thing in itself which lies outside the conditions of possible experience).[1] Unfortunately, this Kantian construction tends to remove the unconscious mind from the province of investigation to the realm of metaphysical speculation. But to the scientific investigator there is nothing metaphysical or mysterious about unconscious mind. It is merely a nonreporting organization of causative links between processes of which we are aware. These nonreporting causative links have to be psychodynamically inferred from, and may be verified by examination of, these conscious processes. The point is that these inferred causative links bridge the gaps and thus make motivational dynamics a workable scheme for the psychodynamic analysis of behavior.

The success of such extrapolated motivational dynamics encouraged the introduction of an extrapolated psychodynamic structure, and pointed to the need for a more explicit consideration of hedonic and adaptive efficiency. This widened dynamic scheme is the conceptual foundation upon which Freud built the science of human behavior known as "psychodynamics." He also suggested the name "metapsychology," an obvious allusion to Kant's metaphysics. In our context, the term "metapsychology" can only be interpreted to mean psychology advanced to a science of behavior through the methodical use of extrapolation.

In the spirit of a true pioneer, Freud himself believed that if a new line of an investigation has proved itself by its success, no time need be wasted in examining its methodologic presuppositions. Amused by people who "keep cleaning their eyeglasses instead of using them," he thus went to the opposite extreme of not cleaning his glasses at all. This omission left him in a state of methodologic uncertainty which is exemplified by the following characteristic passages:

To begin with, it would appear that in the products of the unconscious—spontaneous ideas, phantasies, symptoms—the conceptions *faeces* (money, gift), *child* and *penis* are seldom distinguished and are easily interchangeable. We realize, of course, that to express oneself in this way is incorrectly to apply to the sphere of the unconscious terms which belong properly to other regions of mental life; in fact, that we have been tempted by the advantages offered by an analogy. To put the matter in a form less open to objection, these elements in the unconscious are often treated as if they were equivalent and could replace one another[2].

. . . We then come to speak, in a condensed and not entirely correct manner, of "unconscious feelings," keeping up an analogy with unconscious ideas which is not altogether justifiable[3].

. . . But this new discovery, which compels us, in spite of our critical faculties, to speak of an "unconscious sense of guilt" . . . [4]

It would seem important to realize that unconscious mind is an extrapolated concept rather than a thing in itself. For only through methodological clarification such as this can the investigator hope to avoid spurious problems and effectively advance Freud's own scientific objectives.

To, From, and At Nonreporting Levels

Today, I believe, the main forms of activity to, from, and at, nonreporting levels, may be outlined as follows.

1. Some phases of the behavior mechanism may be lowered to nonreporting levels through automatization, which saves conscious effort, and increases the speed, dependability, and predictability of performance.

2. Memories must be stored at nonreporting levels because they would clutter up the awareness level which must be kept free for the arriving sensory messages. But they are on recall like the information stored in an office file.

3. Thoughts that have "sunk in," such as the multiplication table, convictions, clichés, and more complex sequences, are on preferential recall. This mechanism may be used to rush old solutions into service, rather than to think afresh.

Automatization, storing, recall, and preferential recall are efficiency mechanisms.

4. By automatically excluding painful memories from recall, repression guards the awareness level against the onslaught of paralyzing, if not killing, pain. Repression is therefore an effective hedonic mechanism. By vetoing the recall of recorded information, repression interferes with the mechanism of rational thought.

5. Excluded from awareness by repression, unwanted tension may either subside or linger at nonreporting levels. In the latter event, it may contact repressed memories, gather momentum, and elicit activities of goal-finding and illusory goal-attainment at nonreporting levels. However, a relative overflow of such latent tension will force its way upward to the awareness level, or downward to lower physiologic levels, or both.

Emotional tension which thus has become manifest, pushes for outward bodily expression and actual goal-attainment. It is from the events of this reporting phase that one can infer the events of the preceding nonreporting phase.

The discharge of latent emotional tension forced downward via the autonomic nervous system may be detected from the changes it precipitates in the affected physiologic functions. Whether or not latent thought by itself may direct the discharge into a particular organ is an open question.

To study and control the causes and consequences of the stray discharge of a relative overflow of emotional tension is the task of comprehensive medicine.

Departmental medicine was a product of the nineteenth century. Comprehensive medicine is a product of our time.

6. The overflowing tension of a repressed desire may be discharged in a dream or daydream about the desired action. However, the repression, or in other words, the fear of painful consequences, may be strong enough to inhibit even this illusory expression and fulfillment of the repressed desire. In this event, the overflowing tension of the repressed desire may precipi-

tate discharge through some imagined or real action involving the use of psychoanalytic symbols that do not arouse this fear. For instance, in a dream, a man's fascination with a certain type of landscape may express and fulfill his strongly repressed desire for encountering a woman in the nude; his dream of the King or Queen, President or First Lady, may fulfill his strongly repressed longing for his own parents upon whom he would wish to rely for loving care just as he did in early life, etc.

The overflowing tension of a repressed fear also may be discharged with the aid of psychoanalytic symbols; such riddance from fear is achieved by undergoing the symbolic equivalent of the dreaded event.

Some of the symbols used in these ways of discharge are typical, recurring in different languages and cultures; some others are strictly personal, coined for the occasion.

In either case, logical reasoning, with its high standards of reality testing, consistency, and discrimination, plays no part in the creation of these psychoanalytic symbols. They are, on the contrary, the products of an emotional, anthropomorphic, and altogether rudimentary mode of thought which tends to identify with one another things which are rationally unrelated. Every human being passes through an infantile stage of development marked by this mode of thought. But this abandoned, archaic mode of thought is firmly deposited in the mind at nonreporting levels, where it subsequently generates for the individual symbols whose archaic meaning will be unintelligible at the awareness level. When these symbols arrive at the awareness level, it will therefore require special effort to understand their meaning. Such understanding is of course facilitated if the individual has a faint awareness of his repressed yet overflowing emotional tension.

Whether or not a certain thought or action of an individual has a symbolic meaning can be determined psychoanalytically through the associative exploration and disclosure of its hidden motivational context. In the absence of a sexual context a wooded hill (even with a brook below) is not a symbol of the mons veneris; nor are, in the absence of a dependency context a King and Queen symbols of the individual's own parents.

Psychoanalytic symbols are rudimentary expressions of repressed yet overflowing emotional tension. Accordingly, the mechanism under consideration may be called *discharge through rudimentary expression*. This mechanism acts as a harmless safety valve for tension at nonreporting levels; however, in certain circumstances, it may result in disorded behavior.

7. Presumably, all conscious thought is preceded by preparatory activity at nonreporting levels. In the personal experience of the French mathematician H. Poincaré and other creative scientists, complex new problem solutions may flash suddenly into one's awareness in an almost completed form and are then merely implemented at the awareness level[5].

8. Freud inferred the characteristics of the fluid type of nonreporting thought from the study of dreams. At still lower levels, nonreporting thought is increasingly stereotyped. All these levels of nonreporting activity were formed during the early years of life.

9. Abandoned adaptive patterns of childhood, particularly of the child-parent dependency relationship, may later reappear in the mechanism of disordered behavior. The reparative process elicited by adaptive failure tends to reactivate them automatically, although they have long since lost their adaptive value. Naturally, repair thus miscarried tends to increase the adaptive failure.

To study and control the failures of psychodynamic adaptation is the task of psychoanalytic medicine.

10. Presence of a characteristic set of nonreporting patterns shared by members of the same culture results from institutionalized indoctrination during the period of growth. Reappearance of this set of patterns in subsequent generations mirrors the historical continuity and cohesiveness of the culture.

Through like reactions of brains tooled alike, much the same organizing principles of culture are bound to emerge and re-emerge from the perennial conditions of existence.

REFERENCES

[1] FREUD, S.: *Collected Papers, 4:* 104. London, 1925.
[2] ——: *Collected Papers, 2:* 165. London, 1924.
[3] ——: *The Ego and the Id.* London, 1927, p. 26.
[4] ——: *The Ego and the Id.* London, 1927, p. 33.
[5] HADAMARD, JACQUES: *The Psychology of Invention in the Mathematical Field.* Princeton, 1945.

An Adaptational View of Sexual Behavior*

> We must bear in mind that some day all our provisional formulations in
> psychology [*psychologische Vorläufigkeiten*] will have to be based on an
> organic foundation. It will then probably be seen that it is special chemical
> substances and processes which achieve the effects of sexuality and the
> perpetuation of individual life in the life of the species.
>
> —Sigmund Freud[10]

THE STANDARD PATTERN

The scientific picture of sexual behavior has become so distorted with
artificialities that we must make a serious attempt to rediscover the obvious. In any attempt of this kind it is always well to begin again at the
beginning,—in this case with a brief re-examination of the evolutionary
differentiation of the sexes, and the physiologic basis of sexual activity. In
this way we may be able to discuss the psychodynamics of sexual behavior
free from such distorting artificialities.

The evolutionary differentiation of the sexes and of sexual behavior originates with reproduction, the mechanism by which the species survives.

In the most primitive protozoa, the individual propagates by its lone
self. The evolutionary advance from solitary reproduction to reproduction
by pairs, that is, in an arrangement of mutual aid, has been brought closer
to our understanding through recent biologic work. According to Johannes
Meisenheimer, this advance was preceded by an apparently earlier form of
mutual aid, the formation of devourer colonies around a common prey.[25]
By exchanging their chemical tools of digestion in cytoplasmic fusion, the
individuals of these colonies increased their alimentary potentialities and
thus their fitness for survival. In certain rhyzophoda we can see these devourer colonies under the microscope. A later protozoic stage brought the
creation of new hereditary potentialities through the combining of the
nuclear material of two individuals. In all subsequent evolutionary stages,
the nuclear fusion of a pair of germ cells, differentiated into male and female,
became the almost universal mechanism of reproduction.†

---

* First published in *Psychosexual Development in Health and Disease*, New York,
Grune and Stratton, 1949. Revised, 1955.

† Recent reports indicate that both mechanisms of mutual aid, fusion and reproductive fusion, occur already in bacterial viruses, the lowest known forms of life. If
these observations prove correct, they would demonstrate even more forcefully the
fundamental significance of these biological mechanisms.[6]

Reproductive activity in the male-female pair is organized to ensure the union of sperm and egg. Each phase in the sequence of reproductive events serves this end. Here we are interested mainly in the coital phase, which effects the transport of sperms from the testicles into, or to, the uterus.

Taken in its entirety, the male-female reproductive pair is an emergent entity, a biologic organization of a higher order. Produced by evolutionary differentiation, male and female germ cells, coital organs *and individuals,* are but so many component parts of this new entity. Its biologic effectiveness is achieved by a vast network of adaptations among its component parts, as indicated in figure 1.

Figure 1 is the first result of our venture to rediscover the obvious. It shows that we cannot describe reproduction, that we cannot understand

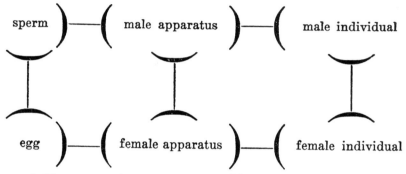

FIGURE 1. NETWORK OF ADAPTATIONS IN THE MALE-FEMALE REPRODUCTIVE PAIR. The connecting lines represent increasing multitudes of mutual adaptations.

the sexes, at the individual level. We must view them at the higher level of pair, or twosome, or group of two, at which the individual himself appears as a component part. Similarly, during the dependency period, child and mother, and then again, child and father, must be viewed as groups of two. We have here more than a formal analogy. As will be seen, the pattern of these early alimentary pairs is destined to exert a powerful influence upon the individual's future sexual behavior. The significance in psychodynamics of the hierarchical levels of organization has been shown elsewhere.[30]

In the evolutionary process, differentiation into male and female individuals appears to have followed a push and pull principle. This is shown in figure 2.

In this tabulation, the characterization of the behavior of the germ cells is based on the work of Franz Moevus who showed in certain algae, that the copulatory fusion of cells is controlled by chemotaxis; he identified the chemical substances responsible for this mechanism.[26]

As regards the suction pump action of the female organ, it should be recalled that the mouth is also a suction pump, and that the anus and the hand can also be made to act like one.

Physiologically, coition may be described as a patterned sequence of mutual stimulatory activities designed to elicit the reflex of orgastic peristalsis in both male and female. Orgastic peristalsis of the penile urethra effects the ejection of the semen; orgastic peristalsis of the vaginal walls facilitates this function by "milking" the penis. The spread of excitation to adjacent structures and beyond may involve muscles of the entire body in orgastic convulsions, thereby producing a generalized "push and pull"

	Push ♂	Pull ♀
Germ cell	seeks egg	attracts sperm
Copulatory apparatus	penetrates: acts as pressure pump; through orgasm reflex, injects semen into vagina	accommodates: acts as suction pump; through orgasm reflex, facilitates insemination and transport of semen into uterus
Whole individual: bearer of germ cells and copulatory apparatus	seeks out, conquers, secures consent of, and seizes female	by "presentation," if not by more forceful means, attracts and holds male

FIGURE 2. THE "PUSH AND PULL" PRINCIPLE IN THE EVOLUTIONARY DIFFERENTIATION OF THE SEXES.

toward the union of sperm and egg. Orgastic peristalsis is the insemination phase of reproduction.

Reproduction is safeguarded by auxiliary mechanisms; orgastic peristalsis of vagina and cervix may fail, without impairment to fertilization. There is also a super-abundance of supplies, for instance the release of millions of sperms when but one can do the job.

We shall now turn to the psychodynamic levels.

Through the comparative study of animals lower in the evolutionary scale, Frank A. Beach and other investigators have thrown into conspicuous relief the part psychodynamic integration plays in sexual behavior. Beach points out that during the evolution of vertebrates, with the development of the brain, mating behavior has undergone a gradual change.[2] Stereotyped inherited forms, organized at lower levels, have broken down and the pattern has become increasingly modifiable and dependent for its completion upon the animal's individual experience.

In man, we have direct investigative access to the psychodynamic levels. Here, the cultural pattern enters the picture as a new and powerful determinant. Through its laws, mores, and other institutions, society controls the behavior of its members from birth to death. The human individual is born with responses constituting his mammalian heritage; and he is born into a web of social institutions which came into being through cumulative tradition and constitute his cultural heritage. Accordingly, his sexual pattern is shaped by highly complex cultural forces in perpetual interaction with his mammalian heritage.* There ensues a degree of variability unknown in other species whose psychodynamic and social levels are less developed.

The physical methods of the animal investigator stop short of the decisive event in the psychodynamic integration of sexual behavior. But in man we see that coition is dominated by the desire for orgastic pleasure. This hedonic motivation is independent of reproductive intent, which may be combined with it, or not. The human female continues to have orgastic desires, even when pregnant, or after the menopause. Orgasm, an intermediary phase in reproduction, is the final goal in this hedonic pursuit. Moreover, the orgastic pleasure scheme is considerably enlarged through contributions derived from extra-genital sources. This hedonic organization of the pair appears to be superposed at psychodynamic levels upon its reproductive organization at physiologic levels. From the physiologic concept of reproductive pair we thus derive the psychodynamic concept of orgastic pleasure pair.

In the two sexes, orgastic pleasure is based upon different genital structures. On grounds of this differentiation, we identify "orgastic pleasure" with "sexual pleasure," and "orgastic pleasure pair" with "sexual pair."

In the sense of this interpretation, the term sexual will be applied first to behavior motivated by the desire for orgastic pleasure, and second to orgasm elicited by mechanisms other than pleasurable stimulation in a sexual motive state, and therefore experienced as a surprise. We have suggested this view previously and repeat it here with renewed emphasis.[27] Independently of our studies, Alfred C. Kinsey, Wardell B. Pomeroy, and Clyde E. Martin have based their invaluable research project on a substantially identical concept of sexual behavior.[20]

As a further step toward clarification, we introduce the concept of standard coital pattern. In this pattern, carrying out the indications of anatomy, the male organ penetrates the female organ at some point before orgasm in the male is evoked. Though motivated by pleasure, this activity is also

---

* A. Kardiner was the first to analyze variations of the sexual pattern in primitive societies from the comparative cultural point of view.[19]

effective for reproduction. The schematic organization of this pattern is shown in figure 3.

It is generally assumed that the direct impact of humoral factors upon the brain is the physiologic basis of sexual arousal. The problem is complicated by the fact that, in order to become effective, such internal stimulation must be psychodynamically "received" and built up to a sexual motive state. Obviously, the strength of stimulation from within varies widely in different individuals, and in the same individual, from time to time; and so does the degree of attention paid by the individual to the arriving internal stimuli. He may foster his sexual desire almost to the exclusion of other pursuits. Or, by subduing this desire, he may save for other purposes the emotional and intellectual resources which would have been absorbed by this desire. But there is no evidence to show that the minimum orgastic requirement of a given organism could be adequately met by means other than the climactic release of sexual tension.

Presumably, the sensory mechanisms of arousal rest upon innate elements which are organized and completed through individual experience. However, in man, the sensory mechanisms of arousal are almost eclipsed by stimulation through memory and wishful thought. Past experience may establish preferred or exclusive modes of stimulation.

In the standard coital pattern, pleasure mechanisms of extragenital regions are utilized as sources of tributary pleasures. The fact that here these pleasure mechanisms work toward an orgastic, i.e. a sexual, end, must not obscure their remarkable flexibility of organization. Pending upon the motivational context, one and the same pleasure mechanisms of the organism also may work toward alimentary ends, or creative artistic ends, or may subserve relief from tension, struggle for power, or still other goals.[27]

Freud's own fundamental discovery that interpretation of a psychodynamic event must be based upon its motivational context,[11] exposed the scientific shortcomings of the Libido Theory in which all modalities of pleasure (and love) are interpreted as being sexual in *themselves*. Disregarding this indiscriminate sexual interpretation the term "libido," as used by Freud, means the love of pleasure; hence, "genital libido" is love of orgastic pleasure; "oral libido" is love of oral pleasure; "narcissistic libido" is pride, or love of self as a source of pleasure, etc. Though it is not a "theory of sex," the libido theory nonetheless occupies an important place in the history of psychoanalysis, for it taught the investigator to look everywhere for hidden pleasure behavior. But the material thus accumulated must be re-examined, and its interpretation put firmly on the basis of motivational context.

Internal stimulation establishes receptivity to psychodynamic stimulation.

↓

Arousal by sensory and intellectual stimulation of each other.

↓

In both mates, this sets up sexual motive state which mobilizes and organizes the organism's emotional and other resources for orgastic pleasure.

↓

In both mates, this state elicits automatic responses of preparedness:
sensory: selective mechanism of attention
intellectual: selective mechanisms of memory and wishful thought
motor: engorgement of erectile structures
glandular: release of sperms; secretion of vehicular and lubricative fluids.

↓

Male woos and secures consent of the female.

↓

Foreplay: mutual stimulation of responsive extra-genital regions sends tributary streams of pleasure into orgastic main stream in both mates.

↓

Male: rise of impetus to penetrate—Female: rise of desire to be penetrated.

↓

Inplay: intramural stimulation by pelvic thrust.

↓

This reflexly evokes pleasurable orgastic peristalsis of genital structures and brings mounting emotional tensions to a climactic discharge in both male and female.

↓

Sleep.

↓

Pride.

FIGURE 3. STANDARD COITAL PATTERN.

The foreplay phase of the coital pattern differs from culture to culture; and from individual to individual, depending on the relative richness or paucity of innervation of his various body parts as well as his past experience. Extensive participation of extragenital parts in the sexual act transforms the entire organism into a single instrument of sexual expression and gratification.*

According to F. A. Beach, pelvic thrust is based on an innate neural pattern which is part of man's mammalian heritage.

The profound differences in the reproductive organization of male and female are reflected in their sexual behavior. The reproductive function plays an incomparably larger role in the life of the female; the same applies to sexual gratification. Clinical observation corroborates this by showing that chronic sexual frustration is far more damaging to the female organism than to the male. Orgasm in the male is attendant upon the production and delivery of sperms; in the female, upon the active reception of sperms. Since the female organism contributes the ovum through the separate process of ovulation, in the sexual act its only reproductive task is sperm collection. This helps to explain the fact that the orgastic requirement of the sexually strong healthy female by far exceeds that of the sexually strong healthy male. Orgastic requirement is measured here in terms of desire and capacity for frequency, in particular for serial or multiple orgasm. Cultural dominance of the male tends to obscure, and of the female to accentuate, this biologic difference between the two sexes.

Through the ages, poets have told us that their simultaneous orgasm gives lovers the awareness of having become completely one. This awareness seems to foreshadow the impending union of sperm and egg. Simultaneous climax is the outcome of mutual adjustment; this, however, frequently means that the male must be able to supply the need for more prolonged stimulation characteristic of the culturally more inhibited female.

The orgastic mechanism has the added responsibility of relieving the organism from all kinds of psychodynamic tensions; as Ferenczi clearly saw, it shares this characteristic with all the other pleasure mechanisms of the organism.[9], †

The human emancipation of its pleasure reward from reproduction was duplicated in the area of alimentary behavior. In 1926 I suggested that satiation is an orgasm-like alimentary event akin to phylogenetically younger sexual orgasm; also that the pleasure-effect of narcotic drugs is a

---

* Bertram D. Lewin has shown that in sexually inspired thought, the body as a whole may serve as a symbol of the male copulatory organ.[23]

† Franz Alexander interprets "genital sexuality (sexuality proper)" as "the expression of surplus energy of the mature organism as a whole."[1]

slightly modified form of the emotional pattern of satiation produced without the intake of food.[28] By tracing reproductive union to alimentary fusion in the devourer colonies, Meisenheimer then added a further link to this chain of evolutionary correlations.

Pride feeds on the pleasures the individual derives from his own successful activities. It expresses his appreciation of himself as a proven provider of pleasure.

Elementary orgastic desire enters into combinations with additional motive forces. This expands the standard coital pattern into what may be called the expanded versions of the standard sexual pattern, as shown schematically in figure 4.

In the outline illustrated by figure 4, love is considered a sustained emotional response to the source of pleasure received and expected.* It finds motor expression in the trend to keep that source close, in readiness to supply the expected pleasure whenever desired. And, love inspires thought that will idealize its source of pleasure, by making it appear as desired, full of perfections and stripped of imperfections. There are as many kinds or currents of love, as there are sources of pleasure.

Language usage makes a psychodynamically meaningful distinction between love and the state of being in love. The latter arises from the confluence of orgastic desire with at least two currents of love: one sensual, the other, magical. If both mates share these emotions, they are said to form a pair in love.

Sensual love is an appreciation of the orgastic value of the mate; it holds the mate in readiness for future occasions.

Magical love, chiefly alimentary in its implications, stems from deeper sources; its secret lies in a triumphant revival of the security system of infantile dependence. To be loved by one's parents meant to be fed and taken care of by them by way of magic, that is, instantaneously and without effort of one's own. By substituting each other for the parent, the lovers achieve the illusion of incestuous fulfillment in a state of impervious security. This makes them self-sufficient and oblivious to the rest of the world. They tend to fill the intervals with carefree activities of companionship. Obviously, this kind of love deserves the designation "magical": it works magic by *parentifying* the mate.

These two currents of love have different destinies. Magical love, emotional dependence upon one another, tends to increase. Sensual love tends to decrease. Its easy availablity and repetition tend to exhaust the value of an orgastic stimulus.

---

* Cf. Honoré Balzac in *Père Goriot*, chapter 8: "Love . . . , the warmth of gratitude that all generous souls feel for the source of their pleasures . . . "

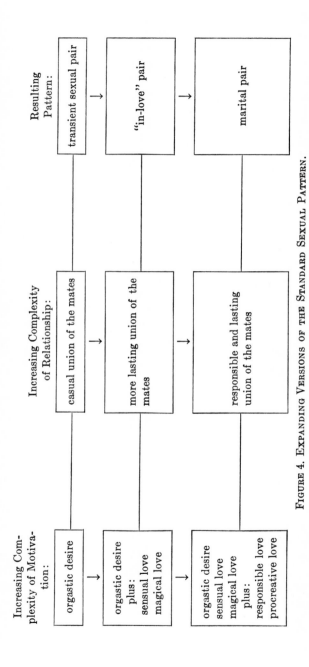

FIGURE 4. EXPANDING VERSIONS OF THE STANDARD SEXUAL PATTERN.

Responsible love rests upon the rational as well as emotional interest in adequate economic security and standing in the community; it works toward survival and cultural self-realization of the mates. By providing for the other like a parent, one of the mates may achieve a reflected sense of security.

Procreative love is one of the instruments by which nature ensures the survival of the species. Reproduction comes close to satisfying the individual's primordial belief in his personal immortality. And, it opens up the rational hope for old age support from the offspring.

While these four currents of love readily blend with one another, conflicts may also arise among them, disrupting pairs or making the choice of mate difficult.

The marital order is different in different cultures. As used in our outline, the concept of "marital pair" refers to the marital order of Western civilization.

The state of being in love may bring about a curious exacerbation of the desire for omnipotence which shows the pair in a new light. At the height of passion and mutual devotion, the lovers may suddenly feel frightened by their utter dependence upon one another for procreative delight. In such moods, the male envies the hidden female cavity, that port of nostalgic re-entries and new departures, just as he envies her privilege of bringing forth and nourishing the young. The female envies the proud male organ, in whose likeness he created the scepter, his emblem of sovereignty. And both envy each other's unfathomable pleasure sensations. This mood may have inspired one Hindu mystic of antiquity to invent the doctrine of bisexuality. To be both male and female, a pair by oneself, is a perfect dream: it leaves nothing to be envied and little to be feared. Illusions of this sort never die.

THE IMPACT OF EARLY THREATS, FEARS AND RAGES

Sexual organization has an early start: its development begins soon after birth. But in our culture, its completion takes fifteen or more years. Since in *homo sapiens* the sexual function is so highly encephalized, it is the responsibility of society to furnish the young with knowledge and experience needed to set up their pattern intelligently. It was Freud's epochal achievement, that he awakened society to this responsibility. Freud's work had a profound influence on contemporary thought. But investigation in this field has hardly begun; we have as yet no answers to most of the problems arising from the fact that orgastic, reproductive and social maturity and economic security are each attained at a different time. And changes in the cultural pattern are very slow; in the upbringing of their children people still tend to follow tradition rather than science. Parents use wishful thinking and prohibitive measures that defeat themselves. They prefer to think that prior to puberty a "nice" child has no orgastic desires, and at any rate sexual information may be postponed until marriage. When they catch the boy in self-stimulation, in so many words, they threaten to cut off his penis; he is sensitive to this threat because his parents have often taken away from him the very things that give him fun. And when the parents catch the girl, they impress upon her that she inflicts irreparable damage upon herself.[29] They also teach the girl to interpret the male's sexual approach as an assault. This view takes root in both sexes. By chancing upon the marital act, or discovering bloodstains in the mother's bed, or by other "telling" experiences, both boy and girl inevitably arrive at the violence misconception of sexual intercourse.

Left to their own intellectual resources, children tend to place reproduction in the digestive tract. Fantasies of oral impregnation, abdominal pregnancy and anal birth may serve to pour sexual fears into the alimentary, and alimentary fears into the sexual area. The fantasy of umbilical birth is inspired by the idea of sexual violence.

The cultural pattern is often stronger than parents; even if some parents are "enlightened," this pattern may still reach their children through indoctrination from playmates or servants.

The frightened boy sees in the little girl a victim of the threatened genital mutilation. The persistence of this dreadful feeling may cause him to avoid the "wound-like" female organ ever after; or if he salvages some capacity for penetration, he will be forced to perform as if in a hurry to get out of that dangerous place.*

The intimidated girl recognizes in the male organ that dangerous weapon which is to damage her by penetration, causing her to lose her bodily, personal, and social integrity. In her sexual dreams, the male organ will be represented by snakes, daggers, firearms, and the like. She is slated, years later, to undergo sexual intercourse in a state of vaginal anesthesia and emotional non-participation which may cause her to reflect: "I wonder what's going on down there?" (From this, however, it must not be concluded that frigidity is always due to a purely emotional etiology.) For-

---

* *Precipitous* ejaculation may turn into a *retarded* one. The patient is then capable of performing with full erection for a lengthy period of time—at the cost of losing all sexual sensation. The return of sensation at once precipitates release. This disorder is, in fact, *delayed* precipitous ejaculation. From the point of view of the female, it is a mechanism of highly successful repair; from the point of view of the male himself, a mechanism of miscarried repair. Some twenty-five years ago, I saw a patient who was unable to regain sensation; upon eventual withdrawal he used pin pricks to rouse his deadened organ to sensation and climax. In the same situation, a schizophrenic used to inject morphine into the cavernous bodies of his penis.

tunately for her, the clitoris, and, as evidenced by the findings of Richard L. Dickinson, the urinary meatus, often escape the incapacitating action of her penetration fear; the orgasm-reflex may then be elicited by stimulation of these areas.[8]

These emotional preoccupations with the threatened mutilating consequences of sexual activity may be generally designated as *fears of genital degradation*. To achieve the desired submissive effect, the parental threats are given sufficient strength to repress the child's defiant rages and resentments.

These fears come to play a crucial part, when the orgastic desire invades the child's dependency relation to the parents. There is a powerful, though unrecognized, sexual undercurrent in the parents' own attitude toward their children. Giving him, as she has to, her natural love and affection, the mother unwittingly also arouses her son's sensual desire; the father courts his daughter's favor. The father then tends to become hostile to the boy, and the mother to the girl, each parent punishing the children for what are actually the consequences of the other parent's unrecognized temptations. Eventually, the explicit or implied threats of genital degradation force the children to renounce or inhibit *their* incest temptation. In later life, this temptation may still influence the choice of mate; or, if the individual shies away from sexual contacts, and yet desires the emotional security of a mate, it may be reactivated as a move of miscarried repair.

When the child develops an orgastic desire for the beloved parent of the opposite sex, the parent of the same sex, whom the child thus would wish to replace, inevitably becomes the target of his jealous resentment. This emotional constellation of the child was designated by Freud as the Oedipus complex.

The child's experiences in the family group lay the foundations of what will later emerge as his Established Pattern of Psychodynamic Adaptation (EPPA). This includes the individual's attitudes toward cooperation and competition, his proneness to domination or submission, his aspirations, social fears and resentments. This lasting adaptive organization has of course profound bearings on the individual's sexual behavior as well.*

The child depends upon the parents' loving care; and the parents insist that whenever he is disobedient he should reconcile them by expiation. By the operation of this educational system the child's defiant rages and resentments are in part repressed, in part turned into self-reproaches. The latter mechanism transforms his sexual fears into *guilty* sexual fears. In

---

* Of the child's situation in the family, "sibling rivalry" and "maternal overprotection" are the most carefully investigated phases; this work was carried out by David M. Levy on extensive clinical material, with comparative methods.[21, 22]

some children these fears and guilty fears persist through life in a conscious or unconscious state; we do not know why. Their innate predisposition to fear may have been too strong, or their experiences too severe. The problem is still unsolved.

To an individual filled with such persistent fears and guilty fears, sexual activity is not a promise but a threat; he is predisposed not to sexual fulfillment but to sexual failure and frustration which in turn increase his plight. By inhibiting any or all of its phases, these fears and repressed yet overflowing rages and resentments may inflict lasting damage upon his sexual organization. The range of the ensuing consequences may be surmised from figure 5.

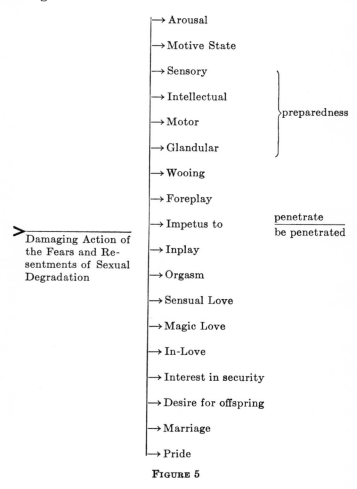

FIGURE 5

If the inhibition from sexual fears and repressed yet overflowing rages is severe enough to incapacitate the individual for standard performance, he suffers a serious loss of function which endangers his health and happiness and depresses his pride to the vanishing point. However, this loss of inner stature may help him to meet the challenge of adaptive failure. For his desire to regain his lost stature elicits unconscious processes of repair which mobilize his psychodynamic resources. As a consequence, he may discover that he can obtain orgastic satisfaction, if not through standard performance, then through some modified form of sexual activity. These reparative patterns of the sexual organization belong to the wider class of modified patterns which will be discussed in the next section.

Modified Patterns

In the modified patterns, no penetration of the male organ into the female organ occurs; orgastic peristalsis of genital structures is elicited by other kinds of stimulation, which may be applied either to the genital itself, or to some other part of the body near or far, or to the mind alone. Accordingly, these patterns are ineffective for reproduction.

Obviously, the criterion of motor behavior by itself suffices to differentiate the modified patterns from the standard one. However, in order to understand the modified patterns, we must also examine the underlying *motivations* and *mechanisms*. This is also of practical importance, for clinical observation proves that much the same motor behavior may ensue from a variety of motivations and mechanisms.

From this point of view of underlying motivation and mechanism, we may subdivide the class of modified patterns into three groups of *reparative*, *situational*, and *incidental* or *variational* patterns.

Reparative patterns. As already mentioned, reparative patterns are ushered in by the inhibition of standard performance through sexual fears and repressed yet overflowing rages; these patterns arise from processes of repair which are, in the main, unconscious. Due to this unconscious developmental history, these modifications are marked by a high degree of inflexibility; the individual depends on them for full orgastic gratification in all circumstances. Though he may force himself to go through the motions of standard performance, he cannot thereby obtain satisfaction.

Situational patterns. Lack of opportunity, segregation, and other circumstances may force even the healthy individual to seek orgastic satisfaction by temporarily adopting a modified pattern. These expedients are the products of conscious deliberation rather than of an unconscious process, and are as as a rule dropped as soon as the situation changes.

Variational patterns. The healthy individual even under ordinary circumstances, may yield to the desire for variation in performance. In some cultures, such surplus activity is part of the established sexual order. In others, it is individual enterprise.

Most if not all the motor features seen in the reparative patterns reappear in the situational and variational patterns as well. But here, resting on altogether different grounds, they are flexible and show a marked tendency toward combination.

In this paper we shall examine only the reparative patterns.

These patterns may enable the individual to recapture his losses in function, pride and social usefulness. However, Western civilization has not yet recognized this medical fact. Our normative codes, as did the laws of medieval times, still prohibit these reparative patterns. For the improvement of his health the individual thus must pay the price of guilty fear, if not legal punishment. Since, on a willing partner, these reparative patterns inflict no more harm than does the standard pattern, the benefit society derives from these penal provisions is nil. On the contrary, these laws create an opportunity for blackmail and other true crimes. It is a responsibility of the medical profession to lift the fog of ancient superstition so that the light of reason may prevail.

The task of systematizing the reparative patterns is facilitated by the concept of standard sexual organization. If this concept is used as a frame of reference, the reparative patterns may be classified as follows:

1. Organ replacement.
2. Sexual pain-dependence.
3. Contact avoidance:
    (a) the self-exposure pattern;
    (b) the voyeur, or peeping, pattern;
4. Patterns of solitary gratification:
    (a) the fetishistic pattern;
    (b) orgastic self-stimulation in cross-dressing;
    (c) orgastic self-stimulation in the illusory twosome of a day-dream or dream;
    (d) blank orgastic self-stimulation in the waking state;
    (e) surprise orgasm in the waking state or in sleep, in particular, the paradoxical orgasm.
5. Homogeneous pairs.
6. Adult-child pairs.
7. Human-animal pairs.
8. Patterns involving more than two mates.

In the following outline of psychodynamic mechanisms, we shall pay close attention to those items which have been obscured by erroneous theories, briefly discuss others, and omit those not yet sufficiently clarified.

1. Organ replacement

(a) *Replacement of the genital organ by some other bodily part*, in one mate or in both, such as in the various contacts of mouth-genital, genital-anus, petting, etc. Avoidance of the opposite organ is due to persistent genital fears and resentments; the choice of replacement follows pleasure preferences acquired in early life, possibly on innate grounds, such as the relative abundance of nerve supply. In the forced avoidance of imaginary dangers, real dangers may be ignored; for instance, the male may replace the *vagina dentata* by the mouth.

2. Sexual pain-dependence

Pain-dependence develops in early life in response to disciplinary stress. If restrictive upbringing defeats the child's defiant rage, his pursuit of forbidden pleasure may take the roundabout way of pain-dependence. We define this mechanism as the forced and automatized pursuit of advance punishment as the only means by which the individual can attain license to gratify his forbidden desires. Here, the anticipation of pleasure overrules the deterrent action of pain. Through this expectation, pain becomes a paradoxical stimulus for pleasure, enhanced in its value by the unique aesthetic effect of contrast.

Pain-dependence is seen in every area of pleasure behavior. It is but a special instance of a general principle of repair, that of recapturing lost pleasure. The pleasure which pain-dependence tends to recapture was of course lost through the prohibitive attitude of the parents. Since pain-dependence may involve self-damage, we interpret it as a deficient adaptation.

The high moral pride the individual takes in his suffering is one of the pleasures, sometimes the only pleasure, which the mechanism of pain-dependence achieves. This pleasure helps the individual to hold his dangerous, defiant rage in check.

The development of pain-dependence may be forestalled, or its action mitigated, by releasing defiant rage and facing its consequences.

Sexual pain-dependence, that is, the individual's dependence for orgastic pleasure upon the stimulation which pain as pre-punishment provides, occurs in two forms. In one, the old guilty fear of the disciplinary authority is stronger than the defiant rage; the individual, with his rage depleted by this fear, cannot help pursuing the necessary punishment in open submission. In the other, the same forced pursuit of punishment prevails, but here, the rage is stronger than the fear; the individual, still enraged against the disciplinary authority who caused him to become dependent upon this pursuit, defiantly conceals this pursuit by shifting the brunt of its burden upon the mate.

In the frightened or submissive form of sexual pain-dependence, the individual achieves orgasm by inviting the required painful stimulation from the mate; and in the angry or defiant form, by venting his rage upon the mate, and thus hiding his own vicarious suffering, his true source of orgastic stimulation, beneath his sense of triumph.

In the more severe cases, painful stimulation tends to become both dramatized and stereotyped, and the individual is fully aware of his pain-dependence. In milder cases, the forced pursuit of pain may remain a hidden phase of the coital pattern, unsuspected by the individual. These latter cases are extremely common.

In the female, a rather frequent form pain-dependence takes is the hidden desire to be raped, which derives from the old violence misconception of sexual intercourse. The hidden desire for rape is then bound to elicit an open dread of rape, or intensify this dread if it already exists on other grounds. In a state of pain-dependence the male too may develop a hidden desire to be raped by a female, and then have an open dread of such rape. Of course, here rape is meant in a social rather than physical sense, referring to loss of male stature, public sexual humiliation, and the like. In individuals of paranoid predisposition, this dread of being raped by an individual of the opposite sex may give rise to sexual delusions of persecution and reference.

Pain-dependence is also the clue to the problem of sexual jealousy. This complex emotional response is elicited by the real or imagined danger of losing the beloved mate to a successful rival, with all the damaging consequences to the individual's own pride, prestige, and security, which this loss would entail. Fearful of this threat, the individual is enraged against both the (supposedly) successful rival and the (supposedly) disloyal mate. At the same time, he secretly envies the successful rival for his presumed sexual superiority. Beneath this envy lurks his own desire for sexual ventures, held in check by his fears of sexual inferiority. While in the grip of these humiliating emotions, he visualizes the successful rival in intimate contact with the disloyal mate. These fantasies throw him into a state of sexual excitement: he is now again, as he once was (as a child in the bedroom of his parents), the sexually aroused but excluded third. Jealousy is a pain-dependent aphrodisiac, precisely the kind of stimulant the sexually pain-dependent individual craves.

Abundant gratification of the desire for love, affection, warmth, appreciation and respect, combined with a periodic release of repressed yet over flowing rage, is bound to bring about a sharp rise of inner stature and self-respect. This combined overcompensatory mechanism may give the organism a respite from the burden of its sexual pain-dependence, notably in the female. In favorable circumstances, it may even enable her to overcome her crippling vaginal anesthesia.

The two contrasting forms of sexual pain-dependence were first described clinically by von Krafft-Ebing. However, the names he invented for them, "masochism" and "sadism," respectively, were seen to be objectionable from the outset. Schrenck-Notzing's attempt to replace them by "passive and active algolagnia" did not succeed, though these terms were better than those of von Krafft-Ebing, because they stressed the basic element of suffering common to these apparently opposite conditions.

Freud envisaged a "sexual instinct" which always includes "masochistic and sadistic components"; and so, in order to explain the clinical phenomena under consideration, he had only to assume that in certain instances one of these components rises to dominance over the "genital component." In the final version of his theory, Freud equated the sexual instinct with Plato's divine Eros and added a satanic antagonist called "death instinct," or "instinct of self-destruction and destruction." He then viewed "masochism" and "sadism" as the "eroticized" manifestations of this death instinct.[15, 12]

However, the simple fact is that those who depend for orgastic pleasure upon sexual arousal through pain do not thereby seek death or pleasure-coated self-damage. They seek pleasure and pay their inescapable price: punishment in advance. The mechanism of pain-dependence has been analyzed into its constituents and there is no gap left to be filled by the postulation of an "instinct of self-destruction." Nor does death come by a special operation of instinct; it comes by a failure of adaptation. In environments that do not tax their adaptive powers, primitive organisms can be kept alive indefinitely. The germ cells of the extant metazoa have been alive for about one billion years. Freud's interpretation of life as a titanic struggle between the two forces, Eros and the death instinct, perpetuates ancient mythology: it depicts once again the eternal war between Vishnu, the Preserver, and Shiva, the Destroyer, of the Hindu Trimurti; between the Persian Ormazd, the Lord of Light, and Ahriman, the Lord of Darkness; between God and Satan, the personified forces of Love and Hate, Attraction and Repulsion, etc. This perennial strife of the gods is continually fed by perennial human passion, or as Freud himself would put it, by the id. The battle of Eros and Death, as unfolded by Freud, is a moving spectacle, filled with suspense, agony and hope. The scientific investigator quietly reduces this Olympian drama to the observation that pleasure is the source and fulfillment of life, and death is its problem. For, as Freud himself would put it, science is a business of the ego, not of the id.

3. Contact avoidance

In this group, the reparative process hardly goes beyond perpetuating an arousal pattern established in childhood. The mechanisms which arrest development by fixation are not sufficiently understood.

(a) *The exhibitionist* is incapacitated for standard performance through persistence of his genital degradation fears. He brings about orgasm by the abrupt exposure and manipulation of his genital in the chance presence of a strange and preferably juvenile female. This is an act of vengeance and triumph. As a boy, by self-exposure, he attempted to seduce his mother to give him orgastic stimulation, but she failed to live up to this expectation. Now, vindictively, he makes any strange woman see that he can do it himself. And he prefers young girls, because as a boy he was frightened by their nakedness. Now, triumphantly, he shows them that *his* penis is still there.

(b) *The voyeur* advances himself to orgastic satisfaction by spying on a woman's sexual privacy. Often enough, he is sexually still the frightened little boy dependent for arousal on peeping into the bedroom of his parents. In one of the other versions of this pattern the male depends for arousal on watching women squat and urinate.

4. Patterns of solitary gratification

In this group, orgasm is achieved in the absence of a mate.

(a) *The fetishist* elevates some bodily part or characteristic possession of the beloved female to his exclusive orgastic stimulus. According to Freud, such a sexual fetish is a symbol for the penis attributed to the female by the fetishist in order to allay his dread of the "mutilated" female organ.[13] As a boy, looking furtively at his mother in orgastic excitement, he stopped short of her genital region by fastening his view to some other point which subsequently became his fetish.

(b) *The sexually significant wearing of clothes of the opposite sex*, first called "transvestitism" by Magnus Hirschfeld, was later renamed "cross-dressing" by Havelock Ellis. The female may cross-dress not only for sexual reasons, but also for certain social purposes.

I was able to observe the use of cross-dressing in orgastic self-stimulation only in the male; by this undertaking, he impersonates to himself as well as to others the orgastically unattainable female, the mother, to whom he remained inseparably attached by ties of alimentary affection. Consequently, he becomes resentful if a male, mistaking his cross-dressing for an invitation, makes advances to him. The orgastic desire is enfeebled, and the mechanism schizophrenic.

(c) *Orgastic self-stimulation in the illusory twosome of a day-dream or a dream* may be looked upon as the "normal" form of gratification during the entire period of sexual immaturity. In the healthy adult, it may be a situational expedient; in the sexually inhibited adult, it may be a true reparative pattern, that is, the only way in which the individual can achieve gratification.

(d) *In early life, blank orgastic self-stimulation* is a chance development. In later years, it may be either a reparative pattern, or the product of schizophrenic disintegration.

(e) *Surprise orgasm*, awake or asleep, is released by an automatic mechanism acting altogether below the level of conscious awareness. It may be a true reparative pattern, i.e., the only way in which the individual can achieve satisfaction. Otherwise, the mechanism acts as a safety valve for repressed sexual tension.

Paradoxical orgasm, the most significant version of surprise orgasm, is elicited by the rising tension of fear. We interpret this mechanism as pleasurable riddance. It can be shown that it is a developmental forerunner of pain-dependence. It is seen as an occasional mechanism but also as a reparative pattern. Responses of this kind were observed in the "neurotic" dog by W. Horsley Gantt.[17]

5. *Homogeneous pairs*

Male pairs and female pairs. Individuals, deterred by fears and resentments from the opposite sex, may find orgastic satisfaction with a mate of the same sex, thus forming a homogeneous pair. The theory of constitutional bisexuality, evolved by von Krafft-Ebing and Freud, explains this by assuming that besides an innate desire for the opposite sex, every human being also has an innate desire for the same sex.[14, 32] However, this theory fails to explain the most conspicuous facts of observation. If male desires male, why does he seek out a male who pretends to be a female? Why does a male impersonate a female, if all he wants is to express a male's desire for a male? Why need a female act like a male in order to attract a female? The theory of constitutional bisexuality makes the observed facts appear far more puzzling than they are by themselves.

Freeing ourselves from such preconceptions, we see at once that the male-female sexual pattern is not only anatomically outlined but, through the marital order, is also culturally ingrained and perpetuated in every individual since early childhood. Those forced to take a mate of their own sex still strive to fulfill this pattern—by approximation. Such is the hold upon the individual of a cultural institution based on biological foundations. Naturally, neither the individual, nor society are aware of the operation of this mechanism; the individual develops guilty fears, and society is ready to prosecute him under its laws.

Freud himself discovered the early presence of male-female desire in these individuals who later formed homogeneous pairs. Had he not mistaken bisexuality for a proven biologic tenet, he would not have failed to trace the activities of these homogeneous pairs to an original male-female desire and thus recognize its unbroken continuity. By adopting instead the bisexual interpretation that the formation of homogeneous pairs was prompted by a genuinely "homosexual desire," he lost the fruits of a great discovery.

The desire to fulfill the male-female pattern is a sexual characteristic shared by all members of our civilization. Fear and resentment of the opposite sex may drive this desire underground, but neither these feelings nor any other force, save for schizophrenic disorganization, can break its strength. Individuals with mates of their own sex are impelled by this underground desire to generate a spurious male-female pattern that will achieve for them the illusion of having, or being themselves, a mate of the opposite sex. It must be emphasized that this mechanism is often deeply buried in the individual's mind under a mass of rationalizations calculated to justify his actual avoidance of the opposite sex.

Male pairs are based on the reassuring presence, female pairs on the reassuring absence, of the male organ.

In the male pair, where one male plays the part of a male, and the other assumes the role of a female, the characteristic activity is anal mount. This male pair is an openly simulated male-female pair; their sexual activity approximates the standard pattern as closely as the available anatomical structures permit.

The developmental history of these two mates is very different. The one playing the male part tends demonstratively to overemphasize his masculinity. He is then domineering, demanding, somewhat irascible and, in sexual contexts, given to flurries of anger that reveal a degree of hidden sexual pain-dependence; though unawares, he is therefore prone to inflict painful humiliation upon his mate. Unconsciously, he longs for a female with a penis and finds her in the sexually effeminate male. The latter is incapacitated for standard performance, because his sexual fears and resentments destroyed his "push," his power of penetration, completely. But he knows how to elicit pleasurable orgastic peristalsis of his genital structures through stimulation from the anus, which, by variational richness of innervation, may have been anatomically predisposed to this vicarious function. Consequently, he has assumed the "less demanding" role of the female, by vaginalizing his anus and dramatizing himself for "pull." In such males, we may speak of psychodynamic sex reversal. In recent years, some of these men, presumably all schizophrenic, proceeded to have their male organ removed by surgery.

Homogeneous mates often remain in a strong but expurgated, that is, purely alimentary, attachment to the mother; though she did have an early orgastic value for them, this was lost the instant they discovered her "mutilated" state.

The infantile history of these types may include orgastic contacts with other boys, fantasies of being in the female role, and other experiences foreshadowing their subsequent retreat into homogeneous pairs. However, we must remember that in other men infantile experiences of the same kind have no such consequences. Upon maturation, these men find their way to women and live an impeccably healthful sexual life. Obviously, the biologic and social forces of the male-female design overrule the conditioning power of their juvenile experiences discordant with this design. Only men incapacitated for the love of women by their unsurmountable fears and resentments become dependent for gratification upon the escape into homogeneous pairs, a pattern which those childhood experiences then help to evolve. Such men cherish and emphasize the memory of those childhood experiences in order to hide their fear and resentment of women from themselves and to persuade themselves (and others) that they were born that way.

In the analogous female pair, the same male-female trend prevails. In frightened fascination with the threat of penetration, the female who pretends to play the male role develops an "illusory penis," and on the strength of this equipment, pretends herself to be the lucky penetrator.[29] In actual performance, she must be content with anatomical structures less suited to serve as a male-organ, or resort to artificial substitutes. In turn, her female mate accepts stimulation from the "harmless" female, which she would be afraid to accept from the "dangerous" male. These women usually harbor bitter resentment against their fathers or mothers or both, because they denied them their affection, and preferred a son.

In other homogeneous pairs, expression of the underlying male-female design may take less obvious, or even abortive forms. Such relations may begin as a strictly companionate pair, based upon the child-parent dependency pattern, which affords the illusion of alimentary security. The orgastic impetus, which by its appearance transforms companionship into sexual mateship, may then be too feeble to generate the male-female design. Such mates often employ mouth-genital contact reminiscent of sucking at the breast, or manual stimulation. This type of development is more frequently seen in female pairs.*

---

* Re-enactment of the mother-child relationship in female pairs was first described by Helene Deutsch.[7]

Fading of the male-female design may also result from the integrative deterioriation of the sexual organization. This is notably the case in latent or overt schizophrenics.

The pattern of homogeneous pairs may include peeping, cross-dressing and other activities.

Generally, in the in-love state of homogeneous pairs, three kinds of love compete for dominance: orgastic love, seeking to fulfill the male-female design; magical love, striving in the main to re-instate the alimentary child-parent design; and the love of economic security. Here, too, by providing for the other like a parent, one of the mates may achieve a reflected sense of security.

The psychodynamics underlying the formation of homogeneous pairs sheds further light on a disorder of the male-female pattern which we have previously discussed. In the male patient, decline or loss of the capacity for standard performance may precipitate a diffuse panic which derives from the patient's unrecognized dread of anal rape. His failure as a male causes him to envy the female's "less demanding" role; secretly he longs to play her role himself. However, the menace of a potent rival rekindles his male pride; he cannot bear to be cuckolded, perhaps even defiled in person, to have his organ exposed as a decoration, as horns for his head. Humiliated by his failure, the patient dreads more humiliation to come. He does not dread voluntary, tranquil self-transmutation and fulfillment in the female role; he dreads being shamed into it. The more pain-dependent the patient is, the more he tortures himself with this vision. This is the true meaning of his overt panic, of his hidden dread of anal rape. On the other hand, in individuals of paranoid predisposition the dread of anal rape may grow into sexual delusions of persecution and reference.

The term "homogeneous pair" should be limited to the human species, for in animals, the investigator can ascertain only motor behavior; as soon as he interprets the animal's motives, he cannot but apply human psychodynamics. In order to derive full benefit from comparative studies, we should bear in mind, first, that experimental animals are less encephalized than man, and second, that the differentiation into male and female is incomplete; each sex includes *fragments* of the organization of the opposite sex. We suggest these constituents be given some descriptive name, perhaps *counterfragments*. Activity based upon them could then be conveniently referred to as *counterfragmentary* behavior.

Observations by Frank A. Beach and others would seem to indicate that in experimental animals a relative overflow of sexual excitation may be vicariously discharged through counterfragmentary channels.[3] However, man is more encephalized than these animals. In the formation of homogeneous pairs, counterfragmentary responses can hardly play more than a minor role. So far, not a trace of evidence has been presented to show that any counterfragment plays any part in the causation of this pattern. Different types of homogeneous pairs have different developmental histories; on psychodynamic grounds, we rather suspect that if innate factors are involved in certain of these developmental processes, they do not fall within the classification of counterfragments.

In a paper presented in 1940 we attempted to trace faulty sexual terminology to its historic origins.[27] In the human embryo, Nineteenth Century biologists discovered gonadal material of the other sex. On this ground, the embryo was labeled first "hermaphroditic," then "bisexual." The label stuck to the organism for good. Obviously, this term by far exceeds in its structural and functional implications the observed facts. It must be remembered that its originators were cellular biologists, wont to define the individual's sex solely by the gonadal cells, and not, as we do today, by the reproductive system as a whole.[26, *] Moreover, they were undoubtedly influenced by the well-known Platonic myth of Hindu origin, which depicted the human individual as being both male and female, a pair by itself.

Biologists also discovered that in certain lower species, as for instance in earthworms, each individual has a complete male and female sexual apparatus and uses both of them effectively for reproduction. Thus, the evidence appeared to be conclusive; bisexuality rose to the dignity of an unquestioned biologic generalization.

No wonder, then, that psychiatrists rushed to use "bisexuality" to explain "homosexuality." They took it for granted that in our species, too, each individual is both male and female—either more male and less female, or the other way around. Accordingly, they assumed that each human individual has innate sexual desires for both sexes.

Since the sexes are evolutionary products of reproductive differentiation, the anatomy of the reproductive apparatus as a whole is the only criterion by which we can tell who is what. In the human species, the male reproductive apparatus and the female reproductive apparatus are mutually exclusive, despite the fact that they develop from a common embryonic origin. Hence, a human being is either a male, or a female, or due to a failure of differentiation, a sex-defective. It is common knowledge that these malformed individuals are possessed by the desire to be of but one sex. In 1940 we attempted to show that "bisexuality" and "homosexuality"

---

* Cherau: *"Propter solum ovarium mulier est, quod est."*
  Virchow: *"Das Weib ist eben Weib durch seine Generationsdrüse."*
  (The woman is a woman precisely through her reproductive gland.)[31]

are deceptive concepts, misleading when applied in medical theory and practice.*

To fall under the spell of "bisexuality" is an occupational hazard of students of sexual behavior. This is illustrated by the following title of a paper by an investigator, noted for outstanding work and meticulous care: "Execution of the Complete Masculine Copulatory Pattern by Sexually Receptive Female Rats." Those female rats must have done it with a borrowed penis, on borrowed sperms.

In his recent book "Biological Actions of Sex Hormones" (1945), Harold Burrows makes the following statements[4]:

> It may be thought, too, that the term "bisexual" as applied to the activities of the gonadal hormones is of little real service and might be discarded with advantage.
>
> The writer has already criticized the use of the phrase "bisexual action" in connection with the gonadal hormones. He would ask permission here to disagree with the term "intersexual" as applied in physiologic and clinical literature. For clear thinking straight-forward, undeceptive language is required, because false terminology tends to confuse the mind.

It is safe to assume that the pitfalls of "bisexuality" will inevitably be discovered and its influence removed from every branch of sexual inquiry. The bi-reproductive organization of some species, and the part played by counterfragments in some other species, will then be described in objective terms like other subjects, and the protean concept of general bisexuality will take its rightful place in fairytale and folklore.

To sum up: in the view here presented, there is no such thing as an innate orgastic desire for the same sex. Three discernible causes may prompt the individual to develop mechanisms of orgastic arousal involving the same sex: hidden but incapacitating fears and resentments of the opposite sex; situational inaccessibility of the opposite sex; and desire for variation. Accordingly, the fear voiced by many patients that their genetic constitution includes a "homosexual component" has no foundation in fact.

8. Activity involving more than two mates

Freud described the plight of the male in whom desire and love are mutually exclusive; hence he is forced to shower his love upon a woman who appears to him dignified, and to seek physical satisfaction with another woman, who he feels is not dignified. These men fear that a woman worthy of being loved would be degraded by physical contact and would avenge

---

* In his not infrequent self-critical moods, Freud expressed doubts about bisexuality. For instance, in 1930, twenty-five years after he had "borrowed" this concept "from biology," he wrote: "The concept of bisexuality is still very obscure. . . . If we assume it to be a fact that each individual has both male and female desires which need satisfaction in his sexual life. . . ."[16]

herself for the indignity. They are still under the sway of the violence misconception of sexual intercourse.

There are any number of reparative patterns involving simultaneous physical contact of more than two mates.

Sex in the Schizophrenic

In individuals of inherited schizophrenic predisposition, the sexual organization remains at a rudimentary level because at least two of its essential constituents, pleasure and love, are innately defective. The ensuing schizo-sexual behavior is marked by blurred awareness and floundering activity.

The delusions of rape seen in schizophrenics of the paranoid type are similar to those produced by individuals who are paranoid but not schizophrenic.

Clinical observation leaves little doubt that the sexual differences between the schizophrenic and other human beings are fundamental. Also, that these differences exist throughout the entire life cycle. This is true of schizophrenics of all descriptions, overt or latent. It follows that sexual concepts derived from the study of healthy and neurotic individuals cannot be applied indiscriminately to the schizophrenic. Sex in the schizophrenic must be studied separately, and on its own terms.

Adaptation and Mechanism

In conclusion, I should like to say a few words about our investigative method.

Biology has developed from the structural to the functional point of view, and is at present in the process of recognizing the adaptive aspect of life. The adaptational point of view permeates the writings of Charles Darwin and, more recently, the work of such men as Julian Huxley and Walter B. Cannon.[18, 5] In the very area of this study, Frank R. Lillie stressed its indispensability for the understanding of sexual behavior.[24] Despite these examples, the new orientation makes slow headway because it is still confused with teleology in the old discredited sense. But teleology is no longer considered an ontologic proposition. Today it has become a methodologic principle. In this sense, then, adaptation, or fitness for survival, is but a frame of reference. We hold that this frame of reference is fundamental to all biology.

Adaptation and mechanism are correlate principles of investigation. Adaptationally, we view behavior of the organism in the relation of means to ends; mechanistically, in the relation of cause and effect. In the mechanistic laws governing behavior, the means appear as the causes, and the ends as their effects. But we must know where to look for laws; this we find out by adaptational search. Adaptational analysis is the reconnaissance arm; causal analysis, the task force of biologic inquiry.

By applying this combined approach in human biology, we may achieve a consistent and verifiable conceptual scheme which will enrich our lives and increase our fitness for survival. This is the goal of science.

REFERENCES

[1] ALEXANDER, FRANZ: *Our Age of Unreason*. New York, 1942.

[2] BEACH, F. A.: Central nervous mechanisms involved in the reproductive behavior of vertebrates. *Psychol. Bull., 39:* 200, 1942.

[3] ——: A review of physiological and psychological studies of sexual behavior in mammals. *Physiol. Rev. 27:* 240, 1947.

[4] BURROWS, HAROLD: *Biological Actions of Sex Hormones*. Cambridge, 1945, p. 114.

[5] CANNON, WALTER B.: *Bodily Changes in Pain, Hunger, Fear and Rage*. New York, 1934.

[6] DELBRÜCK, MAX AND MARY: Bacterial viruses and sex. *Scientific American*, 179, 5: 6, 1948.

[7] DEUTSCH, HELENE: *The Psychology of Women*. New York, 1944.

[8] DICKINSON, RICHARD L.: *Human Sex Anatomy*. Baltimore, 1933.

[9] FERENCZI, SANDOR: *Thalassa, A Theory of Genitality*. New York, Psychoanal. Quart. Inc., 1933.

[10] FREUD, S.: Zur Einführung des Narcissmus. *Ges. Schriften, 6:* 161. The passage quoted is my own translation. The translation in Freud's *Collected Papers, 4:* 36, is inaccurate.

[11] ——: *A General Introduction to Psychoanalysis*. New York, 1935.

[12] ——: The Economic Problem in Masochism. *Collected Papers, 2:* 255. London, 1924.

[13] ——: Fetishism. *Internat. J. Psycho-Analysis, 9:* 161, 1928.

[14] ——: Three Contributions to the Theory of Sex. *The Basic Writings of Sigmund Freud*. Modern Library.

[15] ——: *Beyond the Pleasure Principle*. London, 1922.

[16] ——: *Civilization and its Discontents*. New York, Ballou, 1930.

[17] GANTT, W. HORSLEY: *Experimental Basis for Neurotic Behavior*. Psychosomatic Medicine Monographs No. 3, 1944.

[18] HUXLEY, JULIAN: *Evolution, the Modern Synthesis*. New York, 1942.

[19] KARDINER, A.: *The Individual and His Society*. New York, 1939.

[20] KINSEY, ALFRED C., POMEROY, WARDELL B., AND MARTIN, CLYDE E.: *Sexual Behavior in the Human Male*. Philadelphia, 1948.

[21] LEVY, DAVID M.: *Studies in Sibling Rivalry*. American Orthopsychiatric Association Monograph, New York, 1937.

[22] ——: *Maternal Overprotection*. New York, 1943.

[23] LEWIN, BERTRAM D.: The body as phallus. *Psychoanal. Quart., 2:* 24, 1933.

[24] LILLIE, F. R.: General Biological Introduction. *Sex and Internal Secretions*, (E. Allan, ed.). Baltimore, 1931.

[25] MEISENHEIMER, JOHANNES: *Geschlecht und Geschlechter im Tierreich. 2:* 521, Jena, 1930.

[26] MOEVUS, FRANZ: Carotinoide als Sexualstoffe von Algen. *Naturwissenschaften, 27:* 97, 1939.

[27] RADO, SANDOR: A critical examination of the concept of bisexuality. *Psychosom. Med. 2:* 459, 1940.

[28] ——: The psychic effects of intoxicants: an attempt to evolve a psycho-analytical theory of morbid cravings. *Internat. J. Psycho-Analysis, 7:* 396, 1928.

[29] ——: Fear of castration in women. *Psychoanal. Quart., 2:* 425, 1933.

[30] ——: Psychodynamics as a basic science. *Am. J. Orthopsychiat, 16:* 405, 1946.

[31] TANDLER, JULIUS, AND GROSZ, SIEGFRIED: *Die biologischen Grundlagen der sekundären Geschlechtscharaktere.* Berlin, 1913.

[32] VON KRAFFT-EBING: *Psychopathia Sexualis.* New York, 1931.

EMERGENCY BEHAVIOR*
With an Introduction to the Dynamics of Conscience

In our present symposium on anxiety I am about to present a paper in which the term anxiety does not occur. By the way of introduction, I should like to explain why.

In common English usage anxiety means distress of the mind caused by the apprehension of danger but softened by the hope that the danger will pass. Fear, on the other hand, is the perfect English rendering of the German *Angst*. However, Freud's early translators suggested that in technical usage anxiety be adopted as the English equivalent of the German *Angst*, for both words derive from the same Latin root *angustia*. Also, they wished to reserve the word fear for the German *Furcht*[11].

But the fact is that Freud himself ignored the German idiomatic distinction between *Furcht* (which was said to have an object), and *Angst* (which was supposed to have none). He showed that *Angst* may have, and as a rule does have, a repressed, unconscious object. Dynamically, such *Angst* is *Furcht*. And again, the strength of *Furcht* may be due, and often enough is due, not to its avowed object but to its repressed unconscious object. Dynamically, such *Furcht* is *Angst*. Freud used *Angst* even in places where the German idiom required *Furcht*, e.g., *Kastrationsangst, Gewissensangst, Vergeltungsangst, Angst vor dem Liebesverlust.*

In current psychiatric usage anxiety denotes fear with some qualification which, however, differs from school to school if not from writer to writer. Unless used in its nontechnical sense, there is no sound basis upon which to differentiate it from fear. In order to aid clear thinking we ought to discard this unhappy word from our technical language and revert to the exclusive use of the word fear. The present writer has done so for years.

EMERGENCY BEHAVIOR

Everyday observation shows that fear is a response to danger. Both pain from external causes and rage are responses of the same kind. Obviously, these responses are alerting events in the perpetual interaction of organism and environment, because they in turn prompt the organism to

---

* First published in *Anxiety*, New York, Grune and Stratton, 1950. Revised, 1955.

engage in further activities designed for the prevention and repair of damage. Activities in this area may be designated as *emergency behavior*. This concept was inspired by the classical work of Walter B. Cannon. Through the study of laboratory animals, Cannon disclosed a long list of physiological changes in pain, fear, and rage[1]. He interpreted most of these changes as "adjustments" because they have a definite "utility" or "survival value" for the animal:

Respiration deepens, the heart beats more rapidly, the arterial pressure rises, the blood is shifted away from the stomach and intestines to the heart and central nervous system and the muscles, the processes in the alimentary canal cease, sugar is freed from the reserves in the liver, the spleen contracts and discharges its content of concentrated corpuscles, and adrenin is secreted from the adrenal medulla. The key to these marvelous transformations in the body is found in relating them to the natural accompaniments of fear and rage—running away in order to escape from danger, and attacking in order to be dominant. Whichever the action, a life-or-death struggle may ensue.

The emotional responses just listed may reasonably be regarded as preparatory for struggle. They are adjustments which, so far as possible, put the organism in readiness for meeting the demands which will be made upon it. The secreted adrenin cooperates with sympathetic nerve impulses in calling forth stored glycogen from the liver, thus flooding the blood with sugar for the use of laboring muscles; it helps in distributing the blood in abundance to the heart, the brain, and the limbs (i.e., to the parts essential for intense physical effort) while taking it away from the inhibited organs in the abdomen; it quickly abolishes the effects of muscular fatigue so that the organism which can muster adrenin in the blood can restore to its tired muscles the same readiness to act which they had when fresh; and it renders the blood more rapidly coagulable. The increased respiration, the redistributed blood running at high pressure, and the more numerous red corpuscles set free from the spleen provide for essential oxygen and for riddance of acid waste, and make a setting for instantaneous and supreme action. In short, all these changes are directly serviceable in rendering the organism more effective in the violent display of energy which fear or rage may involve.

We can best understand [these remarkable arrangements] by reference to racial history. For innumerable generations our ancestors had to meet the exigencies of existence by physical effort, perhaps in putting forth their utmost strength. The struggle for existence has been largely a nerve and muscle struggle[2].*

---

* These passages are reprinted here by permission of W. W. Norton and Company.

Cannon accumulated a solid mass of experimental evidence to show that peripheral systems of the organism perform "emergency functions" favoring the animal's survival. While his individual results may have varying degrees of accuracy, on the whole this conception is impregnable.

The emergency adjustments of the peripheral systems of the organism are seen to originate at the psychodynamic levels of central integration. To explore the emergency functions of these levels is a major responsibility of psychodynamics. I made a groping attempt in this direction in 1933, without knowing at that time of Cannon's work[16]. My subsequent conceptual scheme of "emergency control," published in 1939 and 1942, traced neurotic behavior to the inadequacies of emergency adjustment[17, 18]. In recent years this scheme has been expanded through the addition of new material. The crucial part played by the failures of emergency adjustment in disordered behavior is now definitely established.

In general, our understanding of emergency behavior was deepened through advances in our knowledge of hierarchic organization and of the adaptational principle of investigation.

Listed in ascending order, we distinguish the hedonic, emotional, emotional thought and unemotional thought levels, and the unit of action-self. Though this organization has undoubtedly an intricate evolutionary history, nonetheless, it would seem that in the human species it corresponds in its entirety to physiologic activity of the cerebrum[21]. As we shall see, every one of the psychodynamic levels, as well as the unit of action-self participates in the integration of emergency behavior.

A few words have to be said about the adaptational principle. Under this principle, we examine behavior both in relation of "means to ends" and in relation of "cause and effect." In end-relating, the question is "what does it lead to?"; in cause-searching, "where does it come from?" End-relating is our preparatory reconnaissance, cause-searching is our task. The point is that this principle applies not only to psychodynamics. In spelling out the methodological implications of Cannon's work one can not fail to realize that this principle is fundamental to physiology as well.* With the establishment of this common principle psychodynamics and physiology are on the road to the construction of a unified science of human behavior.

In contradistinction to old-time teleology, the adaptational principle does not assume that all behavior of the organism is inherently purposive. Evaluation of the adaptive value of behavior is the job of the observer and must not be confused with the work done by the organism itself. In the class of "goal-directed behavior" the organism is seen to do its own goal-

---

* The adaptive aspect of the functions of the central nervous system is stressed by Stanley Cobb[3], R. W. Gerard[10], and other recent writers.

searchings, goal-findings, goal-pursuits, and goal-attainments. This class of behavior is distinguished by the fact that here the organism's own expectancies enter as components into the causal mechanism of its behavior. To appraise the adaptive efficiency of the organism's own goal-mechanism is naturally a task for the investigator. In other classes of behavior no goal-directing mechanism is demonstrable. Acting upon clues, the organism may repeat blindly an established pattern. It is then once again the task of the investigator to determine the adaptive value the pattern had when it was established, and the adaptive value it has here and now.

We may now survey the organization of emergency behavior with the aid of a series of tables.

TABLE 1. *Emergency Behavior: Over-all Aspects of Organization.*

Evolutionary basis:
The effective use of pain as a warning signal of damage.
Adaptive purposes:
(1) To prevent damage—or, in the presence of damage, to prevent further damage —to the organism through the alerting action of pain (fear of pain).
(2) To repair damage through the regeneration of structure, and restoration or replacement of function.
Order of operation:
Prevention is the first line of defense, repair the second.
Rule of precedence:
Emergency as a rule takes precedence over all other kinds of motivation: SAFETY FIRST.

Table 1 shows certain over-all aspects of the organization of emergency behavior.

It is true that damage to the organism does not always cause pain, nor is pain always attributable to damage. Nevertheless, their linkage is so frequent and dependable that the organism can use pain effectively as a warning signal of damage. This signaling arrangement, developed at an early stage of evolutionary history, is the very basis upon which the entire organization of emergency behavior has evolved.

In the further course of evolution more and better equipment appeared, the range of *foresight* (anticipation of pain from damage) increased, and so also, through the cumulative effect of repetition, did the *automatization* of patterns. Although in actual operation, prevention precedes repair, in historical development repair came earlier and prevention later.

In the event of conflicting motivations, generally the emergency motivation is the strongest. This rule of precedence is enforced by natural selection which eliminates differently organized species. If the individual violates this rule, he is bound to incur damage or to pay the penalty of death. In disordered behavior the rule of precedence is either neglected, or more often, misapplied.

Table 2 shows the basic emergency mechanisms at the hedonic, emotional, and emotional thought levels.

By observing moribund or gravely ill patients in semi-comatose states, one may form an approximate idea of mental life reduced to the hedonic level.

TABLE 2. *Emergency Behavior: Basic Mechanisms at the Hedonic, Emotional, and Emotional Thought Levels.*

Level	Alerting Signal	Emergency Move	Evolutionary Aspects	
			Expanding Range of Anticipation	Improved performance due to more and better equipment
Emotional thought	Angry thought	Combat, defiance	Long-range anticipation of pain from damage	Intellectual exploration of past and future, from near to far: cortical system
	Apprehensive thought	Escape, submission, cry for help		
Emotional	Brute rage	Combat, defiance	Anticipation of pain from impending damage	Sensory exploration of "shell of immediate future surrounding the animal's head": distance receptors
	Brute fear	Escape, submission, cry for help		
Hedonic	Pain	Riddance (prevention of further pain)	Anticipation of further pain	Sampling of pain from damage incurred: contact receptors

Insofar as our ancestral line is concerned, some forerunner of the hedonic level may have been present already in the protozoa. We must not shrink from evolutionary extrapolations such as this; though not accessible to direct proof, they can aid our investigative work in indirect ways. But if we read pleasure-like and pain-like sensations into the protozoan, we must also assume that these sensations guide the animal's responses to external stimulation.

At this evolutionary stage the animal does not yet have the equipment with which to foresee the next situation it will meet. Nevertheless, its behavior already reveals a minimum degree of foresight. When pained it makes every effort to rid itself of the source of suffering, as if expecting that otherwise the pain will continue. We termed this the riddance response. This elementary characteristic of all animal existence was noted by Charles Darwin:

> Great pain has urged all animals during endless generations to make the most violent and diversified efforts to escape from the cause of suffering[4].

The riddance response is ingrained in our organization. Such responses as scratching, shedding of tears, sneezing, coughing, spitting, vomiting, colic bowel movement, are riddance reflexes, designed to eliminate pain-causing agents from the surface or inside of the body.

"Mental pain" may precipitate riddance just as readily as does "bodily pain." Repression is automatized riddance of painful thought and emotion. This fundamental mechanism tends to exclude painful processes from the range of awareness. The existence of this mechanism conclusively proves that the activities of the human organism are subject to hedonic self-regulation.

Repression of thoughts and emotions is a less effective riddance mechanism than those designed to rid the organism of foreign bodies within or things without. But the principle is the same. Moreover, inhibition in the psychodynamic sense also is automatized riddance.

The great emergency emotions fear and rage work in the same adaptive direction as pain but with the increased facilities of a much higher level of organization. Psychodynamically, both are based on the anticipation of pain from impending damage. Both warn the organism that a threat of damage exists and prompt it to preventive measures; in fear the goal is to escape from the threat, and in rage, to eliminate it by combat. In social dependency relationships escape may take the form of submission to the authority, and rage that of defiance. In the infant and the helpless fear tends to elicit a cry for help.

The appearance on the phylogenetic scene of the emergency emotions must have been preceded by the evolution of distance receptors, whose adaptive function we may best characterize in Sir Charles Sherrington's words:

> The animal's locomotion carries it with one end foremost and habitually so. That leading end, the head, has receiving stations signaling from things at a distance, things which the animal in its forward movement will next meet. A shell of its immediate future surrounds the animal's head[28].*

Clearly, fear and rage presuppose the sensory exploration of this shell of the immediate future surrounding the animal's head. In man, the presence

---

* This passage is reprinted here by permission of the University Press, Cambridge, England.

of an immediate threat may of course be detected by intellectual analysis or recall.

Clinical observation favors the view that while fear is an immediate response to the threat of damage, rage is not; it looks as if the organism would have to be primed to rage by a shot of fear. It is said that one shrinks with fear and swells with rage. This figure of speech depicts well the contrast between one set to escape and desirous of presenting as small a target as possible, and one set to fight and desirous of appearing as large and formidable as possible. Moreover, shrinking and swelling are also phases of one and the same behavior sequence during which the organism first yields to an impact and then counters it with resilience.

However, the organism is often seen to oscillate between fear and rage until the one or the other prevails. Certain phenotypes rarely react with pure fear or pure rage; their characteristic responses are rage over (repressed) fear, and fear over (repressed) rage.

Since all fear is fear of pain to come, the organism tends to respond to present pain with fear of more pain to come. By being thus feared, the pain becomes more severe. Moreover, present pain may also elicit rage.

With the evolution of the cerebral cortex, intellectual activity rose from an adjunct to the emotions to a superimposed organization of increasing complexity and significance. In its highest forms, freed more and more from the influence of the emotions, thought became an exploratory tool of ever increasing dependability. With the aid of this tool man became able to calculate and foretell dependably events lying beyond the "shell of the immediate future" surrounding his head, and has thus vastly expanded the spatial and temporal range of his expectancies.

However, between emotion on the one hand and unemotional thought on the other, there is the intermediate level of emotional thought. At this level, emotion still tends to control reason rather than the other way around. By comparison with unemotional thought, emotional thought is an inferior instrument for the interpreting of what one is actually exposed to; it is not objective but selective; it tends to justify and thus to feed the emotion from which it springs, and by which it is controlled.

At this level, brute fear and rage are "humanized," i.e., softened down to apprehensive thought and angry thought. There is more discrimination, analysis, combination, and greater flexibility and diversity of motor performance. Yet, the moves prompted by the new set of warning signals remain substantially the same: escape, submission and cry for help on the one hand, combat and defiance on the other.

Fear and rage, like the other basic emotions, become here the points of departure for the differentiation of new arrays of derivative emotions, specialized for the mastery of diverse environmental situations.

Frustration elicits rage or angry thought which is either punitive (aimed at eliminating the opponent), or coercive (aimed at forcing him to consent). The rage of frustration, augmented by a sense of injustice, may give rise to sustained resentment.

Repeated fear and rage teach the organism how to hate the one who aroused these emotions. Hate may be described as a sustained emotional response to the object of repeated fear and rage. This was known to Shakespeare: "In time we hate that which we often fear." (Antony and Cleopatra, III, 12). Hate finds motor expression in the trend to move away from its object or keep it at a safe distance, or remove it for good. And, hate inspires thought that will make its object appear more hateful, by ignoring it as a source of possible pleasure, and overstating its importance as a cause of pain. (The contrasting characteristics of love were described elsewhere[20, p. 167].)

Table 3 shows the basic emergency mechanisms at the level of unemotional thought. Here the heavy machinery of emotional response is superseded by purely intellectual activity. The organism aims at detecting threatening damage well in advance; this done, it weighs its own power against the threat. In the event that the threat exceeds its own power, and it can obtain the help of no sufficient allies, it cannot but choose the lesser evil. In the opposite case, it will protect itself by dominating the opponent. The latter move sets the stage for the entry of additional motivations, such as the one leading to gainful domination.

TABLE 3. *Emergency Behavior: Basic Mechanisms at the Unemotional Thought Level.*

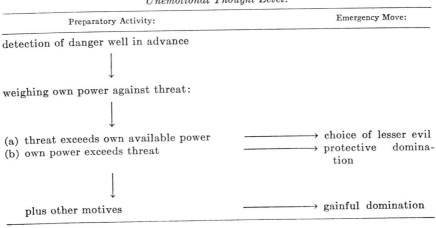

Table 4 shows the responses of the action-self to the organism's emergency behavior. The self responds to its rage, angry thought, acute awareness of own strength, with rising pride; and, on the contrary, to its fear, apprehensive thought, acute awareness of own weakness, with falling pride. The self's want of pride may cause it to respond with rage, or to fancy itself as the stronger one, when the proper response would have been fear or the awareness of its own weakness.

TABLE 4. *Emergency Behavior: Responses of the Action-self.*

Warning Signal of Emergency	The Action-self's Reactive Appreciation
Rage, angry thought, acute awareness of own strength	Rising pride
Fear, apprehensive thought, acute awareness of own weakness	Falling pride

The capacity always to handle emergency at the level of unemotional thought is an asset of the few. Most of us can do so only under particularly favorable circumstances, or perhaps under no circumstances at all. The individual then responds to the emergency with apprehensive or angry thought, if not with a violent outburst of brute fear or rage.

The predictable ways in which the individual responds to emergencies must be recognized as a significant trait of his Established Pattern of Psychodynamic Adaptation (EPPA).

Insupportable pain tends to reactivate the riddance response. We are all familiar with the impulse to tear away a severely aching part of the body. Similarly, the suspense of a (presumably) impending disaster may become so unbearably painful, that it will blindly drive the individual into the very misfortune he dreads. He may then act automatically, or yield to the irrational impulse "to get it over with."

Mark Twain wrote a remarkable description of riddance behavior:

When I was twelve and a half years old ... the summer came and brought with it an epidemic of measles. For a time a child died almost every day. The village was paralyzed with fright, distress, despair. Children that were not smitten were imprisoned in their homes to save then from the infection. ... I was a prisoner. My soul was steeped in this awful dreariness and in fear. At some time or other every day and every night a sudden shiver shook me to the marrow, and I said to myself, "there, I've got it! and I shall die." *Life on these miserable terms was not worth living, and at last I made up my mind to get the disease, and have it over*, one way or the other. I escaped from the house and went to the house of a neighbor where a playmate of mine was very ill with the malady. When the chance offered I crept into his room and got into bed with him. I was discovered by his mother ... But I had the disease[24].*

---

* Reprinted by permission of Harper & Brothers. The italics are mine. I am indebted for this reference to Dr. Thomas A. Loftus.

Riddance is a mechanism of grave importance in disordered behavior. Clinical examples were cited on previous occasions[16, 17, 18]. It was also shown that in a delusional state the patient may suddenly remove one of his vital organs (eye, genital, etc.) and perceive this act of riddance as a triumph. Here I should like to add a war observation on "combat fatigued" pilots. Overwhelmed by the almost uncontrollable dread that their "number would turn up," these men struggled with the temptation to crash their airplanes into the ground.

DYNAMICS OF CONSCIENCE

In a previous paper it was suggested that moral self-restraint is a higher form of emergency behavior[17]. This point of view proved rather helpful as our work advanced. Here, however, we shall be able to discuss only a few major points.

If a society is to survive, it must impose moral self-restraint upon its members, in order to increase their fitness for peaceful cooperation with one another and with the group as a whole. The mechanisms of moral self-restraint are rational and emotional; we must recognize them as the mechanisms of conscience.

These mechanisms originate in the child's relationship to his parents (and other disciplinary authorities), and continue to grow and operate in the individual's relationship to his society. Their development and operations are governed by the following biological principles:

prevention and repair of damage;
anticipation of requirements to be met;
automatization of responses through the cumulative effect of repeated experience;
continuous reinforcement of automatizations;
care of the young;
mutual aid.

The latter principle is manifested in the desire to be loved and cared for, and to contribute to the best of one's ability and be appreciated. Man, the "social animal," depends for his emotional security upon the satisfaction of these desires.

The awareness of being loved entails at least the illusion of (alimentary) security. This mechanism was described elsewhere([20], p. 167).

The prohibitions and requirements imposed on the child by his parents form an integral part of the social and cultural system under which the family lives. These parental rules, while varying in different societies, must be, and are, enforced everywhere, by reward (pleasure) and punishment (pain).

To the parental threat of punishment the child responds with fear of punishment which exerts a restraining influence upon his activities. The parents then reward the child's obedience with loving care, to which he responds with the self-reward of rising moral pride. These mechanisms become automatized to varying degrees. In adult life, they continue as fear of social punishment, and as rising self-respect and pride in social recognition.

As long as the child's fear of punishment remains contingent upon being caught, it operates as a *fear of detection*. Hence, whenever he yields to his temptations, augmented as a rule by his defiant rage, he will try to "get away with" his disobedience by hiding it from the authorities. An adult who never rose above this mechanism of self-restraint will behave in much the same way.

Self-restraint for fear of detection is not yet a mechanism of conscience; we may call it a mechanism of preconscience. On the other hand, the self-reward of self-respect and rising moral pride is already a mechanism of conscience.

These mechanisms are shown schematically in table 5.

TABLE 5. *The Restraining Mechanism of Preconscience and its Failure.*

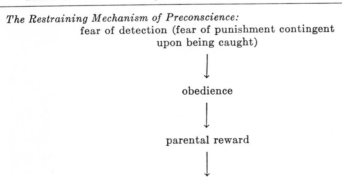

The Restraining Mechanism of Preconscience:
　　　　　　fear of detection (fear of punishment contingent
　　　　　　　　　upon being caught)

↓

obedience

↓

parental reward

↓

self-reward of self-respect and rising moral pride.

Failure of this Mechanism:
　　　　　　temptation plus defiant rage overrule
　　　　　　　　fear of detection

↓

disobedience

↓

effort to escape detection.

At some point, the child arrives at the conviction that punishment is inescapable because his parents see, hear, and know everything. The stronger the child's primordial belief in his own omnipotence was, the more powerful will be the hold of this idea on his mind. The automatized version of this fear of inescapable punishment must be recognized as the *fear of of conscience. The fear of conscience is the most effective, and socially the most valuable mechanism of self-restraint we possess.*

Immanuel Kant was overwhelmed by the existence of what he called the "moral law within." Our analysis shows that such a law can exist because the fear of conscience is a fear of inescapable punishment. While hiding it from himself, Kant nonetheless gave this secret away in his famous passage:

Two things fill the mind with ever new and increasing admiration and awe, the oftener and the more steadily we reflect on them: *the starry heavens above and the moral law within*[12].

Poetry and folklore praise the sun and the stars as the eyes of God; for instance, in his sonnet "Shall I compare thee to a summer's day?" Shakespeare calls the sun the "eye of heaven." The "two things" juxtaposed in Kant's conscious thought, may have been causally connected in the *non-reporting forephase* of this thought: "With those all-seeing eyes above me, there must be the moral law within me."

Belief in divine omnipotence strengthens the child's fear of conscience; if he later turns agnostic, this effect may be lost if not reversed.

With progressing automatization, obedience tends to elicit at once the self-reward of self-respect and rising moral pride; but this mechanism must be reinforced from time to time by parental reward.

Temptation may release the child's repressed rage or elicit a rage of frustration, and thus make him defiant. By defeating his fear of conscience, this combination may drive him to disobedience. However, he soon discovers that it was one thing to override a fear of detection, and quiet another to override a fear of conscience. Although both satisfied a prohibited desire, the difference is that fear of conscience leaves absolutely no hope for escape. There is no problem of detection, *he* knows he did wrong, that due punishment is inescapable. The pain of this awareness is intensified by his desire to reinstate himself in the good graces of his parents. Thus defeated, even his defiant rage recoils and turns inward against him, causing him to heap self-reproach upon self-reproach. In contra-distinction to fear of conscience, we call this ensemble of feelings and thoughts *guilty fear*. The phrase is taken from Shakespeare. Guilty fear brings self-respect and moral pride down to a low ebb.

The child is taught by his parents what to do about his guilty fear. He must make a confession, show remorse, receive his due punishment and ask for forgiveness. Thereupon his parents take him back into their loving care. We call this sequence *expiatory behavior;* it is an emotional mechanism of repair. Accordingly, guilty fear is not a preventive signal, but a reparative one. By successive stages of anticipation and automatization the expiatory pattern becomes firmly fixed. In one of its versions, the child seeks forgiveness by self-punishment, which he may execute automatically, i.e., without conscious intent or recognition.

The relief that guilty fear seeks is not punishment or self-punishment for its own sake, but for the sake of forgiveness, and the recapturing of the love of the parents, which it entails[13, 14]. Clinical experience disproves the classical theory which envisaged only a "masochistic need for punishment" and a corresponding "sadism of the superego." The retroflexion of rage is one of the brilliant factual findings of Freud. He described it as "sadism (aggression) turned upon the self."

The "voice of conscience" is an inner experience of high dramatic effectiveness. But why does conscience need to resort to this dramatic effect? If, in order to defeat temptation, conscience must speak in a loud voice, and repeat time and again "don't do it!" this shows that its automatic restraining power is inadequate. Self-restraint is then achieved by the inner reproduction of the original auditory experience which should have led to the automatization of this response in the first place. In general, the more automatically conscience works, the finer an instrument it is from the point of view of social cooperation.

The automatization of conscience has, however, limits to its adaptive usefulness. Over-automatization produces the untoward mechanisms of nonreporting fear of conscience, imagined guilt, nonreporting guilty fear, automatic self-punishment for imagined guilt, the mechanisms of pain-dependence, in which the pain of advance punishment is sought as a license for the fulfilment of prohibited desires, etc.[21]. But these complications lie beyond our present purpose.

We have seen that both preventive signals, fear of detection, and fear of conscience, may be overruled by defiant rage. The same applies to the reparative signal of guilty fear, but the mechanism is different.

The crucial component of guilty fear is retroflexed rage; it is the component which humbles the self most. If this rage becomes once again environment-directed and defiant, the self turns from self-reproach to reproaching the very person he guiltily fears, from expiation to attack: "You are to be blamed (not I)." The self then believes it is acting purely in "self-defense." Actually, this is a mechanism of miscarried repair; we call it rage over guilty fear, or guilty rage. "Guilt projection" is an inadequate term both from the descriptive and the dynamic points of view.

These mechanisms of conscience are shown schematically in tables 6 and 7.

The "voice of conscience" may have inspired the concept of the superego which Freud outlined as follows: Arising from an internalized replica of the

TABLE 6. *The Restraining Mechanism of Conscience. Failure, Repair, and Miscarried Repair.*

The Restraining Mechanism of Conscience:

fear of conscience (fear of *inescapable* punishment) → self-restraint mirroring prohibitions imposed upon the child → obedience (law-abiding behavior) → rising self-respect and moral pride → . . . parental (social) reward.

Failure and Repair:

temptation plus defiant rage overrule fear of conscience → disobedience → guilty fear → falling self-respect and moral pride.

Dynamic Composition of Guilty Fear:

awareness of guilt + agonizing suspense of inescapable punishment + longing for parents' loving care + venting of retroflexed rage upon self.

Repair:

guilty fear → expiatory behavior → parental (social) forgiveness → rising self-respect and moral pride.

Miscarried Repair:

retroflexed rage in guilty fear → defiant rage over repressed guilty fear (guilty rage) → reproachful behavior.

TABLE 7. *The Signaling Arrangements of Preconscience and Conscience.*

Warning Signal	Characteristic	Reaction of the Action-self
Fear of detection	Preventive	Falling pride
Fear of conscience	Preventive	Rising self-respect and moral pride
Guilty fear	Reparative	Falling self-respect and moral pride
Rage over repressed guilty fear (guilty rage)	Supposedly, "self-defense"; actually, miscarried repair	Rising self-respect and moral pride

father, the superego uses its "borrowed power" to keep the ego under control. The ego welcomes this development which will help it to withstand and defeat the incestuous desires of its id, so firmly prohibited by the father.

In this concept of the genesis of conscience, the internalization of the external father-son relationship is the dramatic event, the one stressed by Freud himself. But in order to arrive at this climax, Freud quietly internalized the whole triangle. It is unmistakable that in this intra-psychic drama the id's relationship to the ego is the same as Jocasta's to Oedipus— or that of Potiphar's wife to Joseph.

Apart from this blueprint of the "psychic apparatus," Freud's momentous thesis is that the individual is ruled by his conscience from within in much the same way and for much the same purposes as he is ruled from without by the patriarchal institutions of our Western civilization. It is this remarkable insight that has opened up new vistas in psychodynamics and to an even greater degree in the social sciences.

Freud insisted that in both the species and the individual the rise of conscience is to be traced to the father's sexual prerogatives. The father's prerogatives without qualification would seem to be more consistent with the facts of both history and clinical observation.

FAILURES OF EMERGENCY ADJUSTMENT

We are now prepared to consider briefly the failures of emergency adjustment.

The organism may overreact to danger or make emergency responses in the absence of actual danger. Its excessive or inappropriate responses are due to an overproduction of fear, rage, and to a lesser degree, of pain. Designed to warn the organism of damage, the emergency emotions thus become a damage to the organism in themselves. In consequence, the organism is forced to struggle with its own overreactions.

This disordered state of emergency control is designated as *emergency dyscontrol*. Its immediate clinical manifestation is the outward discharge of the excessive emotions in fits of fear or rage. These fits, designated as the *pattern of emotional outflow*, must be recognized as the simplest form of disordered behavior. It may, notably in children, stay on for a while and then disappear without further consequences.

However, the organism may seek to stop the overproduction, or at least the outflow, by its own psychodynamic means. It will then try to figure out what to do; if conscious thought is of no avail, it will resort to processes of nonreporting thought; eventually, it may fall back for help on repression and the other automatic mechanisms of riddance.

As Freud conclusively demonstrated, disordered behavior rarely appears for the first time in adulthood; its roots and first manifestations are as a rule found in childhood and are then carried over into adult life as a predisposition.

Suppose the child experiences a violent attack of fear. He would wish to forestall the recurrence of such an attack. How is this to be done? He has not read any textbooks, and would not have gotten the answer even if he had. All he can do is to remember, and thus interpret, the attack in the *sensory context* of its occurrence. If his memory stresses the visual picture, he will henceforth be forced to avoid the situation branded by the crucial attack. Through automatization of this mechanism, he develops the *phobic pattern* of emergency dyscontrol.

If, on the other hand, the child's memory stresses the kinesthetic (proprioceptive) aspect of the experience he will henceforth be forced to retreat from the motor activity branded by the crucial attack. Through automatization of this mechanism, he develops the *inhibitory pattern* of emergency dyscontrol.

In the adult, strong emotion may block intellectual activity at higher levels. Consequently, his thinking, too, may get stuck in the sensory material of an overwhelming experience. We can see this in patients with acute inhibitions or phobias.

In the development of the phobic pattern, an overreactive child may become crucially frightened and subsequently phobic not only if he has a mishap himself, but also if he chances upon the mistreatment or misfortune of someone else. This is notably the case if he was previously warned or threatened with punishment; the attack of fear is then elicited by his sudden realization: "It can happen to me, too." When the mother threatened to beat "little Hans"[5, 6] with the carpet beater (Vienna, around 1900), he was not particularly impressed; yet he became sensitized to this danger. Subsequently, seeing a coachman bearing down on a fallen horse with his whip, he identified himself with the horse, became terrified and developed a street phobia. He was, he admitted to his mother, afraid of the horse; he meant, of course, of *the example* of the horse. But in an obvious attempt to rationalize his fear he said he was afraid the horse would bite him. Unfortunately, this rationalization was taken at its face value and the interpretation made that the boy identified the horse with his father, and that this identification was the pivotal mechanism of his phobia.

Hans had good reasons to see himself in the place of the mistreated horse. In other circumstances, overreactive children may look at an animal that frightened them as if it were their feared parent, and subsequently avoid its sight. So did the "Wolf-man"[6, 7]. But this apparently phobic response actually initiates a wholesome release of repressed rage: the child can "tell off" the animal but not the parent. He may even be encouraged by sensible people to go on with this "innocent" game. It was precisely in order to qualify the animal for the function of *scapegoat* that the child, exploiting some chance occurrence, began to respond to it with increased fear and "phobic avoidance."

To go back to the inhibitory pattern of emergency dyscontrol, we find that this pattern may also evolve by a different mechanism. Suppose the first signs of the child's dyscontrol are not conspicuous enough to be noticed by the child himself, but may be noticed by his parents. What do the parents do about these symptoms? Sensing that something is wrong, they link the symptoms to some supposedly dangerous thing the child has done and forbid him to do it again. They thus teach the child to blame his overreaction—on himself. With the automatization of this response, the child develops nonreporting fears of conscience (and, guilty fears). These nonreporting responses may become so overwhelmingly strong that they inhibit not only those activities which were actually tabooed, or which the child believes were tabooed, by the parents, but also the *approaches* to these activities, on an ever widening scale. The result is again the inhibitory pattern of emergency dyscontrol.

Let us now turn to an adult patient. His life has become miserable because he is firmly convinced that he has, or is threatened by, a serious (physical) illness. Analysis then shows that this semi-delusional idea stems from his nonreporting belief, that such illness is past due punishment which now is catching up with him. We can omit complicating details: this is the essential mechanism of the *hypochondriac pattern* of emergency dyscontrol.

Imagined dangers, threatening from the environment, may be mastered by the phobic mechanism of avoidance. But against imagined dangers, threatening from within the organism, the patient is helpless. Hence, the hypochondriac runs to the doctor and literally cries for help.

The hypochondriac mechanism increases rather than decreases the overproduction of the emergency emotions. With the growing suspense, the condition tends to climax in an act of hypochondriac riddance. The patient then misleads the physician into performing unnecessary surgery on him; or, in constant dread of a heart attack, goes down with an actual attack of coronary thrombosis.

In coping with the overreaction, the organism may stop the outflow of the emergency emotions by repression. Resort to this mechanism is usually, but not necessarily, prompted by nonreporting fears of conscience, and produces the *repressive pattern* of emergency dyscontrol. This, however, is an unstable condition, bound to give rise to a large variety of further disturbances. We shall revert to this topic and discuss one borderland group of these derivative disturbances in a moment.

These failures of emergency adjustment are of paramount importance. They are seen to be the basic factors in the etiological psychodynamics of all forms of disordered behavior. The mechanisms of emergency dyscontrol are phases of a process of miscarried prevention, which entails losses in utility, pleasure, and social usefulness. These losses in turn elicit a process of miscarried repair, which disorders behavior still more. The Dynamics of Behavior, containing the extensive material upon which these generalizations are based, has been presented over a period of years in my lectures at Columbia University and will be published.

The significance of emergency dyscontrol extends far beyond the psychodynamic realm of behavior disorders. Its repressive mechanism provides the setting for further multidirectional developments which we call *descending dyscontrol*.

Descending dyscontrol results from what we suggest be called the Walter B. Cannon phenomenon, namely, the discharge via the autonomic nervous system of the repressed yet overflowing emergency emotions into the various component systems (respiratory, circulatory, alimentary, endocrine, etc.) of the whole organism. Descending dyscontrol comprises the disordering effects which the Cannon phenomenon produces in the physiology (and anatomy) of these systems. The clinical manifestations of descending dyscontrol belong to the domain of comprehensive medicine. The new resource that has made, or rather promises to make, medicine comprehensive is the addition of psychodynamics to the established basic sciences.

Independently, Hans Selye developed his physiological theory of "The General-Adaptation-Syndrome and the Diseases of Adaptation"[22].

The basic failures of emergency adjustment just discussed are shown schematically in table 8. A tentative classification of the more complex forms of disordered behavior will be proposed elsewhere.

HISTORICAL REMARKS

The views here presented continue the line of development taken by Freud's own classical theories. Freud at first assumed that fear was a product of repressed love, or more precisely, of a vicarious discharge of the tensions created in the organism by its own frustrated and repressed desires. All his writings were based on this premise until he realized in 1926 that, regardless of the ways in which the organism generates its fear, this construction misses the point. He then accepted the common-sense view that fear is a response to danger; hence, it must first be understood in terms of the organism's relationship to the environment. At the same time, he stated with utmost emphasis that in the last analysis fear alone is responsible for all neurotic disturbances; that fear is not a consequence of repressive developments, but their very cause[7].

The next logical step would have been to realize that pain and rage, too, may play a part in the causation of neurotic disturbances. But the libido theory directed the investigator's attention to "masochism" and "sadism,"

TABLE 8. *The Basic Failures of Emergency Adjustment.*

EMERGENCY DYSCONTROL

overproduction of fear, rage and, to a lesser degree, of pain.

Pattern of Emotional Outflow
Overproduction + emotional outflow mechanism

Outward discharge of excessive or undue emergency emotions.

Phobic Pattern
Overproduction + phobic mechanism

Remembering his crucial attack of fear in its visual context, the child hence-forth will be forced to avoid the situation branded by that attack.

Inhibitory Pattern
Overproduction + inhibitory mechanism

Remembering his crucial attack of fear in its kinesthetic (proprioceptive) con-text, the child henceforth will be forced to retreat from the motor activity branded by that attack.

(Nonreporting) fear of conscience inhibits not only the activities (actually or supposedly) tabooed by parents, but also their approaches, on an ever widening scale.

Hypochondriac Pattern
Overproduction + hypochondriac mechanism

The patient's semi-delusional idea that he is threatened by some serious (physical) illness stems from his nonreporting belief that this illness is past due punishment which now is catching up with him; tends to climax in an act of hypochondriac riddance.

Repressive Pattern
Overproduction + repressive mechanism
Outflow of emergency emotions stopped by repression.

DESCENDING DYSCONTROL
Overproduction + repression + Cannon phenomenon

Autonomic discharge of the repressed yet overflowing emergency emotions into component systems (respiratory, circulatory, alimen-tary, endocrine, etc.) of the whole organism produces disordering effects in the physiology (anatomy) of these systems.

MORE COMPLEX FORMS OF DISORDERED BEHAVIOR

---

not to pain and rage. In 1930, in discovering "nonerotic aggression," Freud was on the verge of discovering rage[8].

Until 1926, the psychoanalytic theory of neurotic disturbances stood on its head. In 1926, with the realization of the true function of fear, Freud put it on one foot. Had he in 1930 discovered that rage, like fear, must first be understood in terms of the organism's relationship to the environment, this theory would have come to stand on both feet. What he actually did in 1930 was to interpret "nonerotic aggression," and with it rage, as an expression of a "death instinct."

Our own psychodynamic construction, that *the failures of emergency adjustment lie at the bottom of all disordered behavior*, takes up Freud's thread at the very point where Freud himself dropped it in 1930.

More imagination was spent upon the psychoanalytic misconstruction of relatively simple facts than went into the writing of the Arabian Nights. This exuberance, in which we early workers had a humble share, was a natural product of the pioneering era. Not the early mistakes, but the isolation and detachment of psychoanalysis from the other branches of knowledge damaged Freud's epochal discoveries and impeded the growth of psychoanalysis.

In admirable self-criticism, Freud wrote in 1933: "The theory of instincts is, as it were, our mythology. The instincts are mythical beings, superb in their indefiniteness." ([9], p. 131). The same applies to the so-called "structural theory" in which a jealous father (the superego) drives a wedge (repression) between a seductive mother (the id) and an opportunistic son (the ego) who would wish to get along with everybody: father, mother, and the rest of the world.

We must heed Freud's own warning, re-establish psychodynamics on a sound biological foundation, and above all, *safeguard intuition by learning how to apply the scientific method to psychoanalytic work.*

REFERENCES

[1] CANNON, WALTER B.: *Bodily Changes in Pain, Hunger, Fear and Rage.* New York, Appleton, 1934, pp. 227–229.

[2] ——: *The Wisdom of the Body.* New York, Norton, 1932.

[3] COBB, STANLEY: *Foundations of Neuro-psychiatry.* Baltimore, Williams & Wilkins, 1949.

[4] DARWIN, CHARLES: *The Expression of the Emotions in Man and Animals.* New York, Appleton, 1910.

[5] FREUD, SIGMUND: A phobia in a five year old boy. *Coll. Papers 3.* London, Hogarth, 1925 (Published in German, 1909.)

[6] ——: From the history of an infantile neurosis. *Coll. Papers 3.* London, Hogarth, 1925 (Published in German, 1918.)

[7] ——: *The Problem of Anxiety.* New York, Norton, 1936. (Published in German, 1926.)

[8] ——: *Civilization and its Discontents.* New York, Ballou, 1930.

[9] ——: *New Introductory Lectures on Psychoanalysis.* New York, Norton, 1933.

[10] GERARD, RALPH W.: Physiology and psychiatry. *Am. J. Psychiat., 106:* 161, 1949.

[11] JONES, ERNEST (Ed.): *Glossary for the Use of Translators of Psychoanalytical Works.* London, Balliere, Tindall & Cox, 1924.

[12] KANT, IMMANUEL: *Critique of Practical Reason.* 4th Ed. London, Longmans, Green, 1889, vol. *2*, p. 260.

[13] RADO, SANDOR: An anxious mother: a contribution to the analysis of the ego. *Internat. J. Psycho-Analysis 9:* 219, 1928. (Published in German, 1927.)

[14] ——: The problem of melancholia. *Internat. J. Psycho-Analysis, 9:* 420, 1928. (Published in German, 1927.)

[15] ——: The psychoanalysis of pharmacothymia (Drug addiction). *Psychoanal. Quart., 2:* 1, 1933.

[16] ——: Fear of castration in women. *Psychoanal. Quart., 2:* 425, 1933.

[17] ——: Developments in the psychoanalytic conception and treatment of the neuroses. *Psychoanal. Quart., 8:* 427, 1939.

[18] ——: Pathodynamics and treatment of traumatic war neurosis (Traumatophobia) *Psychosom. Med., 4:* 362, 1942.

[19] ——: Psychodynamics as a basic science. *Am. J. Orthopsychiat., 16:* 405, 1946.

[20] ——: An adaptational view of sexual behavior. *Psychosexual Development in Health and Disease,* Ed. Hoch and Zubin. New York, Grune & Stratton, 1949.

[21] ——: Mind, unconscious mind, and brain. *Psychosom. Med., 11:* 165, 1949.

[22] SELYE, HANS: The general-adaptation-syndrome and the diseases of adaptation. In *Textbook of Endocrinology.* Montreal, Canada, Montreal University, 1947.

[23] SHERRINGTON, SIR CHARLES: *The Brain and its Mechanism.* Cambridge Univ. Press, 1933.

[24] TWAIN, MARK: The turning point of my life. *What is Man? and Other Essays.* New York, Harper, 1917, 130–131.

Psychodynamics of Depression from the Etiologic Point of View*

In the study of disordered behavior we will find our chief help is the etiologic point of view. In order to keep etiology the center of investigative interest, we have evolved the working concept of "pathogenic phenotypes." The problem thus posed is to disclose the causative chain of events which produces each of these disease-prone phenotypes as its effect. Genetically, this etiologic chain is a chain of interactions of genotype and environment. We must learn to correlate more effectively clinical observation and material drawn from genetics, pathologic anatomy, physiology, biophysics, biochemistry, and psychodynamics. There can be no true progress unless we leave our cozy pigeon-holes and join forces for the common task.

Within this framework we tentatively speak of the "class of moodcyclic phenotypes," which is characterized, among other manifestations, by the high incidence of depressive spells. These depressive spells are the topic of our present symposium. My assignment is to outline their specific psychodynamics which presumably represent the terminal links in the etiologic chain.

In the circumstances we must resort to schematic presentation and limit ourselves to the essentials. First we shall sketch the clinical picture of a spell of depression:

The patient is sad and in painful tension. He is intolerant of his condition, thereby increasing his distress. His self-esteem is abased, his self-confidence shattered. Retardation of his initiative, thinking, and motor actions makes him incapable of sustained effort. His behavior indicates open or underlying fears and guilty fears. He is demonstratively preoccupied with his alleged failings, shortcomings, and unworthiness; yet he also harbors a deep resentment that life does not give him a fair deal.

He usually has suicidal ideas and often suicidal impulses. His sleep is poor; his appetite and sexual desire are on the wane or gone. He takes little

* Read at the Research Symposium on Depression, given by the Joint Staffs of the Psychoanalytic Clinic of Columbia University, and of the Department of Research Psychiatry of the New York State Psychiatric Institute and Hospital, October 14, 1950. First published in *Psychosomatic Medicine, 13:* 51–55, 1951.

or no interest in his work and ordinary affairs and shies away from affectionate as well as competitive relationships. All in all, he has lost his capacity to enjoy life. He is drawn into a world of his own imagination, a world dedicated to the pursuit of suffering rather than to the pursuit of happiness.

Such attacks may be occasioned by a serious loss, failure, or defeat; or may seem to come from the clear blue sky. Their onset may be sudden or gradual; their duration, from a few days or weeks to many months. Their severity ranges from mildly neurotic to fully pyschotic.

Often in the neurotic and almost always in the psychotic cases there are conspicuous physical symptoms, such as loss of weight and constipation.

In some patients spells of depression alternate with spells of elation while in others no spells of elation occur.

The depressive spell has a hidden pattern of meaning. Since the patient's subjective experience contains only disjointed fragments of this pattern, the observer must penetrate psychoanalytically into the unconscious (or, as we prefer to say, "non-reporting") foundations of the patient's subjective experience[8]. In this light, the depressive spell is a desperate cry for love, precipitated by an actual or imagined loss which the patient feels endangers his emotional (and material) security. In the simplest case the patient has lost his beloved one. The emotional overreaction to this emergency unfolds, unbeknown to the patient himself, as an expiatory process of self-punishment. By blaming and punishing himself for the loss he has suffered, he now wishes to reconcile the *mother* and to reinstate himself into *her* loving care. The aim-image of the patient's repentance is the emotional and alimentary security which he, as an infant, enjoyed while clinging to his mother's feeding breast. The patient's mute cry for love is patterned on the hungry infant's loud cry for help. His most conspicuous morbid fears (such as his fear of impoverishment, his hypochondriac concern for his digestive organs) are revivals of the infant's early fear of starvation[4, 5]. The expiatory process is governed by the emergency principle of repair: in the organism the pain of lost pleasure tends to elicit activity aimed at recapturing the lost pleasure.

However, the patient's dominant motivation of repentance is complicated by the simultaneous presence of a strong resentment. As far as his guilty fear goes, he is humble and yearns to repent; as far as his coercive rage goes, he is resentful.

In the forephase of the depressive spell the patient tends to vent his resentment on the beloved person, the one by whom he feels "let down" or deserted. He wants to force this person to love him.* When the patient feels that his coercive rage is defeated, his need for repentance gains the

---

* According to an anecdote, the father of Frederick the Great was overheard shouting as he beat one of the lackies, "You must love me, you rascal."

upper hand; his rage then recoils and turns inward against him, increasing by its vehemence the severity of his self-reproaches and self-punishments. As a superlative bid for forgiveness, the patient may thus be driven to suicide. When he attempts to finish his life, he appears to be acting under the strong illusion that this supreme sacrifice will reconcile the mother and secure her nourishing graces—forever[6, 7].

A significant feature must be added to the characterization of the love-hungry patient's coercive rage. This rage proposes to use the patient's teeth as coercive weapons. The infant's teeth enhanced his alimentary delight; but rage remembers the destructive power of biting and chewing. In the non-reporting reaches of his mind, the enraged patient is set to devour the frustrating mother herself as a substitute for food. Moreover, her disappearance from the scene will enable the smiling mother to reappear with her dependable offerings of food. In dire need, prehistoric tribesmen may have devoured their chieftain (later, their totem animal) with similar ideas in mind. Sometimes this "cannibalistic" feature is clearly revealed in the depressed patient's dreams. Fasting, the temporary cessation of biting and chewing, is in turn one of the earliest and most enduring forms of punishment and self-punishment in our civilization ("tooth for tooth"). It appears in the cultural patterns of expiation and reappears in the depressive version of expiation for the same psychodynamic reasons.*

The patient takes pride not in his repentance, but in his coercive rage, even after defeat has retroflexed and forced this rage to subserve his repentance. Thus he punishes himself not only for his defiance, but also, in continued defiance, for his inexcusable failure to terrorize the beloved one (the mother) in the first place. Furthermore, the retroflexion of rage is never complete; the expiatory process is continuously complicated by a residue of straight rage which remains directed against the environment. The merciless, though unconscious, irony with which the patient blames even the failings of the beloved one on himself demonstrates spectacularly this residue of straight rage. By reducing his self-reproaches to absurdity, he succeeds in venting his resentment on the beloved one at the height of his forced contrition and self-disparagement.

The extreme painfulness of depression may in part be explained by the fact that in his dependent craving the patient is torn between coercive rage and submissive fear, and thus strives to achieve his imaginary purpose, that of regaining the mother's love, by employing two conflicting methods at the same time.

The struggle between fear and rage underlies the clinical distinction between retarded depression and agitated depression. If rage is sufficiently

---

* Another version of morbid fasting is known to the medical profession as "anorexia nervosa."

retroflexed by the prevailing guilty fear, the patient is retarded; if the prevailing guilty fear is shot through with straight environment-directed rage, he is agitated. Whenever antagonistic tensions of equal or nearly equal strength compete for *immediate* discharge, they tend to produce an interference pattern of discharge. We call this psychodynamic mechanism discharge-interference. His retarded behavior, on the other hand, is explained as an inhibitory effect of the combined action of guilty fear and pain.

Based on these findings, we view depression as a process of miscarried repair. To a healthy person a serious loss is a challenge. He meets the emergency by calming his emotions, marshalling his remaining resources, and increasing his adaptive efficiency. Depressive repair miscarries because it results in the exact opposite. Anachronistically, this repair presses the obsolete adaptive pattern of alimentary maternal dependence into service and by this regressive move it incapacitates the patient still more[12].

Historically, this theory developed as follows. Retroflexed rage is one of Freud's early clinical discoveries; he described it as "sadism (aggression) turned against the self." In 1917, Freud[2] suggested that the depressed patient's ego metamorphoses into a replica of the lost love-object. This replacement by identification, Freud continued, serves the patient's ambivalence, his hate as well as his love, for at the same time he turns his sadism against himself and thus hits the love-object in himself.

In 1924, a significant paper by Abraham[1] initiated a tacit reconsideration of this hypothesis of "identification with the lost love-object." Abraham showed that the identification amounts to a forceful fantasy of devouring and thus destroying the hated love-object.

In 1927, the present writer[4, 5] introduced three points. First, that the depressed patient reverts to the infant's first love-object (source of security), the mother. Second, that the patient has the same idea as had the infant: to destroy the *frustrating* aspect of the beloved one (formed in the split-off image of the "frustrating mother"), while retaining the *gratifying* aspect of the beloved one (formed in the split-off image of the "gratifying mother"). Third, that the depressive process is a process of expiation, overcharged by retroflexed rage. In 1932, he added[6] that when the depressed patient voices his reproaches as self-reproaches, he does so ironically. In recent years, closer study of the failures of emergency adjustment[10] has shown that the entire depressive process must be evaluated from the adaptational point of view, and interpreted as a process of miscarried repair.

The motivational organization which we hold to be specific of the depressive spell is composed of three primary constituents: the alteration of mood to one of sustained gloomy repentance; the regressive yearning for the alimentary security of the infant; and, the struggle between the excessive emergency emotions, in which submissive fear defeats coercive rage. The first two of these three constituents are altogether peculiar to the depressive spell, but the third is not. A similarly grave conflict between the excessive emergency emotions is a primary constituent also in the obsessional and the paranoid patterns. However, in these contexts the relative strength of the contending forces is different, and so is their disordering effect.

In the nonreporting foundations of the obsessional pattern the coercive use of the teeth is eclipsed in actual effectiveness by the coercive use of the hands and of the trampling feet. In certain circumstances, the infant may also resort to the coercive use of defecation. In the infant's experience, the hands could be used both ways, to fondle or to beat; and the control of reputedly poisonous feces too could be used either to obey and accommodate or to have fun and defy. The coercive use of the extremities (which includes the infant's "murderous" impulses as well) was the enraged infant's response to maternal discipline in general; enraged bowel defiance his reaction to the mother's particular effort to impose bowel "regularity" upon him. With the progressing biologic maturation of the infant, the struggle for power between him and the mother is thus extended and intensified. In the pattern under consideration the combined forces of straight rage and prohibited desire are about as strong as the combined forces of guilty fear and retroflexed rage. This makes the struggle between obedient submission and defiant coercion interminable. Must he let mother have her way, or can he force her to let him have his way and still love him? Although the emotions concerned are repressed to an astonishing extent, their conflicting tensions penetrate into the range of awareness and raise havoc with the patient's intellect. The see-saw of the patient's doubts, doings and undoings, sidetracked precautions and side-tracked temptations, token transgressions and token self-punishments, is a product of discharge-interference. The function of these symptoms is to insure discharge. The formation of interference patterns explains the puzzling fact that the discharge, though forced, is nonetheless slow and torturous. Wherever the desire or demand is irrepressible or inescapable, such as in the areas of evacuation, sex and work, the patient may obtain satisfaction through "pain-dependent pleasure behavior"[9]. The patterns of pain-dependence are interference patterns of discharge, composed of two antagonistic sets of tensions: guilty fear and retroflexed rage on the one hand and, on the other, defiant rage and inhibited desire. Each of these patterns derives its special characteristics from the particular pleasure organization involved; the inhibition of desire is automatized, varies in severity, and results from parental prohibition in early life. To sum up: the obsessive patient experiences less emotional turmoil; but he tends to become pain-dependent and is forced to squander his finest resources on a hopeless and unending task.*

* By using the concept of emergency behavior,[10] adaptational psychodynamics supplies the answers to the questions Freud raised in 1926.[8]

In the paranoid pattern on the other hand, straight environment-directed rage rises to dominance; hence the patient's proneness to violence[11, 12]. This differential dynamics may help to explain the clinical observation stressed already by Abraham[1], that during the intervals between depressive spells the behavior of moodcyclic patients often shows an obsessive pattern; and we may add, occasionally a paranoid pattern. These patterns tend to disappear during the depressive spell; but the patient's pain-dependence persists.

Knowledge of the specific dynamics of depression has proved helpful in treatment. Here I shall mention but one point of technique which this dynamics has put into sharp relief.

The therapist's intuitive reaction to the depressed patient is to treat him with overwhelming kindness. This may indeed reassure the patient and lessen his predicament, but it also may defeat completely the therapist's purpose and drive the patient into utter despair. If, at the moment, the patient's craving for affection is stronger, kindness will win. If his guilty fear and retroflexed rage are stronger, kindness will lose; because in the latter case the patient will feel: "This man is so kind to me and I am such an unworthy person." The fresh bout of self-reproaches thus provoked may increase the danger of suicide. When the therapist finds that retroflexed rage has reached an alarming degree, he may therefore treat the patient harshly in order to provoke a relieving outburst of rage. Here the danger is that the patient may break the treatment. These are, of course, hardly more than palliative measures designed to keep the patient alive and the treatment going[10, 11].

Concerning the psychodynamic aspect of shock treatment, observers have suggested that in the patient's unconscious mind such treatment registers as a punishment. Even if it does, the question of the physiologic mode of action of shock treatment still remains.

In order to balance the picture, I shall now enumerate some of the unsolved problems:

Our tentative generalizations derive from the psychoanalytic study of a limited number of cases. In order to establish their range of validity it will be necessary to repeat such studies on a much larger scale.

The strength of fear and rage in relation to one another, and the strength of both in relation to the patient's capacity for love, joy and happiness in life, are problems almost untouched. A closely related task is to explore the *physiologic* basis of such psychodynamic mechanisms as *discharge-summation* through the joint action of confluent tensions, and *discharge-interference* through the alternate action of competing tensions.

In the case of unoccasioned depression a "precipitating loss" exists only in the patient's unconscious imagination; thus this "loss" is an effect of the atient's emotional disturbance, rather than its cause. Even in occasioned depression, it is not infrequently the patient's emotional overreaction that makes this "loss" appear to him so severe. Hence, the patient's emotional overreaction need not be due to a precipitating loss, failure, or defeat. His sudden guilty fear and hidden craving for alimentary security may be due to other as yet unknown causes. He then may invent a "precipitating event" in order to make the expiatory pattern complete, as if rationalizing his depression. The problem is to disclose the mechanism responsible for the sharp rise in the patient's guilty fear and for his regressive dependence for emotional security on the feeding mother.

There is a good deal of work to be done at the *physiologic* level of inquiry. Even the expiatory process itself may be the human elaboration of a biologic pattern formed at lower stages of the evolutionary scale.

Treated or untreated, after a period of time the depressive spell spends its fury and subsides; we do not know why or how.

Psychodynamics, so far, has offered no clue to explain why some depressed patients are subject also to spells of elation and others are not.

The incidence of depressive spells is not limited to the class of moodcyclic phenotypes. Such spells also occur in almost every other pathogenic type. We encounter depressions in drug-dependent patients, neurotics, schizophrenics, general paretics, patients afflicted with severe physical illness, etc. The question arises whether or not significant psychodynamic differences exist between depressive spells that occur in different pathogenic contexts. Further psychoanalytic investigation may provide an answer to this question.

In the failures of emergency adjustment the ultimate factor discernible by psychodynamic analysis is the patient's emotional overreaction to danger in terms of pain, fear, and rage. This trait is traceable to early life; the most constant among its early manifestations is the infant's emotional overreaction to parental discipline with its threats of punishment. At the present stage of inquiry an investigative program must include the *physiologic* and *genetic* aspects of this emotional overreaction. In our view, this problem is of surpassing importance to the psychodynamics of all disordered behavior[s]. Concerning depression, the program must also include the problem of the moodcyclic *genotype*.

The value of the cooperation of the geneticist depends on the degree of precision with which the psychiatrist can classify the clinical material and formulate the problem for him. The same applies to the cooperation expected from our colleagues in the fields of pathologic anatomy, physiology, biophysics, and biochemistry. Hence, the first item on our agenda must be to improve the scientific standards of clinical observation and description, and put the interpretation of the patient's behavior firmly on the basis of adaptational psychodynamics. We must abandon obsolete methods and concepts without costly delay. Semantics and cybernetics warn us with increasing urgency that by using undefined (and often enough, undefinable) language we can communicate nothing but confusion. Our responsibility is to keep pace with the general advance of science, evolve a sound, consistent, and verifiable conceptual scheme, and keep it continuously up to date.

REFERENCES

[1] ABRAHAM, K.: Manic-depressive states and the pregenital levels of the libido. *Selected Papers*. London, The Hogarth Press, 1927, p. 418. (Published in German, 1924.)

[2] FREUD, S.: Mourning and melancholia. *Collected Papers, 4.* London, The Hogarth Press, 1925. (Published in German, 1917.)

[3] ——: *The Problem of Anxiety*. New York, Norton, 1936. (Published in German, 1926.)

[4] RADO, S.: An anxious mother: A contribution to the analysis of the ego. *Internat. J. Psycho-Analysis, 9:* 219, 1928. (Published in German, 1927.)

[5] ——: The problem of melancholia. *Internat. J. Psycho-Analysis, 9:* 420, 1928. (Published in German, 1927.)

[6] ——: *Patterns of motivation in depression.* 12th Internat. Psychoanal. Congress, Wiesbaden, 1932.

[7] ——: The psychoanalysis of pharmacothymia (drug addiction). *Psychoanal. Quart. 2:* 1, 1933.

[8] ——: Mind, unconscious mind, and brain. *Psychosom. Med. 11:* 165, 1949.

[9] ——: An adaptational view of sexual behavior. In *Psychosexual Development in Health and Disease* (Hoch and Zubin, Eds.). New York, Grune & Stratton, 1949.

[10] ——: Emergency behavior: With an introduction to the dynamics of conscience. In *Anxiety* (Hoch and Zubin, Eds.). New York, Grune & Stratton, 1950.

[11] ——: The border region between the normal and the abnormal: Four types. In *Ministry and Medicine in Human Relations* (I. Galdston, ed.). New York, International Universities Press, 1955.

[12] ——: Lectures at Columbia University.

On the Psychoanalytic Exploration of Fear and Other Emotions[*]

Since, in my opinion, we cannot meaningfully split off so-called anxiety from the entity of fear, I should like to present the topic under consideration in terms of fear.

In adaptational psychodynamics, we do not study fear as an isolated phenomenon, as a feeling in and of itself. We study fear mainly by the method of contextual inference.[4] The over-all context in which we seek to understand fear is the interaction of organism and environment. We begin with the everyday observation that fear is a response to danger. So is pain, and so is rage. Each of these responses in turn prompts the organism to further activities designed to prevent and repair damage to its organic integrity. We call the context of activities concerned with danger, emergency behavior.[5] This designation was inspired by the work of Walter B. Cannon.[1]

I have attempted to show elsewhere that the organization of emergency behavior is hierarchically ordered and reflects the course of evolutionary history. In this organization, pain is the warning signal of damage. Though pain and damage are not inevitably connected, nevertheless, their linkage is so frequent and dependable that the organism can use pain effectively as a warning signal of damage. This signaling arrangement, developed at an early stage of evolutionary history, is the very basis upon which the entire organization of emergency behavior has evolved. In the further course of evolution, as more and better equipment appeared, the range of foresight (expectancy of pain from damage) increased, and so also, through the cumulative effect of repetition, did the automatization of operating patterns.

At a low evolutionary stage, equipped only with contact receptors, the animal cannot yet foresee the next situation it will meet. Nevertheless, its behavior already reveals a minimum degree of foresight. When pained it makes every effort to rid itself of the source of suffering, as if expecting that otherwise the pain will continue. This elementary characteristic of all

* This paper was presented as part of the panel discussion on the Differences Between Anxiety and other Feelings, at the meeting of the Section on Psychology of The New York Acadamy of Sciences, April 21, 1952. First published in the *Transactions of the New York Academy of Sciences*, series II, *14:* 280–283, 1952.

animal existence was noted by Charles Darwin: "Great pain has urged all animals during endless generations to make the most violent and diversified efforts to escape from the cause of suffering."[2]

I termed these activities elicited by pain the riddance response.[3] This response is ingrained in our organization. Such reflexes as scratching, shedding of tears, sneezing, coughing, spitting, vomiting, and colic bowel movement, are riddance reflexes, designed to eliminate pain-causing agents from the surface or inside of the body.

Repression is automatized riddance from painful thought and feeling. Moreover, inhibition of motor activity that has become dangerous is also automatized riddance.

At subsequent stages of philogenetic history, there evolved the distance receptors, whose adaptive function we may best characterize in Sir Charles Sherrington's words: "The animal's locomotion carries it with one end foremost and habitually so. That leading end, the head, has receiving stations signaling from things at a distance, things which the animal in its foreward movement will next meet. A shell of its immediate future surrounds the animal's head."[7]

Exploration of this shell by the distance receptors enables the animal to foresee pain from an impending damage. Clearly, fear is a warning signal elicited by this expectancy. The same applies to rage. These two emergency emotions in turn spur the organism to muscular activities, but of the exactly opposite direction and kind. The response to fear is escape (flight), and to rage, combat (fight). Clinical observation indicates that fear is an immediate response to the threat of pain from damage, but rage is not; it looks as if the organism has to be primed to rage by a shot of fear. Moreover, the organism is often seen to oscillate between fear and rage until one or the other prevails.

The emotionally aroused animal's muscular activity, however, is not limited to escape or combat. Already at this evolutionary stage there begins to develop the outward display, or more precisely, the expressive aspect of these emotions, presumably for the purpose of broadcasting the warning to the other members of the herd.

With the further evolution of the central nervous system, in particular of the cerebral cortex, intellectual activity rose from an adjunct to the emotions to a super-imposed organization of growing complexity and significance. In its highest forms, freed more and more from the influence of the emotions, thought became an exploratory tool of ever-increasing dependability. With the aid of this tool, man learned to calculate and foretell dependably events lying beyond his "shell of the immediate future" and has thus vastly expanded the spatial and temporal range of his expectancies.

However, between emotion, on the one hand, and unemotional thought, on the other, there is the intermediate level of emotional thought. At this intermediate level, emotion still tends to control reason rather than the other way around. By comparison with unemotional thought, emotional thought is an inferior instrument for the interpretation of what one is actually exposed to. It is not objective but selective. It tends to justify, and thus to feed, the emotion from which it springs, and by which it is controlled.

At the intermediate level of emotional thought, brute fear and rage are in a measure "humanized," i.e., softened down to apprehensive thought and angry thought. There is more discrimination, analysis, combination, and greater flexibility and diversity of motor performance. At the high level of unemotional thought, the organism responds to danger with a purely intellectual expectancy of pain from threatening damage. Unhampered by the emergency emotions, the intellect safeguards the organism in the superior manner of a computing machine. Yet, the moves prompted by these new sets of warning signals remain substantially the same: escape on the one hand, and combat on the other.

In the infant and in the helpless, fear tends to elicit a cry for help. In social dependency relationships, escape may take the form of submission to the authority; and rage, that of defiance.

During cultural history, long before the stage of unemotional thought was attained, there developed those more complex elaborations of fear known as fear of conscience and guilty fear. Fear of conscience elicits conscious restraint, or automatic repression of dangerous thought and desire, and automatic inhibition of dangerous action. Guilty fear, on the other hand, elicits the reparative pattern of expiatory behavior, a pattern often complicated by rage retroflexed and vented on the self.

In order to place the theory just outlined in the proper perspective, let me remark here that in adaptational psychodynamics we contrast the emergency emotions with the welfare emotions, such as strong desire, joy, love, and pride.

After this theoretical preparation, we may now proceed to the methodology of actual psychoanalytic work with the patient. How do we detect in him the presence of fear, or for that matter, of any other emotion?

We listen to the patient's running account of his life performance, observe his treatment behavior and, aided by the technique of free association, trace the patterns of his thoughts and actions. We know the characteristic patterns of emotionally-inspired thought and action (we learned them by advancing from the simple to the complex, from the crude to the refined, from the open to the hidden) and can readily infer from the emerging patterns the emotions that inspired them. We thus detect the presence of fear and other emotions by inference from their motivating (integrative) action, that is to say, by inference from the behavior context. I must add, however that the drawing of such inferences is not a purely intellectual process: the investigator is guided therein by his own emotional resonance. The gross manifestation of resonance is known in everyday life as the contagiousness of emotions. In this procedure of exploration by inference, the expressive aspect of the patient's emotion and even the patient's subjective feeling, which he may describe to us, are often enough used only as controls. Our theory reflects this exploratory procedure. In general, we view the emotions as a class of instrumentalities of the organism for the integration of its behavior.

Clinical experience conclusively proves that the feeling aspect of fear or of rage may be completely absent, as we say, removed from the patient's awareness by repression, and yet the emotions of fear and rage may nonetheless be present in the organism and exert their motivating (integrative) influence on the patient's actions and thoughts. In these instances we speak of unconscious, or better, of non-reporting fear and rage.[4] Sometimes, but not always, the presence of such non-reporting emotions is also indicated by a feeling of qualitatively undifferentiated tension.

The patterns of thought and action motivated (integrated) by the various emotions characteristically differ from one another. We speak of escape pattern, combat pattern, submission pattern, defiance pattern, brooding pattern, expiatory pattern, pattern of self-damaging defiance, *etc.* Hence, the same method of contextual inference also enables us to tell the various emotions apart.

We now have our answer to the first two of the questions posed for this panel discussion. First: the differences between fear and other emotions can best be defined by their motivating (integrative) action. Second: these differences can be objectively recognized by examining the patterns of the patient's actions and thoughts.

As we see, the contextual study of the emotions dwarfs the significance of their feeling aspect. This is most fortunate indeed, because we have no dependable means for the comparative study of other people's feelings. Even our capacity for understanding the feelings they describe depends on our own emotional experiences. This answers the third question posed for this panel discussion: though the subjective differences between emotions, say between fear and joy, are of overriding importance for our well-being, the scientific study of the verbal accounts of these differences in feeling is still in an elementary stage. We speak of differences in "specific feeling quality," hedonic tone (pleasant–unpleasant), intensity (mild–strong), *etc.*

Let me call your attention to an important difference between feeling and thought. Though both belong to the private phase of behavior, the patient can communicate his thought verbatim, but he cannot communicate his feelings directly. This is why emotionally-inspired action is so helpful to the investigator: it moves the emotion from the private phase to the public phase of behavior. Moreover, emotionally-inspired thought is often enough fantasied action and hence renders the investigator a similar service. From the point of view of the investigator, emotionally-motivated action and emotionally-motivated fantasied action act as amplifiers of the motivating emotion.

The theory of emergency behavior proves helpful in clarifying the variety of pathological fears and other faulty emergency responses encountered in psychoanalytic work. The patient is seen to develop fear in the absence of danger, to respond with excessive fear to trivial danger, to suffer from guilty fear arising from imagined guilt, *etc.* His fear may become so severe that its inhibitory action defeats its emergency function, and damages, rather than aids, the organism. When fear thus becomes a threat to the organism it elicits a new round of preventive and reparative measures which often enough miscarry completely. I termed the resulting disturbance emergency dyscontrol. This disturbance may include the simultaneous arousal of fear and rage, which then compete with one another for immediate discharge, and thus create a discharge interference.[6] In obsessional cases, this is seen in the see-saw of the patient's broodings and in the see-saw of his rituals. In great psychotic excitement, with the breakdown of hierarchic regulation, the contrasting action patterns elicited by simultaneous fear and rage may produce a pattern of motor confusion. So far, clinical observation has fully justified the proposition that failures of emergency adjustment lie at the bottom of disordered behavior.

The theory of emergency behavior depicts an exceedingly complex subject in first approximation. But it organizes facts scattered over vast areas under a common point of view, and points up ever new problems that can be explored by observation and experiment. Without a fruitful conceptual scheme we could undertake neither research nor treatment.

REFERENCES

[1] CANNON, W. B.: *Bodily Changes in Pain, Hunger, Fear and Rage.* New York, Appleton, 1934, 227–229.

[2] DARWIN, C.: *The Expression of the Emotions in Man and Animals.* New York, Appleton, 1910.

[3] RADO, S.: Developments in the psychoanalytic conception and treatment of the neuroses. *Psychoanal. Quart., 8:* 427, 1939.

[4] ——: Mind, unconscious mind, and brain. *Psychosom. Med., 11:* 165, 1949.

[5] ——: Emergency behavior: With an introduction to the dynamics of conscience. *Anxiety* (Hoch and Zubin, Eds.). New York, Grune and Stratton, 1950.

[6] ——: Psychodynamics of depression from the etiologic point of view. *Psychosom. Med., 13:* 51, 1951.

[7] SHERRINGTON, C.: *The Brain and its Mechanism.* Cambridge Univ. Press, 1933.

Psychiatric Aspects of Sweating*

I feel fortunate in having been invited to discuss before you the psychiatric aspects of sweating, for your symposium shows remarkable advance in knowledge of the physiological changes that underlie the clinical pictures. We psychiatrists, too, are making strides in tracing our clinical findings to the underlying psychodynamics; but then we still face the supreme task of comprehensive medicine: to correlate psychodynamics and physiology.

The physiologist views sweating as one of the homeostatic mechanisms concerned with temperature regulation. However, the sweat mechanism is known also to respond to emotional stimulation. Emotional sweating may aid or disturb temperature regulation; in any case, it may also be charged with functions other than thermal and may have an adaptive value on these other grounds.

In the physiological study of the sweat mechanism one focuses his attention on the interaction of the organism and its physical environment. In the psychiatric study of sweating the focus is on the interaction of the organism and its human environment, for emotions are responses to social situations, arising in the main in the relationship of human beings to one another. The emotions that are known to affect the sweat mechanism are shown in the following paragraphs:

Emergency Emotions.—In this class, emotions are based on (1) the foresight of painful (damaging) experience and (2) the intent to avoid such experience.

Fears: Appropriate or inappropriate fears, fears of conscience, guilty fears. These responses may be manifest or latent. The presence of latent fears can be inferred psychoanalytically from the motivational context.

Rages: Appropriate or inappropriate resentments, angers, and rages. These responses may be manifest or latent. The presence of latent rage can be inferred psychoanalytically from the motivational context. An important automatic discharge of latent yet overflowing rage is self-harming defiance.

Welfare Emotions.—In this class, emotions are based on (1) the foresight of pleasurable (beneficial) experience and (2) the desire for such experience.

Desire: Recognized or unrecognized.

---

* Discussion in a Symposium on the Sweat Apparatus, Dermatological Society, New York, Dec. 20, 1951. First published in the *A. M. A. Archives of Dermatology and Syphilology, 66:* 175–176, 1952.

Sexual Excitement: Recognized or unrecognized.

This class further includes emotions (joy, love, pride, etc.) which are not known to affect the sweat mechanism.

Comment.—This classification is based on the adaptive function of the emotions. In my opinion, adaptation is the most helpful point of view we have so far developed in all biology. The psychodynamics of the emergency emotions harmonizes well with Walter B. Cannon's physiological work, which is based on the same point of view.

From among the emergency emotions the varieties of fear just listed have the most conspicuous action on the sweat mechanism. The cold sweat, the clammy palms of the man in fear are generally known. Here we are puzzled by individual differences. We see patients with a healthy capacity for thermal sweating who show no marked emotional sweating when shaking with fear. Other patients may sweat profusely when it requires skillful psychoanalytic exploration to detect their fear. Sweating from fear must be considered a physiologic constituent of the organismic event we call fear, even though the adaptive function of this constituent is unknown; however, excessive sweating from fear must be considered pathological: it is a descending involvement.

The adaptive significance of such descending involvements is open to biological speculation. It is a vital interest of the organism to keep its psychodynamic nervous system, its highest level of central integration, free from the burden of excessive excitation. By utilizing the established physiological patterns of the Cannon phenomenon, this system may dump the excessive excitation of emergency emotions at lower physiological levels. The disturbance thus created at the point of dumping is, as a rule, the lesser of two evils. In the light of this hypothesis, descending involvements, such as profuse sweating from fear, originate with a central mechanism for the peripheral disposal of excessive excitation.

Rage frankly expressed appears to have little if any stimulating effect upon the sweat mechanism. But latent rage, if discharged automatically in self-harming defiance, may on the contrary produce profuse emotional sweating. To give a clinical example, there are patients whose manual performance or work requires completely dry fingers; their sweating hands render performance impossible or ruin the material with which they work. The patient thus automatically spites the demanding authority by "cutting off his own nose." After the mechanism of sweating from self-damaging defiance has been established in the organism, it becomes difficult to demonstrate it because of the then added fear of the damaging consequences of the sweating. It then looks as if the sweating would be caused by this fear, which in fact merely intensifies it.

Turning now to the welfare emotions, the sweat-eliciting action of desire appears to have little practical importance. There are reports on performers capable of producing sweating in certain circumscribed areas at will. I myself have never seen this feat. However, I do not think that it can be done by a mere "concentration of thought"; if it can be done at all, one must presume, it is done by the action of desire.

The influence of sexual excitement on apocrine sweating seems to be a controversial question among physiologists. There is nothing controversial about it to the psychiatrist. The huge apocrine sweat glands are strategically located—certainly not for temperature regulation, but for the production of odoriferous sweat. As mentioned by Dr. Shelley, the activity of these glands begins after puberty and is controlled by the hormonal machinery of the organism. There can be little doubt that odoriferous apocrine sweating in the female is a mechanism for the sexual attraction of the male. It may be, as Dr. Shelley has suggested, a vestigial mechanism; however, psychoanalytic observation shows that men in unsuspected numbers and often unbeknown to themselves depend for adequate sexual arousal on this olfactory stimulus. The cultural pattern seeks to make odoriferous sweat sexually repulsive rather than attractive; capitalizing on an idea borrowed from the flowers and the bees, it offers perfume as a vicarious olfactory stimulant.

In reverting to the emergency emotions, let me say a few words about the patient's own emotional reaction to his profuse sweating from fear. This reaction is a composite of shame, embarrassment, and still more fear; the added fear is fear of the damaging social consequences of the profuse sweating. Thus, a vicious circle is brought into play. According to Dr. Herrmann, these patients should be advised to keep cool and calm. Imagine a young man dancing with his "best girl," keeping cool and contemplating calmly the prints his profusely sweating hand will leave on her pink dress. Though Dr. Herrmann's advice is sound, it does not seem to fit every psychological situation. To break these vicious circles is a difficult task even in psychiatric treatment.

Closer correlation of the psychodynamics of the emotions with the physiology of the emotions is still a task for the future.

Recent Advances in Psychoanalytic Therapy*

Freud's motivational theory of behavior, known as classical psychodynamics, is the basis of the classical technique of psychoanalytic therapy. Adaptational psychodynamics, a consistent development of the classical theory, seeks to place the analysis of behavior on a sound biological foundation, and to depict motivation in a close-to-the-fact language that facilitates its clinical verification. This revised theory sheds new light on the therapeutic mechanisms by which the various treatment procedures operate, discloses the imperfections of the classical technique as well as its lasting achievements, and leads to the development of a new technique of psychoanalytic therapy which I call the adaptational technique.

Limiting the scope of my assignment to this line of recent development, in the present paper I shall introduce a conceptual scheme for the comparative study of diverse psychotherapeutic methods, take a fresh view of the chief therapeutic ideas evolved in the past, outline the new adaptational technique and finally glance at the problems that lie ahead.

THE CONCEPTUAL SCHEME

Psychotherapy is a medical procedure; it may be defined as the use of human influence for the treatment of behavior disorders. We distinguish between the patient's *treatment behavior* and his *life performance*. The term treatment behavior refers to his co-operation with the physician; the term life performance, to the rest of his activities in daily life.

The patient's treatment behavior can be understood only in terms of his own shifting *designs for co-operation* whether he is aware of them or not. The various designs for co-operation encountered in our patients fall into a hierarchically ordered scheme of levels; this order is shown in table 1.

These designs for co-operation are subject to complications. For example, instead of co-operating the patient may wish to take the place of the physician; or he may be divided against himself and secretly prefer to stay ill. However, such complications do not affect the validity of our hierarchical scheme.

---

* First published in *Psychiatric Treatment*, Vol. 21 of the *Proceedings of the Association for Research in Nervous and Mental Disease*, Baltimore, Williams & Wilkins, 1953, pp. 42–58.

At the self-reliant and aspiring levels the patient's treatment behavior is based on common sense. In contrast, at the parentifying and magic-craving

TABLE 1. *Hierarchic order of the patient's designs for co-operation*

ASPIRING Level: Available only in the adult who is capable and desirous of self-advancement by extensive learning and maturation.	"I am delighted to co-operate with the doctor. This is my opportunity to learn how to make full use of all my potential resources for adaptive growth."

↑ ↓

SELF-RELIANT Level: Available in the average adult who is capable of learning the simple know-how of daily life.	"I am ready to co-operate with the doctor. I must learn how to help myself and do things for myself."

↓

Adult
_____
Child-like

↑

PARENTIFYING Level: When the adult feels like a helpless child, he seeks parental help and therefore parentifies the therapist.	"I don't know what the doctor expects of me. I couldn't do it anyway. He should cure me by *his* effort."

↑ ↓

MAGIC-CRAVING Level: The completely discouraged adult retreats to the hope that the parentified therapist will do miracles for him.	"The doctor must not only cure me, he must do everything for me—by magic."

↑ = advance.   ↓ = regression.

levels his treatment behavior reveals excessive emotional dependence on the physician, befitting a child more than an adult. Often unknown to himself he sees in the physician an idealized re-incarnation of his own parent, brought back to the scene by the power of his desire. Accordingly, his co-operation aims at obtaining the privileges of a favorite child, not at learning and maturation. Thus in our hierarchical scheme the sharp dividing line runs between the self-reliant and parentifying levels: above this line the patient's co-operation is adult, below it, child-like.

While the aspiring and self-reliant levels are not available in every patient, proneness of the helpless adult to regress to parentifying or magic-craving behavior is ineradicable and universal.

The fundamental clinical fact is that patients can be successfully treated at every level of treatment behavior. However, the goals and techniques of treatment are so different from level to level that it becomes an important technical task to counteract the patient's inclination to shift from one level to another, in particular, to cross the line that divides the levels of adult co-operation from the levels of child-like co-operation.

The physician must seek to stabilize the patient's co-operation at the level selected for his treatment. For this purpose he uses measures devised to regulate the patient's treatment behavior; we call these *priming measures*. In contradistinction, we call the measures devised to modify the patient's life performance *modifying measures*. Measures intended to prime and modify at the same time are called *double duty measures*.

Each particular method of psychotherapy has its own *plan for priming* and its own *plan for modifying*. Of course, its plan for modifying depends upon its plan for priming. These two plans may be conveniently used as a basis for classification of all methods of psychotherapy.

LINEAGE OF PSYCHOTHERAPEUTIC METHODS

Comparative analysis shows that the historical development of the major psychotherapeutic methods has an inherent logical consistency. To demonstrate this instructive fact, in our re-examination of these methods we shall follow the order of their historical appearance. The lineage of psychotherapeutic methods is shown in table 2.

HYPNOTHERAPY

Priming

Hypnotherapy's plan for priming is to put the patient into a hypnotic state by taking full advantage of his craving for magical help[7, 11, 12]. As a child the patient knew the ironclad rule that he must purchase the "magical" ministrations of his parents with his own obedience. When told by the physician that he should go to sleep though he is not sleepy at all, the patient senses that the ironclad rule is still in force. Hence, by the action of his own desire the patient lapses into a hypnotic state, a state of almost *automatic obedience* to the parentified physician. Far from resenting this necessity, the patient feels hopeful, even triumphant: his dream of magical help is coming true. Therefore he will act upon the physician's orders as if acting upon his own intentions.

Magic-craving of the distressed is craving for security through obedience. Hypnotherapy works at the magic-craving level of treatment behavior.

TABLE 2. *Lineage of psychotherapeutic methods*

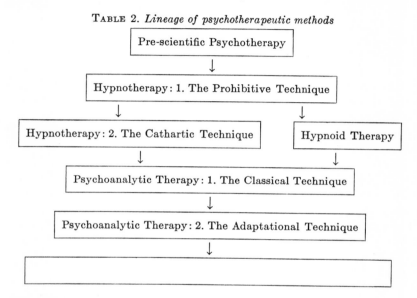

1. The prohibitive technique: modifying

Having thus primed the patient for automatic obedience, the physician must decide what modifying measure to employ. He may choose the most primitive modifying measure known, the exercise of disciplinary authority. In effect, the physician tells the hypnotized patient: "Stop this nonsense! You are not ill! You feel fine!" The proper designation of this procedure is the prohibitive technique of hypnotherapy.

This technique tries to cure the patient with parental discipline. Therapeutic results are obtained at the cost of increased inner tension; their collapse is only a question of time. Nonetheless, this technique may still be used to tide the patient over an emergency.

2. The cathartic technique: modifying

In 1880–82 a patient of Dr. Joseph Breuer of Vienna taught the medical profession how to make better therapeutic use of the hypnotic state. This young lady knew that hypnosis is but a means to an end: what she sought to obtain by her almost automatic obedience was *permission to disobey*. She wished to have *her* say while under hypnosis. With Breuer's consent she revived forgotten emotional experiences, and the emotional relief freed her from her symptoms. She called this procedure "chimney sweeping". In 1893, Breuer, by then in collaboration with Freud, called it the cathartic method of hypnotherapy, or hypnocatharsis[1]. In contradistinction to the prohibitive technique, it is a permissive technique, the first one to appear in scientific psychotherapy.

That the wholesale discharge of pent-up emotions has an unburdening effect has been appreciated since Aristotle. What Breuer discovered was a new and more specific therapeutic principle, but his true discovery was lost in a shuffle of unwarranted generalizations.

In a hot summer, Breuer's patient was unable to drink a drop of water because she could not touch the tumbler with her lips. Under hypnosis she related that once when she entered the room of her hated English governess, she saw the latter's "disgusting" little dog drinking out of a tumbler. She said nothing because she "wanted to be polite". Breuer describes the rest of this hypnotic session as follows:

> After she gave energetic expression to her anger, she asked for a drink, and without any inhibition drank a great deal of water, awakening from the hypnosis with the glass at her lips ([1], p. 23).

This therapeutic mechanism is not an emotional purge in general, but the *release of repressed rage* in particular. This mechanism can remove only symptoms that serve as a vicarious outlet for rage *recently* repressed. The inability of Breuer's patient to touch the tumbler with her lips gave pantomimic expression to her bitter resentment of the governess: "You see what your inconsiderate action did to me! For all I know this may be the same tumbler you allowed your disgusting pet to use. How can you expect me to touch it with my lips? If I die of thirst it will be your fault."

We also learn from this case that release of rage is therapeutic only if certain additional criteria are satisfied. It was with Breuer's approval that the patient released her anger at the governess. This put an end to her humiliation, restored her pride, and assuaged her guilty fear of the governess. Had Breuer reprimanded her for her disrespect of the governess, he would have destroyed the therapeutic success. Another crucial point is that the patient felt free to recall the incident responsible for her rage. Had she feared that Breuer might criticize her, she would have remained silent or vented her anger on Breuer; in either case she would have retained her symptom.

Today we may formulate the modifying measure discovered by Breuer as follows:

The release of repressed rage is a decompressive procedure comparable to the opening of a blind abscess. To release the repressed rage, one must first locate and revive it in the memory context of the life experience that provoked it. Furthermore, to be successful, the release must retrieve the patient's lost pride; this effect can be obtained only if the patient feels that the physician approves of his released rage.

HYPNOID THERAPY

The hypnoid state is a wakeful counterpart of the hypnotic state. In the hypnoid state the patient displays a degree of *uncritical obedience* to the parentified physician, that makes him act upon the latter's propositions as if acting on his own intentions. The degree of uncritical obedience varies in a wide range. Uncritical obedience may result 1) from the patient's craving for magic, or 2) from his craving for a helpful ersatzparent, helpful in a more or less realistic sense. Thus hypnoid therapy may work 1) at the magic-craving level, or 2) at the parentifying level.

1. Priming and modifying at the magic-craving level

Magic-craving may be a fleeting episode evoked by distress in the healthy or the sick. Priming must sustain the patient's craving and belief that the physician is the person he needs. The means used may be crude or subtle; they amount to a reassuring display of what the patient believes to be the superior powers of the physician.

Modifying is done by disguised hypnoid orders; the vehicle used may be a placebo or a measure of true medical value. The magic-craving patient may supply himself with the desired hypnoid orders regardless of the physician's own intentions. This applies to all physicians and all medical procedures.

Hypnoid therapy at the magic-craving level is known as suggestive therapy or as the suggestive component of all medical procedures.

What enables the magic-craving patient to act upon the physician's hypnoid orders, whether these are explicit, implied or simply presumed by the patient? By parentifying the physician at the cost of uncritical obedience, the patient experiences an uplift, increased self-confidence and sense of emotional security; these changes relax his inhibitions, allay his fears and facilitate his life performance. Owing to the patient's own desire, the parentified physician may thus be able to induce him to do things he was unable to do by himself. However, the physician must first comfort the patient and help him to unburden himself by discharging his pent-up emotions. He may help the patient over the hump by sound advice and other supportive measures.

2. *Priming and modifying at the parentifying level*

Priming follows the same principles as above; but here the physician must be more subtle because the patient is more critical. As compared with the magic-craving level, here the physician's opportunity for modifying is greatly increased. By utilizing the patient's desire for security through obedience he may employ modifying measures that will induce in the patient true processes of emotional learning. Many of the therapeutic results thus achieved may survive even if later the patient loses his hypnoid faith in the physician. However, the patient will then have to find another ersatzparent.

We have no descriptive name for this type of treatment; the term "brief psychotherapy" has some currency.

PSYCHOANALYTIC THERAPY: 1. THE CLASSICAL TECHNIQUE

Freud's conception of psychoanalytic treatment

Freud's discovery of free association—thinking out loud—was a fruit of the bold initiative of Breuer's patient. With the introduction of this new investigative method it has become a psychodynamic principle that the patient shall have *his* say in his treatment. Safeguarded by the Hippocratic oath of the physician and prompted by his own need for help, he may be more candid with the physician than he ever dared to be with himself. The new investigative method disclosed the patient's life history in intimate detail and enabled Freud to organize this hitherto inaccessible material in terms of motivation and development. This type of work, he said, may relieve the patient from the necessity of sustaining inner resistances; he may recall his forgotten past, his repressed desires, and handle them in the superior manner of conscious control. Since conscious desires can produce no vicarious activity (viewed at the time as the general mechanism of symptom formation) "the continuance and even the renewal of the morbid condition is impossible"[3]. As this statement shows, Freud attributed almost unlimited therapeutic power to the undoing of the patient's repressions, hence his vision of psychoanalysis as a therapy of total reconstruction that would lift the patient to a higher level of psychodynamic organization.

Freud's threefold formulation of the mode of action of psychoanalytic therapy is basic to the classical technique. He advanced it in 1904, repeating it unchanged throughout his life[3-6]:

> The aim of our efforts may be expressed in various formulas—making conscious the unconscious, removing the repressions, filling in the gaps in memory; they all amount to the same thing.
> We do nothing for our patients but enable this one mental change to take place in them; the extent to which it is achieved is the extent of the benefit we do them ([5], p. 377).

Freud's discovery and interpretation of parentifying treatment behavior

To explain the unexpected fact that the patient turns child-like in his treatment behavior, Freud introduced a hypothesis of far-reaching consequences. The patient, he said, is subject to an inner force that compels him to *transfer* his infantile responses from his past relationship to his parents to his present relationship to the physician. He thus viewed parentifying treatment behavior as a forced repetition of the patient's past, and called it *transference*. This hypothesis made parentifying treatment behavior a phenomenon independent from and unmotivated by the patient's present situation in treatment and life.

This hypothesis enabled Freud to consider parentifying treatment behavior as but another form in which the patient reproduces his past. Recollections and repetitions complement one another, each revealing the patient's past in its own way. Freud's classification of transference and the meaning of his terms are shown in table 3.

TABLE 3. *"Transference": terms and meaning*

Terms *Forms of transference:*	Meaning *Patient behaves the way he did when he was:*
Positive transference	An obedient child
Resistant transference	A disobedient child
1) Negative transference	1) A defiant child
2) Sensual transference	2) A child bent on sexual gratification

Priming

In Freud's view, positive transference is the force—the only force—that enables the patient to absorb and act upon the interpretations proposed to him by the physician:

> The outcome in this struggle [between repression and therapeutic undoing of re-

pression] is not decided by his [the patient's] intellectual insight—it is neither strong enough nor free enough to accomplish such a thing—but solely by his relationship to the physician. In so far as his transference bears the positive sign, it clothes the physician with authority, transforms itself into faith in his findings and in his views. Without this kind of transference or with a negative one, the physician and his arguments would never even be listened to. Faith repeats the history of its own origin; it is a derivative of love and at first it needed no arguments. Not until later does it admit them so far as to take them into critical consideration if they have been offered by someone who is loved. Without this support arguments have no weight with the patient, never do have any with most people in life (⁵, p. 387).

This passage is the basis of Freud's three rules for the handling of transference: 1) Positive transference must be preserved intact throughout the treatment. 2) Resistant transference must be dissolved and the patient restored to positive transference. This can be done, he said, by showing the patient that it is a now senseless repetition of his infantile behavior towards his parents. 3) At the conclusion of the treatment positive transference "must be dissolved"; Freud did not say how this could be done.

Freud's rules, translated into the language of our conceptual scheme, might read as follows: Only in a state of child-like dependence upon the physician, a state of uncritical obedience, can the patient absorb and act upon the interpretations proposed to him by the physician. Therefore his child-like dependence, his uncritical obedience, must be preserved intact throughout the treatment. His disobedience—defiance—must be broken: he must be shown that it is a repetition of his infantile behavior, now disturbingly injected into his relationship to the physician. At the conclusion of the treatment he must be induced to terminate his uncritical obedience.

To sum up: the classical technique primes the patient for uncritical co-operation with the physician. The classical technique is a technique of child-like emotional dependence; it works at the parentifying level of treatment behavior.

Modifying

An adequate plan for modifying the patient's life performance must first consider the relation of available means to desired ends. It must include an itemized list of the problems; an itemized list of the tools; a set of instructions as to how to put the latter to work.

The classical plan for modifying includes no itemized list of the problems; it merely implies that the problem is to cure the patient of his psychoneurosis. This limits the plan to an outline of the relationship of the tools to one another.

The modifying measures used by the classical technique fall into three groups:

1. Interpretation of the patient's recollections for the purpose of undoing his repressions; reinforcement of the emerging insights by repeated "working-through" of the material.

2. Interpretation, for the same purpose, of the patient's resistant transference, particularly his negative transference. Translated into the language of our conceptual scheme: the physician must trace selected phases of the patient's parentifying treatment behavior to comparable phases of his childhood behavior; in particular, he must trace the patient's present defiance to his defiance of his parents in early life. The objective is to familiarize the patient with his repertoire of defiance and incestuous desires; awareness will enable him to control these infantile impulses in his life performance.

Since interpretation of the patient's resistant transference is also used to regulate his treatment behavior, it is a double duty measure in the sense of our conceptual scheme.

3. Measures of so-called "activity" on the part of the physician, such as pledging the patient to abstain from making crucial decisions while under treatment, persuading him to make an effort to fight his phobic avoidances, setting a deadline for the treatment.

In the classical technique, interpretation is based on classical psychodynamics. The emphasis is on making the patient understand his development, that is his libidinal development, his temptations, fears and mechanisms of defense. In classical psychodynamics, neurotic and psychotic behavior are described and explained in terms of libidinal development; so is, for that matter, all behavior. In the classical technique excessive preoccupation with questions of libidinal meaning and development has completely dwarfed the basic question of all psychotherapy: the ascertaining of the adaptive value (positive or negative) of the patient's life performance. The disclosure of motivation and development is notoriously mistaken for an evaluation of performance. Let me make this clear with an example. A piece of writing may be a work of art or the senseless effusion of a deranged mind; which it is can be ascertained only by critical evaluation in the cultural context, not by disclosure of its author's motivation and development.

Critical evaluation of the classical technique

The aim of psychoanalytic therapy is to increase the patient's capacity for enjoyment and active achievement in life by lifting him to a higher level of psychodynamic organization. The pre-analytic methods of psychotherapy could not even conceive the possibility of such total reconstruction. To have evolved this objective is a lasting achievement of the classical technique. How far has it advanced towards the attainment of its goal? Measuring it by its own yardstick, this is what we find:

1. The classical technique works at the parentifying level of treatment behavior. To the extent of his uncritical obedience to the physician the patient continues practicing child-like emotional dependence throughout his treatment. Therefore, this technique cannot lift him to a higher level of psychodynamic organization. By offering the patient a singular opportunity for emotional learning over a lengthy period of time, it may achieve unmatched therapeutic results; but it cannot significantly reduce his proneness to inappropriate emotional dependence. If the burden of his adaptive task increases he will seek shelter with an ersatzparent.

2. Parentifying treatment behavior is a product of the patient's therapeutic situation. The transference theory views it as a product of repetition-compulsion[4], a hypothetical force exempt from the hedonic self-regulation of the organism, operating "beyond the pleasure principle". Thus parentifying treatment behavior appears on the scene like a *deus ex machina*. Attributing parentifying treatment behavior to the intervention of an almost supernatural force has rendered its true understanding impossible. Ultimately, it threatens to strip psychoanalytic therapy of its unique scientific and practical value, and to turn it into a ritual.

3. Analysis of the patient's parentifying treatment behavior in terms of negative transference, variously featured in psychoanalytic literature as erlebnistherapie, neocatharsis[2], corrective experience, and the like, is an inadequate procedure for the all-important therapeutic release of the patient's resentments. In Breuer's catharsis the released rage retains its true object; therein lies the therapeutic efficacy of Breuer's procedure. In the transference procedure whenever the patient vents his rage on the physician, there follows a penetrating search for the infantile origins of his rage resulting as a rule in the finding that he has again repeated his rage against his father. This procedure relieves neither the patient's true resentment of the physician nor his true resentment of his father; still less does it relieve the resentments of his current life situation which are in no small measure responsible for his present suffering. In therapeutic efficacy the scapegoat principle of negative transference lags far behind the true-release principle embodied in Breuer's procedure.

4. A one-sided developmental frame of reference of whatever kind is inadequate for the purposes of psychodynamic understanding and therapeutic interpretation. It tends to concentrate all interest and effort on the patient's past, to the neglect of his present. This fact is reflected in psychoanalytic literature, which refers neatly to the entirety of the patient's present life as his "current conflict".

5. The modifying power of the undoing of repressions is overrated. To

overcome repressions and thus be able to recall the past is one thing; to learn from it and be able to act on the new knowledge, another. It is the patient's undue inhibitions that make him unable to act and learn by acting. These undue inhibitions develop in childhood and are carried over into adult life as automatizations. Undoing the repression of thought and desire does not by itself remove the automatized inhibition of executive action.

However, such shortcomings of the classical technique are not final. Psychoanalytic therapy surges with values and therapeutic resources; in its development, the classical technique is not the end but the beginning.

Psychoanalytic Therapy: 2. The Adaptational Technique

Patients lastingly incapable of adult co-operation are not eligible for a therapy of total reconstruction. They require other treatment methods. The adaptational technique is designed to work at the self-reliant or preferably the aspiring level of treatment behavior.

In the adaptational psychodynamics of behavior disorders we encounter organized sequences of events which we have come to recognize as processes of miscarried prevention and miscarried repair[8, 13-16]. They are brought into play in early life by the child's faulty emergency responses, his over-reaction to danger, particularly to the parental threat of punishment. The early phase of behavior disorder, emergency dyscontrol, appears in the child's dependency relationship to his parents; its products are carried over into adult life. The ensemble of the patient's faulty emergency responses includes excessive or inappropriate fears, rages, guilty fears and guilty rages; most damaging are the undue inhibitions which have arrested function, growth and development in the affected areas, pre-eminently in group membership and sexual behavior. In the treatment of behavior disorders, the critical task is to bring the patient's emergency emotions under control; to remove his damaging inhibitions; to generate in him an emotional matrix dominated by welfare emotions (pleasurable desire, joy, love and pride) and controlled by adaptive insight, a matrix conducive to a healthy life performance. In the adaptational technique the plans for priming and modifying seek to fulfill this task.

Priming

The adaptational plan for priming is to hold the patient as much as possible at the adult levels of co-operation with the physician. When his treatment behavior turns or threatens to turn child-like, we seek to bring him back to the adult level without delay.

Child-like co-operation, that is, parentifying treatment behavior, must be understood in the context of the here and now. Adaptational psychodynamics views the patient's search for an ersatzparent as a process of miscarried repair, a cardinal feature of behavior disorders. Before he entered treatment, he moved in disillusion from one ersatzparent to the next. During treatment, as soon as he loses his self-confidence, he parentifies the physician. Resorting to the adaptive pattern, the goals and tactics, of a child, he then plies the parentified physician with smiles, tears and lashings, as shown schematically in table 4.

We know the patient's personal program for parentifying behavior from his life history; he performed this program time and again in his relationship to his parents and ersatzparents. The adaptational technique seeks to forestall the unnecessary repetition of this program in the patient's treat-

TABLE 4. *Plying the parentified physician with smiles, tears, and lashings*

Ingratiating:	"I am courting your favor, doing everything you wish, be nice to me."
Impatient:	"It's time for you to cure me (by magic)."
Seductive:	"Meanwhile, make love to me (the magic of your love will cure me)."
Upon feeling rejected by the physician:	
Expiatory:	"Your aloofness fills me with guilty fear. I should like to expiate for my disobedience and promise to be obedient—please forgive me."
Resentful:	"When I was a child my parents never let me have my way. You said yourself that's how they started my intimidation and illness. It's *your* job to undo the wrong they did me. True, you urge me 'to get it off my chest,' but you hold me in your clutches just the same. You can't fool me."
Coercive:	"Now I am really furious. Stop this double talk and cure me."
Vindictive:	"I shall get even with you . . . I never wish to see you again."

ment behavior by the priming measure of *interceptive interpretation*. This is an intricate procedure; to succeed, the physician must first bolster up the patient's self-confidence on *realistic grounds*. Interpretation is a double duty measure: it is used for modifying the patient's life performance as well as regulating his treatment behavior. We shall deal with it under the next heading.

Modifying

The adaptational technique's plan for modifying is too elaborate to be presented here in detail. I shall touch only upon a few major points.

We interpret to the patient his treatment behavior and life performance in an adaptational framework of meaning. By adaptations we mean improvements in the organism's pattern of interaction with its environment; these are composed of changes undergone by the organism itself ("autoplastic" adaptations) and changes brought about by the organism in the environment ("alloplastic" adaptations).

The patient must learn to view life, himself, and others in terms of opportunities and responsibilities, successes and failures. He must learn to understand his doings in terms of motivation and control, to evaluate his doings in terms of the cultural context, and to understand his development in terms of his background and life history.

The meaning of non-reporting (unconscious) motivation can be stated only in extrapolated terms of conscious motivation[11, 15]; the strength of non-reporting motivation can be determined only in relation to the strength of conscious motivation. Therefore interpretation must always embrace the conscious as well as the non-reporting phases of motivation. Even when the biographical material on hand reaches far into the past, interpretation must always begin and end with the patient's present life performance, his present adaptive task. The significance of this rule cannot be overstated.

A mathematical interpretation may be a purely intellectual process. A therapeutic interpretation must engender in the patient an emotional process or else miss its purpose. Freud described psychoanalytic therapy as a process of re-education; I should like to stress that it is pre-eminently a process of *emotional* re-education. In behavior disorders emotions control reason; a crucial goal of treatment is to adjust emotion to reason. Insight alone has little if any therapeutic effect. This is pre-eminently true of painful insight which is at the mercy of the patient's next emotional upheaval. Using the material of his own life experience, we show the patient how brute emotions, emotional thought, and unemotional thought differ from one another in integrative action[13, 14]. He can learn to change his faulty pattern of emotional responses in one way only: by practice; he must begin to do this before the eyes of the physician. Thus, the process of emotional re-education always begins with the therapeutic release of the resentments of his current life situation. Rage glues the patient's attention to the past, to the damage he believes to have suffered; he must learn to look to the future, learn from the damage and seek repair if and when possible. If the patient arrives in the physician's office in a state of acute emotional distress, the first order of busines is of course to relieve his distress.

Let me show with one example how emotional re-education works. Suppose the patient is in a state of apprehension, unable to tackle an inescapable task. Asked to give free rein to his thought, he piles up his memories of failure at comparable tasks. Emotional thought tends of course to justify and thus to feed the emotion from which it springs and by which it is controlled. We can indeed see that his apprehension grows. Suppose further that by a stroke of good luck he not only arrives at the historical origin of this particular apprehension but also discovers its connection with a latent fear of damage to his sexual anatomy. In whatever frame of reference the physician interprets this material, with whatever skill, the patient will leave the office more disheartened than he was when he came. I have seen this often enough in my patients and in patients of other analysts.

There is a silver lining in every cloud. Memories can be looked at from many angles. More often than we think, even memories of true failure, not to speak of memories of presumed failure, do contain elements of success. The therapeutic task is to neutralize the perturbing power of memories of failure by playing up the elements conducive to pleasure[10]. If this is done on a sufficiently large scale the patient advances from unwarranted despair to warranted hope. We need not fear that we will becloud his judgment and teach him how to deceive himself. On the contrary, it is only when this emotional neutralization succeeds and his fears and rages subside that he becomes capable of clear thought and realistic judgment. This procedure, the *emotional redefinition of memories*, is a powerful aid in the task of transforming the patient's emotional outlook or, as we may put it, his field of emotional expectation, and restoring his lost self-confidence. These changes are a prerequisite of all further emotional learning.

One need not fear that treatment at the adult level of co-operation deprives the patient of the requisite emotional incentive. At first the child learns only if he loves those who teach him. Later he discovers the intellectual and practical value of the subject matter to which he is exposed. He then develops the proper emotional incentives for learning by taking pleasure and pride in his growing knowledge and skills. If the patient missed out on this development he must acquire the proper emotional mechanism of learning in his treatment.

A unique instrument of emotional re-education is the therapeutic analysis of the patient's dreams; the proved value of dream analysis is considerably increased by a revised procedure. Other innovations are the preventive handling of the patient's riddance impulses[8, 13], known in the psychoanalytic literature as "acting out"; the reversal of the vicious circles of disorder into benign ones, and the dissolution of still accessible inhibitions. Here I can do no more than mention these subjects. The same applies to the development of special procedures for the treatment of the patterns of self-damaging defiance and sexual pain-dependence, other common sexual disorders, and the obsessive and depressive patterns[16].

Concluding remarks on the adaptational technique

Viewed in its entirety, treatment with the adaptational technique takes place in a different intellectual and emotional climate. As elsewhere in medicine, this change can be ascertained only through the physician's own practical experience. This of course requires thorough familiarity with all the details and finenesses of the adaptational technique.

Scientific psychotherapy has undergone a process of gradual liberalization that has lifted the patient in status from subject to citizen. Breuer's patient must be recognized as the pioneer of this development. It was her good fortune and the good fortune of psychotherapy that she sought help from a physician of the scientific stature of Joseph Breuer. Breuer replaced the ancient prohibitive technique of hypnotherapy with his permissive technique. There followed the emancipation of psychotherapy from the hypnotic state, and its advance to the various forms of suggestive therapy. Freud's catharsis in the waking state led to his discovery of free association and of the patient's biography as a proper subject of medical study. This marked the beginning of a new epoch of psychotherapy based on psychodynamic principles. Freud's discovery of parentifying treatment behavior opened up the patient's emotional relationship to the physician and posed it as a crucial problem of all psychotherapy. However, under the metaphysical guise of a repetition-compulsion, the classical technique relapsed: it re-introduced the authoritarian principle in the treatment of the patient. The adaptational technique is an attempt to restore the line of development initiated by Breuer's patient.

THE TASK AHEAD

Digging in the patient's past yields diminishing returns. This fact poses a host of unexplored problems. Our technical skill in dealing with emotions is still in its infancy. Emotional resonance, known in everyday life as the contagiousness of emotions, is a significant mechanism in the therapeutic interaction of patient and physician; it awaits experimental investigation. Work on the patient's completely automatized inhibitions has hardly begun; as yet we have only glimpsed the mechanism of reinforcement.

The adaptational technique pursues the Freudian goal of total reconstruction. However, adaptational psychodynamics and some of the new principles of the adaptational technique can be used to develop a variety of other treatment procedures that would attain lesser goals in much shorter time. The social need for what I call trouble-shooting and easing methods of treatment is pressing.

Though therapy is obviously a process of interaction of patient and physician, the psychodynamics of the physician is still a rather neglected chapter of inquiry. We have viewed the patient's designs for co-operation in terms of a four-level scheme; we shall have to view the therapeutic intentions of the physician in terms of a corresponding scheme. We shall have to explore how the physician's own emotional matrix influences his choice of method, and how the fluctuations in his own emotional state influence his conduct of the treatment.

We may look forward with confidence to the future development of psychoanalytic therapy.

REFERENCES

1 BREUER, J. AND FREUD, S.: *Studies in Hysteria.* New York, Nervous and Mental Disease Publishing Company, 1936. (Published in German, 1895.)

2 FERENCZI, S.: The principle of relaxation and neocatharsis. *Internat. J. Psycho-Analysis, 11:* 428, 1930.

3 FREUD, S.: Freud's psychoanalytic method. *Collected Papers, 1:* 264. London, 1924. (Published in German, 1904.)

4 ——: Papers on technique. *Collected Papers, 2:* 285. London, 1924. (Published in German, 1910–1919.)

5 ——: "Transference" and "the analytic therapy." In *A General Introduction to Psychoanalysis.* New York, 1935. (Published in German, 1917.)

6 ——: Analysis terminable and interminable. *Collected Papers, 5:* 316. London, 1950. (Published in German, 1937.)

7 RADO, S.: The economic principle in psychoanalytic technique. *Internat. J. Psycho-Analysis, 6:* 35, 1925.

8 ——: Developments in the psychoanalytic conception and treatment of the neuroses. *Psychoanal. Quart., 8:* 427, 1939.

9 ——: The relationship of patient to therapist. *Am. J. Orthopsychiat., 12:* 542, 1942.

10 ——: Pathodynamics and treatment of traumatic war neurosis (traumatophobia). *Psychosom. Med., 4:* 362, 1942.

11 ——: Mind, unconscious mind, and brain. *Psychosom. Med., 11:* 165, 1949.

12 ——: Between reason and magic. 105th annual meeting of the Am. Psychia. Ass., Montreal, Quebec, 1949.

13 ——: Emergency behavior; with an introduction to the dynamics of conscience. In *Anxiety* (Hoch and Zubin, Eds.), New York, Grune and Stratton, 1950.

14 ——: On the psychoanalytic exploration of fear and other emotions. *Trans. N. Y. Acad. Sc. II, 14:* 280.

15 ——: Hedonic control, action-self, and the depressive spell. In Press. [Published 1954 in *Depression* (Hoch and Zubin, Eds.). New York, Grune & Stratton.]

16 ——: Behavior disorders: their dynamics and classification. To be published. [Published 1953 in *Am. J. Psychiat., 110:* 406.]

Dynamics and Classification of Disordered Behavior*

ORGANISMIC UTILITY: THE ADAPTATIONAL FRAMEWORK OF
MEANING

I deeply appreciate the opportunity to address this general session. First may I define my concepts. Adaptations are improvements in the organism's pattern of interaction with its environment that increase the organism's chances for survival, cultural self-realization, and perpetuation of its type. "Autoplastic" adaptations result from changes undergone by the organism itself; "alloplastic" adaptations, from changes wrought by the organism on its environment. Phylogenetic adaptations are based on genetic mechanisms, such as *favorable* mutation—the appearance of potentially valuable new equipment. The phylogenetic accumulation of *unfavorable* mutations may lead to adaptive degradation, if not extinction of the organism and the species. In ontogenetic and situational (here and now) adaptations the psychodynamic master mechanisms are learning, creative imagination, and goal-directed activity.

Adaptational psychodynamics studies the part played in behavior by motivation and control. It deals with pleasure and pain, emotion and thought, desire and executive action, and interprets them in terms of organismic utility, that is, in an adaptational framework of meaning. Its foremost objective is to discover the mechanisms by which the psychodynamic cerebral system accomplishes its integrative task.

Adaptational psychodynamics is a development of classical psychodynamics, the theoretical system originated by Sigmund Freud, and is based on the psychoanalytic method of investigation. Looking forward to the achievement of a comprehensive, unified science of human behavior, adaptational psychodynamics places the analysis of behavior in the genetic, physiologic (biochemical, biophysical), and cultural contexts of the organism. It seeks to replace undefined and undefinable concepts by defined ones and to evolve a close-to-the-fact scientific language that will convey the most information in the fewest words. Even though the introduction of

---

* The Academic Lecture read at the 109th annual meeting of The American Psychiatric Association, Los Angeles, Calif., May 4–8, 1953. First published in *American Journal of Psychiatry, 110:* 406–416, 1953.

numerous new terms makes communication difficult at first, this is a crucial step toward an increasingly rigorous application of the scientific method.

Behavior disorders are disturbances of psychodynamic integration that significantly affect the organism's adaptive life performance, its attainment of utility and pleasure. They are thus marked by either (1) adaptive impairment, (2) adaptive incompetence, or (3) transgressive conduct. The term impairment indicates psychoneurosis; the term incompetence, psychosis; and the term transgressive conduct, psychopathic state.

In the analysis of behavior disorders we encounter organized sequences of events which we have come to recognize as processes of miscarried prevention and miscarried repair. They are brought into play by a disordered response of the organism which we can relate to an environmental situation and trace to comparable exposures in the past. Our analysis may thus penetrate to the point where, instead of an adaptive response, a disordered one made its first appearance. This difference cannot be explained by further psychodynamic analysis, which reaches here its terminal point. Nonetheless, we can continue the etiological inquiry. We can seek to disclose the cerebral mechanism of such a disordered psychodynamic response; we can study its broader physiologic context; and we can search for its genetic context.

The ideal etiological classification of behavior disorders will draw on their genetics and physiology as well as on their adaptational psychodynamics. Today our knowledge of the genetic and physiologic phases of etiology is too scanty to attain this goal. The best we can do is experiment with provisional classifications based mainly on the psychodynamic phase of etiology. This is what I have attempted to do in the following scheme.

SCHEME OF CLASSIFICATION*

Class I. *Overreactive Disorders.*—(1) Emergency Dyscontrol: The emotional outflow, the riddance through dreams, the phobic, the inhibitory, the repressive, and the hypochondriac patterns. (2) Descending Dyscontrol. (3) Sexual Disorders: Disorders of the standard pattern. Dependence on reparative patterns: the patterns of pain-dependence; the male-female pattern modified by replacements; the eidolic and reductive patterns. Firesetting and shoplifting as sexual equivalents. (4) Social Overdependence. (5) Common Maladaptation: A combination of sexual disorder with social overdependence. (6) The Expressive Pattern: Excessive elaboration of common maladaptation: ostentatious self-presentation; dream-like interludes; rudimentary pantomimes; disease-copies and the expressive complication

---

* [A revised version of this scheme of classification appears on page 343 of this volume.]

of incidental disease. (7) The Obsessive Pattern: Obsessive elaboration of common maladaptation: broodings, rituals and overt temptations. Tic and stammering as obsessive equivalents; bedwetting, nail-biting, grinding of teeth in sleep, as precursors of the obsessive pattern. (8) The Paranoid Pattern.—Paranoid elaboration of common maladaptation: the nondisintegrative version of the Magnan sequence.

Class II. *Moodcyclic Disorders.*—Cycles of depression; cycles of reparative elation: the pattern of alternate cycles; cycles of minor elation; cycles of depression masked by elation; cycles of preventive elation.

Class III. *Schizotypal Disorders.*—(1) Compensated Schizo-adaptation. (2) Decompensated Schizo-adaptation. (3) Schizotypal Disintegration marked by Adaptive Incompetence.

Class IV. *Extractive Disorders.*—The ingratiating ("smile and suck") and extortive ("hit and grab") patterns of transgressive conduct.

Class V. *Lesional Disorders.*

Class VI: *Narcotic Disorders.*—Patterns of Drug-dependence.

Class VII. *Disorders of War Adaptation.*

EXAMPLES OF ADAPTATIONAL DYNAMICS OF BEHAVIOR DISORDERS

This classification is a by-product of studies in the adaptational psychodynamics of behavior disorders, developing from the fact that the organism's first survival concern is safety. Walter B. Cannon has shown how, by their emergency function, the peripheral systems serve the whole organism's interest in safety. Following this clue, I have attempted to outline the emergency function of the psychodynamic cerebral system, terming it "emergency control."

However, if an *overproduction* of the emergency emotions such as fear, rage, and guilty fear is the organism's response to danger, it will be unable to handle effectively the exigencies of daily life. These disordered—excessive or inappropriate—emergency responses impede rather than aid, the organism in its adaptive task. They elicit processes of miscarried prevention and miscarried repair that produce further disordering effects. These failures of emergency control lead to the simplest forms of behavior disorder, which I term "emergency dyscontrol."

With emergency dyscontrol as a point of departure, it was possible to arrange the clinically observed forms of behavior disorder according to the increasing complexity of their psychodynamic mechanisms. The resulting scheme somewhat resembles the known patterns in organic chemistry, where, starting with a simple compound, we may derive increasingly complex ones through rearrangement of the components or the addition of new components.

The various psychodynamic mechanisms of behavior disorders belong to different physiologic and genetic contexts. With advancing knowledge of these contexts the apparent inconsistencies of classification may be expected to disappear. For example, in time we should be able to characterize every behavior disorder by "lesions" of the underlying physiologic (biochemical, biophysical) functions; the separate class of Lesional Disorders will then have outlived its usefulness. Our present difficulties with classification derive from lack of etiological knowledge, not from lack of logic.

To illustrate the material listed in the above classification scheme, I shall begin with the simplest psychiatric problem, the dynamics of emergency dyscontrol and descending dyscontrol (subclasses 1 and 2 of Class I. Overreactive Disorders), and follow with perhaps the most complex psychiatric problem, the dynamics of the schizotypal disorders (Class III). The pivotal task is the same in the dynamic study of all behavior disorders: to reduce a mass of observational data to an outline of their hierarchical organization.

Class I. Overreactive Disorders

The basic emergency emotions are pain, fear, rage, and, in a wider sense, guilty fear enhanced by retroflexed rage, and guilty rage. These emotions prompt the organism to emergency moves: pain elicits riddance, *i.e.*, activities aimed at getting rid of its cause; fear prompts moves of escape or submission to authority; rage evokes combat or defiance; guilty fear produces expiatory behavior aimed at recapturing loving care; guilty rage leads to violence in presumed self-defense. Retroflexed rage is defeated rage turned by the organism against itself; its self-reproach is usually assimilated with the prevailing pattern of remorse. By preparing the organism to meet emergencies, these emotions play a significant part in biologically effective emergency control.

Overproduction of these emergency emotions results in disordered—excessive or inappropriate—emergency responses which, instead of aiding the organism, threaten to damage it. The infantile organism is unable to control these disordered responses by its own psychodynamic means and enters upon a state of emergency dyscontrol. Proneness to overreaction and dyscontrol develops in childhood, presumably on a genetic basis, and is carried over into adult life.

1. *Emergency Dyscontrol.*—Failure of the organism to control its over-reaction by its own resources results in the following patterns of emergency dyscontrol: the emotional outflow, the riddance-through-dreams, the phobic, the inhibitory, the repressive, and the hypochondriac.

In the *emotional outflow* pattern the organism seeks to rid itself of its excessive emergency emotions by fits of fear or outbursts of rage.

In the *riddance-through-dreams* pattern the same result is accomplished by means of enraged dreams or terror dreams.

Phobic behavior or phobic avoidance is a pattern of miscarried prevention. It usually originates in childhood, in the child's dependency relationship to his parents. The child is terrified by a chance experience, which would not produce such an overreaction in other children. To forestall the recurrence of this crucial attack of terror, he will henceforth automatically avoid the situation—the visual context—in which the terror occurred. Sometimes the child's overreaction is the consequence of a previous parental warning and threat of punishment. Magical thinking may make this mode of prevention retroactive; the child then forgets that the parental threat and his terrifying experience ever occurred. Once the avoidance mechanism is established, the child may, by generalization, use it for the magical control of other parental threats as well. If the object of the child's phobic avoidance is a "dangerous" animal, he may have a further gain: he may actually vent his repressed rage—his resentment of the threatening parent—on this "scape-goat." Phobic avoidance in the adult retains these infantile features.

The *inhibitory* is also an infantile pattern of miscarried prevention, but with 2 different mechanisms. The first prevents the recurrence of a crucial attack of fear by the organism's automatically inhibiting the motor activity—the proprioceptive context—in which the attack occurred. The other shows an even higher degree of foresight misapplied: to play safe, the organism automatically inhibits not only the activities tabooed by the authorities, but on an ever-widening scale, also the *approaches* to those activities.

In the *repressive* pattern, while unable to stop the overproduction of emergency emotions, the organism succeeds in automatically cutting off these emotions from consciousness and outward discharge. This mechanism is of course powerless to halt an eventual overflow of the repressed emotions, which are thus bound to produce further disordering consequences.

Since fear and rage are antagonistic responses, open fear is often accompanied by repressed rage; I call this dynamic formation fear over rage. Similarly, open rage may be accompanied by repressed fear; this is called rage over fear. The battle between fear and rage is strongly influenced by the conflict between the organism's desire for security through dependence and its pride in cultural self-realization. Fear over rage shows victory of the dependency need; the resulting combination of repressed rage and hurt pride is a prolific though less conspicuous source of the patient's suffering. The contrary outcome—rage over fear—shows victory of the organism's pride in having its own way. Incomplete repression of fear and rage may produce qualitatively undifferentiated chronic tension states, marked by apprehensiveness or irascibility or both.

The *hypochondriac* pattern is marked by an excessive outflow of unrecognized guilty fear. Frantically, the patient dreads illness: in his nonreporting (unconscious) belief illness is a long overdue punishment for past disobediences (sexual self-stimulation, truculence) now catching up with him. Often the attack climaxes in an act of riddance (unnecessary surgery, precipitation of actual illness, etc.). This pattern defeats its preventive and reparative intents completely: it increases rather than decreases the overproduction of hypochondriac (that is, guilty) fear. Beneath hypochondriac (guilty) fear there is always repressed rage and hurt pride.

Following the pattern of its desires, the healthy organism seizes opportunities to attain utility and pleasure. Emergency dyscontrol interferes with these pursuits; it reduces the adaptive value of the patient's life performance and tends to make him dependent on external help. If his life situation —his relatives and friends—permits, he capitalizes on his illness; he vents his repressed rage and recaptures his pride by exploiting the privileges of the sick in the manner of a child. The same infantile and vindictive exploitation of relatives and friends may occur in every form of disordered behavior, or for that matter, in every illness. *Emergency dyscontrol enters as a basic etiological factor into the emotional dynamics of almost all behavior disorders.*

2. *Descending Dyscontrol.*—The autonomic overdischarge of excessive or inappropriate emergency emotions may precipitate disease processes in the peripheral systems affected. The psychodynamic cerebral system becomes aware of the peripheral disease thus precipitated, and responds to this internal event just as it responds to events in the environment. Descending dyscontrol thus brings into play a circular operation of responses, which I call the *psychodynamic circuit of peripheral disease*. The same circuit eventuates if a peripheral disease of purely peripheral origin elicits emergency overreaction with autonomic over-discharge. Clearly, psychodynamic circuit and purely peripheral physiology are interdependent and inseparable components of the same organismic context. By including the concept of psychodynamic circuit in its body of theory, purely physiological medicine advances to comprehensive medicine.

Class III. Schizotypal Disorders

The conceptual scheme of schizotypal organization evolved from the concept of schizophrenia; we shall first briefly review this development.

In 1911, E. Bleuler defined schizophrenia as follows: "This disease is characterized by a specific type of alteration of thinking, feeling, and relation to the external world, which appears nowhere else in this particular fashion."

The current genetic theory of schizophrenia traces its etiology to an inherited predisposition, transmitted to an offspring from both parents by a Mendelian mechanism.

In Dobzhansky's formulation genotype is the inherited cause of development, and phenotype—the organism as it appears to our senses in structure and function—the actual outcome of development. In this sense the patient suffering from an open schizophrenic psychosis is a schizophrenic phenotype, engendered by a schizophrenic genotype in its interaction with the environment. A phenotype changes continuously throughout the life span; its development is circumscribed by the genotype's "norm of reaction" to changing environmental influences.

For psychodynamic purposes I shall abbreviate the term schizophrenic phenotype to *schizotype*. Can we diagnose the patient's inherited predisposition before he develops an open psychosis or even if he never develops an open psychosis? In other words, are we prepared to view him as a schizotype from birth to death, or only during his open psychosis? Clinical observation gives us the answer.

The manifold clinical pictures—symptoms and syndromes—of the schizophrenic psychosis have been described and classified by many clinical investigators; there is substantial agreement on almost all cardinal points. But when we subject these gross manifestations of the open psychosis to minute psychodynamic analysis, we discover an underlying ensemble of psychodynamic traits which, as we shall presently see, is demonstrable in the patient during his whole life. This finding will define him as a schizotype from birth to death, and will allow us to view his life history as a sequence of schizotypal changes. The ensemble of psychodynamic traits peculiar to the schizotypes may be called *schizotypal organization*. It is this organization which is meant by the prefix *schizo-* because this organization constitutes the psychodynamic expression of the schizophrenic genotypes. Conversely, we may define a genotype as schizophrenic if its norm of reaction is schizogenic.

Before outlining this concept of schizotypal organization I shall review some relevant propositions of adaptational psychodynamics. On evolutionary as well as clinical grounds I have suggested elsewhere that in the psychodynamic cerebral system integrative activity is spread over a hierarchy of 4 levels. In ascending order, we speak of the hedonic level, the levels of brute emotion, emotional thought, and unemotional thought.

At the hedonic level the pattern for hedonic self-regulation is established: the organism moves towards the source of pleasure and away from the cause of pain. It relies on the expectation that pleasure signals the presence of needed supplies or conditions otherwise favorable to its survival, and pain the presence of a threat to its organic integrity.

At the next 2 levels the emotions are the controlling means of integration. Emotions are central mechanisms both for the arousal of the peripheral organism, and for the peripheral disposal of superabundant central excitation. We divide them into the emergency emotions based on present pain or the expectation of pain, such as fear, rage, retroflexed rage, guilty fear, and guilty rage; and the welfare emotions based on present pleasure or the expectation of pleasure, such as pleasurable desire, joy, love, and pride.

Unemotional thought forges the tools of common sense and science. By teaching the organism to support present pain for the sake of future pleasure, foresight increases the flexibility of hedonic self-regulation.

Behavior of the whole organism may be integrated at any of these 4 levels or at any combination of them. Integrative activity may be in part nonreporting (unconscious), in part self-reporting (conscious); accordingly, the psychodynamic cerebral system falls into the nonreporting and self-reporting ranges. To advance from the nonreporting to the self-reporting range, cerebral activity must pass the pain-barrier, an organization of precautionary mechanisms upon which hedonic control rests. Communications of the organism to the environment must pass the social pain-guard, an analogous organization of precautionary mechanisms, superimposed on the pain-barrier.

The conscious range is dominated by the supreme integrative system of the entire organism, which I call its *action-self*. Of proprioceptive origin, the action-self emerges from the circular response pattern of self-awareness and willed action. It then integrates the contrasting pictures of total organism and total environment that provide the basis for the selfhood of the conscious organism. These integrations are fundamental to the organism's entire orientation and represent highly complex organizations composed of sensory, intellectual, emotional, and motor components. At first the organism attributes unlimited power to its willed actions; hence its first thought-picture of itself is one of an omnipotent being. This early thought-picture—designated as its primordial self—remains the source of its indestructible belief in magic. Recognizing the difference between attainment and aspiration, present and future, the maturing organism differentiates its thought-picture of self into a tested self and a desired self. However, under the pressure of strong desire, this forced and precarious differentiation tends to disappear.

Using this framework of meaning, I can state in simple terms the basic observation upon which the conceptual scheme of schizotypal organization rests. *In the schizotypes the machinery of psychodynamic integration is strikingly inadequate, because one of its essential components, the organizing action of pleasure—its motivational strength—is innately defective. My term for this crucial defect is "integrative pleasure deficiency."*

This formulation derives from 2 sets of data. First, the patient himself often realizes that his pleasure, his pleasurable emotions and thoughts, are inadequate if not rudimentary. "I am," said one of our clinic patients, "incapable of giving and sharing love"; and again, "I do not know how to react with people." Secondly, we can conveniently observe the motivational strength, the integrative action and scope, of the patient's emotions. We then see that the integrative action of his welfare emotions as well as of his pleasure is significantly diminished. We shall now explore the far-reaching consequences of this condition.

It is generally known that pleasurable emotions facilitate performance, keeping our zest to live at a high level. Insufficient pleasure hinders performance; the schizotype's zest for life is reduced. The welfare emotions also counterbalance the pain-connected emergency emotions. In the schizotypes, motivational weakness of the welfare emotions causes an emotional disbalance; without this adequate tempering influence the emergency emotions tend to grow excessive in motivational strength and integrative scope. The extraordinary strength of fear in the schizotypes so impressed some observers that they called it *existentialangst* (fear of existence); the same excessive strength marks schizotypal rage, once it has free rein.

Integrative pleasure deficiency impairs the ontogenetic development of the action-self. Pleasure is the tie that really binds. An action-self deficient in connective pleasure is brittle, prone to break under stress, to lose control of the contrasting integrations, total organism, and total environment. This weakness of the action-self is the basis of the patient's oversensitivity and profound insecurity in relation to himself, to his bodily parts, and to his environment. His insecurity in human relationships is aggravated by further consequences of the patient's pleasure deficiency. Because his capacity for affection and human sympathy is reduced he cannot reciprocate when receiving them, still less elicit them. Small wonder he finds it difficult to get a firm emotional foothold in family or other groups.

The patient's limited capacity for pleasure and love renders the ontogenetic development of a healthy sexual function impossible. The resulting sexual organization is rudimentary, ill-proportioned, lacking in genuine love and tenderness, subject to fragmentation and formation of miscarried reparative patterns.

The integrative pleasure deficiency is indeed fundamental and all-pervasive: it leaves no phase of life, no area of behavior unaffected. As anticipated in Bleuler's first definition, the schizotypes differ fundamentally from other human types. Often enough the patient knows this himself: he longs to be like other people. To stress the radical importance of schizotypal organization, we must describe the life performance of the patient so organized in terms not of adaptation, but of a schizotypal system of adaptation, or, briefly, schizo-adaptation.

The degree of the innate integrative pleasure deficiency and the consequent task of schizo-adaptation vary widely from patient to patient. The outcome of the patient's struggle for human existence depends upon the relation of his adaptive resources to the adaptive burden of his changing life situation. To take care of its deficiencies, the organism must evolve (1) a scarcity economy of pleasure, (2) a security pattern featuring compensatory dependence, and (3) a replacement technique of integration in which the job ordinarily done by pleasurable feeling and thought is shifted to unemotional thought. It is, I suggest, the combination of these 3 reparative processes upon which the entire system of schizotypal adaptation rests.

Though we have not yet succeeded in reducing the scarcity economy of pleasure to its elementary mechanisms, its beneficial results are readily observable. Its efficacy appears to depend on the available degree of intelligence, foresight, capacity for learning, and the absence—successful avoidance or control—of emergency overreactions detrimental to pleasure. While an endowment for superior performance facilitates the task of husbanding pleasure it may introduce new complications. The schizotypes show the same variety in endowment as the rest of the population; some of them have superior intelligence, special artistic, scientific, or other gifts. The favored pursuit of a patient belonging to this elite group tends to absorb whatever capacity he has for pleasure, leaving him disastrously vulnerable to failure, actual or presumed.

The need for compensatory dependence accompanies the schizotypes throughout the life span. Often without realizing it, the patient leans heavily on external support, his relationship to others remaining that of the child to his parents. Perpetuation of this infantile need is further complicated by the fact that in a schizotype, the child's security pattern of dependence is defective from the outset. As a child a schizotype is terrified by conflict and resents the necessity of engaging in sibling rivalry or having to play one parent against the other; he would prefer to lean on everyone within his reach. He cannot give affection, the means of ingratiation; hence his response to parental demands is chiefly limited to fear or rage, obedience or defiance, yes or no; the all-important range of "between" is undeveloped or atrophied by disuse. Under stress the adult patient tends to revert to his infantile belief that an ersatzparent can and will supply his needs by magic.

The replacement technique shifts the integrative task from pleasurable to cold thought. Schizotypes lack the feel for the simple pleasures, the affectionate give-and-take of daily life. In lieu of immediate emotional grasp the baffled patient presses his intellect into service, as if trying to pick up something at a distance with lazy tongs. For the spontaneous pleasurable responses he lacks he substitutes mechanical imitations. If highly sophisticated, he may ridicule the conventional forms of affectionate behavior, dissecting and examining them as though they were the technological performance of a machine.

In favorable circumstances this system of adaptation may hold the schizotype in a compensated state. He may, in fact, go through life without ever suffering a breakdown. However, his sensitivity to loss of affection and pleasure is extreme. Because he knows only rudimentary pleasure, such warmth as he is capable of deriving from being loved has for him a unique facilitating and reassuring value. Any change in his life situation that deprives him of this help, thus undermining his pleasure, security and self-confidence, becomes a threat of decompensation. Every shred of activity he enjoys plays an important part in his equilibrium; every loss of pleasure is a tragedy which he blames on his parent or ersatzparent. He may feel harassed from without, though the fact is that it is he who drives himself too hard. Under growing pressure he develops excessive fears, guilty fears, and rages, blurred awareness and magic thought. These inordinate emergency responses signify the onset of decompensation. In a self-defeating effort to cope with these responses, to recapture his pleasure and security from dependence, he develops a scrambled form of emergency dyscontrol which is peculiar to the decompensated schizotypes. Ordinary dyscontrol seen in other types eventuates in phobic, hypochondriac, expressive, obsessive, paranoid, and other overreactive patterns which are circumscribed and intricately organized. In the decompensated schizotypes these mechanisms appear in a scramble and are much more simply organized, springing directly from the patient's obedience-defiance conflict.* He may feel profoundly humiliated or disgusted with himself, experiencing diffuse and strange bodily sensations or even fearing that his body undergoes a revolt-

---

* In 1914, exploring the value of the libido theory for the interpretation of schizophrenia, Freud contrasted the neurotic (overreactive) pictures developed by schizophrenics with those developed by patients other than schizophrenic: "The difference between the transference neuroses arising in this way and the corresponding formations where the ego is normal [i.e., non-schizophrenic] would afford us the deepest insight into the structure of our mental apparatus."

ing decomposition. He may sense the threat of disintegration and fear that he is losing his mind. He struggles desperately to retain adaptive control; this struggle is pathognomonic of the decompensated schizotypes. When he is overcome by the impatience of a hungry infant and in addition his remorse defeats his resentment, he may develop a facade of depression or find "relief" in alcohol-dependence. Decompensation often includes endocrine or other peripheral disturbances; in the female patient a conspicuous symptom is arrest of the menses.

As distinguished from the various forms of adaptive impairment, schizotypal decompensation is a state of threatening adaptive incompetence. The decompensated patient is left with but one remedial resource, his integrative machinery of unemotional thought. This machinery may hold firm or it may slowly or rapidly break down. Should it collapse, the patient enters upon a process of schizotypal disintegration marked by adaptive incompetence.

The first sign of disintegration which the patient cannot hide from the environment is his thought disorder. Apparently this disorder is a direct consequence of the overburdening of the cognitive function. However, closer scrutiny reveals the presence of a less conspicuous but all the more important factor that complicates this untoward development. In actual fact the process of disintegration begins not with a thought disorder, but with an extensive *proprioceptive disorder*, a distorted awareness of bodily self. Usually its first manifestations have already appeared at the stage of decompensation.

This proprioceptive disorder eludes psychodynamic explanation. We understand neither its cause and course of development, nor its relation to the integrative pleasure deficiency. But we can see that it disorganizes the action-self with fateful consequences. The organism now ceases to have a definite selfhood, for the disorganized action-self cannot sustain the 2 basic integrations—total organism and total environment—upon which selfhood depends. Psychodynamic life is now the interaction of a *fragmented* organism with a *fragmented* environment.* The patient loses his grasp and control of himself as well as of the environment. I suggest that proprioceptive awareness is the deepest internal root of language and thought. By increasing the integrative burden of the already overtaxed cognitive function, proprioceptive disorder precipitates its breakdown. The patient glides into a many-faceted thought disorder that can be understood only by a comparison with normal thinking.

The healthy organism, moving from desire towards fulfillment, analyzes experience into cause and effect so that it can find the means that will

---

* The term "fragmentation" was first used by William A. White; he meant by it a "molecular splitting of the psyche."

lead to the ends it desires. Normal thinking is like a suspension bridge between organism and environment. Schizotypal thinking, if severely disordered, buckles this bridge and lifts it into the air; in Bleuler's terms, it is then both de-reistic and de-personalized.

Stressing the adaptive function of thinking, physicist Ernst Mach pointed out that thought organization proceeds in 2 consecutive steps: we adjust our thoughts first to the facts and then to one another, achieving a dependable degree of objectivity, logical consistency, and thought-economy. However, Mach's formulation applies only to unemotional (objective, rational, realistic) thought. In emotional thinking the adjustment of thoughts to facts is inadequate and the adjustment of thoughts to one another aims not at logical but at *emotional* consistency. Furthermore, since thought processes take place in both the nonreporting (unconscious) and the self-reporting (conscious) ranges of the psychodynamic cerebral system, simultaneous processes of emotional thought in the nonreporting range, though consistent in themselves, may be at variance with one another as well as with the facts. The characteristics of nonreporting thought-organization (Freud's "primary process") are revealed through the analysis of dreams; emotional thoughts marked by the characteristic features of primary organization and a total lack of adjustment to the world of facts may be called prime thoughts.

The raw material of conscious thinking comes in part from the sense organs, in part from the nonreporting range. On their way, as stated above, prime thoughts must pass the pain-barrier; intended communications to the environment, the social pain-guard. We also stated that pain-barrier and social pain-guard are precautionary mechanisms of hedonic control; let us now add that conscious thought-adjustment is the rational mechanism of adaptive control of both the environment and the organism itself.

These 3 mechanisms are wrecked by the disintegrative process. Prime thoughts may then enter freely the self-reporting range, escape conscious adjustment and be blurted out or acted out. There appear hallucinations and delusions which preclude the adjustment of thought to fact even if the requisite machinery is still available. Hallucinations are prime thoughts perceived as data of the senses; therefore they have the factual reality of perceptions. Delusions are prime thoughts exalted to the plane of fact-adjusted thought by the magic of the strong emotions from which they spring and by which they are controlled; for this reason they are impervious to refutation by the true facts.

Often the earliest sign of incipient thought disorder is the loss in hierarchical depth: thought organization tends to be replaced by thought aggregation, vertical meaning by horizontal irrelevance, sense by sound. As rationality dwindles to the vanishing point, infantile tonality emerges as an ordering principle.

Disintegration of the machinery of adaptive thinking renders the patient incapable of sustaining effective human relationships. He has no facilities to handle a many-sided group situation; in his fragmented field there is room for but one protagonist at a time. He seeks to operate on a child-parent dependency pattern stripped to the bone. His choice of response is now rigidly limited to yes or no (obedience or defiance); the range of "between" disappears completely. Moreover, he tends to perceive both alternatives as equally undesirable: he faces not a choice but a dilemma of yes or no. This applies to the entire gamut of his responses, intellectual, emotional, and motor.

At the same time, almost identical changes take place in the patient's relationship to himself, to his mode of handling his own impulses. To understand these changes, we shall again take a comparative view of the healthy organism.

During the period of growth the psychodynamic cerebral system builds a semiautomatic organization of self-restraining and self-prodding responses known as our conscience. The child learns to anticipate certain parental and other authoritarian demands to which he is continuously exposed, and to meet them automatically.

The same applies to the system of enforcement used by the parents. Parental reward gives rise to automatized self-reward known as self-respect and moral pride; parental punishment, to automatized self-punishment as a means of expiating one's presumed wrongdoings and reinstating oneself in the loving care of the authority thus reconciled. The adaptive gain of conscience is security through obedience; its main problem is the handling of defiant rage.

In the disintegrating schizotype, impairment of the action-self breaks up the context in which the mechanisms of conscience operate. Subsequently, it is no longer his conscience that admonishes him but once again the disciplinary authority of his present or past. Freud discovered this regressive replacement of conscience by the original child-parent relationship in paranoid behavior. Today we realize that this regression, a disintegration of the "voice of conscience," takes place in all disintegrating schizotypes; the paranoid is its most conspicuous manifestation. Continuing the reparative intent of the voice of conscience, this regression seeks to reinforce the faltering mechanisms of conscience by reactivating the infantile experiences from which they originate. To the extent to which the true mechanisms of conscience fail to operate, the patient loses his ethos—his system of shared emotional values upon which cultural group membership rests. As we have seen, the disintegrating patient's human relationships are reduced to the scant residues of his infantile dependency pattern; this same pattern replaces his conscience, his human sympathy, integrity, and standards as well. As a consequence, when the patient has to act upon his own impulses, he faces the same yes-or-no dilemma as he does in his vestigial relationships to others.

The yes-or-no dilemma ushers in the yes-or-no disturbance which is peculiar to schizotypal disintegration and forms the core of what is known as the patient's activity disorder. In a challenging situation, be the stimulation external, internal, or both, the patient may be completely blocked by his dilemma and respond only with paralyzed perplexity. Or he may try to obey and defy simultaneously, presenting a picture of intellectual, emotional, or motor confusion. Or if he gets going in one direction he may be unable to stop, continuing or repeating the same response regardless of the changing situation. Whether the resulting behavior shows automatic obedience or automatic defiance, it is unrelated to the adaptive task and is as a rule terminated by a sudden and unpredictable shift.

The symptoms resulting from the yes-or-no disturbance are well known to the clinician. They include perseveration, echolalia, echopraxy, negativism, overtalkativeness, mutism, akinesia, hyperkinesia, inappropriate emotional or motor response, stereotypes, gesturing, posturing, grimacing, extreme muscular and postural flexibility or rigidity, and finally, schizotypal excitement and stupor.

The yes-or-no disturbance, though dominated by the obedience-defiance conflict of the infantile dependency pattern, has still deeper roots in the functional design of the sensory-motor organism, notably in the contrast and persistence principle of perception and in the principle of reciprocal innervation of muscles.

The disintegrating patient may retreat into a magic universe of his own creation. Unlike the magic world of ordinary day-dreaming, the magic universe of the disintegrating schizotype is split off into irreconcilable fragments. Creative imagination disintegrates as soon as the organism loses the unity and coherence of its thought-picture of self. This is reflected in the patient's regression to archaic sources of pleasure, in his excitements, hallucinations, delusions, posturings, and other activities detached from the actual environment. Fragmentation of his magic universe may be directly represented in his dreams and artistic creations which with telling frequency feature dismemberment, isolated or dead bodily parts, and related motifs.

The patient's subjective experience, his awareness of his own disintegrating activity, eludes our comprehension. He may show signs of what Jaspers calls "double orientation": while interpreting his perceptions (thoughts, hallucinations, actions) in a disrupted context of irrationality, he simultaneously records them in the context of residual enfeebled rationality. This shadowy perpetuation of the true environmental context may enable the delusional patient suddenly to recapture realistic contact without relinquishing his delusions or, if the thought disorder subsides, to see his delusions in retrospect against the world of facts.

The remarkable phenomena of double orientation show that the disintegrating patient still struggles to maintain adaptive control. However, the disintegration of function prepares the ground for a cessation of function. This malignant turn occurs if the organism, tiring of the struggle, gives up and withdraws. There follows a process of deterioration, a progressive functional shrinkage of the psychodynamic cerebral system. The process may lead to a total retreat from the adaptive task: the patient becomes a living corpse. His withdrawal from the struggle for existence is the ultimate consequence of the disease process, not its cause.

I have shown that the characteristics of the schizotypes stem from an integrative pleasure deficiency. This defect is a basic and, in my view, innate trait of schizotypal organization. However, proprioceptive disorder, with its highly disintegrative effect, cannot be traced to this pleasure deficiency. Thus one must assume that *a predisposition to proprioceptive disorder, a sort of proprioceptive diathesis, is another basic trait of schizotypal organization.* The significance of proprioceptive disorder underscores the necessity of correlating the psychodynamic mechanisms just described with the broader context of the still unknown physiologic mechanisms in which they operate. Only through such cross-interpretation can we hope to arrive at a comprehensive theory of schizotypal organization.

On psychodynamic grounds I view schizotypal disorders as developmental stages of schizotypal organization:

III. 1. *Compensated schizo-adaptation.*—This is a relatively stable stage, marked by adequate operation of the schizotypal system of adaptation. Though there is a liability to decompensation, the patient may remain at this stage throughout life. The so-called schizoid is viewed here as a well-compensated schizotype.

III. 2. *Decompensated schizo-adaptation.*—This stage is precipitated by emergency dyscontrol and its consequences, which overtax the security pattern of compensatory dependence and destroy the scarcity economy of pleasure. The patient develops a scramble of overreactive mechanisms (as distinguished from organized overreactive patterns seen in other types) and the first signs of proprioceptive disorder. Though he may remain at this stage for an indefinite time or recover spontaneously, he is now threatened by disintegrative breakdown. This is the stage labeled recently by P. Hoch and P. Polatin "pseudo-neurotic schizophrenia."

III. 3. *Schizotypal disintegration marked by adaptive incompetence.*—This is the stage known as open schizophrenic psychosis. The focus of the disintegrative process is disorganization of the action-self which, brought about by a psychodynamically unexplainable proprioceptive disorder, in turn precipitates disorders of thought, activity, etc. There is a chance of spontaneous remission, and, on the other hand, a liability to progressive deterioration.

This developmental outline suggests how pressing is the need to find the criteria for the stability of the compensated stage; and the criteria for determining the patient's liability to decompensation, disintegration, and deterioration as against his chances for spontaneous remission.

CONCLUDING REMARKS

The adaptational theory of disordered behavior, examples of which I have just presented, has evolved gradually over a period of years and rests upon clinical data. This is also true of the adaptational psychodynamics of healthy behavior, a subject to which I could make only scanty references in this paper.

My hope is that an adaptational dynamics of disordered behavior will stimulate physiologic and genetic studies, but the main task will be to test its fruitfulness in psychodynamic and therapeutic quests.

REFERENCES

Concepts used but not fully defined in this paper are further expounded in the author's following publications:

[1] Developments in the psychoanalytic conception and treatment of the neuroses. *Psychoanalyt. Quart., 8:* 427, 1939.

[2] Pathodynamics and treatment of traumatic war neurosis (Traumatophobia). *Psychosom. Med., 4:* 362, 1942.

[3] Psychodynamics as a basic science. *Am. J. Orthopsychiat., 16:* 405, 1946.

[4] An adaptational view of sexual behavior. In *Psychosexual Development in Health and Disease,* (Hoch and Zubin, Eds.). New York, Grune & Stratton, 1949.

[5] Mind, unconscious mind, and brain. *Psychosom. Med., 11:* 165, 1949.

[6] Emergency behavior; with an introduction to the dynamics of conscience. In *Anxiety,* (Hoch and Zubin, Eds.). New York, Grune & Stratton, 1950.

[7] Psychodynamics of depression from the etiologic point of view. *Psychosom. Med., 13:* 51, 1951.

[8] On the psychoanalytic exploration of fear and other emotions. *Trans. N. Y. Acad. Sc. II, 14:* 280, 1952.

⁹ Recent advances of psychoanalytic therapy. *Psychiatric Treatment*, Vol. XXI, Proceedings of the Assoc. for Research in Nervous and Mental Disease. Baltimore, Williams & Wilkins, 1954.

¹⁰ Hedonic control, action-self, and the depressive spell. *Depression*, (Hoch and Zubin, Eds.). Grune & Stratton, New York, 1953.

Other publications referred to in this paper:

¹¹ BLEULER, EUGEN. *Dementia Praecox or the Group of Schizophrenias*. New York, International Universities Press, 1950.

¹² BUMKE, OSWALD. *Handbuch der Geisteskrankheiten*. Vol. 9, Die Schizophrenie. Berlin, Julius Springer, 1932.

¹³ DOBZHANSKY, THEODOSIUS. *Genetics and the Origin of Species*. New York, Columbia University Press, 1951.

¹⁴ FREUD, SIGMUND. *On Narcissism, An Introduction*. London, Hogarth, 1925.

¹⁵ HOCH, PAUL AND POLATIN, PHILIP. Pseudoneurotic forms of schizophrenia. *Psychiat. Quart.*, *23:* 248, 1949.

¹⁶ KALLMANN, FRANZ J. The genetic theory of schizophrenia. *Am. J. Psychiat.*, *103:* 309, Nov. 1946.

Hedonic Control, Action-Self, and the Depressive Spell*

THE DEPRESSIVE PATTERN

In a previous paper[31] I outlined an adaptational theory of the depressive spell. Let me here summarize its salient features.

The depressive spell is a mood-cyclic disorder. We interpret it as a particular form of emergency dyscontrol.[31] The patient has suffered a severe loss, or in any case, behaves as if he had suffered one. His emotional reaction to this actual or presumed emergency is overwhelming and threatens to destroy his capacity for adaptive control. At first he is torn between coercive rage and guilty fear, which drive him in opposite directions. Then his mounting guilty fear gains the upper hand. It splits his defeated coercive rage into two unequal parts that undergo different vicissitudes. The smaller part—the stubborn core—is forced underground. There it remains what it was, coercive rage directed against the environment. The larger part of defeated rage escapes repression because its flexibility permits its assimilation to the now prevailing pattern of guilty fear. This portion of defeated rage is turned against the patient himself and is vented in remorseful bouts of self-reproach. Though such self-punishment from retroflexed rage is excruciatingly painful, the patient's remorse is but a facade. Beneath this facade he has utmost contempt for himself because of his inability to live up to his expectations. Bitter with wounded pride, he thus punishes himself—not in contrition—but for his failure to gain his coercive ends. This deeply hidden meaning of self-punishment from retroflexed rage makes mockery of the patient's remorse and reveals the real root of his sense of unworthiness.

The emotional storm deprives the patient of his capacity for mature life performance. Subjectively, he is reduced from a self-reliant adult to a frightened and helpless child. The patient's adaptive degradation—a consequence of his loss of self-confidence—is our decisive clue to the understanding of his depressive spell. He senses in the present emergency a threat of starvation and responds to it by reproducing the hungry infant's cry for his mother's help.[24, 25] But the patient's situation, as compared with

---

* First published in *Depression*, Proceedings Forty-Second Annual Meeting American Psychopathological Association, New York, Grune & Stratton, 1954.

that of the hungry infant, is complicated by his guilty fear. Excessive guilty fear, heightened by retroflexed rage, forces him into expiation. Thus, it is by means of punishing himself that he hopes to regain his mother, her loving care, and above all, her feeding breast. This resort to obsolete technics of mastery, limited altogether to the patient's imagination, is a type of miscarried repair. It makes the patient's suffering more severe, and his adaptive impairment more serious.

The patient is unaware of the complex motivational pattern of his illness. What he actually experiences are disrupted fragments of the total pattern; and he experiences them in a downward swing of mood, a state of gloom punctuated by hammering blows of pain. As he says himself, he feels "blue," and understands why we call his illness a spell of depression.

The longer a depressive cycle lasts the more gravely does it violate the minimal pleasure requirements of human existence. In the balance between pleasure and pain, there is a shift resulting in a disastrous dominance of pain. We must give close attention to this fact, for it points to a hitherto unrecognized etiologic factor in this illness—a basic disturbance in the hedonic control of the organism.

The exploration of this disturbance ought to shed new light on the problem of depression. In the present paper I shall therefore examine the part played in the rise and fall of the depressive cycle by the hedonic self-regulation of the organism. This task requires several steps of preparation. First, I shall review the relationship between psychodynamic and physiologic studies of the organism, and outline the concept of hedonic control.

Toward a Unified Science of Human Behavior

The nervous activity of the cerebrum is in part self-reporting, in part nonreporting. Only to the extent to which it is self-reporting is the organism conscious of what its brain does for (or against) it. Though self-reporting activity may issue from, and terminate in, nonreporting activity, the latter has by itself no effect on consciousness.

Self-reporting activity forms the self-reporting range of cerebral nervous activity; nonreporting activity, its nonreporting range. The self-reporting range is the range of awareness or, as we may also say, the range of consciousness. In our usage, awareness and consciousness are equivalent terms.

Utilizing Bridgman's operational point of view,[5] we may say that the activity of the self-reporting range has two distinct aspects: the *psychodynamic* awareness process and the *physiologic* reporting process. The relationship between these two aspects was clearly seen by Spinoza: "The order and connection of ideas is the same as the order and connection of things." [37] Since we need an operational hypothesis—and this is the simplest one to make—I have assumed that the psychodynamic awareness process and the physiologic reporting process are exactly synchronous and exactly congruent.[29]

The psychodynamic "meaning" or, in other words, the motivational significance, of some activity of the nonreporting range may be disclosed by the psychoanalytic method of contextual inference. The area that lies within reach of this method is the psychodynamic sector of the nonreporting range. The classical theory refers to this sector as "the unconscious." Together, the range of awareness and the psychodynamic sector of the nonreporting range constitute the psychodynamic range of cerebral nervous activity. We also refer to this range as the psychodynamic cerebral system.

We state the meaning of nonreporting activity disclosed by inference in an extrapolated language of psychodynamics. We speak of nonreporting tension, nonreporting desire, nonreporting thought, and so forth. In this language such adjectives as unconscious, hidden, latent, tacit, are used in the same sense as is nonreporting.

Nonreporting activity is called awareness-prone when, by its organization, it is prone to elicit reporting activity, i.e., activity in the range of consciousness. Conscious activity regularly elicits after-activity in the nonreporting range, such as the storing of memories in the filing cabinet of this range.

Let me stress the fact that this conceptual scheme is not ontological, but operational. It is summarized in figure 1.

The organism seeks to satisfy its desires—to attain its goals—by effective control of its environment. The awareness process serves this purpose by its integrative action. It is the conscious phase of cerebral integration. Hence, the awareness process occupies the foremost place in the hierarchic design of the organism.

Though concerned with the same organism, the student of psychodynamics on the one hand, and the physiologist on the other, use different methods of investigation and different frames of reference. The student of psychodynamics explores the psychodynamic range of cerebral nervous activity chiefly by communicated introspection. To make his findings meaningful, he views them in an adaptational framework, in a context of motivation and control. But the physiologist explores all activities of the organism (including those of its cerebrum) chiefly by methods based on inspection. To make his findings meaningful, he views them in a general framework of matter, space and time. For the achievement of a unified science of human behavior, physiology will have to be assimilated to psychodynamics to a much greater extent than psychodynamics will have to be assimilated to physiology. The physiologist will have to evolve still further his matter-space-time formulation of the organism so as to bring it into the closest possible correspondence with the special adaptational framework of motivation and control. I consider the latter framework fundamental to all biology.[28, 29]

There are hopeful signs of progress in the direction of unification. One is the emergence of new theories, such as L. Bertalanffy's "organismic" conception of biology.[4] Another, that both sides voice their dissatisfaction with the present state of affairs. The physiologist complains that the theories of classical psychoanalysis, still unrivaled in popular appeal, are unrelated to

Nonreporting Range (includes psychodynamic sector—"the unconscious" of the classical theory)

Self-reporting Range (Range of Awareness or Range of Consciousness)

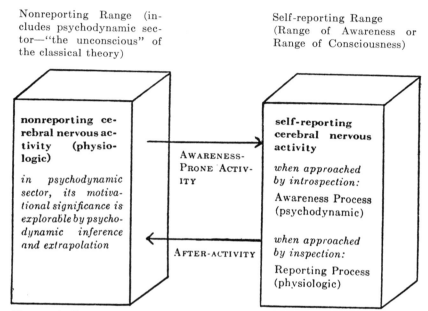

FIGURE 1. SUMMARY OF CONCEPTUAL SCHEME: CEREBRAL NERVOUS ACTIVITY

Range of awareness + psychodynamic sector of nonreporting range = psychodynamic range of cerebral nervous activity = psychodynamic cerebral system.

the physiologic organism. The student of adaptational psychodynamics, in turn, complains that the physiologist still tends to view consciousness as an epiphenomenon, presumably installed by nature in the brain for decorative purposes. Even the brilliant automaton theory of the organism, proposed by cybernetics, appears to take the same position.[15, 39] Natural selection favored the evolution of consciousness because of its eminent value for the improvement of life.

The road to unification will be long and arduous. It will be necessary then, to develop a new branch of knowledge, *physiologic psychodynamics*, concerned with the broader physiologic context as well as the cerebral mechanisms of motivation and control.

THE MACHINERY OF HEDONIC CONTROL

Levels, Signals, and Performance

The organism is a biologic system that perpetuates itself and its kind by means of its environment (its surrounding system). It supplies its systemic requirements, known as its "needs," by transforming stored potentials into an adaptive control of the environment. At the level of the psychodynamic cerebral system the needs of the organism give rise to tensions and desires, the sum total of which constitutes what Sherrington calls the "zest to live." [36]

Dobzhansky defines genotype as the inherited cause, and phenotype— the organism in appearance, structure, and function—as the actual outcome, of development. Utilizing this genetic distinction, one sees that the needs and desires of the phenotype, like its other traits, are an outcome of the interaction of genotype and environment. Roughly speaking, the needs and desires of the organism are either aboriginal or acculturated. The former show *predominantly* the influence of the genotype, and the latter *predominantly* the forming influence of the culture in which the organism lives. The acculturated needs and desires of the organism are complex and imperfectly known. The slow maturation of the human organism accounts for the strength of its aboriginal dependency needs.

The rise of appropriate desires (tensions) makes the organism aware of its needs and urges it to do what it can to supply them. The organism organizes its doing, exploring, planning and effecting, in the psychodynamic cerebral system.

On evolutionary as well as clinical grounds, I suggested elsewhere[27, 30, 34] that the psychodynamic cerebral system includes an *integrative apparatus* in which activity is spread over a hierarchy of four levels. Of these the lowest and most primitive one is the hedonic level. In ascending order there follow the levels of brute emotion, the intermediate level of emotional thought, and the top level of unemotional thought.

The hedonic level may have its evolutionary origin in the organization of the protozoan. The design of this level makes the organism move *toward* the source of *pleasure*, and *away* from the cause of *pain*. Hence, at the hedonic level the organism relies on the expectation that pleasure signals the presence of needed supplies or of conditions otherwise favorable to its survival; and pain the presence of a threat to its organic integrity. Thanks to the biologic effectiveness of this system of hedonic control, primitive species survived and evolved into higher ones. Where this system failed, the organism (species) died.

In pleasure and pain the animal organism thus possesses a dependable system of signals for the *yes* or *no* evaluation of its encounters and the self-regulation of its behavior. The activities described as "moving toward" and "moving away from" are mechanisms evolved in response to these *yes* and *no* signals. They are, in fact, the basic executive operations of the organism under this simple system of hedonic control. The further development and specialization of these operations may then be regulated by "feedback." [39] Hedonic self-regulation extends over the organism's entire operating pattern: pleasure is the reward for successful performance, and the memory of pleasure invites repetition of the beneficial activity. Pain is the punishment for failure and the memory of pain deters the organism from repeating the self-harming activity. Nature has placed massive pleasure rewards on the operations which supply the organism's aboriginal needs; such as, intake of food, evacuation of waste and reproduction. The perennial problem of cultural development is to extend this system of pleasure rewards to the operations that will supply the organism's acculturated needs, i.e., where it will have adaptive utility, in a given culture. At the same time, pleasure-yielding yet socially undesirable activity must be vigorously combatted by the threat of punishment or, in other words, the infliction of pain. The reward and punishment system of society is based upon, and is but an extension of, the hedonic self-regulation of the biologic organism.

The philosopher Jeremy Bentham[3] saw the hedonic self-regulation of the organism with admirable clarity:

> Nature has placed mankind under the governance of two sovereign masters, *pain* and *pleasure*. It is for them alone to point out what we ought to do, as well as to determine what we shall do. (Bentham's italics)

Freud recognized the same fact in his "pleasure and pain principle" which was later abbreviated to "pleasure principle."

In the class mammalia, labor precipitates the expulsion of the foetus and impresses upon the mother the arrival of the young. Pain here is a signal of danger to the species. If it were neglected by the mother, the newborn would die. Once the mother is aware of the newborn, and the pain is gone, a subsequent set of pleasure signals directs her to the job to be done.

The levels of brute emotion and emotional thought may have appeared during the evolution of the metazoa. The level of unemotional thought is peculiar to man. From level to level, the organism acquired more and better operating equipment, increased its foresight and grasp of its environment. Conceptual thought, group cooperation and cumulative tradition multiplied the adaptive utility of its performance, and its control of the environment. Its growing foresight taught it to pursue pleasurable ends by painful means, that is, to accept present pain for the sake of future pleasure. Nevertheless, despite the evolution of the level of unemotional thought, the elementary desire for the source of pleasure and aversion to the cause of pain have continued to limit man's activities and determine his goals and desires. Moreover, no man can function continuously at the level of unemotional thought. The organism has a multiplicity of emotional needs. It must take time out to satisfy them by recreation and play. To reduce the tensions of its frustrated desires, it turns to *illusory fulfillment*: it indulges in the wishful imagery of emotional thought. Dreaming, as Freud has shown, is such a hedonic mechanism for the prompt disposal of sleep-disturbing tensions. During work, the organism has its moments of "distraction" that act as safety valves for the discharge of its neglected tensions. If the organism is an automaton, it is one designed to operate under hedonic control.

At each of the four levels, integrative activity may be either conscious or nonreporting. As a rule, it is composed of both conscious and nonreporting phases. But this machinery is not in its entirety subject to hedonic control. It is important to realize that hedonic control operates only at the entrance to, and within, the range of awareness. This fact requires more thorough treatment.

The Pain-Barrier

Everyday observation shows that the organism is afraid of memories, thoughts, and feelings that are either painful in themselves or have painful consequences. It dislikes to harbor such dangerous material in its consciousness, and it learns to refrain from divulging such material to others. Hence, whenever possible, the organism intentionally suppresses painful or pain-connected tensions, feelings, and thoughts. Or, as Freud discovered, it removes them automatically from its consciousness. Moreover, as a matter of preventive precaution, the material thus removed remains excluded from consciousness. Freud called this lock-out mechanism repression.

Intentional suppression and automatic repression are hedonic functions. I interpret them as riddance mechanisms.[27, 29] Intentional suppression is used when automatic repression fails. But selective removal is by no means the only precautionary technic used by the organism. There are still other technics, such as selective combination.

Precautionary mechanisms effect hedonic control in every area of human behavior. Science, to give an example, is our rational mechanism for exploring the universe, including ourselves. It works by the logical ordering of conceptual thought and the systematic testing of such thought against our sense-data. Even this rational mechanism has a hedonic aspect: to the intellectually sensitive organism a logical or experimental error may be just as painful as an aching wound. Hence, the scientist seeks to avoid such errors not only for the sake of science, but also in order to avoid intellectual pain.

In the ramified organization of precautionary control one discerns a trunk-system, located strategically between the nonreporting and self-reporting ranges, and thus exposed to pressures and tensions from both sides. This trunk-system regulates selectively the flow of nonreporting yet awareness-prone activity into the self-reporting range (range of conscious-

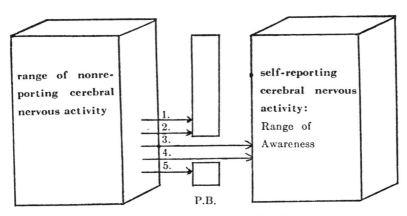

FIGURE 2. THE ACTION OF THE PAIN-BARRIER

P. B. The pain-barrier.

1 to 5. Trains of nonreporting yet awareness-prone cerebral nervous activity hit upon the pain-barrier. Some of them, marked here as trains 1, 2, and 5, are stopped by it; others, marked here as trains 3 and 4, pass it, and enter the range of awareness.

ness). On the whole, control by this trunk-system is flexible, attuned to the fluctuation of pressures and tensions in the two ranges. However, it also includes the rigid lockout action of repression. I call this fundamental trunk-system of precautionary organization the *pain-barrier*. Its action is shown schematically in figure 2.

A branch-system of the pain-barrier is our *social pain guard*. It consists of a special set of precautionary mechanisms that controls the communications of the organism to its social environment. Another specialized branch-system of the pain barrier is our *sensory pain guard*. It is composed of the precautionary mechanisms that protect the sense organs from painful stimulation (Freud's *Reizschutz*). The concept of hedonic control may help psychodynamics to utilize the Aristotelian insight that the organism is a hedonic system, dedicated to the pursuit of happiness: "Happiness . . . is the End at which all actions aim." [2]

Thinking Out Loud

In a psychoanalytic treatment we have a unique opportunity to study the working of hedonic control under experimental conditions. In the treatment situation the patient is obliged "to associate freely" or, to put it more descriptively, to think out loud. Let me contrast this particular mode of thinking with the routine of daily life.

Thinking is a process of self-reporting of the brain; talking, a process of reporting one's thoughts verbally to an audience. Ordinarily both processes are under hedonic control. They are subject to the preventive, selective, and reparative action of precautionary mechanisms. The most conspicuous of these mechanisms is riddance of our hedonic errors of thought and talk. We quickly repress or suppress painful thoughts that should have been but were not kept out of consciousness; we try quickly to explain away what we should not have blurted out in the first place.

The psychoanalytic patient behaves differently. When he thinks out loud, he does become aware of painful (or pain-connected) thoughts. He utters them, and he is also able to hold onto them. Though recognized as fundamental to the psychoanalytic method, this phenomenon has remained a puzzle just the same.

Close observation reveals the dynamics of thinking out loud. The patient is pressed by his illness. He wants to cooperate with the physician, and he hopes to be cured. He may look forward to the results of his self-exploration with a measure of intellectual curiosity and an even stronger longing to satisfy his frustrated pride. These and similar desires create and sustain in him an active motivational state, or, as we shall say, a field of pleasure expectation with respect to the material to be uncovered. This field then interacts with the awareness-prone material of the nonreporting range.

By its cushioning effect it so softens the pain of painful thought that such thought can enter consciousness and remain there without eliciting the riddance response. Thus, his field of pleasure expectation enables the patient to think out loud and circumvent his precautionary mechanisms, that is, his pain-barrier.

The material of the patient's self-exploration must be organized and interpreted for him. The physician does this by the method of contextual inference. He discloses to the patient his hidden patterns of motivation and shows him how to evaluate the significance of these patterns for the purposes of adaptive control. This work too depends for its success upon the presence in the patient of a field of pleasure expectation of adequate strength.

Experience further proves that the field of pleasure expectation cannot hold the riddance response indefinitely in abeyance. The patient must soon reinforce his painful insight by actual gain, or rather by appropriate welfare emotions—love, joy, pride—derived from actual gain. Otherwise the field of pleasure expectation sooner or later disappears. This change, when it comes, restores the patient to his old sensitivity, and thus puts an end to his painful awareness and painful insight.

The Nonreporting Range

As we have seen, the pain-barrier effectively safeguards the range of consciousness against pain by withholding painful material in the nonreporting range. In the light of this fact one is tempted to visualize the nonreporting range only as a depository of painful tensions, feelings, and thoughts. To correct this one-sided picture let me stress the fact that the nonreporting range includes an even greater abundance of potentially pleasurable material. It is the *fons et origo* of creative imagination. All conscious activity, pleasurable or painful, has its fore-phase and after-phase in the nonreporting range.

Furthermore, we have been considering so far only what I call *fluid* activity of the nonreporting range. Though spectacular, this is by far the smaller part of its total activity. The bulk of nonreporting activity is not fluid, but on the contrary fixed and stereotyped by automatization. These automatic patterns, regardless of the extent to which they were inherited or to what extent modified by learning, must have in their development passed through a stage of conscious formation. They were custom-made, so to speak, to fit the pleasure requirements of the organism.

As we see, from the point of view of hedonic control, the psychodynamic cerebral system falls into three parts. The conscious range is under hedonic control; the stereotyped section of the nonreporting range is so organized as to meet hedonic requirements; the fluid section of the nonreporting range shows neither hedonic organization nor hedonic control. Aside from potentially pleasurable tensions, feelings and thoughts, it also holds quantities of nonreporting tensions, feelings and thoughts that would be experienced as exceedingly painful were they to enter consciousness. This section is a potential threat to the conscious range. One may view the psychodynamic cerebral system as the experimental behavior laboratory of the organism, in which the fluid section of the nonreporting range is reserved for work with explosive material. For the organism to maintain such a section in its cerebrum is a dangerous business.

PUNCTURE OF THE PAIN-BARRIER

We are now prepared to examine the psychodynamic state of the depressed patient from the point of view of hedonic control.

Let me revert to the fact that the patient's consciousness is flooded with pain and painful thought derived from fear, rage, guilty fear and retro-flexed rage. He struggles with a sense of unworthiness, his self-confidence is shattered, his appetite and sex desire are on the wane or gone.

This state of consciousness may continue for a long time. The ordinary function of the precautionary mechanisms is suspended; preventive selection is swept aside and the arriving masses of pain cannot be handled by riddance. The inescapable conclusion is that the patient's *pain-barrier has been, and still is, extensively punctured.*

This finding raises numerous questions of immediate theoretical and clinical importance. Here I propose to inquire into the following three: How does the puncture of the pain-barrier come about? How does the organism deal with the painful material that invades consciousness because of the puncture? How does the organism repair the puncture when the depressive spell subsides?

ANTECEDENT EVENTS

The pain-barrier controls the passage of cerebral nervous activity from the nonreporting range to the range of consciousness. To plot the course of events that climaxes in the puncture of the pain-barrier, we must first glance at these two ranges in the state of health.

The emotional matrix of healthy life performance is dominated by welfare emotions; such as, pleasurable desire, joy, love and pride. While these emotions saturate the range of consciousness, the organism maintains a hopeful attitude or, as I call it, a field of over-all pleasure expectation. By eliciting the emotional resonance of others,[32] its radiance facilitates its struggle for cultural self-realization. It has no trouble with the painful tensions arising from time to time in the nonreporting range. They do not reach explosive strength; and their occasional overflow can be readily discharged by spells of fear in the waking state or by fear-ridden dreams.

In the depressive spell, the welfare emotions are swept aside by waves of resentment, followed by heavy counter-currents of fear tinged by guilty fear. Fear makes the patient's outlook increasingly hopeless. By this token, his field of over-all pleasure expectation is now superseded by a field of over-all pain expectation. Simultaneously, in the nonreporting range there is a fresh turbulence of emergency emotions. They are awareness-prone and thus threaten to invade the range of consciousness in full force. The interaction of the two ranges sets up a vicious circle. The field of pain expectation exerts a suction-like action upon the nonreporting range. This accelerates the inflow into consciousness of painful tensions, feelings and thoughts that justify, and therefore enhance, the patient's prevailing pain expectation which, in turn, increases the inflow, and so forth. This vicious circle more and more weakens and eventually punctures the pain-barrier. As a result, consciousness becomes flooded with painful material.

I have traced the puncture of the pain-barrier back to the patient's first overreaction, which ushered in his depressive spell. This overreaction appeared to be precipitated by the loss he suffered. However, this construction doesn't bear closer scrutiny. In the case of unoccasioned depression, the "precipitating loss" is obviously a figment of the patient's nonreporting imagination, perhaps an attempt at rationalizing his overreaction. Even in occasioned depression it may be the patient's overreaction that makes his "loss" appear to him so severe. Possibly this overreaction has no true psychodynamic cause. It may be a psychodynamic effect produced in the self-reporting range by a chain of nonreporting events that in turn originates at lower physiologic levels.

The Failure of Hedonic Self-Regulation in Miscarried Repair

After the puncture of the pain-barrier, more pain, fear, and impotent rage enter consciousness. To spare itself, the organism slows down and reduces its activities, thereby incapacitating itself still more. The patient dreams of miraculous help but none is forthcoming. He feels forsaken, puts the blame on himself, and interprets his situation as a deserved punishment.

The switch from objectively unjustified fear to objectively unjustified guilty fear is our point of interest. The patient's tolerance for fear and impotent rage is limited. When escape and combat are of no avail, fear becomes hopeless and so does rage. But guilty fear, the fear that knows the technic of expiation, offers hope. By punishing himself for his presumed wrongdoings, he can win forgiveness and unfailing help. This hope persuades the patient to switch from fear to guilty fear. But this hope is a mirage. It lures the patient into a trap. With the passage of time, he tries to *force* fulfillment by increasing the severity of self-punishment. The remedial procedure upon which he relies enhances rather than relieves his suffering. The mounting tension of guilty fear and retroflexed rage is the work of false hope.

Hopeless fear and rage are common human experiences, and so is the counsel of despair. Accordingly, the resort to the automatized repair-pattern of guilty fear is by no means limited to the depressive spell. But there is one characteristic that sets aside true depression from the various forms of unrecognized atonement. This feature is the patient's nonreporting fear of starvation, voiced usually as a fear of impoverishment. I have stressed the significance of this fear ever since I caught a glimpse of the depressive pattern.[25] One can trace this fear to two momentous experiences of the infant: his hunger and his intoxicating pleasure of satiation when he gorges at the mother's breast. I once labeled the latter phenomenon, "alimentary orgasm." [23]

The patient develops true depression when, in his nonreporting imagination, he begins to dramatize his "emergency" as a threat of starvation. We see that the patient loses his appetite, that he loses weight and, paradoxically, even punishes himself by fasting. But these manifestations merely rationalize and augment his mortal fear. Though this fear is based on an oversensitivity to the threat of alimentary deprivation developed in early life, its onset may be precipitated by current influences from lower physiologic levels. The patient may be subject to an actual metabolic disturbance that spoils his appetite and scares him in still other ways. Dependent for his well-being on the pleasure of satiation, he then blows up his scare to a fear of starvation. In fact, the assumption has been made repeatedly that the depressive spell is due to underlying metabolic changes,[18] but to my knowledge no such causative changes have yet been demonstrated.

Alimentary orgasm is assuredly the best means of dissipating the fear of starvation. But the patient's desire to regain his mother's feeding breast merely intensifies his contrition and, with it, his suffering.

Expiatory repair invoking the patient's image of his mother may be supplemented by repair invoking the image of the person whose loss precipitated his depressive spell. Unbeknown to himself, the patient may seek to acquire traits he loved and admired (and envied) in the one he lost, so as to be able to continue their enjoyment.[8] At the same time, by means of ironic self-reproaches, he may vent his rage on the same person. These two mechanisms are feeble attempts at reducing the patient's pain; the first by hedonic replacement, and the second by a partial restoration of his pride. As I have shown elsewhere[25, 31] their simultaneous appearance is made possible by the fact that in the patient's imagination the lost person is represented by two contrasting images: the one—wholly adorable—is a creation of his love; the other—wholly detestable—is a creation of his hate. This double-image technic of emotional thought, characteristic of the child's early relationship to his mother, is here carried forward into adult life.

So far we have dealt with miscarried repair in *retarded* depression. In the *agitated* form of depression the picture is slightly modified by the fact that here the patient makes an additional attempt at repair. With coercive intent, he tries to release his repressed stubborn rage. The hedonic motivation of this move is clear. The patient's pride feeds and grows on his stubborn rage, but not on his repentence. Were his stubborn rage to succeed, he would regain his lost pride. But the patient's guilty fear is of forbidding strength. The result is abortive rage that keeps the patient agitated and worsens his plight.

Repressed stubborn rage may also cause equally stubborn constipation; due to a belated defiance of the patient's mother, who used to incense him, when he was a child, with her insistence on bowel regularity.

Let me make here a passing reference to physical disease as a depressive equivalent. Beginning with the common cold[17] and culminating in disturbances of the gastrointestinal tract, there is a series of illnesses that may forestall the onset of an impending spell of depression or intercept its course. As a rule, when sick, the patient gets nursing care reminiscent of maternal care; but here, adaptive degradation of the patient is convincingly rationalized in his own eyes and in the eyes of the physician. Alexander and his collaborators duly stressed the part played by the patient's dependency needs in gastrointestinal disturbances.[1] From the adaptational point of view, the depressive patient's flight into the nursing care of physical illness is, of course, miscarried repair.

A few chance observations I was able to make showed to my amazement that in *ulcerative* disorders of the gastrointestinal tract, repair may be miscarried to an extreme. I have shown elsewhere[25, 31] that in depressive atonement, fasting is the paramount mode of self-punishment. But pangs of hunger may tempt the patient to break his fast. Hunger, the S.O.S. signal of the organism to itself, is thus, paradoxically, turned into a threat. The situation is analogous to that of the sexually incapacitated schizophrenic who experiences the genital urge—the S.O.S. signal of the species to the individual—as a threat rather than an opportunity. He responds with the "remedial" impulse to amputate his own genitals.[26] The gastrointestinal patient, bent on fasting, and perturbed by his hunger which he refers to his stomach, may respond to his predicament by the "remedial" impulse to get rid of his stomach or some other portion of his gastrointestinal tract. What part this impulse plays in ulcerative processes of the gastrointestinal tract will have to be ascertained by a thorough study of larger clinical material. Ulceration as a form of gastrointestinal riddance may yet prove to be a counterpart of genital riddance in the schizophrenic. The general significance of riddance responses has been shown elsewhere.[27, 30]

It is known that in the rare psychotic form of depression (marked by total adaptive incompetence rather than by adaptive impairment), the patient's hypochondriac delusions are mostly concerned with his gastrointestinal tract. The patient thinks, for instance, that he has lost his stomach or intestines. Delusional ideas of this sort may arise in response to the patient's own hidden impulse to get rid of that nuisance, his gastro-intestinal tract.

THE ACTION-SELF

We shall turn again to the healthy organism and take a view of its relationship to itself. Working only with adult material, I have been probing into this relationship since 1926,[23] searching for its infantile origins. Slowly I have evolved a reconstruction. What follows is a bare outline of this reconstruction, stripped of the clinical evidence on which it rests.

We start with the fact that the organism is aware of itself as a unitary entity. Self-awareness is a remarkable function of the conscious organism. Presumably, in the infant, this function begins with *proprioceptive* sensations. The infant organism discovers (we do not know how) that the muscular activities it perceives are *doings*, and that the doer is itself. The infant's most vigorous, and most emotional, muscular activity is sucking at the mother's breast. Thus, in our mammalian species, it is sucking that brings the organism to awareness of itself. Could the infant speak, he would jubilantly announce: *"succo ergo sum,"* "I suck, hence I am."

Since this hypothesis derives from the observation of disordered behavior, let me adduce as further evidence the following self-observation by William James:

> The self . . . when carefully examined is found to consist mainly of the collection of these peculiar [bodily] motions in the head or between the head and the throat. (James' italics)

Sucking can do no more than bring an inherited functional pattern (innate nervous organization) into play and thereby start its ontogenetic development. This inherited organization is, in essence, a circuit, a circular response pattern, of self-awareness and willed action:

The particular psychodynamic system built upon this circuit integrates the conscious organism into a self-aware and intentionally acting whole. In full, this system may be designated as the *integral action-self system* of the conscious organism. For convenience, I shall refer to it as the *action-self*. Located axially to the four levels of the psychodynamic integrative apparatus, the action-self is obviously the pivotal system of the entire organism. Guided by voluntary muscular activity, the action-self ascertains the boundaries of the organism, distinguishes between "within" and "without," between the doings of the organism and events in its environment. This distinction is then further elaborated by other sense-data. Through its action-self the organism thus evolves the two fundamental and contrasting integrations *total organism* and *total environment*, upon which its selfhood rests.

H. Helmholtz[13] saw the significance of voluntary muscular activity in the organism's separation of within from without:

> The changes which we can make and unmake, by our conscious volitional impulses, separate themselves from those which do not result from, and cannot be eliminated by, impulses of the will. The latter definition is a negative one. Fichte expressed this appropriately by saying that opposite to an "I" a "non-I" has to be recognized.

Sherrington called mind the manager of muscle.[35] Phylogenetically, the action-self must be an ancient portion of "mind"; in the infant, we see its rise from the ranks.

Total organism is a complex integration, an essential component of which is the highly emotional thought-picture the organism evolves of itself. At first this thought-picture is altogether dominated by wishful thought. Intoxicated by its ability to move, the young organism attributes *unlimited power* to its willed actions, and pictures itself as an *omnipotent being*. I call this fundamental thought-picture its primordial self. It is sustained by a sense of all-might, which the organism learns to externalize in an imagery of bodily size. To let it be known that it possesses such superior powers, it will soon seek to exhibit itself in as gigantic dimensions as possible.

When the child discovers the sad truth that his actual powers are limited, he safely removes his primordial self—that precious thought-picture of an omnipotent being—to the nonreporting range where it will be preserved for the rest of his life. As an adaptive corollary, he delegates his secret omnipotence to his parents, expecting them to do his magic for him. At the same time he must learn to distinguish between his being and his becoming. From a reality-tested picture of the organism the action-self then separates a thought-picture of what the organism desires to become (Freud's Ego-Ideal).

This thought-picture is the desired self of the organism, its blueprint for cultural self-realization. At the transmigratory state of self-realization the child projects himself into the place of those whom he envies and admires. His action-self takes, so to speak, credit for their achievements. Then follows the blueprint stage, the desire to copy or surpass them. However, the dividing line between the thought picture of what one is (tested self) and the blueprint of what one would like to be (desired self) remains precarious throughout the life-span.

Our primordial longing for omnipotence is the mainspring of civilization. The worship of omnipotence in religion is only one of its expressions. The cultural effort to *achieve* omnipotence has produced the scientist, who gives laws to the universe[22]; the artist, who recreates the universe in samples of his choosing; and the technologist, who is about to perfect the electronic robot that may come close to running our productive system for us with no effort of our own. To rise from hunger and toil to comfort and leisure is the next aim of man's quest for omnipotence. The final goal is his conquest of death.

The organism appreciates itself as a proven provider of pleasure. This emotional appreciation, mediated by the action-self, is known as pride. Itself a derivative of sucking, the action-self continues to feed on pleasure. It absorbs the pleasure of all activity and success, above all the pleasure of loving, being loved and respected, loving and respecting oneself. The action-self expands and contracts, and the pride of the organism rises and falls, with the amount of pleasure the action-self consumes, just as the bodily weight of the organism rises and falls with its intake of food. Pride, the emotional stature of the organism, is thus determined by the size of the action-self.

The bodily expression of pride corroborates this view. Let me quote Charles Darwin:

A proud man exhibits his sense of superiority by holding his head and body erect. He is haughty (*haut*), or high, and makes himself appear as large as possible; so that he is said to be swollen or puffed up with pride.[6]

To increase this effect of physical stature, proud chieftains wore towering headgear; proud kings seated themselves on a throne, and wore a crown; the Emperor in *Gulliver's Travels* wore heels taller than the heels of his subjects by almost the breadth of a fingernail. On Jonathan Swift's authority, this alone sufficed to "strike an awe into the beholders." [38] In contrast to the imperious gesture of the outstretched arm, worshipful humility is expressed by a head bent slightly forward, shoulders, arms and hands curved in towards the subject's own body.

Language abounds with idioms that bear out our construction. The organism is said to swell with rage and shrink with fear. This reflects the swelling and shrinking of its pride, and, in turn, of its action-self. Presumably, fear becomes paralyzing when it paralyzes the action-self.

The organism has its established sources of pride; *but it may shift these sources and manipulate its pride. Its management of pride is a highly significant determinant of its behavior in health and disease.*[28, 30, 34]

In addition to pride, the organism evolves, through the expansion of its action-self, a whole series of more exalted emotions, such as triumph, ecstasy, elation, and narcotic intoxication. Their common root is the intoxicating pleasure of satiation at the mother's breast.[23]

Parental reward and punishment force the young organism to seek security through obedience. Anticipating parental criticisms and demands, the psychodynamic cerebral system develops a semi-automatic organization of self-restraining and self-prodding responses known as our conscience.[30, 32] The action-self, though restricted in its freedom of action by conscience, is forced to make it a more or less autonomous part of its own organization. With this momentous development of the action-self, the organism becomes better fit for peaceful cooperation with other members of the group. Now it must, and can, accept full responsibility not only for its action, but often for its thoughts and intended actions as well.[30, 32]

Variations in the extension of the action-self directly influence the self-restraining and self-prodding responses of conscience.[30] By expanding, the action-self increases our sense of self-reliance; by contracting, it increases our sense of dependence. Accordingly, the expansion of the action-self weakens the restraining action of conscience; contraction of the action-self strengthens it.

Certain disorders force the action-self to expand in a move of miscarried repair. The organism is then prone to mistake the picture of its desired self, or even that of its primordial self, for a picture of its tested self, and act accordingly. It is then said to suffer from a delusion of grandeur.

Awareness of ordinarily "willed" action may be stripped of the self-attributive effect of the action-self. This is seen in thoughts and feelings elicited under experimental conditions by direct electric stimulation of the brain.[21] Obviously, such stimulation bypasses the action-self and its established channels for willed activity. In dreams, presumably for similar reasons, the whereabouts of the dreamer is often uncertain, and his identity confused or completely lost.

The fact that the action-self works under hedonic control has far-reaching consequences. "The mind," observed Spinoza, "shrinks from conceiving those things, which diminish or constrain the power of itself and of the body."[35] It is, of course, the action-self that rids consciousness of certain thoughts and feelings thrust upon it from within or without. Moreover, to satisfy its pride, the action-self continuously edits and re-edits the entire remembered history of the organism. This was sensed by Nietzsche:

'I did this,' says my memory. 'I cannot have done this,' says my pride, and remains inexorable. In the end—memory yields.[20]

During sleep or in the presence of serious disorder, the action-self may treat certain thoughts as if they were forced upon the organism by the environment. Hallucinations are such thoughts, disowned and transformed by the action-self into what appear to the organism as sense-data of external origin.

Let me now give a rounded summary of these features of the action-self.

Of proprioceptive origin, the action-self is the pivotal integrative system of the whole organism. Guided by willed action, it separates the organism's awareness of itself from its awareness of the world about it, and completes this fundamental separation by building up the unitary entity of total organism in contrast to the total environment. It is upon these contrasting integrations that the selfhood of the organism depends, as well as its awareness of its unbroken historical continuity. In accord with these functions, the action-self plays a pivotal part in the integrative action of the awareness process. This part is enhanced by its automatized organization of conscience, which increases the fitness of the organism for peaceful cooperation with the group. By its expansion and contraction, the action-self serves as the gauge of the emotional stature of the organism, of the ups and downs of its successes and failures. In its hunger for pride, it continuously edits for the organism the thought-picture of its present, past and future.

The depressive patient, severely inhibited in pleasurable activity by his inappropriate emergency emotions, is starved of pleasure and pride. In consequence, his action-self contracts, interacting thereby with the inhibition that has precipitated its contraction, in a vicious circle. This mechanism is an added obstacle to recovery.

Browbeaten by retroflexed rage, the contracting action-self revises the thought-picture of the organism in the direction opposite to grandeur. The resulting picture of a disappointed, worthless being may be called the patient's despised self. Mistaking this picture for a picture of his tested self, the patient develops a sense—if not a delusion—of unworthiness. Assimilated to the facade of remorse, this then becomes a sense—or delusion —of moral unworthiness.

THE ROAD TO RECOVERY

Recovery, spontaneous or therapeutic, sets in when the patient begins to recapture his lost capacity for pleasure, for the enjoyment of life. But this statement must be qualified. From the point of view of adaptive value, there are two kinds of pleasure: one true, and the other spurious. True pleasure is the earned reward of successful effort. It stems from the transformation of stored organismic potentials into adaptive control. Spurious pleasure on the other hand is obtained by little or no effort. It springs from the mere illusion of control. The action-self responds to true pleasure with due pride; to spurious pleasure, its reaction is exalted. This effortless pleasure appears to it as an actual proof of its magic powers. It responds with triumph and may even lift the organism to a state of intoxication or elation. As we now see, the patient is on the road to recovery only when he begins to achieve *true* pleasure. This fact makes it advisable first to examine spurious recovery based on the attainment of spurious pleasure.

On the rebound from depression, the organism may seize the opportunity to recapture its lost pleasure. If undertaken precipitously, this reparative move defeats its purpose. The organism outmaneuvers its residual retardation, tears holes in its inhibitions and repressions, jumps without discrimination from stimulus to stimulus, from one incompleted act to the next, as if afraid of missing out on an opportunity to enjoy life again. The immediate result of this frantic effort is a *scattering disorganization of its routine operating procedures*. At this price, the organism succeeds in generating not pleasure but *spurious* pleasure. During the depression it expected pain to be followed by more pain. Now it expects pleasure to be followed by more pleasure. During depression, the organism shrank in emotional stature almost to nothingness, and the adaptive task appeared in gigantic dimensions. Now its emotional stature appears in gigantic dimensions and the adaptive task shrinks almost to nothingness. As if intoxicated, the organism becomes overconfident and experiences a new exuberance of life, an upward swing of mood. It enters upon a cycle of elation.

The exuberant activity of the elated patient is wasteful if not self-damaging; but it is sustained by a deceptive spirit of unrivaled prosperity. We trace these manifestations of elation to the fact that spurious pleasure inflates the action-self and at the same time manipulates the gauge by which hedonic control operates. One may compare this with a defective steam engine. While the pressure gauge indicates optimal pressure, the actual pressure in the boiler is at the point of explosion. I suggested elsewhere that elation is a developmental derivative, a morbid counterpart of a basic human experience—the infant's intoxicating satiation at the mother's breast.[25, 26] Recently, B. D. Lewin discussed elation from the latter point of view.[19]

The depressive spell may subside without being followed by a spell of elation. If elation occurs the pattern of alternate cycles is established. Elation may set in while the depressive cycle is still at its height. The patient is then in a mixed state, a depression masked by elation. In other circumstances, the organism may forestall depression by a spell of preventive elation.

Our medical predecessors may have intuitively grasped the reparative intent of elation when they began to treat depression with the administration of opiates. *Tinctura opii* is the old time remedy for depression.

Let us see what the opiates can do for the patient. Their analgesic (pain-killing) and soporific (sleep-inducing) action relieves the patient from the almost physical pain of depression. Their euphoric effect is produced in two steps: they induce pleasure beyond the mere relief from pain, and then cause the patient to become intoxicated with the spurious pleasure he thus experiences. Narcotic intoxication is closely related to elation. It derives from the same infantile origin.[26]

Though the opiates have little or no effect on the overproduction of the emergency emotions, transiently they may quiet these emotions and cover up the depression by their intoxicating effect. The patient may win a breathing space, and under favorable circumstances may even pull out of his depression.

The danger of this medication is that the patient may develop opium-dependence. Writing about the opiates, Goodman and Gilman[12] point out that there is a definite relationship between the severity of pain and the amount of opiate required and tolerated. If the nature of the patient's illness is such that his pain suddenly subsides or disappears, then the amount of opiate he required and tolerated while in severe pain, may produce in him signs of opiate poisoning. Similarly, one sees that the less the patient's actual pain, the greater the combined pleasure-inducing and intoxicating action of the opiate, and, in the long run, the greater also the risk of addiction. These considerations apply to the use of any other narcotic drug.

In emerging from his depression, the patient may pass through a minor spell of elation, usually referred to as a hypomanic state. In contrast to his previous retardation, his relatives and friends may mistake his elevation of mood and scattering disorganization of activity for a greater ease, and interpret it as a sign of improvement. Unrecognized elation is a dangerous phase of mood-cyclic disorder. Soaring above ordinary bounds, the overactive and overconfident patient may at a moment's notice inflict severe social damage upon himself and others.

Both nature and the physician are trying to fight depression with the wrong kind of pleasure. Their failure is due to the fact that the pleasure they employ is spurious. The true antidote to depression is true pleasure, derived from the liberation of healthful activity, from the natural re-expansion of the contracted action-self. Although the patient may feel better, the dependable sign of recovery is the dwindling of his inhibitions, and increasing fullness of his life performance.

To bring about this result is the task of the psychotherapy of the depressive spell. The patient's inhibition, his inability to cope with his fears, guilty fears, and retroflexed rages, show that the over-activity of his emergency emotions is a radical etiologic factor in his illness. The task of causal therapy would be to remove these emotions, or rather to reduce their excessive strength. It is of utmost importance to realize that psychotherapy cannot do this while the tide of these emotions is still rising. During this phase, we can hardly do better than shield the patient from avoidable damage, otherwise biding our time until the tide passes its peak. From this point on, our therapy may accelerate the recession of the emergency emotions and the re-expansion of the contracted action-self. One can now lure the patient subtly to take an active interest again in his own life, and help him to perceive those opportunities most likely to yield him a quick but true reward in terms of gratification. If this emergency phase of the work is successfully completed and the depressive spell subsides, then, in a second phase of treatment, one may aim at the patient's preventive readjustment by the adaptational technic of psychoanalytic therapy.[33]

In 1918, Freud's position was that the therapist should wait until the depressive spell subsides and then "during the lucid interval," start treatment in order to prevent its recurrence.[9] This is still sound clinical judgement. In contradistinction, the practice of penetrating into the life history of the patient and feeding him so-called psychoanalytic insight while the tide of his emergency emotions is still rising, is contrary to the scientific rationale of treatment.

In the psychotherapy of the depressive spell, what we need most is a wonder drug that would reduce the patient's fears, guilty fears, and rages without the slightest pleasure-inducing and intoxicating effects. Such a truly non-narcotic drug would revolutionize the psychotherapy of the depressive spell (and, for that matter, psychotherapy altogether).

This is the place to stress the value of the electro-convulsive treatment of the depressive spell.[16] If successful, this treatment quickly readies the patient for psychotherapy. In mode of action it resembles the wonder-drug to come. It seems to reduce the patient's emergency emotions without pleasure-inducing and intoxicating effects. However, since it leaves the patient's action-self contracted and his pain-barrier punctured, there is a considerable danger of relapse. The task of subsequent psychotherapy is to re-establish in the conscious range a field of true pleasure expectation and gradually bring the machinery of initiative and sustained effort into play.

The problem of electro-convulsive treatment is far from solved. We do not know its physiologic mechanism. Also, in some cases the patient's response is excellent, and in others disappointing. We do not know why.

It ought not to be difficult now to form an idea of the "healing" of the punctured pain-barrier. As we saw, the puncture was caused by the sudden rise of inordinate tensions in the two adjoining ranges, pressure in the non-reporting range and suction in the self-reporting range—tensions that interacted in a vicious circle. Obviously, what the puncture requires for its healing is rest from the demands that are made upon the pain barrier far in excess of its functional strength. The process of healing cannot begin until the excessive tensions in both ranges *simultaneously* subside. The next phase of healing may be an interaction of the two ranges now in a benign circle.

The Predisposition to Mood-cyclic Disorder

I have shown that the depressed and elated cycles of mood are directly traceable to impairments of the hedonic control of the organism. An overwhelming emergency response, culminating in the fear of starvation, punctures the pain-barrier. This damage brings forth the depressive cycle. In order to end the depressive cycle or to prevent its threatening onslaught, faulty self-regulation turns to producing spurious pleasure and thus manipulates the gauge of hedonic control. This damage brings forth the elated cycle. In depression, the therapeutic use of narcotic intoxication is an artificial counterpart of this natural process of miscarried repair.

In this light, proneness to mood-cyclic disorder must include the following three phenotypic traits:

1) Proneness to emergency overreaction and dyscontrol.

2) Critical significance of alimentary security in the hedonic pattern of the organism. This implies a high susceptibility to the threat of alimentary deprivation.

3) Intolerance of pain,[52] marked by an acute fear of pain that increases pain in a vicious circle. Moreover, intolerance of pain may be a direct expression of an underlying vulnerability of the pain-barrier, and therefore of the entire machinery of hedonic control.

In phenotypes prone to mood-cyclic disorders the ontogenetic development of these traits may be based on the presence of predisposing factors in their genotypes. Actualization of these presumably inherited factors would then be the outcome of their interaction with the sequence of environments to which the organism is exposed. In this respect most significant of course are the environments encountered during the early years of growth. I called attention elsewhere[25] to the part played by the hunger pains of the infant in the etiology of mood-cyclic disorders. In this sense, loss of the alimentary security of loving maternal care may be the earliest environmental influence capable of starting the actualization of an inherited mood-cyclic predisposition.

Looking Ahead

Recently Daniel H. Funkenstein published biochemical data[11] that appear to support the emergency overreaction theory of depression as outlined in my previous paper.[31] His work opens the door for a long overdue cooperation between the representatives of allied disciplines struggling with different aspects of the same problem. We have the beginnings of a physiology of pain, but not of pleasure. It is to be hoped that it will be possible to test the depressive pattern, now including the puncture of the pain-barrier, by biochemical methods, and thus begin to establish its physiologic context.

The working concept of inherited mood-cyclic predisposition, which I have introduced in the preceding chapter, must await its validation by genetic studies. The general significance of concepts of this type is brought into sharp relief by Dobzhansky's succinct formulation[7] that genetics is the physiology of inheritance and variation. In line with this, concepts of behavior predisposition aim at an adaptional psychodynamics of human inheritance and variation. They thus seek to outline some of the problems for human genetics to solve.

Overspecialization has split human biology into a loose collection of isolated and self-contained sciences that are less and less capable of capturing the infinite organizational complexity of the life of Man. Looking ahead, we may anticipate the rise of a comprehensive dynamics of human behavior. To achieve this comprehensive science, the adaptional psychodynamics of behavior will have to be correlated with its physiology, and this in turn with its genetics. The component sciences of the new structure may be visualized as three interconnected strata of an inverted pyramid: the adaptational psychodynamics of behavior, situated at the inverted base; the genetics of behavior, at the inverted apex; and the physiology of behavior, between them. While working in one of these component fields, it may be of value to see beforehand where the problem on hand will fit into the picture of the whole.

References

[1] ALEXANDER, FRANZ AND FRENCH, THOMAS M.: *Studies in Psychosomatic Medicine.* New York, Ronald Press, 1948.

[2] ARISTOTLE: *Nichomachean Ethics*, 1.7.8. Loeb Classical Library, Harvard, 1939, p. 31.

[3] BENTHAM, JEREMY: An Introduction to the Principles of Morals and Legislation. *The English Philosophers from Bacon to Mill.* New York, Modern Library, 1939, p. 791.

[4] v. BERTALANFFY, L.: *Problems of Life.* New York, Wiley, 1952.

[5] BRIDGMAN, P. W.: *The Nature of Some of Our Physical Concepts.* New York, Philosophical Library, 1952.

[6] DARWIN, CHARLES: *The Expression of the Emotions in Man and Animals.* London, Watts and Co., 1934, p. 134.

[7] DOBZHANSKY, THEODOSIUS: *Genetics and the Origin of Species.* New York, Columbia University Press, 1951.

[8] FREUD, SIGMUND: Mourning and Melancholia. *Collected Papers, 4:* 30, London, Hogarth, 1925.

[9] ——: *A General Introduction to Psychoanalysis.* New York, Liveright, 1935.

[10] ——: *An Outline of Psychoanalysis.* New York, Norton, 1949, p. 21. (Published in German, 1940.)

[11] FUNKENSTEIN, DANIEL H., GREENBLATT, M. AND SOLOMON, H. D.: Norephrine-like and ephrine-like substances in psychotic and psychoneurotic patients. *Am. J. Psychiat., 108:* 9, March 1952, 652–662.

[12] GOODMAN, LOUIS AND GILMAN, ALFRED: *The Pharmacological Basis of Therapeutics.* New York, Macmillan, 1941, p. 218.

[13] HELMHOLTZ, H.: *Schriften Zur Erkenntnistheorie.* Berlin, Springer, 1921.

[14] JAMES, WILLIAM: *The Principles of Psychology.* New York, Henry Holt, 1890, *1:* 301.

[15] JEFFRESS, LLOYD A., Ed: *Cerebral Mechanisms in Behavior.* New York, Wiley, 1951.

[16] KALINOWSKY, LOTHAR B. AND HOCH, PAUL H.: *Shock Treatment.* New York, Grune and Stratton, 1952.

[17] LANDAUER, KARL: Aquivalente der Trauer. *Int. Ztschr. f. Psychoanal., 11:* 194, 1925.

[18] LANGE, JOHANNES: Die endogenen und reaktiven Gemütserkrankungen. *Bumke's Handbuch, 7:* 2. Berlin, Springer, 1928.

[19] LEWIN, BERTRAM D.: *The Psychoanalysis of Elation.* New York, Norton, 1950.

[20] NIETZSCHE, FRIEDRICH: *Jenseits von Gut und Böse. 4:* 68.

[21] PENFIELD, WILDER AND RASMUSSEN, THEODORE: *The Cerebral Cortex of Man.* New York, Macmillan, 1950.

[22] RADO, SANDOR: The paths of natural science in the light of psychoanalysis. *Psychoanal. Quart., 1:* 683, 1932. (Published in German, 1922.)

[23] ——: The psychic effects of intoxicants: An attempt to evolve a psycho-analytical theory of morbid cravings. *Internat. J. Psycho-Analysis, 7:* 396, 1926. (Published in German, 1927.)

[24] ——: An anxious mother: a contribution to the analysis of the ego. *Internat. J. Psycho-Analysis, 9:* 219, 1928. (Published in German, 1927.)

[25] ——: The problem of melancholia. *Internat. J. Psycho-Analysis, 9:* 420, 1928. (Published in German, 1927.)

[26] ——: The psychoanalysis of pharmacothymia (drug addiction). *Psychoanal. Quart., 2:* 1, 1933.

[27] ——: Developments in the psychoanalytic conception and treatment of the neuroses. *Psychoanal. Quart., 8:* 427, 1939.

[28] ——: An Adaptational View of Sexual Behavior. *Psychosexual Development in Health and Disease* (Hoch and Zubin, Eds.). New York, Grune & Stratton, 1949.

[29] ——: Mind, unconscious mind, and brain. *Psychosom. Med., 11:* 165, 1949.

30 —— : Emergency Behavior: With an Introduction to the Dynamics of Conscience. *Anxiety* (Hoch and Zubin, Eds.). New York, Grune & Stratton, 1950.

31 —— : Psychodynamics of depression from the etiologic point of view. *Psychosom. Med., 13:* 51, 1951.

32 —— : On the psychoanalytic exploration of fear and other emotions. *Trans. N. Y. Acad. Sc., II, 14:* 280, 1952.

33 —— : Recent Advances of Psychoanalytic Therapy. *Psychiatric Treatment* (Wortis, Hare and Herman, Eds.). Baltimore, Williams & Wilkins, 1953.

34 —— : Lectures at Columbia University.

35 SHERRINGTON, SIR CHARLES: *The Brain and its Mechanism.* New York, Macmillan, 1937.

36 —— : *Man and his Nature.* Cambridge University Press, 1940.

37 SPINOZA: *Ethics*, Part 3.

38 SWIFT, JONATHAN: *Gulliver's Travels.* London, Oxford Univ. Press, 1933, p. 30.

39 WIENER, NORBERT: *Cybernetics.* New York, Wiley, 1948.

Evolutionary Basis of Sexual Adaptation*

In the human adult we speak of the standard or reproductive pattern of sexual performance marked by the following features: close physical contact and climactic genital union of male and female; pleasure and welfare emotions (desire, joy, affection, love and pride); absence of pain and of emergency emotions (fear, rage, guilty fear and guilty rage)[12, 13]. We view this pattern as the healthy form of sexual adaptation.

Standard performance may be impaired by debilitating or incapacitating inhibitions; these are cases of impaired adaptation. In another class of cases a modified pattern takes the place of the standard pattern. From the point of view of motivation, the appearance of such modified patterns may be incidental, situational or reparative.

Incidental modifications are motivated by the desire for variation. The individual has adequate capacity and opportunity for standard performance.

Situational modifications occur in limiting conditions such as segregation or other lack of opportunity. When the situation changes, as a rule the individual reverts to the standard pattern. Incidental and situational modifications show the elasticity of healthy sexual organization.

Reparative modifications are the more rigid consequence of a disordered ontogenetic development of the sexual function. Incapable of standard performance, the individual depends for satisfaction on a modified pattern forced upon him by automatic processes of repair, working for the most part outside his range of consciousness. In our society such individuals are branded as offenders even if their sexual activity involves no damage and is carried out by mutual consent. These reparative modifications are true psychiatric disorders, complicated by the patient's justified fear of the consequences. We view them as deficient though more or less effective forms of sexual adaptation.

Modified patterns of courtship and mating also occur in subhuman species

---

* Portions of this paper were presented in the panel discussion on "Sexual Perversions" at the Mid-Winter Meeting of the American Psychoanalytic Association, December, 1953. The entire paper was read before the Seventh Annual Institute in Psychiatry and Neurology, Veterans Administration Hospital, North Little Rock, Arkansas, February 24, 1955. First published in the *Journal of Nervous and Mental Disease, 121:* 389, 1955.

under natural conditions. However, when opportunity arises, the animal reverts to the pattern characteristic of its type. It does not develop dependence on a modified pattern spontaneously. The persistence of deficient sexual adaptations appears to be peculiar to the human species.

Recent advances in the biological and cultural sciences have considerably increased the value of the evolutionary point of view, recognized in psychoanalysis from the outset. Phylogenetic, cultural and individual history, and genetics deal with different aspects and phases of the same evolutionary process. In the present paper an attempt will be made to trace the healthy, impaired and deficient forms of sexual adaptation to their biological and cultural origins, and to arrive at a *unified evolutionary framework of meaning*.

EVOLUTION OF THE NERVOUS SYSTEM IN THE VERTEBRATES

In the evolutionary line from fish to man, the successive forms have changed from life in water to life on land, from the mass movement of swimming to standing and running, first on four feet, then on two. The latter transformation has been followed by the emergence of manipulative skills, the use of tools, conceptual thinking, talking and writing. During this evolution, the nervous system has grown and new brain parts have appeared. More and more the forebrain has come to cover, overshadow and dominate the nervous structures from which it has developed. In the words of C. Judson Herrick, the forebrain has evolved as a "synthetic apparatus of control" that integrates the activities of all the other parts of the nervous system and increases the animal's capacity to modify its performance in the light of previous experience. Its "explosive" phylogenetic growth has made the forebrain the supremely distinctive organ of the human species[8].

MAMMALIAN EVOLUTION OF THE SEXUAL PATTERN

In recent decades a novel type of experimental work has been done on mammalian species ancestral to man, designed to explore, by the method of comparative analysis, the *physiological* organization of sexual behavior. Frank A. Beach has had the largest share in these investigations, fitting their results into a comprehensive theory and publishing a critical review of the literature[2, 3].

Two lines of investigation were followed: one concerned with the central nervous mechanism of courtship and mating; the other, with their hormonal control. In the course of mammalian evolution, with the phylogenetic development of the brain, several changes have taken place in both. In the lower vertebrates the nervous machinery of courtship and mating is in its entirety innately organized. In the adult animal with no previous sexual experience a simple set of stimuli suffices to bring into play a stereotyped and automatized operating pattern. Nor is there any margin for significant modification by experience. To this automatic nervous organization, one may fittingly apply Claude Bernard's remark: "Nature thought it prudent to remove these important phenomena from the caprice of an ignorant will." However, during mammalian phylogenesis, this rigid innate nervous organization has gradually broken down, and the pattern has become increasingly modifiable and dependent for its completion upon experience. The sexually inexperienced adult male chimpanzee, when aroused, is unable to effect union with a receptive female without first undergoing "a long period of practice and learning"[2]. In our species, only a few discrete fragments of the total pattern have remained innate reflexes: erection, orgasm, and perhaps pelvic thrust. The rest of the pattern has to be learned.

Gonadal secretions exert powerful and specific effects upon the patterns of courtship and mating in all mammalian forms. Their mode of action on the nervous system is imperfectly known. They seem to strengthen the effects produced by nervous mechanisms in a selective fashion, presumably depending upon the differential biochemical composition of the nervous structures involved. In any case, at lower evolutionary levels, sexual behavior is strictly controlled by gonadal hormones. But with the advancing phylogenetic status of the species the controlling significance of hormones is gradually reduced and limited to certain discrete components of the total nervous mechanism. At the same time, control over the total pattern shifts to the "synthetic apparatus" located in the forebrain.

In both lines of experimental study the available evidence points to the same conclusion: *the human male and female do not inherit an organized neuro-hormonal machinery of courtship and mating. Nor do they inherit any organized component mechanism that would—or could—direct them to such goals as mating or choice of mate.* In the light of this evidence, the psychoanalytic theory of sexual instincts evolved in the first decades of this century becomes an historical expedient that has outlived its scientific usefulness. Each of the sexes has an innate capacity for learning and is equipped with a specific power plant and tools. But in sharp contrast to the lower vertebrates, and as a consequence of the encephalization of certain functions first organized at lower evolutionary levels of the central nervous system, they inherit no organized information or directions concerning the use of this equipment.

The Standard Sexual Pattern of Contemporary Man

Observation shows that the healthy human adult periodically enters upon a sexual motive state—a state of acute desire—that readies the organism for sexual performance. The goal desired is the climactic genital union of male and female. Extensive participation of extragenital parts in this union shows that the sexual motive state transforms the entire organism into a single instrument of sexual expression and gratification. The motivation is thus preponderantly hedonic, often even to the complete exclusion of reproductive intent. Nonetheless the fact remains that orgasm is a reflex effect produced by the reproductive systems; in both sexes, it is nature's massive hedonic reward for insemination[15]. The reproductive systems are the *raison d'être* of the sexes; orgasm serves the process of reproductive integration that alone renders evolutionary differentiation into male and female biologically effective.

Beginning with its gross peripheral *physiology*, orgasm is a reflex response, evoked in both sexes by the reciprocal stimulation of genital union. It may be described as a cycle of peristaltic contractions of genital (and adjacent) structures. In the male, its reproductive function is to transport and eject the seminal fluid, and in the female, to facilitate this act of ejection by the stimulative effect of *active* reception. Less well understood is the complex *psychodynamic* organization that rests upon this peripheral physiology. Reciprocal stimulation leads to the accumulation of pleasurable tensions, and orgasm to their climactic release. The psychodynamic effectiveness of the entire mechanism depends upon quality and volume of the tensions accumulated and upon the completeness of their discharge. Both vary widely from individual to individual and at different times in the same individual. Pleasurable tensions may be generated by stimulation of contact receptors and distance receptors, and through the activation of pleasant memories and wishful expectations. Desire and love give rise to a stream of emotional tensions composed of many currents.* The same is true of pride[12, 15]. These welfare emotions increase the pleasurable tension and the value of its release. But an admixture of unpleasant tensions, stemming from inappropriate emergency emotions, is an unwelcome cultural complication of the standard pattern because their inhibitory action renders release incomplete.

In human life the climactic union of male and female is an overwhelming shared emotional experience. Apart from its reproductive function, it must be recognized as the *master-mechanism for the pleasurable accumulation and discharge of superabundant emotional tensions.*† Evolution of the forebrain

---

* The pair "in love" reactivates the child's blissful reliance on loving parental care and blends it with mature sensual desire. The female becomes an idealized version of the feeding mother; the male, of the protecting father. By this magic, they may achieve the illusion of incestuous fulfillment in a state of impervious security. Their triumph makes them self-sufficient, oblivious to the rest of the world.

† The superabundance of tensions was pointed out by Sandor Ferenczi[5]; subsequently, Franz Alexander[1] proposed to explain this fact by his concept of "surplus energy."

has increased the adaptive value of this emotional mechanism, an increase that reflects the extent to which our emotional life has risen—in differentiation, refinement and complexity—above that of our subhuman forebears.

Of course, the genital union of male and female may be completely unaffectionate, achieving no more than a rudimentary orgasm that relieves pressing but isolated sexual tensions and serves as an outlet for glandular secretions.

Cultural Evolution

Retracing our steps, we shall now describe the cultural evolution of the sexual pattern.

Through the ages our species has lived in societies that have handed down their achievements and possessions from parent to offspring in a continuous chain. Cumulative tradition is a cultural mechanism of inheritance, an external counterpart of the genic mechanism of inheritance. Some of the innate reflexes and automatized patterns of activity may be interpreted as "built-in" centers of information and direction. Our cultural resources of learning—such as parents, teachers, libraries—are similar centers established in the environment. In the evolution of the central nervous system certain lower-level functions have been in part encephalized, in part externalized, i.e., lifted to the societal level of the species.

Once this stage of central nervous organization has been attained, education becomes a biological necessity. Through the millenia, primitive societies have carried out sexual education of the young in a ritualized fashion. While such instruction has featured the evolutionary pattern of male-female pair, societies have also evolved normative codes imposing cultural restrictions upon the sexual activity of their members. Penalty of extinction compelled them to abide by the evolutionary pattern of the male-female pair; but why did they invent and perpetuate the system of normative codes?

In dealing with this question, we must rely on the method of evolutionary extrapolation that aims at reconstructing ancient man's thoughts, feelings, and doings on the patterns of motivation known to us from the study of contemporary human behavior.

Let me begin with the psychodynamic proposition that a society is an organized group held together by the forces and mechanisms of *competitive cooperation*. Group organization is always hierarchical, marked by relationships of dominance and subordination, centralized control and local independence. These hierarchical relationships change from time to time in a perennial contest of supremacy fought with a combination of forces: emotional, intellectual, spiritual, muscular, and material[16].*

At the dawn of civilization—presumably some hundred thousand years ago—contests of supremacy may have been decided by the muscular strength of emotionally aroused men. Aside from Darwin's observation on the life of higher apes, this assumption may have inspired Freud's[7] brilliant hypothesis that in primeval human groups the strongest male monopolized every female in his reach.† His boundless jealousy—desire for exclusive possession—his drunken pride of self-importance and his fists led to the establishment of the first sexual taboos, and with them to the cultural institution of sexual laws and mores.

In the course of time, sexual behavior became enmeshed in a network of rivalries. To the struggle between fathers and sons were added the fight of sons with one another; the female's battle with the male, her scheming for sexual self-determination and privilege; the conflict of mothers and daughters and of daughters with one another, etc. From the integration of sexual desire with the need for food, shelter, protection and parental care of the young emerged the institutions of tribe, household, family and the diverse marital orders of polygyny, polyandry and monogamy.

The emotional dynamics of polygyny and polyandry has been profoundly influenced by abundance or scarcity of food, exposure to attack or safety of geographical isolation, relative wealth or poverty, making it desirable if not imperative to increase, or on the other hand to limit, the size of population[9]. These marital systems brought new sexual prohibitions and restrictions, but at the same time also growing foresight, wisdom and readiness for compromise. Comparative historical study of the three marital systems lies beyond our present purpose; it suffices to say that in Western civilization monogamy has prevailed. Monogamous marriage is a partnership based on the idea of non-competitive cooperation with one another.

Primitive societies excel in accepting the emotional nature of Man and

---

* Competition is adaptive only to the extent to which it improves cooperation; ruthless competition tends to destroy the group. In general, the more a group organization respects the individual's dignity as a human being, the greater its chances for survival and healthy growth. Members of a group may have three kinds of emotional relationship to one another: contemptuous hate, indifference, and affectionate respect. The first is self-liquidating, the second inadequate; the biological optimum for creative cooperation may be achieved only by the third. Intuitive recognition of this biological fact—variously formulated as the golden rule of conduct, the categorical imperative, the doctrine of brotherly love or the humanistic ideal of peaceful cooperation—is the basis upon which the great ethical systems of mankind have been built[16].

† Congratulated on this achievement Freud remarked: "I should like to see it in the cinema." He did not live to see Walt Disney's documentary film, *Seal Island*.

making provisions for it. They reinforce the stability of the established order by a periodic relaxation of their sexual taboos in the excesses of religious feasts. Similarly, Western civilization has safeguarded the institution of monogamy by substituting *tacit* relaxations for the ritualized ones.

In contemporary societies the sexual laws and mores derive from the same dynamics of competitive cooperation as they have done since time immemorial. The weapons used range from tradition to reason, from cunning to guns.

Ontogenetic Development: the Campaign of Deterrence

Our cultural tradition requires that children be reared for a monogamous life mitigated by the tacit relaxation known as the double standard. Though since World War I the emancipation of women has ushered in an era of spreading enlightenment and change, the influence of tradition is still overwhelmingly strong.

How does traditional education seek to achieve its goal? It first keeps children ignorant of sexual matters. Later, it seeks to deter them from sexual activity and interests. The open tactical measures employed in this long drawn-out campaign of deterrence derive from a hidden strategical plan that abounds with historical (if not prehistorical) connotations. By far exceeding the intent of the incest taboos of society, this plan makes the sexual act appear as an act of violence perpetrated by the male upon the reluctant or foolishly consenting female. It may be denounced as a sin or something that a nice child should not even think of doing. The threat of severe and inescapable punishment is extended to genital self-stimulation with its attendant imagery of sexual union. The boy is threatened with punitive removal of his offending organ or sinning hand, or with some dreadful disease in consequence of his evil doing. If caught in sexual play with a girl, he is warned that he will inflict fateful damage on her, leading to merciless retaliation. And she is warned that such contact with a boy will destroy her anatomic and emotional integrity and social standing. This indoctrination is reinforced by the chance observation of parental intercourse and its misconception as an act of violence; and by the discovery that sexual activity causes bleeding (menstruation, defloration, birth). As a consequence, the boy comes to believe that the female organ is an open wound, resulting from the violent removal—cutting off or tearing out—of the missing penis; the girl comes to believe that the male organ is a destructive weapon. Naturally, each is also influenced by the other's misconceptions.

To this campaign of deterrence boys and girls respond with diverse fears of sexual degradation culminating uniformly in both sexes in a *fear of penetration*. At the same time, the brutal interference with their sexual desires unleashes in them defiant rage against the disciplinary authorities—above all the mother—soon to be repressed by their fear of parental punishment and need for loving parental care. The resulting dynamic formation of prevailing fear over repressed yet overflowing rage is unstable; the overflowing portion of rage must be retroflexed and vented in self-reproaches that transform the prevailing sexual fears into *guilty* sexual fears[12, 14]. In its entirety, in both sexes, the child's emergency response is composed of fear, guilty fear, distrust, suspicion and resentment of the mother (disciplinary authorities), of the opposite organ, and eventually of the opposite sex. Instead of helping the child to evolve a biologically and culturally healthful pattern, the agencies of society spoil the welfare context of sexual union by injecting into it the idea of violence and the corresponding emergency emotions.

Historically, the need to place violence in the center of sexual education and thus turn it into a campaign of deterrence may have originated with women. In the perennial battle of the sexes, women may have invented this strategic though self-defeating scheme in order to avenge their sexual servitude; the men who ruled them may have consented because it has obviously strengthened their own jealously guarded prerogatives.

THE OUTCOME: HEALTHY, IMPAIRED AND DEFICIENT SEXUAL ADAPTATION

As a rule, primitive societies elevate the young to sexually full-fledged members of the community by the initiation rites of puberty. In modern societies, traditional education seeks to continue the child's early antisexual adaptation throughout puberty and adolescence. Then this infantile adaptation is expected to transform itself into a sexually mature adaptation to the conditions of adult existence.

In fact, traditional sexual education results in the three forms of sexual adaptation briefly defined in the opening section of this paper. We are now prepared to examine them in greater detail.

One part of the population achieves a more or less healthy sexual adaptation—if not in the beginning, then after marriage. In this event, the early violence conception and the corresponding emergency emotions are repressed and reduced to rudiments.

In the second part of the population sexual adaptation is impaired by open inhibitions of varying severity, which may debilitate desire, performance, love and marriage. The patient may suffer from lack of desire, failure of erection, faltering or rushed performance, and—particularly the female—from failure of sensation or climax. Though not always aware of it, the patient suffers profound humiliation from his inadequacy. These disorders are traceable to the persistence or recrudescence in the adult of the sexual fears and resentments of childhood, now overlaid by an array of more or less realistic worries, apprehensions and grudges. Characteristically exaggerating the sexual laws and mores, the patient lives in constant dread of violating them. The distorted outlook of childhood may include faulty marital expectations which, persisting into adulthood, destroy the cooperative relationship essential to marriage, producing such disruptive consequences as irrational jealousy, intra-marital competition and struggle for dominance or, on the other hand, compensatory over-dependence modeled on the infant's alimentary pattern. Sexual impairment of both spouses brings a vicious circle into play.

The hidden pathogenic factors directly responsible for the inhibitions, and less directly for the other symptoms, are the same in both sexes: the old guilty fears of penetration and the old resentments of the opposite organ and the opposite sex. The powerful persistence of these infantile responses is an unsolved problem. As we have seen, the healthy child "outgrows" them; their tenacity in the others may be due to the innate strength of fear and rage or to the harshness of parental discipline. Also, there may be present some innate weakness in the organization of pleasure, love and the orgasm reflex that increases their vulnerability to the impact of emergency emotions of excessive strength[12, 14].

The third part of the population emerges from ontogenic development with deficient although more or less effective sexual adaptation. The pattern of standard performance is both undeveloped and inhibited. To obtain satisfaction, the patient must abide by a modified pattern forced upon him by automatic processes of repair. Under our present laws these reparative patterns bring the patient into conflict with society. This fact gives rise to further compensatory developments aimed at assuaging his social fears. Here we shall consider these reparative patterns under three headings: reparative organ replacement and organ avoidance; sexual pain-dependence; reparative formation of homogeneous pairs.

Reparative Organ Replacement and Organ Avoidance

In a group of reparative patterns the dreaded and resented genital organ of the opposite sex is either replaced by other body parts or, by means of still other arrangements, avoided altogether. The extreme form of avoidance is replacement of the human mate. The reparative processes often evolve these patterns by reverting to a mode of arousal discovered and successfully used during the early period of growth. The organism's innate sensory susceptibilities to sexual arousal have a spectacular compass; depending upon the circumstances, almost any person, animal, object or activity may come to play the part of an effective stimulant. Due to anatomic variation, a body part may have a richer nerve supply; its stronger pleasure response to stimulation may then establish a site of preference.

Sexual Pain-Dependence

Modeled on the violence conception of the sexual act, the pain-dependent patterns are triggered by a mechanism of *preliminary riddance*, interpreted as *advance punishment*[12]. Standard performance is inhibited by the patient's guilty fear of inescapable punishment. To free himself from the crippling inhibition, he undergoes beforehand the dreaded punishment by inviting humiliating treatment from the mate. Or, in an outburst of repressed yet overflowing rage, he inflicts on the mate the punishment he dreads, sharing vicariously the latter's suffering. The response of sexual climax is made possible by these mechanisms of preliminary riddance from fear through advance punishment.

The forms of sexual pain-dependence fall into three groups: criminal, dramatized and hidden.

In the criminal forms, pain-dependence precipitates what amounts to a savage execution of the violence conception of the sexual act. Lust-murderers—some twenty of them—examined for the German courts by the late Johannes Lange, were without exception incapable of standard performance, reaching sexual climax through the act of violence[10]. The prototype of the criminal form of sexual pain-dependence is rape.

The dramatized forms of sexual pain-dependence first came to public attention through the literary output of the Marquis de Sade (1740–1814) and von Sacher-Masoch (1835–95). In these forms two consenting mates enact, *short of severe pain and serious physical injury*, a dramatized version of the violence conception of the sexual act. Both forms—the fear-ridden and the enraged—are staged performances. The daydreams attendant upon pain-dependent genital self-stimulation often draw their material from literary sources.

The hidden forms of sexual pain-dependence are extremely common. They are revealed in a large variety of clinical manifestations: quarrelling as a prelude to a truly happy embrace; lack of sensation or climax due to an unconscious desire to be raped, betrayed by a corresponding conscious dread of rape; use of the self-tortures of irrational jealousy as an aphrodisiac; surprise orgasm elicited by latent or open fear in the absence of sexual desire, etc.

Reparative Formation of Homogeneous Pairs

The campaign of deterrence causes the female to view the male organ as a destructive weapon; and the male to see in the "mutilated" female organ a reminder of inescapable punishment. Fear and resentment of the opposite organ, though unrecognized, may be so insurmountable that the individual escapes from the male-female pair into a homogeneous pair. Male pairs are based on the reassuring presence, and female pairs on the reassuring absence, of the male organ. However, the crucial facts are that in male pairs on male impersonates a female, and in female pairs one female impersonates a male; they pretend to be a male-female pair. The anal mount practiced by male pairs openly imitates the pattern of male-female union; the phallic artifices used by female pairs serve the same purpose. Homogeneous pairs satisfy their repudiated yet irresistible male-female desire by means of shared illusions and actual approximations[12]. One sees now the true significance of Freud's momentous discovery that in childhood these individuals were closely attached to persons of the opposite sex and had strong sexual desires for them[6].

The male's sexual desire for a male—and the female's for a female—are blinds that enable them to represent their sexual defeat as a triumph of sexual self-realization. This revised motivational analysis of so-called "homosexuality" should not come as a surprise. The anatomy of the sexes outlines the evolutionary pattern of male-female pairs; and the cultural institution of marriage ingrains the same pattern in every human being since early childhood. No force, save for schizophrenic disorganization, can break its strength. If driven underground, the male-female desire achieves *imaginary* fulfillment through homogeneous pairs, despite the fact that such pairs are formed in forced avoidance of the opposite sex. Such "return of the repressed," by way of the very bulwark erected against it, is one of the best known Freudian mechanisms.

In societies that prohibit the formation of homogeneous sexual pairs, the individual dependent for gratification on this pattern lives in constant dread of detection and punishment. To restore his equilibrium he often clings to the myth that he belongs to a third sex, superior to the rest of mankind.

For emotional security, homogeneous pairs, like male-female pairs, tend to fall back on the resources of the system of infantile dependence. Chiefly alimentary in its motivation, this mutual dependence is patterned on the mother-child (by substitution: father-child) relationship[4].

Dependence on the formation of homogeneous sexual pairs is a deficient adaptation evolved by the organism in response to its own emergency over-reaction to the "campaign of deterrence." Since the 1880's, so-called "homosexuality" and "heterosexuality" have been interpreted as manifestations of a supposed "general constitutional bisexuality." However, the latter concept proved to be an unwarranted biological generalization. It is true that in certain lower species, as for instance in earthworms, each individual has a complete male and female sexual apparatus and uses both of them effectively for reproduction. But in human anatomy the two reproductive systems are mutually exclusive; the functional pattern of the sexually mature human individual bears no significant causal relation to the zygote's bipotentiality of embryologic differentiation[11, 12]. A human being is either a male or a female, or, due to a failure of embryonic differentiation, is anatomically deformed. It is common knowledge that these malformed individuals are possessed by the desire to be of but one sex.

The unified conceptual scheme here outlined may be applied to problems of evolutionary adaptation in other behavior areas.

REFERENCES

[1] ALEXANDER, FRANZ: *Our Age of Unreason*. New York, Lippincott, 1942.

[2] BEACH, F. A.: A review of physiological and psychological studies of sexual behavior in mammals. *Physiol. Rev.*, *27:* 240–307, 1947.

[3] ———: Reproductive activities. In *Steven's Handbook of Experimental Psychology*. New York, John Wiley and Sons, 1951.

[4] DEUTSCH, H.: *The Psychology of Women*. New York, Grune & Stratton, 1944.

[5] FERENCZI, S.: *Tahlassa, a Theory of Genitality*. New York, Psychoanal. Quart. Inc., 1938.

[6] FREUD, S.: Three contributions to the theory of sex. *The Basic Writings of Sigmund Freud*. Modern Library.

[7] ———: Totem and taboo. *The Basic Writings of Sigmund Freud*. Modern Library.

[8] HERRICK, C. J.: *The Brain of the Tiger Salamander*. Univ. of Chicago Press, 1948.

[9] KARDINER, A.: *The Individual and His Society*. New York, Columbia Univ. Press, 1939.

[10] LANGE, J.: *Personal communication*.

[11] RADO, S.: A critical examination of the concept of bisexuality. *Psychosomat. Med.* *2:* 459, 1940.

[12] ———: An adaptational view of sexual behavior. In *Psychosexual Development in Health and Disease* (Hoch and Zubin, Eds.). New York, Grune & Stratton, 1950.

[13] ———: Emergency behavior: with an introduction to the dynamics of conscience. In *Anxiety* (Hoch and Zubin, Eds.). New York, Grune & Stratton, 1950.

[14] ———: Dynamics and classification of disordered behavior. *Am. J. Psychiat.*, *110:* 406, 1953.

[15] ———: Hedonic control, action-self, and the depressive spell. In *Depression* (Hoch and Zubin, Eds.). New York, Grune & Stratton, 1954.

[16] ———: Lectures at Columbia University.

The Border Region Between the Normal and the Abnormal: Four Types*

More than twenty years ago I participated in a series of conferences called the *Arbeitsgemeinschaft für Mediziner und Theologen* (A Study Group for Medical Men and Theologians). Half of the members were psychiatrists, the other half clergymen. A philosopher sat in the chair. The medical men talked mostly about religion, the ministers mostly about medicine. We hoped to find a common ground for practical ends, but, actually, our discussions soared to the highest levels of abstraction. In order to find a common ground for practical ends, I am afraid that one has to come down to earth.

Our medical knowledge of the workings of the mind is greater today than it was at any time in the past. If we psychiatrists make the fundamentals of psychodynamics available to the minister, he will be better equipped to help the parishioner who comes to him for help. Among those who come to the minister, there will be individuals suffering from serious mental pathology. These individuals are actually or potentially dangerous to themselves, to the minister, and to the entire community. We must help the minister to detect these individuals, and to turn them over to a psychiatrist. They urgently need psychiatric treatment, if not custodial care.

It is my assignment to treat of the signs of dangerous mental illness. Unfortunately, there is no list of signs against which one might check a dubious case. We must look at the entire clinical picture of individuals, and then look deeper into their psychodynamics. In order to be able to do this, we shall have to proceed in a schematic manner and limit ourselves to the essentials.

We may divide disordered behavior into three clinical forms: neurotic, extractive (so-called "psychopathic"), and psychotic. They have one outstanding characteristic in common. The patient's behavior is controlled, without his being aware of it, by emotional patterns which overrule his reason. However, the consequences of such disordered behavior are quite different in the three groups. Generally speaking, the neurotic hurts him-

* Read at the Conference on Ministry and Medicine in Human Relations at the New York Academy of Medicine, May 11, 1950. First published in *Ministry and Medicine in Human Relations*, New York, International Universities Press, Inc., 1955.

self; the extractive type ("psychopath") hurts others; and the psychotic hurts both himself and others.

Before taking up some of the pathological pictures for detailed discussion, we must say a few words about the psychodynamics of the situation which arises when the parishioner enters the minister's office.

Whenever a person in distress turns for help to someone in authority, he is bound, unbeknown to himself, to fall under the sway of strong emotions, which transcend the scope of the situation as rationally conceived. This unconscious emotional involvement of the parishioner with the minister derives from childhood. It represents the revival of the child's dependency pattern; the child wants to lean on the parent and enjoy the loving care of the parent, which the child imagines to be unlimited.

Let me emphasize that this infantile emotional pattern is bound to be revived in every form of counseling or treatment, regardless of whether the person seeking help is mentally healthy or mentally ill. In the latter case the complication is that he brings his mental pathology into a situation which is in itself emotionally highly charged. Hence, it may easily precipitate an explosion, surprising to the observer who is only familiar with the surface aspects of the situation. Furthermore, the parishioner's unconscious emotional involvement with the minister may elicit in the minister an unconscious emotional counterinvolvement with the parishioner; like a devoted parent, he may wish to do more for the parishioner than he actually can, and thus end up by defeating his purpose.

Putting first things first, I shall deal with four pathogenic types which, I feel, are the most important ones to be noted: the depressive, the extractive type ("psychopath"), the paranoid, and the schizotype ("schizophrenic"). In order to avoid misunderstanding, I wish to emphasize that this classification into pathogenic types rests on genetic concepts and thus runs across the aforementioned classification into clinical forms.

We understand only in part the causative chain of events which produces each of these four types. Though we have good reasons to assume that each of these types has specific hereditary determinants, we cannot say what this predisposition consists of or how it operates. Nor can we tell why the depressive, the paranoid, and the schizoid type manifest themselves in two forms: a less severe neurotic form and a much more severe psychotic form. What we do know with a measure of certainty is the specific dynamics of these conditions, presumably representing in each of them the terminal links in the causative chain.

The clinical picture of an attack of *depression* may be schematically outlined as follows: The patient is sad and in painful tension. He is intolerant of his condition, thereby increasing his distress. His self-esteem is abased, his self-confidence shattered. Retardation of his initiative, thinking, and motor actions makes him incapable of sustained effort. His behavior indicates underlying fears, particularly guilty fears. He is demonstratively preoccupied with his alleged failings, shortcomings, and unworthiness; and yet he also harbors a deep resentment that life does not give him a fair deal.

He usually has suicidal ideas and often suicidal impulses. His sleep is poor; his appetite and sex desires are on the wane or gone. He takes little or no interest in his work and ordinary affairs and shies away from affectionate as well as competitive relationships. All in all, he has lost his capacity to enjoy life. He is drawn into a world of his own imagination, a world dedicated to the pursuit of suffering rather than the pursuit of happiness.

Such attacks are either occasioned by a serious loss, failure, or defeat; or may seem to come from the clear blue sky. Their onset may be sudden or gradual, their duration from a few weeks to many months. Their severity ranges from mildly neurotic to fully psychotic.

Often in the neurotic and almost always in the psychotic cases there are conspicuous physical symptoms, such as loss of weight and constipation.

In some patients spells of depression alternate with spells of elation while in others no spells of elation occur. We do not know why.

From the psychodynamic point of view, depression is a desperate cry for love, precipitated by a serious loss which endangers the patient's emotional (and material) security. The emotional overreaction to this emergency unfolds as an expiatory process of self-punishment, undertaken with the unconscious intent of reconciling the mother, and thus regaining her loving care. The patient's unconscious aim-image is the emotional and alimentary security derived from the infant's clinging to the mother's feeding breast. The patient's mute cry for love is thus traceable to the hungry infant's loud cry for help. Similarly, his most conspicuous morbid fears are traceable to the infant's early fear of starvation.[6, 7]

However, the patient's dominant motivation of repentance is complicated by the simultaneous presence of a strong resentment. As far as his fears of conscience and guilty fears go, he is humble and yearns to repent; as far as his coercive rage goes, he is resentful.

At first the patient tends to vent his resentment on the beloved person, the one by whom he feels "let down" or deserted. When the patient feels that his coercive rage is defeated, the repentant mood gains the upper hand; his rage then recoils and turns inward against him, increasing by its full vehemence the severity of his self-reproaches and self-punishments. As a superlative bid for forgiveness, the patient may thus be driven to suicide.

The patient's pride remains on the side of his coercive rage even after defeat has retroflexed and thus forced this rage to subserve his expiation. Thus, he punishes himself not only for his defiance but also, in continued defiance, for his miserable failure to terrorize the mother in the first place.

Retroflexed rage is the essence of the phenomena which Freud discovered and described as the depressive patient's "ambivalence" and "sadism turned against the self." [1]

It must be understood that the unfortunate who commits suicide does not, in the unconscious reaches of his mind, have the intention of actually finishing his life. By reconciling the (presumably mortally offended) mother with his supreme sacrifice, he hopes, on the contrary, to reinstate himself into her nourishing graces—forever.[8, 9]

Based on these findings, we view depression as a process of miscarried repair. To a healthy person a serious loss is a challenge. He meets the emergency by calming his emotions, marshaling his remaining resources, and increasing his adaptive efficiency. Depressive repair miscarries because it results in the exact opposite. Anachronistically, this repair presses an obsolete adaptive pattern into service, and by this regressive move it incapacitates the patient and still more increases his helplessness and plight.

In the case of apparently unoccasioned depression a "precipitating loss" exists only in the patient's unconscious imagination; it is an effect of the patient's changed outlook, rather than its cause.

The grave danger of severe depression is suicide. I wish it were possible to describe clearly the signs indicating that this danger is imminent; but there are no clear rules by which one can safely go. The psychiatrist must base his judgment on his experience and on what we call his "sense of the fingertips." When you have the feeling that your parishioner's inner onslaught on himself is more savage than he cares to reveal, your best course of action is to summon a psychiatrist.

Human sympathy may tempt you to treat your morbidly depressed parishioner with overwhelming kindness, in the hope that you can reassure him and lessen his plight. This treatment may indeed succeed; but it may also happen that, by proceeding thus, you defeat your purpose completely and drive him into despair. If at the moment his craving for affection is stronger, you win. If his guilt and retroflexed rage are stronger, you lose, because in the latter case he will feel: "Here this man is so kind to me and I am such an unworthy person." The fresh bout of self-reproach thus provoked will naturally increase the danger of suicide.

If the psychiatrist finds that retroflexed rage has reached an alarming degree, he may treat the patient harshly, in order to provoke a relieving outburst of rage. I mention this procedure because you may have heard or read about it, and I should like to dissuade you from experimenting with it. It requires a high degree of technical knowledge and skill and is not without danger even in the hands of an experienced psychiatrist.

Our next subject is the *extractive type*. Akin to the criminal, he is com-

monly called the antisocial psychopath. Schematically, this is the clinical
picture he presents: Prompted mostly by the need of the instant, the extractive patient leaps merrily from one desire to the next. As Greenacre
puts it, he lives "in a series of present moments." [3] In contradistinction to
the neurotic and the psychotic, he usually seeks tangible rather than imaginary gains. Being both impatient and intolerant of frustration, he rushes
to immediate pleasures through short-cuts, which may include parasitic
ingratiation and extortion, resorting to physical violence, debauchery, and
the use of alcohol or other narcotic drugs.

Under the pressure of frustration or threat, the extractive patient forgets the lessons of the past, repeating time and again the same transgressions. Acting under such pressure, he is also unconcerned about the consequences of his failings and shows no consideration either for others or for
his own future. His fear of authority has as little restraining influence upon
his conduct as has his conscience. He often professes high moral standards
which he readily applies to others but rarely to himself. He is incapable of
forming strong and lasting affectionate ties, and his loyalty is at the mercy
of his next excitement. Yet, beneath his callousness, he has an insatiable
yearning for affection, which Levy has called "affect hunger." [5] This
yearning and his high vulnerability to frustration make him oversensitive
and irascible, subject to violent rages, but also to strong fears, guilty fears,
and depressive spells.

For his emotional security he depends upon incessant approval and admiration, which he often obtains by a display of magnificent intentions,
pretenses, play-acting, and lying. He excels in self-deceit as well as in the
deceit of others. However, he may also seek thrills through acts of true,
though extravagant, generosity. His intelligence varies in a wide range from
defective to genius. If artistically or otherwise gifted, he may produce outstanding works. His sexual behavior, often impaired by a degree of what I
have suggested be called "pain dependence" and a lack of love, shows
reparative and variational modifications of the standard sexual pattern.[9]
In his life history, extractive bouts may alternate with relatively quiescent
periods. In short, the extractive patient is a disastrously short-sighted,
excitable, irresponsible, parasitic, and showy hedonist who never renounces the grand illusion that he is the son of privilege.

The extractive patient uses, in the main, two techniques, both of which
go back to behavior patterns of the infant. One is the pattern of the infant
who smiles and sucks; in the grownup, this is repeated by the cunning in-
gratiator who softens up his victims and then exploits them. The other
pattern is the hit-and-grab, or threaten-to-hit-and-grab pattern; in the
grownup, this is repeated by the extortionist. Clearly the extractive pa-

tient turns his victim into a replica of the father or mother, on whom one can live as a parasite.

It is a thankless task to attempt to "cure" a patient of the extractive type, for he is inherently incapable of making a normal and lasting adjustment. In addition to his sexual and social pain dependence, the psychodynamic clue to his condition is the fact that he cannot sustain painful tension for any length of time. Suddenly his needs become "imperative," overrule the restraining power of his conscience, as well as his fear of being caught, and cause him to seek relief at almost any price. As compared to the normal, his reactivity is delay-deficient, because in his organization, in contrast to the normal, the hedonic level is dominant over the emotional and intellectual levels.[10, 11]

In favorable circumstances, the psychiatrist may be able to guide the family in creating a setting calculated to keep the extractive patient in a relatively quiescent state. The psychiatrist may thus succeed in adjusting the patient's environment to the patient.

In your dealings with the extractive type, please beware of his false front. He is so plausible; he is a past master in the art of explaining everything under the sun. My colleagues and I have been fooled by them more than once.

Let me now turn to the *paranoid* patient and describe to you schematically his clinical picture.[10] In the initial stage the patient develops morbid fears which increase in strength and irrationality. He interprets events, wholly unrelated to him in fact, as machinations aimed at him. People are after him and they have malicious designs on him. They plot to victimize him by sexual violence. Then his suspicions narrow down to a particular person or group. At some point his righteous indignation over the injustice and the indignities done to him releases his pent-up rage. Going from one outburst to the next, he then will tend to resort to violence, in presumed self-defense. Eventually, he manages to rescue himself from this turmoil by means of a grandiose reinterpretation of himself. He discovers that he is a chosen person; and those acts which before seemed to him to threaten disaster, appear transformed: now they are wonderful acts calculated to bestow on him high distinction or grace. But for the false premises, his delusional thought often falls into a sharp logical pattern. These developments may take place on a scale small or large, forming a neurotic or psychotic process. People around the patient frequently fail to discover that he is mentally ill.

Psychodynamically, the condition shows a high degree of pain dependence which impairs performance in the sexual and social areas of behavior. This then is combined with the puzzling fact of circumscribed and systematized delusions. To rationalize his irrational (infantile) fears the patient invents appropriate threats and then proceeds in his delusion to enact these imagined threats on the stage of reality. Such delusional enactment makes his irrational fears appear to him as objectively justified. His wounded pride, wounded by the "crying injustice" done to him, unleashes his self-assertive rage and threatens to drive him into true disaster. He may in time succeed in restoring his pride by means of a reparative delusion of grandeur. Obviously, this is a process of miscarried repair.

When you encounter a paranoid parishioner, please remember that he may succeed in arousing your compassion by making you believe that the injustice he laments is real rather than a figment of his imagination. If you then become doubtful and he discovers that you no longer side with him, he will at once turn against you and treat you as one of his enemies. Not infrequently, his grandiose delusions have a coloring which you will readily recognize as pseudoreligious. It would be ill-advised to try to dissuade him from his delusions, for they are impervious to both reasoned argument and emotional influence.

The last of the four types I wish to present to you is the *schizophrenic*. However, our knowledge of this type is so meager that I shall have to limit the discussion to a few remarks. The psychiatrist has no serious difficulties in diagnosing a patient as schizophrenic after he has broken down and is in an open psychotic episode, or when he already shows the ominous signs of deterioration. The difficult task is to diagnose him before his first breakdown occurs. At that time, as a rule, he has, as Hoch and Polatin put it, a "pseudoneurotic" façade and is therefore easily mistaken for a true neurotic.[4] Despite this difficulty, noticed by Freud long ago,[2] we should be able to ascertain the fact that he is a schizophrenic.* We are still learning how to do this.

This, in summation, is the advice I can offer you: If you have before you a parishioner in whom the emergency emotions of fear and rage are much stronger than the nourishing emotions of love and affection, who seems to be unable to form any truly deep attachments in his life, who is fearfully dependent, in dire need of love and yet extremely feeble in his reaching out for love, then be on your guard. If, in addition, he has a rather lifeless facial expression, with an absent look in his eyes; he sits, gestures, and moves

---

* In an effort to improve the clarity of thought and language we are using the term "schizotype," an abbreviation of "schizophrenic phenotype." A "latent" schizophrenic may then be described more accurately as a schizotype in a pseudoneurotic phase, with a certain liability to open psychotic breakdown.

The point is that the schizophrenic may break and go into an open psychotic episode even during the course of treatment by a psychiatrist. Also, he may do so on the very occasion of his visits with his minister.

about in a manner that strikes you as uncalled for and strange; he is abstract and slightly incoherent in his talk, and finds it difficult to control onrushes of fantasy and imagination—then you should place him in the care of a psychiatrist.

ADDENDUM

Since the original presentation of this paper (1950), the author has published the following articles on the topics of depression and the psychodynamic organization of the schizotype: Psychodynamics of Depression from the Etiologic Point of View. *Psychosomatic Medicine, 13:* 51, 1951; Hedonic Control, Action-Self, and the Depressive Spell. In *Depression,* ed. Hoch and Zubin. New York, Grune & Stratton, 1954; Dynamics and Classification of Disordered Behavior. *American Journal of Psychiatry, 110:* 406, 1953.

REFERENCES

[1] FREUD, SIGMUND: Mourning and Melancholia (1917). *Collected Papers, 4:* 152. London, Hogarth Press, 1925.

[2] ——: On Narcissism: An Introduction (1914). *Collected Papers, 4:* 43. London, Hogarth Press, 1925.

[3] GREENACRE, PHYLLIS: Conscience in the psychopath. *Am. J. Orthopsychiat., 15:* 495, 1945.

[4] HOCH, PAUL H. AND POLATIN, PHILLIP: Pseudoneurotic forms of schizophrenia. *Psychiat. Quart., 23:* 248, 1949.

[5] LEVY, DAVID M.: Primary affect-hunger. *Am. J. Psychiat., 94:* 643, 1937.

[6] RADO, SANDOR: An anxious mother: A contribution to the analysis of the ego. *Internat. J. Psycho-Analysis, 9:* 219, 1928.

[7] ——: The problem of melancholia. *Internat. J. Psycho-Analysis, 9:* 420, 1928.

[8] ——: The psychoanalysis of pharmacothymia (drug addiction). *Psychoanal. Quart., 2:* 1, 1933.

[9] ——: An Adaptational View of Sexual Behavior. *Psychosexual Development in Health and Disease* (Hoch and Zubin, Eds.). New York, Grune & Stratton, 1949.

[10] ——: Emergency Behavior: With an Introduction to the Dynamics of Conscience. *Anxiety* (Hoch and Zubin, Eds.). New York, Grune & Stratton, 1950.

[11] ——: Lectures at Columbia University (unpublished).

Adapational Psychodynamics:
A Basic Science*

Over two hundred years ago Alexander Pope observed that the proper study of mankind is man. But this insight had no immediate influence on the direction of mankind's quest for knowledge. Marching from triumph to triumph, the physical sciences have left the study of man far behind in development. Still worse, overspecialization has split human biology into a loose collection of isolated and self-contained sciences, less and less capable of capturing the infinite organizational complexity of the life of man. We must now pool our resources and try to reach general agreement upon a suitable design for a unified science of human behavior.

The spectacular success of the physical sciences should not obscure the fact that biologically mankind is better equipped for exploring man than for exploring the rest of the universe. We examine the world about us through our senses, chiefly by *inspection*. As Sir Arthur Eddington remarked, our picture of the physical world rests on our use of the yardstick and the clock; in the last analysis, on pointer-reading. However, the human organism can be examined by *introspection* as well as by inspection. The organism is directly aware of its thoughts, feelings and doings and can communicate them to others. Thus, we can evolve two scientific pictures of the organism, one inspective, the other introspective. Should we succeed in making these two pictures truly complementary, then we could comprehend man more fully than anything else. The proper study of mankind is *indeed* man.

The importance of a unitary conceptual scheme in human biology is not generally recognized. Certain influential schools of thought reject introspection as a method, and consciousness as a subject of science. In their view, science deals only with the phenomena of matter, space and time; consciousness, they suggest, is but an epiphenomenon—presumably installed by nature in the brain for decorative purposes. However, this

---

* Presented at the Decennial Celebration of the Columbia University Psychoanalytic Clinic, March 19 and 20, 1955. First published in *Changing Concepts of Psychoanalytic Medicine*, New York: Grune & Stratton, 1956. In summing up the writer's previous work, this address draws part of its material and formulations from articles included in the present volume.

332

view is untenable. Natural selection has favored the evolution of consciousness. Living in social groups, man at all times is forced to grapple with the problem of his own nature, trying to understand, predict, and control the behavior of other men. Mankind's time-honored knowledge of man, a craft of human relationships, testifies to the unique practical value of introspective inquiry.

In the dim past, thinking about behavior may have begun with the realization that men always wanted certain things and went after them. This led to the concept of motivation: our predecessors learned to view themselves as charged with desires and goals that prompted them to act in certain ways. World literature depicted the vast panorama of human experience in a motivational framework. No one has yet proposed a workable substitute for this mode of understanding.

The idea of motive forces was complemented by the ancient discovery of the regulatory function of pleasure and pain. It was seen that man sought to repeat pleasurable experiences and to avoid painful ones. Aristotle epitomized this insight: "Happiness . . . being found to be something final and self-sufficient, is the End at which all actions aim."[1] Jeremy Bentham formulated it with admirable precision: "Nature has placed mankind under the governance of two sovereign masters, *pain* and *pleasure*. It is for them alone to point out what we ought to do as well as to determine what we shall do."[2] (Bentham's italics.)

With the appearance of Freud on the scientific scene, the introspective study of human behavior became a medical concern. Freud sought to understand the behavior of his patients in the same way as he understood people in daily life, that is, in terms of motivational analysis and the pleasure-pain principle. His epochal feat was the discovery of a new investigative method which he termed "free association." He saw that in the therapeutic situation the patient, pressed by his illness and need for help, could be induced to think out loud. He thus revealed not only his "secrets," but also the material within himself of which he had been previously unaware. Inferences drawn from this previously "unconscious" material explained important phases of the patient's behavior that could not be understood before. In Freud's psychoanalytic method, free association acts as the spearhead for motivational analysis.

With a wealth of clinical observations calling for conceptual clarification and organization, Freud evolved a psychoanalytic theory of the working of the mind which is now known as "classical psychodynamics." This theory has housed a solid mass of empirical findings. To mention only the most important ones, it taught us to view the patient's present behavior in the light of his developmental history; it stressed the lasting significance of the formative period of childhood and the complex role played by the residues of infantile dependence in later life.

However, in the development of a science, facts and theories have different destinies. The established facts remain, but the theories invented to explain them are subject to the impact of new facts and points of view.

This was also true of classical psychodynamics. Freud's most popular creation was his libido theory which traced all behavior to a sexual motivation. Freud saw that sexual desire and sexual frustration influenced human behavior far more profoundly than was commonly recognized. But his subsequent generalization that all desire for and love of pleasure was sexual never had a factual foundation. [3, 4, 7, 10]

The early successes of the libido theory appeared to show the investigative value of the apparently motivational concept of instinct (innate drive). In actual fact, the libido theory succeeded to the extent it did because it was a theory built upon the pleasure-pain principle. Libido was, if anything, a biologic force, endowed with the capacity to seek pleasure and avoid pain. The significance of this was dramatically, though inadvertently, demonstrated by Freud himself when he introduced a revised version of the libido theory.[5] Here, he separated from the libidinal instincts, which he now personified as "Eros," a class of "death instincts" (innate propensities to die), which supposedly operated "beyond the pleasure principle." By this stipulation Freud stripped the "death instincts" of the directive action of pleasure and pain; he was unaware that, thereby, he stripped them of psychodynamic meaning. Nor did the postulated "titanic struggle" of "Eros" with the "death instincts" shed new light on human behavior. It was always known that pleasure is the source and fulfillment of life and death is its problem.

The libido theory did not feature the part played by the emotions in behavior, whether healthy or disordered. Under the name of "affective cathexes," the emotions appeared as one of the manifestations of hypothetic instincts, rather than as elementary facts of clinical observation. Consequently, the clinical problems of emotional motivation were viewed as problems of the "instincts and their vicissitudes."

From the point of view of cultural history, the libido theory thus tended to obliterate the insight of the ancient Greek dramatists who saw clearly that in states of strong emotional excitement men behaved very differently than they did when they were calm and therefore capable of using their judgment and common sense. Their plays, masterpieces not only of art but also of science, showed with merciless realism what excessive fear, blind rage, overmastering passion and the drunken pride of self-importance could do to human conduct and relationships.

Freud's theory of the structure of the "psychic apparatus" depicted the individual's inner life as an intrapsychic drama acted out by the three characters, Superego, Ego and Id—obvious personifications of Conscience, Common Sense and Passion.[6] This theory had artistic beauty and a strong emotional appeal, but it was not an investigative tool. Its attempted application to clinical problems resulted most often in an obscure and unnecessarily complicated description of obvious and simple facts.

With superb detachment, Freud himself referred to his theories as a "scaffolding," and, indeed, his clinical papers abounded in splendid first approximations and brilliant improvisations. At the same time, his general formulations became increasingly abstract and remote.

Freud's overwhelming authority paralyzed fresh inquiry. Gradually his theories were transformed into a definitive and self-sufficient system, isolated both from the biologic organism and its social environment. Physicist J. Robert Oppenheimer has given a pin-point appraisal of this change: "In fact, one of the features which must arouse our suspicion of the dogmas some of Freud's followers have built up on the initial brilliant work of Freud, is the tendency toward a *self-sealing system* . . . which has a way of almost automatically discounting evidence which might bear adversely on the doctrine. The whole point of science is just the opposite."[8] (Oppenheimer's italics.)

The situation called for a combination of three remedial measures: (1) an increasingly rigorous application of the scientific method to psychoanalytic work; (2) a re-examination of Freud's theories and findings; and (3) a complete resystematization of psychodynamics. During the last decades a consistent effort in this direction has led to the emergence of the new conceptual scheme of an adaptational psychodynamics that places the analysis of behavior in the genetic, physiologic (biochemical, biophysical) contexts of the organism. It seeks to replace undefinable concepts with defined ones and to evolve a close-to-the-fact scientific language that will convey the most information in the fewest words. Even though the introduction of numerous new terms makes communication difficult at first, this is a crucial step toward formulating theories that can be verified or refuted by observation.[9-16]

An adaptational psychodynamics capable of fulfilling this program may be viewed as the *basic* component of a comprehensive dynamics of human behavior. The skeleton structure of this science-to-come may be visualized as follows:

ADAPTATIONAL PSYCHODYNAMICS OF HUMAN BEHAVIOR
studies the part played by motivation and
control in the organism's interaction
with its cultural environment

PHYSIOLOGY OF HUMAN BEHAVIOR

GENETICS OF HUMAN BEHAVIOR
studies the physiology
of human inheritance
and variation

COMPREHENSIVE DYNAMICS OF HUMAN BEHAVIOR

Psychodynamics must be recognized as the basic component of this structure, because it alone can discover the behavior problems which await their solution from physiology and genetics.

Let us now review briefly some of the propositions of adaptational psychodynamics. This science is based on the psychoanalytic method of investigation. As we have just seen, it studies the part played by motivation and control in the organism's interaction with its cultural environment. It deals with pleasure and pain, emotion and thought, desire and executive action, interpreting them in terms of organismic utility, that is, in an adaptational framework. In the theory of evolution, the pivotal concept is adaptation; since the organism's life cycle is but a phase of evolution, it is consistent to make the same concept basic to the study of behavior.

We define ontogenetic adaptations as improvements in the organism's pattern of interaction with its environment that increase its chances for survival, cultural self-realization, and perpetuation of its type. Autoplastic adaptations result from changes undergone by the organism itself; alloplastic adaptations from changes wrought by the organism on its environment. In ontogenetic adaptations, the master mechanisms are learning, creative imagination and goal-directed activity.

Corollary to our adaptational framework is our adaptational principle of investigation. Under this principle we examine behavior first from the point of view of "means to end," and next, from the point of view of "cause and effect." In end-relating the question is, what is its purpose? In cause-searching the question is, how does it fulfill its purpose? End-relating is our preparatory reconaissance; cause-searching is our ultimate task.

The adaptive value of behavior is determined by its effect upon the welfare of the organism. A favorable effect makes this value positive; an unfavorable effect, negative. The adaptive evaluation of behavior is a singularly important step in the investigative procedure. It must be undertaken by the observer independently of the self-evaluation of the organism under observation.

We view the organism as the outcome of its evolutionary history and define it as a self-regulating biologic system that perpetuates itself and its type by means of its environment (its surrounding system).

The organism's systemic requirements are known as its needs. Like its other traits, they are an outcome of the interaction between inherited predisposition (genotype) and environment. We speak of aboriginal needs that show *predominantly* the influence of the inherited predisposition, and acculturated needs that reflect *predominantly* the forming influence of the culture in which the organism lives. Due to its slow maturation, the organism has aboriginal dependency needs; it has aboriginal needs for safety, maintenance, growth, repair and reproduction. It has acculturated needs for security, cultural development and self-realization—feeling important and gaining recognition—in an organized group (tribe, society). The needs demonstrable in all known societies, designated by the anthropologists as universals, are the common denominators of human existence.

Need is an explanatory concept rather than an investigative tool. It has proved to be far more fruitful to describe the motive forces of behavior in terms of feelings, thoughts, and impulses to act; and the mechanisms of behavior as organized sequences of feelings, thoughts, and actions. The organism's interaction with its cultural environment may then be analyzed in such terms as behavior areas, mechanisms, and patterns; social institutions and functions.

As a rule, the organism becomes aware of its systemic requirements through such conscious experiences as pleasurable and painful tensions, desires, and aversions. By bringing the neuromuscular system into play, its systemic requirements cause the organism to transform stored potentials into motor activity aimed at controlling the environment. Successful control elicits a sense of satisfaction which usually stops the motor activity. Thus, in a general way, we can say that the cycles of behavior run from desire to fulfillment and back.

The organism integrates its behavior chiefly by what is known as its mind. The old scientific gap between mind and brain has been widened rather than narrowed by the introduction of the ambiguous notion of unconscious mind. We have attempted to bridge this gap by the following concept.

The nervous activity of the brain is in part *self-reporting*, in part *non-reporting*. Only to the extent to which it is self-reporting is the organism conscious of what its brain does for (or against) it. We call the organized sequence of self-reporting brain activity the *reporting process*, and the corresponding stream of consciousness, the *awareness process*. These two processes are not identical. The awareness process is directly known to us and may be studied by introspection; the reporting process is studied by inspection. Hence, from the operational point of view, the former is psychodynamic, the latter, physiologic. In the sense of Spinoza we postulate that they are exactly synchronous and exactly congruent.

Nonreporting activity is called awareness-prone when, by its organization, it is bound to be relayed to the self-reporting range and thus eventuate in awareness. Conscious (i.e., self-reporting) activity regularly elicits after-activity in the nonreporting range, such as the storing of memories.

By far the larger part of the brain's nervous activity is nonreporting. Nevertheless, it too contributes to motivating behavior. From the psychodynamic point of view, it has "meaning" or, in other words, motivational significance that cannot be detected by ordinary means. But free association feeds material into the subject's stream of consciousness which otherwise would have remained repressed. Freud taught us to draw contextual inferences from this material and thus disclose to some extent the unknown motivating action of the brain's nonreporting nervous activity. Let me illustrate this with an example. Suppose, in the analysis of the subject, at some point we fail to find the motivating cause of his behavior. But from the material of his free associations we can draw the contextual inference that the unknown motivating cause has acted as if it had been a desire, though in fact it was a purely physiologic process of his brain; we then refer to the motivating cause thus detected as a *nonreporting desire*. Similarly, we speak of nonreporting tensions, feelings, thoughts and impulses, etc. As these examples show, we qualify psychodynamic terms by the definite adjective "nonreporting" rather than by the hopelessly ambiguous adjective "unconscious" used in classical psychodynamics. Our usage indicates that what we are talking about is the inferred motivational significance of nonreporting nervous activity. Such extrapolated use of the ordinary language of psychodynamics is a uniquely fruitful methodologic device. The information thus acquired approximates the information that the subject would have possessed about himself had the nervous process under consideration advanced in his brain from the nonreporting to the self-reporting stage.

On the grounds of this methodologic clarification we have suggested that in comprehensive terminology, mind and unconscious mind be referred to as the "psychodynamic cerebral system." This proposed concept embraces: (1) the entire self-reporting range of the brain's nervous activity in both its psychodynamic and physiologic aspects and (2) that range of nonreporting activity which is nonetheless accessible to *extrapolative* investigation by psychodynamic methods, as well as to *ordinary* investigation by physiologic methods. We may now state more precisely that the foremost objective of adaptational psychodynamics is to discover the mechanisms by which the psychodynamic cerebral system accomplishes its integrative task.

Roughly speaking, the integrative activity of the psychodynamic cerebral system is dominated by the action of pleasure, pain, emotion, and reason. Adaptational psychodynamics has attempted to clarify the way in which these means of integration operate. Building upon the physiologic work of Hughlings Jackson, Charles Sherrington, J. H. Woodger and others, we have assumed that the psychodynamic cerebral system includes an *integrative apparatus* composed of four units. Each of these has its own distinctive organization. In relation to one another we see in these four units of the integrative apparatus, hierarchically ordered levels that reflect the course of evolutionary history. In ascending order we speak of the hedonic unit (or level), the units (or levels) of brute emotions, emotional thought and unemotional thought.

The term hedonic (from the Greek *hedonikos*, pleasurable) is defined as marked by or working by means of pleasure and pain. In the hedonic unit, the pattern for hedonic self-regulation is established: the organism moves towards the source of pleasure and away from the cause of pain. It is guided by the expectation that pleasure will signal the presence of needed supplies or conditions favorable to its survival, and pain the presence of a threat to its organic integrity.

Hedonic self-regulation may have appeared already in the organization of the protozoan; it has remained basic to the life process at all subsequent stages of evolutionary history, including man. Despite the complications introduced through the emergence and development of higher levels of integration, the human organism, like all other animal organisms, is a biologic system that operates under hedonic control. Recognition of this fact is a cornerstone of the theoretic structure of adaptational psychodynamics.

In the next two units, the emotions are the controlling means of integration. Emotions are central mechanisms both for the arousal of the peripheral organism and for the peripheral disposal of superabundant central excitation. We divide them into the emergency emotions based on present pain or the expectation of pain, such as fear, rage, retroflexed rage, guilty fear, and guilty rage; and the welfare emotions based on present pleasure or the expectation of pleasure, such as pleasurable desire, affection, love, joy, self-respect, and pride.

Emotional thought is a subdued derivative of brute emotion. By comparison with unemotional thought, it is an inferior instrument for interpreting the things to which the organism is actually exposed; it is not objective but selective; it tends to justify and thus to feed the emotion from which it springs and by which it is controlled.

Unemotional thought forges the tools of reason, common sense and science that prepare the ground for intelligent action and self-restraint.

Behavior of the whole organism may be integrated in any of these four hierarchically ordered units or in any combination of them. Furthermore, the integrative process may be in part nonreporting, in part self-reporting; in the nonreporting part the integrative process is dominated by emotional thought. To advance from nonreporting to self-reporting, the integrative process must pass the pain-barrier, an organization of precautionary mechanisms upon which hedonic control rests. Communications of the organism to the environment must pass the social pain-guard, an analogous organization of precautionary mechanisms superimposed on the pain-barrier. These precautionary organizations also include the intellectual mechanisms of (more or less) realistic thought adjustment.

The supreme unit of the psychodynamic integrative apparatus, and in fact of the entire organism, is the action-self, located axially to the four hierarchically ordered units just described. Of *proprioceptive* origin, the action-self emerges from the circular pattern of self-awareness and willed action. It then integrates the contrasting pictures of total organism and total environment that provide the basis for the selfhood of the conscious organism. These integrations are fundamental to the organism's entire orientation and represent highly complex organizations composed of sensory, intellectual, emotional, and motor components. At first the organism attributes unlimited power to its willed actions; hence, its first thought-picture of itself is one of an omnipotent being. This early thought-picture— designated as its primordial self—remains the source of its supreme and indestructible craving for omnipotence. Recognizing the difference between attainment and aspiration, present and future, the maturing organism differentiates its thought-picture of self into a tested self and a desired self. However, under the pressure of strong desire, this forced and precarious differentiation tends to disappear.

During the period of growth the psychodynamic cerebral system builds a semiautomatic organization of self-restraining and self-prodding responses known as our conscience. The child learns to anticipate certain parental and other authoritarian demands to which he is continuously exposed, and to meet them automatically. The same applies to the system of enforcement used by the parents. Parental reward gives rise to automatized self-reward known as self-respect and moral pride; parental punishment gives rise to automatized self-punishment as a means of expiating one's presumed wrongdoings and reinstating oneself in the loving care of the authority thus reconciled. Conscience achieves security through obedience; its main problem is the control of defiant rage.

Man's cultural evolution has rested on the growth and increasing complexity of the unit of unemotional thought. Thanks to this development, intelligence became the foremost adaptive function of the organism, more and more capable of modifying the automatic workings of the organism's hedonic self-regulation. We must take a closer view of this process.

Primitive man was at the mercy of his immediate hedonic responses to his experiences. At a higher stage of development man became capable of taking time out to think and contemplate the *future* consequences of his reactions. His growing foresight thus taught him to absorb present pain for the sake of future pleasure and, conversely, to abstain from such pleasure as would result in future damage and pain. He also learned to subdue pain and substitute for it the anticipation of pleasure, and to substitute the fear of pain to come for deceptive pleasure. It was an important advance in self-preservation when such a *learned* hedonic response became so firmly automatized and spontaneous that it could replace the original one. Throughout the course of cultural history such advances have been initiated by intellectually alert and gifted members of the species and perpetuated by education.

The gradual subordination of the organism's hedonic self-regulation to the dictates of reason in turn increased the adaptive value of intellectual activity. Man could clear the fog of emotional—wishful, fearful, angry—thought that through the ages had limited and distorted his comprehension of himself and the world about him; consequently, his knowledge and control of both himself and his environment became increasingly scientific.

To avoid misunderstanding, let us stress here a fact of paramount importance. Man is not a computing machine; his emotional needs must be met if he is to function in a state of health and to prosper. Science can help us modify the organism's hedonic self-regulation only within the biologic limits of its flexibility. Hedonic control is of the essence of the biologic organism. Moving from desire to fulfillment, the healthy organism analyzes experience into cause and effect so that it can find the means that will lead to the ends it *desires*. If the organism's hedonic self-regulation could be removed, the residual entity would be neither human nor an organism.

As regards the adaptational psychodynamics of cultural groups, I will consider here only the *biologic* characteristics common to *all* human societies.

A society is an organized group held together by the forces and mechanisms of *competitive cooperation*. Group organization is always hierarchical, marked by relationships of dominance and subordination, centralized control, and local independence. These hierarchical relationships change from time to time in a perennial contest of supremacy, fought with a combination of forces: emotional, intellectual, spiritual, muscular, and material.

However, competition is adaptive only to the extent to which it *improves cooperation*; ruthless competition tends to destroy the group. In general, the more a group organization respects the individual's dignity as a human being, the greater its chances for survival and healthy growth. Members of a group may have three kinds of emotional relationship to one another: contemptuous hate, indifference and affectionate respect. The first is self-liquidating, the second inadequate; the biologic optimum for creative cooperation may be achieved only by the third. Intuitive recognition of this biologic fact, variously formulated as the golden rule of conduct, the categorical imperative, the doctrine of brotherly love or the humanistic ideal of peaceful cooperation, is the basis upon which the great ethical systems of mankind have been built.

Classical psychodynamics traced the cultural effort of mankind to the Oedipus complex. In our view, *the mainspring of culture is man's primordial craving for omnipotence*. The worship of omnipotence in religion is only one of its expressions. The cultural effort to *achieve* omnipotence has produced the scientist, who gives laws to the universe; the artist, who recreates the universe in samples of his choosing; and the technologist, who is about to perfect the electronic robot that may come close to running our productive system for us with no effort of our own. To rise from hunger and toil to comfort and leisure is the next aim of man's quest for omnipotence. The final goal is his conquest of death.

Cultural evolution has hinged on man's educational struggle to replace his unenlightened hedonic responses with enlightened ones. In this struggle, the chief adversary has been and still is the innate strength of his own emotional predisposition (genotype). Consequently, learned hedonic control is for the most part emotional control. By the system of reward (pleasure) and punishment (pain), traditional education has, on the whole, achieved phenomenal results in subduing brute emotion, notably the vehemence of defiant rage.

Let us now turn to the adaptational psychodynamics of behavior disorders. We define them as disturbances of psychodynamic integration that significantly affect the organism's adaptive life performance, its attainment of utility and pleasure.

In the analysis of behavior disorders we encounter organized sequences of events which we have come to recognize as processes of miscarried prevention and miscarried repair. They are brought into play by a disordered response of the organism which we can relate to an environmental situation and trace to comparable exposures in the past. Our analysis may thus penetrate to the point where, instead of an adaptive response, a disordered one made its first appearance. The fact that this occured cannot be explained by further psychodynamic investigation, which reaches here its terminal point. Nonetheless, we can continue the etiologic inquiry. We can seek to disclose the cerebral mechanism of such a disordered psychodynamic response; we can study its broader physiologic context; and we can search for its genetic context. Today our knowledge of the genetic and physiologic phases of etiology is too scanty to attain this goal. For the most part we must be content with the study of the psychodynamic phase of etiology.

Paradoxically, the appearance of disordered responses must be traced to the fact that the organism's first survival concern is safety. Walter B. Cannon has shown how, by their emergency function, the peripheral systems serve the whole organism's interest in safety. Following this clue, we have attempted to outline the emergency function of the psychodynamic cerebral system, terming it "emergency control."

However, if an *overproduction* of the emergency emotions such as fear, rage, guilty fear, and guilty rage is the organism's response to danger, it will be unable to handle effectively the exigencies of daily life. For these disordered—excessive or inappropriate—emergency responses are themselves a threat from within, with which it is unable to cope. They elicit processes of miscarried prevention and miscarried repair that produce further disordering effects. These failures of emergency control lead to the simplest forms of behavior disorder which we term "emergency dyscontrol."

An overproduction of emergency emotions, that is, emergency dyscontrol, enters as a basic etiologic factor into the psychodynamics of the more complex behavior disorders, acting here in combination with additional pathogenic agents. With emergency dyscontrol as a point of departure, it has thus become possible to arrange the clinically observed forms of behavior disorders according to the increasing complexity of their patterns and mechanisms. The resulting scheme of classification somewhat resembles the known patterns in organic chemistry where, starting with a simple compound, we may derive increasingly complex ones through rearrangement of the components or the addition of new components. In bare outline, this scheme of classification follows:

CLASS I. *Overreactive Disorders.*

(1) Emergency Dyscontrol: The emotional outflow, the riddance through dreams, the phobic, the inhibitory, the repressive, and the hypochondriac patterns; the gainful exploitation of illness. (2) Descending Dyscontrol. (3) Sexual Disorders: The impairments and failures of standard performance. Dependence on reparative pat-

terns: Organ replacement and organ avoidance; the criminal, dramatic and hidden forms of sexual pain-dependence; the formation of homogeneous pairs. Firesetting and shoplifting as sexual equivalents. (4) Social Overdependence: The continuous search for an ersatzparent; the mechanisms of forced competition, avoidance of competition, and of self-harming defiance. (5) Common Maladaptation: A combination of sexual disorder with social overdependence. (6) The Expressive Pattern (Expressive elaboration of common maladaptation): Ostentatious self-presentation; dreamlike interludes; rudimentary pantomimes; disease-copies and the expressive complication of incidental disease. (7) The Obsessive Pattern (Obsessive elaboration of common maladaptation): Broodings, rituals, and overt temptations. Tic and stammering as obsessive equivalents; bedwetting, nailbiting, grinding of teeth in sleep, as precursors of the obsessive pattern. (8) The Paranoid Pattern (nondisintegrative elaboration of common maladaptation): The hypochondriac, self-referential, persecutory and grandiose stages of the Magnan sequence.

CLASS II. *Moodcyclic Disorders.*
Cycles of depression; cycles of reparative elation; the pattern of alternate cycles; cycles of minor elation; cycles of depression masked by elation; cycles of preventive elation.

CLASS III. *Schizotypal Disorders.*
(1) Compensated schizo-adaptation. (2) Decompensated schizo-adaptation. (3) Schizotypal disintegration marked by adaptive incompetence.

CLASS IV. *Extractive Disorders.*
The ingratiating ("smile and suck") and extortive ("hit and grab") patterns of transgressive conduct.

CLASS V. *Lesional Disorders.*

CLASS VI. *Narcotic Disorders.*
Patterns of drug-dependence.

CLASS VII. *Disorders of War Adaptation.*

During the past two years, I have undertaken with a team of collaborators a more detailed clinical investigation of schizotypal organization. Dr. Buchenholz, a member of the team, will present a preliminary report on this work.[17]

From the point of view of therapeutic modification, most promising are the psychoneuroses or, in our terminology, the class of overreactive and moodcyclic disorders. Caught in the clash between their own defiant rage (violence from within) and the retaliatory rage of their parents (violence from without), these patients have emerged from childhood with an established pattern of adaptation that forces them unawares to damage themselves in order to avoid the dreaded danger of damaging others. Their suffering is increased if they develop pain-dependence. Freud's psychoanalytic therapy was designed to lift these patients out of their predicament by means of a medical technique for re-education; the adaptational development of this procedure into a technique for emotional re-education has further increased its effectiveness. In our present context, it is clear that *psychoanalytic therapy is but a renewed effort toward mankind's most ancient cultural goal: the use of our intelligence for the education of our hedonic control.*

Turning to the world at large, we see that the same failure to resolve our violent emotional conflicts is the chief obstacle to the achievement of peaceful and equitable human relationships. The findings of adaptational psychodynamics as well as the lessons of history confirm the insight of the sages of ancient Greece; we must rise to their vision and lift the hedonic self-regulation of the organism from the level of the beast to the level of our human intelligence. Even a potentially dangerous inherited predisposition could perhaps be rendered harmless, possibly by means of a calculated atrophy of disuse. We can learn how to prevent the ontogenetic growth and development of excessive and irresistible fears, rages, guilty fears and guilty rages; how to transmute what would otherwise result in self-sufficient pride and overpowering passion into refined and socially desirable emotions; how to bring about an adaptive pattern that would make intelligent performance the pride and joyful essence of life. The purpose of life is to enjoy it; the purpose of culture can only be to prolong and increase the vigor and beauty of life by creating ever new capacities as well as opportunities for its enjoyment.

These are the problems; to find their solution is the responsibility of adaptational psychodynamics. Only upon a science of motivation and control can we hope to build up the complex organized body of knowledge that we need to understand human behavior and prevent its disorders.

REFERENCES

[1] ARISTOTLE: *Nichomachean Ethics*, I. Cambridge, Harvard University Press, Loeb Classical Library, 1939, p. 31.

[2] BENTHAM, JEREMY: An Introduction to the Principles of Morals and Legislation. *The English Philosophers from Bacon to Mill*. New York, Modern Library, 1939, p. 791.

[3] FREUD, SIGMUND: Three Contributions to the Theory of Sex. *The Basic Writings of Sigmund Freud*, A. A. Brill, ed. New York, Modern Library, 1938. (Published in German, 1905.)

[4] ——: *A General Introduction to Psychoanalysis*. New York, Horace Liveright, 1935. (Published in German, 1918.)

[5] ——: *Beyond the Pleasure Principle*. London, International Psycho-Analytical Press, 1922. (Published in German, 1920.)

[6] ——: *The Ego and the Id*. London, Hogarth Press, 1927. (Published in German, 1923.)

[7] ——: *An Outline of Psychoanalysis*. New York, W. W. Norton and Co., Inc., 1949. (Published in German, 1940.)

[8] OPPENHEIMER, J. ROBERT: *Physics in the Contemporary World*. Second Arthur D. Little Memorial Lecture at the Massachusetts Institute of Technology, 1947.

[9] RADO, SANDOR: Psychodynamics as a basic science. *Am. J. Orthopsychiat. 16:* 405, 1946.

[10] ——: An Adaptational View of Sexual Behavior. *Psychosexual Development in*

Health and Disease, Hoch, P. H. and Zubin, J., eds. New York, Grune & Stratton, Inc., 1949.

[11] ——: Mind, unconscious mind, and brain. *Psychosom. Med. 11:* 165, 1949.

[12] ——: Emergency Behavior; with an Introduction to the Dynamics of Conscience. *Anxiety*, Hoch, P. H. and Zubin, J., eds. New York, Grune & Stratton, Inc., 1950.

[13] ——: Psychodynamics of depression from the etiologic point of view. *Psychosom. Med. 13:* 51, 1951.

[14] ——: On the psychoanalytic exploration of fear and other emotions. *Trans. N. Y. Acad. Sc.* II, *14:* 280, 1952.

[15] ——: Hedonic Control, Action-Self, and the Depressive Spell. *Depression*, Hoch, P. H. and Zubin, J., eds. New York, Grune & Stratton, Inc., 1954.

[16] ——: Dynamics and classification of disordered behavior. *Am. J. Psychiat. 110:* 406, 1953.

[17] ——: Schizotypal Organization. *Changing Concepts of Psychoanalytic Medicine*, Rado, S. and Daniels, G. E., eds. New York, Grune & Stratton, Inc., 1956.

Adaptational Development of Psychoanalytic Therapy[*]

Healing through the mind is the oldest art and the youngest science. In the nineteenth century, physicians rediscovered the ancient techniques of hypnosis and suggestion and claimed a place for them in modern scientific medicine. These time-honored methods were, in fact, disciplinary measures disguised as medical procedures. The physician told the patient how he should think, feel and act, persuading him that he was capable of doing so.

In the 1880's, in Imperial Vienna, a young female patient of Dr. Joseph Breuer revolutionized psychotherapy. While under hypnosis, she insisted that she should have *her* say. She poured out her deeply repressed resentment of her governess, and lo and behold, some of her symptoms disappeared. This stunning result was in no small measure due to the fact that Dr. Breuer silently approved of her irreverence to the governess. Had he bawled her out, she would hardly have lost her symptoms. But Breuer's attitude enabled her to rise from her humiliation at the hands of the governess and restore her self-respect and pride. Thanks to Breuer's insight prohibitive hypnosis was thus superseded by cathartic hypnosis. This was the first step in the liberalization of psychotherapy[1].

Then came Freud.[2-5] From about 1890 on, he sought to obtain similar results by letting the patient unburden himself in the waking state. He thus discovered the investigative technique of free association and the phenomenon of repression. This was the birth of Freud's psychoanalytic method of treatment, another gigantic step away from the authoritarian spirit of the past. For not only was the patient freed from the dictates of hypnosis in the hands of an arbitrary physician, but he was also permitted, even urged, to undo his repressions, that is, the damage inflicted on him unwittingly by his parents in early life. By becoming aware of his long repressed feelings and thoughts, he could now reconsider them with a more mature mind. And, he could fill in the gaps in his memory and thus make Freud's scientific understanding of his developmental history more

* Presented at the Decennial Celebration of the Columbia University Psychoanalytic Clinic, March 19 and 20, 1955. First published in *Changing Concepts of Psychoanalytic Medicine*, New York: Grune and Stratton, 1956. In summing up the writer's previous work, this address draws part of its material and formulations from articles included in the present volume.

complete. Admittedly, and we may add fortunately, Freud was dominated by his research interest and viewed his new treatment procedure as a means to this end. In his eyes, the patient was a sort of research assistant. Clearly, in Freud's psychoanalytic treatment, the emphasis shifted from the originally intended emotional purge to the gaining of insight.

However, to Freud's distress, the patient got tired of dwelling incessantly on his developmental history. He became impatient and wanted to be cured. In this mood, he behaved more like a defiant child than a research assistant. Freud found an ingenious explanation for this baffling change: the patient, he said, transferred his childish feelings from his parents to the physician. Even more ingenious was Freud's idea of how to utilize this unwelcome change for the investigative purpose of the treatment. When the patient behaved like a child, he unwittingly still continued to reproduce the past—this time, not by recalling it, but by re-enacting it.

Freud classified this transference as positive and resistant; and he subdivided resistant transference into negative and sensual. He handled each of these different forms of transference in a different way. Positive transference, he said, must be preserved intact throughout the treatment. To this end, the two forms of resistant transference, negative and sensual, must be removed by tracing them to their infantile origins. At the conclusion of the treatment, positive transference "must be dissolved." How this could be done, Freud did not say.

Freud attributed almost unlimited therapeutic power to the undoing of the patient's repressions. If, he said, this one mental change takes place in the patient, then "the continuance and even the renewal of the morbid condition is impossible." (See[2]: page 269.) Hence his vision of psychoanalysis as a therapy of total reconstruction that would lift the patient to a higher level of psychodynamic organization.

Thanks to the efforts of decades, psychoanalytic therapy has grown in efficacy and prestige; it became, as Freud put it, a process of "re-education." Today, we call this procedure the "classical technique."

However, this technique had its failures as well as its successes. Re-examination of its theoretic presuppositions gradually revealed the causes of its limitations. Let me review them briefly as follows:

(1) In the classical technique, interpretation was based on classical psychodynamics. The emphasis was placed on making the patient understand his libidinal development, his temptations, fears and mechanisms of defense. Excessive preoccupation with questions of libidinal meaning and development completely dwarfed the basic task of all psychotherapy: the ascertaining of the adaptive value (positive or negative) of the patient's life performance. The disclosure of motivation and development was notoriously mistaken for an evaluation of performance. Let me make this

clear with an example: A piece of writing may be a work of art or the senseless effusion of a deranged mind; which it is can be ascertained only by a critical evaluation in the cultural context, not by disclosure of its author's motivation and development.

While it is absolutely essential to clarify the patient's background and intimate history, prolonged and indiscriminate digging in his past yields diminishing returns.

A purely developmental frame of reference is inadequate for the purposes of therapeutic interpretation. It tends to concentrate all interest and effort on the patient's past, to the neglect of his present.

(2) The modifying power of the undoing of repressions was overrated. To overcome repressions and thus be able to recall the past is one thing; to learn from it and be able to act on the new knowledge, another. One cannot remove the patient's automatized inhibitions by recalling the circumstances that created them.

(3) Even more fundamental were the difficulties arising from the concept and handling of transference. This subject has become surrounded with obscurities. To clear them up, we must first understand what the terms of Freud's transference theory actually mean (table 1).

TABLE 1. "TRANSFERENCE": TERMS AND MEANING

Terms: Forms of transference	Meaning: Patient behaves the way he did when he was:
Positive transference	An obedient child
Resistant transference	A disobedient child
(1) Negative transference	(1) A defiant child
(2) Sensual transference	(2) A child bent on sexual gratification

In the light of this table, we understand better Freud's rule that the treatment should be conducted in a state of positive transference. It meant that the patient should be kept in a childlike, more or less uncritical, emotional dependence on the physician. In Freud's view, this emotional dependence was the only force that enabled the patient to absorb and act upon the interpretations proposed to him by the physician. This is what he said:

"The outcome in this struggle [between repression and therapeutic undoing of repression] is not decided by his [the patient's] intellectual insight —it is neither strong enough nor free enough to accomplish such a thing— but solely by his relationship to the physician. In so far as his transference bears the positive sign, it clothes the physician with authority, transforms itself into faith in his findings and in his views. Without this kind of transference or with a negative one, the physician and his arguments would never even be listened to. Faith repeats the history of its own origin; it is a derivative of love and at first it needs no arguments. Not until later does it admit them so far as to take them into critical consideration if they have been offered by someone who is loved. Without this support arguments have no weight with the patient, never do have any with most people in life." (See[4]: page 387.)

In Imperial Vienna, it was an educational maxim that the child learns because he loves the teacher. By absorbing this maxim, Freud's psychoanalytic technique regressed to the authoritarian principle. Thereby, it defeated its own goal, which was to lift the patient to the highest attainable level of maturity.

But these shortcomings of the classical technique could not be accepted as final. Psychoanalytic therapy surged with unexplored resources and we were confident that in its development the classical technique was not the end, but the beginning.

Adaptational psychodynamics has given fresh impetus to a revision of the classical concept of treatment. With this new dynamics as a foundation, we have gradually evolved a procedure now known as the adaptational technique. Its purpose is to bring psychoanalytic therapy closer to the fulfillment of its Freudian goal of total reconstruction. Furthermore, to meet an urgent practical need, we have sought also to develop less ambitious treatment methods that would attain limited goals in much shorter time. We call them *reparative methods*. Accordingly, today we divide the methods of psychotherapy into two classes: reconstructive, and reparative. *Reconstructive treatment is a shorter designation for the adaptational technique of psychoanalytic therapy.* The reparative methods are still in an experimental stage; they are the subject of Dr. Goldman's paper.[6]

The first step in our program has been to evolve a *conceptual* scheme suitable for a comparative scientific study of all psychotherapeutic methods.[7, 8] We have distinguished between the patient's *treatment behavior* and his *life performance*. The term, treatment behavior, refers to his cooperation with the physician; the term life performance, to his internal as well as external activities in daily life. The patient's treatment behavior depends on his own shifting designs for cooperation, whether he is aware of them or not. The various designs for cooperation encountered in our patients fall into a hierarchically ordered scheme of levels. This order is shown in table 2.

At the self-reliant and aspiring levels, the patient's treatment behavior is based on common sense. In contrast, at the parentifying and magic-craving levels his treatment behavior reveals emotional dependence on the physician, befitting a child more than an adult. Often unknown to himself, he sees in the physician an idealized reincarnation of his own

TABLE 2. HIERARCHIC ORDER OF THE PATIENT'S DESIGNS FOR COOPERATION

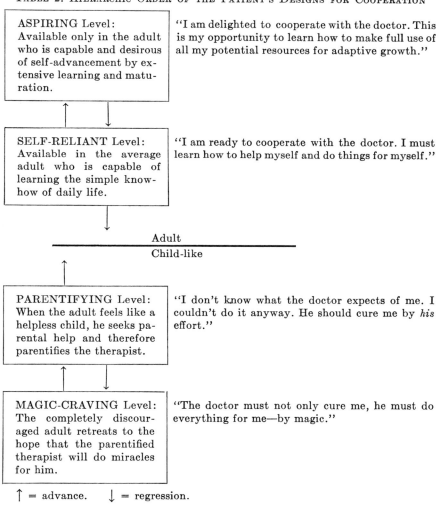

ASPIRING Level: Available only in the adult who is capable and desirous of self-advancement by extensive learning and maturation.

"I am delighted to cooperate with the doctor. This is my opportunity to learn how to make full use of all my potential resources for adaptive growth."

SELF-RELIANT Level: Available in the average adult who is capable of learning the simple know-how of daily life.

"I am ready to cooperate with the doctor. I must learn how to help myself and do things for myself."

Adult

Child-like

PARENTIFYING Level: When the adult feels like a helpless child, he seeks parental help and therefore parentifies the therapist.

"I don't know what the doctor expects of me. I couldn't do it anyway. He should cure me by *his* effort."

MAGIC-CRAVING Level: The completely discouraged adult retreats to the hope that the parentified therapist will do miracles for him.

"The doctor must not only cure me, he must do everything for me—by magic."

↑ = advance.   ↓ = regression.

parent, brought back to the scene by the power of his desire. Accordingly, his cooperation aims at obtaining the privileges of a favorite child, not at learning and maturation. Thus, in our hierarchic scheme, the sharp dividing line runs between the self-reliant and parentifying levels; above this line the patient's cooperation is adult, below it, childlike.

While the aspiring and self-reliant levels are not available in every patient, the parentifying and magic-craving levels are; in a state of helplessness, the reaching out for (magic) help is universal.

Patients can be successfully treated at every level of treatment behavior. However, the goals and techniques of treatment are so different at the different levels that it often becomes an important technical task to counteract the patient's inclination to shift from one level of treatment behavior to another, in particular, his inclination to cross the line that divides the levels of adult from the levels of childlike cooperation.

The physician must seek to stabilize the patient's cooperation at the level selected for his treatment. For this purpose he uses measures devised to regulate the patient's treatment behavior; we call these *priming measures*. In contradistinction, we call the measures devised to modify the patient's life performance *modifying measures*.

Each particular method of psychotherapy has its own *plan for priming* and its own *plan for modifying*. Of course, its plan for modifying depends upon its plan for priming. We use these two plans as a basis for classification of all methods of psychotherapy.

The magic-craving level is used in hypnotherapy; the parentifying level in the classical psychoanalytic technique and in the reparative methods; the self-reliant and aspiring levels in the adaptational technique which, as we have just seen, seeks to advance psychoanalysis to a therapy of total reconstruction.

Let me now give a scanty description of this reconstructive therapy. This method is primarily designed, as was Freud's classical technique, for the treatment of overreactive behavior disorders. However, it presupposes on the part of the patient a capacity for adult treatment behavior. Patients lastingly incapable of cooperating at the self-reliant or aspiring levels are not eligible for this type of treatment; they can be treated only by reparative methods.

In the adaptational psychodynamics of the overreactive behavior disorders, we encounter organized sequences of events which we have come to recognize as processes of miscarried prevention and miscarried repair. They are brought into play in early life by the child's faulty emergency responses, his overreaction to danger, particularly to the parental threat of punishment. The early phase of behavior disorder, emergency dyscontrol, appears in the child's dependency relationship to its parents. Its products are carried over into adult life, where the part originally played by the parents is continued by the pressures of society. The ensemble of the patient's faulty emergency responses includes excessive or inappropriate fears, rages, guilty fears and guilty rages; most damaging are the undue inhibitions which have arrested function, growth and development in the affected areas, pre-eminently in group membership and sexual behavior. In the treatment of behavior disorders, the critical tasks are: to bring the patient's emergency emotions under control; to remove his damaging inhibitions; to generate in him an emotional matrix dominated by the welfare emotions (pleasurable desire, joy, affection, love, self-respect and pride) and *controlled by adaptive insight*, a matrix conducive to a healthy life performance, both internal and external. The final task is to guide the patient in learning how to *act* upon the promptings of his now liberated welfare emotions; by advancing from spectator to participant, he must balance the confined pleasures of inactive reception with the full joys of active achievement in life. In the adaptational technique, the plans for priming and modifying seek to fulfill these tasks.

The adaptational plan for priming is to hold the patient as much as possible at the adult levels of cooperation with the physician. When his treatment behavior turns or threatens to turn childishly emotional, we seek to bring him back to the adult level without delay. We gently discourage his secret hope that *we* can do the job for him. We explain to him that a psychoanalytic treatment cannot be compared with surgery under general anesthesia. Here, *he* is required to make an effort; he is expected, with our help, to learn to understand himself better and develop modes of performance based on new emotional skills.

Childlike treatment behavior must be understood in the context of the here and now. Adaptational psychodynamics views the patient's search for an ersatzparent as a process of miscarried repair, a cardinal trait of behavior disorders. Before the patient entered treatment, he moved in disillusion from one ersatzparent to the next. During treatment, whenever he loses self-confidence, self-respect, and feels helpless, he parentifies the physician. Resorting to his old adaptive pattern, the goals and tactics of a child, he then plies the physician with smiles, tears and lashings, as shown schematically in table 3.

The patient performed his repertory of infantile behavior time and again in his relationship to his parents and ersatzparents. Since we know this repertory from his life history, we try to prevent him from repeating it once again in his treatment behavior. We do this by *interceptive interpretation*. To succeed, we first bolster up his self-confidence on *realistic* grounds by animating him to continuously enjoy even his smallest successes in daily life.

This way of handling the patient's parentifying treatment behavior is our most radical departure from the classical technique. The reason is obvious. If the goal is to make the patient self-reliant in his life performance, we must create for him every opportunity to practice self-reliance in his treatment behavior.

Special mention should be made of the resentful, coercive and vindictive phases of the patient's treatment behavior. Guided by the theory of negative transference, the classical technique helped the patient to unload his repressed infantile rages upon the physician. This procedure, in which the physician played the part of a scapegoat, was then featured as a "corrective therapeutic experience."

However, this procedure is inadequate for the all-important release of the patient's resentments. It relieves neither the patient's true resentment of the physician nor his true resentment of his parents; still less does it relieve the resentments of his current life situation which are in no small measure responsible for his present suffering. The adaptational technique

TABLE 3.

PLYING THE PARENTIFIED PHYSICIAN WITH SMILES, TEARS AND LASHINGS

Ingratiating:	"I am courting your favor, doing everything you wish, be nice to me."
Impatient:	"It's time for you to cure me (by magic)."
Seductive:	"Meanwhile, make love to me (the magic of your love will cure me)."

Upon feeling rejected by the physician:

Expiatory:	"Your aloofness fills me with guilty fear. I should like to expiate for my disobedience and promise to be obedient—please forgive me."
Resentful:	"When I was a child my parents never let me have my way. You said yourself that's how they started my intimidation and illness. It's *your* job to undo the wrong they did me. True, you urge me 'to get it off my chest,' but you hold me in your clutches just the same. You can't fool me."
Coercive:	"Now I am really furious. Stop this double talk and cure me."
Vindictive:	"I shall get even with you . . . I never wish to see you again."

uses the true-release principle embodied in Breuer's procedure; instead of allowing the patient to substitute a scapegoat, it teaches him how to reproduce in his memory the actual rage-provoking scene with the original cast.

The physician is selected for the function of scapegoat through the mechanism of emotional displacement or, as Freud first described it in 1895, of "false [emotional] connection." Emotional displacement occurs in daily life as well as in treatment behavior. In fact, to vent one's rage safely on a scapegoat is one of mankind's oldest ills and pervades every phase of social life. The evidence ranges from the despot who slays the bearer of bad news on the spot, to the husband who unloads his pent-up anger at the boss onto his wife, to the unscrupulous statesman who diverts the people's ire from his regime to an alleged enemy, either foreign or native. The classical technique of psychoanalytic therapy helps the patient to practice in his treatment behavior the very evil which it proposes to remedy. Only Freud's preoccupation with the (erroneous) idea that the scapegoat technique would allow him to explore otherwise inaccessible phases of the patient's past could have persuaded him to consider it a sound therapeutic measure.

The adaptational technique's plan for modifying is too elaborate to be presented here in detail. I shall touch only upon a few major points.

We interpret to the patient his treatment behavior and life performance in an adaptational framework. The patient must learn to view life, himself and others in terms of opportunities and responsibilities, successes and failures. He must learn to understand his doings in terms of motivation and control, to evaluate his doings in terms of the cultural context and to understand his development in terms of his background and life history.

Even when the biographic material on hand reaches far into the past, interpretation must always begin and end with the patient's present life performance, his present adaptive task. We can measure the therapeutic value of our interpretations only by their practical effect, namely, the patient's increasing capacity for healthy enjoyment of the here and now.

A mathematic interpretation may be a purely intellectual process. A therapeutic interpretation must engender in the patient an emotional process or else miss its purpose. Psychoanalytic therapy is pre-eminently a process of *emotional* re-education. In behavior disorders emotions control reason; a crucial goal of treatment is to adjust emotion to reason. Insight alone has little, if any, therapeutic effect. This is especially true of painful insight which is at the mercy of the patient's next emotional upheaval. Using the material of his own life experience, we show the patient how brute emotions, emotional thought and unemotional thought differ from one another in motivating action. He can learn to change his faulty pattern of emotional responses in one way only: by practice. He must begin to do this before the eyes of the physician. Thus, the process of emotional re-education always begins with the therapeutic release of the manifold resentments of his current life situation. Rage glues the patient's attention to the past, to the damage he believes he has suffered; he must learn to look to the future, learn from the damage, and seek repair, if and when possible.

One need not fear that treatment at the adult level of cooperation deprives the patient of the requisite emotional incentive. At first, the child learns only if he loves those who teach him. Later, he discovers the intellectual and practical value of the subject matter to which he is exposed. He then develops the proper emotional incentives for learning by taking pleasure and pride in his growing knowledge and skills. If the patient missed out on this development he must acquire the proper emotional mechanism for learning in his treatment.

A unique instrument of emotional re-education is the therapeutic analysis of the patient's dreams. The adaptational view stresses the fact that dreams are the products of emotional thought, stirred up as a rule by an unresolved emotional conflict of the previous day. Hence, the first task is to detect this conflict. We then turn to a *penetrating motivational analysis of the life situation* in which the conflict occurred, as well as of the patient's current treatment behavior. Armed with this knowledge, we revert to the dream and find that its correct interpretation falls into our lap. No matter how far back into the past the patient's associations may lead, his dream invariably proves to be a mechanism for the disposal of his sleep-disturbing emotional tensions. The point is that our technique gives us invaluable clues. It reveals the patient's current sensitivities; it enables us to use his dreams as a pressure gauge of his latent emotional tensions. A simple wishful dream indicates the absence of fear; a dramatic dream with a happy ending shows the presence of fear manageable by the power of the wish; a nightmare proves the presence of fear unmanageable by the power of the wish. The unmanageable fear forces the dreamer to undergo the dreaded event and get it over with. We classify nightmares as riddance dreams; they usually awaken the dreamer.

Other innovations are procedures aimed at advancing the patient from unwarranted despair to warranted hope, such as the therapeutic reinterpretation of guilty fear and the emotional redefinition of memories; the handling of the patient's riddance impulses—known in psychoanalytic literature as "acting out"—by preventive means; the reversal of the vicious circles of disorder into benign ones; and the dissolution of still accessible inhibitions. Here I can do no more than mention these subjects. The same applies to the development of special procedures for the treatment of the patterns of self-damaging defiance and sexual pain-dependence, other common sexual disorders, and the obsessive and depressive patterns.

Viewed in its entirety, treatment with the adaptational technique takes place in an intellectual and emotional climate profoundly different from that of the classical technique. As elsewhere in medicine, this change in treatment procedure can be fully realized only through the physician's own practical experience. This of course requires familiarity with all the details and finesses of the adaptational technique.

As we have seen, scientific psychotherapy has undergone a process of gradual liberalization that has lifted the patient in status from subject to citizen. Breuer's patient must be recognized as the pioneer of this development. It was her good fortune and the good fortune of psychotherapy that she sought help from a physician of the scientific stature of Joseph Breuer. Breuer replaced the ancient prohibitive technique of hypnotherapy with his permissive technique. There followed the emancipation of psychotherapy from the hypnotic state. Freud's catharsis in the waking state led to his discovery of free association and of the patient's biography as a proper subject of medical study. This marked the beginning of a new epoch of psychotherapy based on psychodynamic principles. Freud's discovery of parentifying treatment behavior opened up the patient's emotional relationship to the physician and posed it as a crucial problem of all psychotherapy. However, the classical technique relapsed; it reintroduced the authoritarian principle in the treatment of the patient. The adaptational technique is an attempt to restore the line of development initiated by Breuer's patient.

We may look forward with confidence to the future development of psychoanalytic therapy.

REFERENCES

[1] BREUER, JOSEPH AND FREUD, SIGMUND: *Studies in Hysteria*. New York, Nervous and Mental Disease Publishing Co., 1936. (Published in German, 1895.)

[2] FREUD, SIGMUND: Freud's Psychoanalytic Method. *Collected Papers*, Vol. I. London, Hogarth Press, 1924. (Published in German, 1904.)

[3] ———: Papers on Technique. *Collected Papers*, Vol. II. London, Hogarth Press, 1924. (Published in German, 1910–1919.)

[4] ———: Transference, Psychoanalytic Therapy. *A General Introduction to Psychoanalysis*. New York, Horace Liveright, Inc., 1935. (Published in German, 1918.)

[5] ———: Analysis Terminable and Interminable. *Collected Papers*, Vol. V. London, Hogarth Press, 1950. (Published in German, 1937.)

[6] GOLDMAN, GEORGE S.: Reparative Psychotherapy. *Changing Concepts of Psychoanalytic Medicine*, Rado, S. and Daniels, G. E., eds. New York, Grune & Stratton, Inc., 1956.

[7] RADO, SANDOR: The relationship of patient to therapist. *Am. J. Orthopsychiat. 12:* 542, 1942.

[8] ———: Recent Advances in Psychoanalytic Therapy. *Psychiatric Treatment, Proceedings of the Association for Research in Nervous and Mental Disease.* (Wortis, Hare, and Herman, Eds.) Baltimore, Williams & Wilkins, 1953.

INDEX

Abraham, K.
on "bad object," 60
on behavior of moodcyclic patients,
240
at Berlin Psychoanalytic Institute, 174
on castration complex in women, 83
on "castrative woman," 108
on homosexuality, 32
on identification, 238
on melancholia, 47–49
on oral erotism, 35
on "primal depression," 93
Abreaction, *see* Catharsis
Accidents
provocation of, 117
Ackerman, N., 176
Action self
as basis of selfhood, 275*f.*, 340
characteristics of, 300*ff.*
and conscience, 303
contracted, 303
contraction of in depression, 304
and depression, 286–311
and emergency behavior, 216, 222
expanded, 303
and pride, 302*f.*
in schizotypes, 276*ff.*
Action, willed
and action self, 275, 340
Activity disorder
in schizotypes, 282
Adaptation
definition of, 268
as principle of investigation, 211, 216*f.*
psychodynamic, failures of, 185
reproductive, 187
in schizotypes, *see* Schizoadaptation
sexual, 312–320, *see also* Sexual
Adaptational point of view as investigative frame of reference, 211
Adaptational psychodynamics, *see* Psychodynamics, adaptational
Adaptive control, struggle for in schizotypes, 279, 283
Adaptive degradation in depression, 286
Adaptive efficiency, 182

Adaptive impairment
as neurosis, 269
sexual, 312, 319*ff.*
Adaptive incompetence
as psychosis, 269, 299
in schizotypal disintegration, 279, 284
Adaptive patterns of childhood, reactivated, 185
Adaptive thinking in schizotypes, 281
Addiction, *see* Drug addiction; Drug dependence; Cravings; Elatants; Pharmacothymia
Adrian, E., on neurophysiology and human behavior, 168
Affection as welfare emotion, 340
Affectomotor level, integration on, 135
Affects (*see also* Emotions)
discharge of in transference, 18
After-activity elicited by self-reporting, 338
Aggression (*see also* Rage)
defense against, 40–46
directed into social channels, 43, 62
directed inward, 39, 42*ff.*, 226, *see also* Rage, retroflexed
directed outward, 114
pleasure in, 41
as reaction to frustration, 52*f.*
repressed, 42*ff.*
Agoraphobia, 103*f.*
Alcohol dependence in schizotypes, 278
Alcohol pharmacothymia, 74
Alcoholics, sadism in, 78
Alcoholism
in extractive type, 328
oral erotism in, 35
Alexander, F.
in American Psychoanalytic Association, 175
at Berlin Psychoanalytic Institute, 174
on genital sexuality, 192
on surplus energy, 315
Algolagnia, passive and active, 203
Alimentary behavior compared to sexual behavior, 192*f.*